# Revenue Statistics in Asia and the Pacific 2022

## STRENGTHENING TAX REVENUES IN DEVELOPING ASIA

**1990-2020**

OECD

dev DEVELOPMENT CENTRE

**Please cite this publication as:**
OECD (2022), *Revenue Statistics in Asia and the Pacific 2022: Strengthening Tax Revenues in Developing Asia*, OECD Publishing, Paris, https://doi.org/10.1787/db29f89a-en.

ISBN 978-92-64-39875-7 (print)
ISBN 978-92-64-93978-3 (pdf)
ISBN 978-92-64-55961-5 (HTML)
ISBN 978-92-64-82386-0 (epub)

Revenue Statistics in Asia and the Pacific
ISSN 2788-9351 (print)
ISSN 2788-936X (online)

**Photo credits:** Cover © some of the graphic elements in the main cover illustration were adapted from Freepik.com

Corrigenda to publications may be found on line at: www.oecd.org/about/publishing/corrigenda.htm.

# Foreword

*Revenue Statistics in Asia and the Pacific* is a joint publication by the OECD Centre for Tax Policy and Administration and the OECD Development Centre with the co-operation of the Asian Development Bank (ADB), the Pacific Island Tax Administrators Association (PITAA), and the Pacific Community (SPC), and with financial support from the governments of Ireland, Japan, Luxembourg, the Netherlands, Norway, Sweden, Switzerland and the United Kingdom. It presents detailed, internationally comparable data on tax revenues for 28 Asian and Pacific economies: Australia, Bangladesh, Bhutan, Cambodia, People's Republic of China, the Cook Islands, Fiji, Indonesia, Japan, Kazakhstan, Korea, Kyrgyzstan*, Lao People's Democratic Republic, Malaysia, the Maldives, Mongolia, Nauru, New Zealand, Pakistan, Papua New Guinea, the Philippines, Samoa, Singapore, the Solomon Islands, Thailand, Tokelau, Vanuatu and Viet Nam. It also provides information on non-tax revenues for Bhutan, Cambodia, the Cook Islands, Fiji, Kazakhstan, Kyrgyzstan, Lao People's Democratic Republic, the Maldives, Mongolia, Nauru, Pakistan, Papua New Guinea, the Philippines, Samoa, Singapore, Thailand, Tokelau, Vanuatu and Viet Nam. Four of these economies are OECD members (Australia, Japan, Korea and New Zealand). The approach used in *Revenue Statistics in Asia and the Pacific* is based on the well-established methodology of the *OECD Revenue Statistics* (OECD, 2021), which has become an essential reference source for OECD member countries. Comparisons are also made with the averages for OECD economies, Latin American and Caribbean (LAC) countries and 30 African countries currently included in *Revenue Statistics in Africa*.

In this publication, the term "taxes" is confined to compulsory, unrequited payments to general government. As outlined in the Interpretative Guide to the Revenue Statistics, taxes are "unrequited" in the sense that benefits provided by government to taxpayers are not normally in proportion to their payments. The OECD methodology classifies a tax according to its base: income, profits and capital gains (classified under heading 1000), payroll (heading 3000), property (heading 4000), goods and services (heading 5000) and other taxes (heading 6000). Compulsory social security contributions paid to general government are treated as taxes, and are classified under heading 2000. Greater detail on the tax concept, the classification of taxes and the accrual basis of reporting is set out in the Interpretative Guide in Annex A.

The publication also presents information on non-tax revenues in 19 economies. The term "non-tax revenue" includes all general government revenue that does not meet the OECD definition of tax revenues. Non-tax revenues include grants (e.g. foreign aid), returns on government market investments, rents on the extraction of resources from public lands, sales of government-produced goods and services, and the collection of fines and forfeits. More details on the definition of these revenues are available in Annex B.

Chapter 1 of this publication provides an overview of the main tax revenue trends in the 28 economies and non-tax revenue trends in the 19 relevant economies from 2010 to 2020. A special feature on options for strengthening tax revenue in developing countries in Asia is found in Chapter 2, while Chapter 3 contains comparative tables on the level and structure of taxation in the 28 economies since 1990. Chapter 4 contains detailed information on tax revenues on a country-by-country basis. Chapter 5 includes information on the level and structure of non-tax revenues in selected economies.

* Note by the ADB: The ADB recognises "Kyrgyzstan" as the "Kyrgyz Republic".

# Acknowledgements

*Revenue Statistics in Asia and the Pacific* is jointly produced by the Organisation for Economic Co-operation and Development (OECD)'s Centre for Tax Policy and Administration (CTP) and the OECD Development Centre (DEV) with the co-operation of the Asian Development Bank (ADB), the Pacific Island Tax Administrators Association (PITAA), and the Pacific Community (SPC), with financial support from the governments of Ireland, Japan, Luxembourg, the Netherlands, Norway, Sweden, Switzerland and the United Kingdom.

The OECD staff with responsibility for producing the publication were: Leonie Cedano, Emmanuelle Modica, Talita Yamashiro Fordelone, Melary Muñoz Rodriguez and Koji Ono of CTP under the supervision of the Director Pascal Saint-Amans, Deputy Director Grace Perez-Navarro, the Head of the Tax Policy and Tax Statistics Division, David Bradbury, Alexander Pick, Acting Head, Tax Data and Statistical Analysis and Michelle Harding, Head, Tax Data and Statistical Analysis; and Jingjing Xia of DEV under the supervision of the Director Ragnheiður Elín Árnadóttir, Deputy Directors Ayumi Yuasa and Federico Bonaglia and Kensuke Tanaka, Head of the Asia Unit. The special feature was written by Yothin Jinjarak, Donghyun Park and Shu Tian (Asian Development Bank) and Sam Hill (World Bank). Elizabeth Nash and Delphine Grandrieux at DEV and Marie-Aurélie Elkurd, Karena Garnier and Natalie Lagorce at CTP assisted with the production and publication of this report.

The authors would like to thank other officials from OECD, ADB, PITAA and SPC for their invaluable help in preparing this publication. Advice and support were provided by Daisuke Miura, Public Management Specialist (Taxation), Sustainable Development and Climate Change Department (SDCC), and Go Nagata, Public Management Specialist (Taxation), SDCC, at the ADB; Nilima Lal, Economic Statistics Advisor at the SPC; Koni Ravono, Head of Secretariat, and Petero Maivucevuce, Training Coordinator at PITAA; Piera Tortora at the OECD Development Co-operation Directorate; Piet Battiau, Bert Brys, Kurt Van Dender, Luisa Dressler, Pierce O'Reilly and Sarah Perret at the OECD Centre for Tax Policy and Administration; and Sean Dougherty at the OECD Public Governance Directorate. The authors would also like to thank colleagues working in national administrations with whom they have consulted regularly. These institutions include finance ministries, national tax agencies and national statistical institutes of the participating countries.

This document was produced with financial support from the governments of Ireland, Japan, Luxembourg, the Netherlands, Norway, Sweden, Switzerland and the United Kingdom. The views expressed herein can in no way be taken to reflect the official opinion or policies of the governments of Ireland, Japan, Luxembourg, the Netherlands, Norway, Sweden, Switzerland and the United Kingdom.

# Table of contents

## FIGURES



## TABLES

# Executive summary

For most countries, achieving the Sustainable Development Goals (SDGs) of the United Nations' 2030 Agenda for Sustainable Development will require the mobilisation of additional public revenues. *Revenue Statistics in Asia and the Pacific* presents key indicators to track progress on domestic resource mobilisation and to inform tax policy reforms that could help close the financing gap to fund the SDGs. This edition of the report provides comprehensive data on public revenues in 2020, the first year of the COVID-19 pandemic.

*Revenue Statistics in Asia and the Pacific 2022* presents detailed, internationally comparable data on tax revenues for 28 economies: Australia, Bangladesh, Bhutan, Cambodia, People's Republic of China, the Cook Islands, Fiji, Indonesia, Japan, Kazakhstan, Korea, Kyrgyzstan, Lao People's Democratic Republic, Malaysia, the Maldives, Mongolia, Nauru, New Zealand, Pakistan, Papua New Guinea, the Philippines, Samoa, Singapore, the Solomon Islands, Thailand, Tokelau, Vanuatu and Viet Nam.

## Tax-to-GDP ratios in Asia and the Pacific

In 2020, the average tax-to-GDP ratio in the 28 Asian and Pacific economies covered in this report was 19.1%, below the averages for the OECD and Latin America and the Caribbean (LAC), of 33.5% and 21.9%, respectively. Tax-to-GDP ratios in the region ranged from 8.9% in Bhutan and Lao PDR to 47.5% in Nauru. Seven of the 18 Asian countries had a tax-to-GDP ratio equal to or above the Asia-Pacific average in 2020: Japan (31.4%, 2019 figure), Korea (28.0%), Viet Nam (22.7%), Mongolia (21.2%), Cambodia (20.2%), China (20.1%) and the Maldives (19.1%). In the Pacific, six economies recorded tax-to-GDP ratios above the Asia-Pacific average (Australia [2019 figure], the Cook Islands, Nauru, New Zealand, Samoa and Tokelau) while four were below this level (Papua New Guinea, Vanuatu, Fiji and the Solomon Islands).

The average tax-to-GDP ratio for the Asia-Pacific region declined by 1.2 percentage points (p.p.) between 2019 and 2020; over the same period, the LAC average declined by 0.8 p.p. while the OECD average increased by 0.1 p.p. Almost three-quarters (19) of the 26 economies in the Asia-Pacific region for which data are available[1] experienced declines in their tax-to-GDP ratio between 2019 and 2020, mainly as a result of the COVID-19 crisis. They decreased by more than 2.0 p.p. in five economies: Kazakhstan and Mongolia (both -2.6 p.p.), Vanuatu (-2.8 p.p.), Fiji (-5.7 p.p.) and the Cook Islands (-8.3 p.p.). The latter three Pacific Islands, heavily reliant on tourism, experienced the largest decreases because of border closures to limit the spread of COVID-19. Seven economies reported increases in their tax-to-GDP ratios in 2020; the largest were observed in Tokelau and Bangladesh at 1.5 p.p. and 1.2 p.p., respectively. The increases in the remaining economies were smaller than 1 p.p.

Over a longer timeframe, tax-to-GDP ratios declined in fifteen of the 28 Asian and Pacific economies between 2010 and 2020. The largest decreases were observed in Fiji (-5.1 p.p.), Bhutan (-5.2 p.p.), Papua

[1] At the time of publication, data for 2020 are not available for Australia and Japan

New Guinea (-5.3 p.p.), the Cook Islands (-7.2 p.p.) and Kazakhstan (-9.7 p.p.). While tax-to-GDP ratios in Kazakhstan, Papua New Guinea and Bhutan were affected by falls in mineral prices between 2010 and 2020, decreases in Fiji and the Cook Islands over this period were attributable to the COVID-19 pandemic. Across the same period, the largest increases in tax-to-GDP ratios were observed in the Maldives (10.1 p.p.), Cambodia (12.9 p.p.) and Nauru (39.2 p.p., since 2014). Samoa, Korea and Japan also reported increases larger than 5 p.p. between 2010 and 2020.

## Tax structures in Asia and the Pacific

Changes in average tax-to-GDP ratios between 2019 and 2020 were driven by different tax categories in Asian and Pacific economies and OECD countries. In Asia-Pacific, revenues from taxes on goods and services decreased in 21 economies and decreased more as a percentage of GDP than in OECD countries, where this tax category did not change on average between 2019 and 2020. Revenues from corporate income tax (CIT) declined in half of the 26 Asia-Pacific economies for which data are available, whereas they declined in two thirds of the OECD countries.

On average, taxes on goods and services were the main source of tax revenues in the Asia-Pacific region in 2020, accounting for 50.6% of total tax revenues, similar to the Africa (30)[2] and LAC averages (51.9%, 2019 figure, and 48.4%, respectively) and higher than in the OECD (32.6%, 2019 figure). However, within this category, the average share of value-added taxes in total revenues was lower in Asia-Pacific (23.1%) than in Africa and LAC (29.3%, 2019 figure and 27.5%, respectively) and similar to the OECD average (20.3%, 2019 figure).

Revenues from personal income taxes (PIT) accounted for 16.0% of total tax revenues on average in Asia-Pacific, similar to the Africa (30) average of 17.7% (2019 figure), above the LAC average (9.8%) and below the OECD average (23.5%, 2019 figure). CIT accounted for a larger share of total tax revenues than PIT in the Asia-Pacific region, on average, at 18.8%, the same as the Africa (30) average (2019 figure) and above the shares in LAC (15.6%) and the OECD (9.6%, 2019 figure). In Pacific economies, PIT accounted for a larger share of total taxation than CIT (except in Fiji), whereas the share of CIT was higher in the Asian countries except for Japan, Kyrgyzstan and Korea.

Social security contributions (SSCs) accounted for a relatively small proportion of tax revenues for most Asian and Pacific economies, at 6.3% of total revenues. None of the Pacific economies levy SSCs and most of the Asian countries in the publication have very low SSCs. However, six Asian countries derived more than 15% of total tax revenues from SSCs: Japan (41.1%, 2019 figure), Viet Nam (30.4%), Korea (28.0%), China (24.2%), Mongolia (18.7%) and the Philippines (15.7%).

## Non-tax revenues in selected economies

This publication also includes data on non-tax revenues for nineteen economies: Bhutan, Cambodia, the Cook Islands, Fiji, Kazakhstan, Kyrgyzstan, Lao PDR, the Maldives, Mongolia, Nauru, Pakistan, Papua New Guinea, the Philippines, Samoa, Singapore, Thailand, Tokelau, Vanuatu and Viet Nam. Between 2019 and 2020, non-tax revenues declined in twelve economies as a percentage of GDP while they increased in seven economies.

In 2020, non-tax revenues exceeded 10% of GDP in Samoa (11.6%), Bhutan (19.8%), Vanuatu (24.0%), the Cook Islands (27.4%), Nauru (67.5%) and Tokelau (218.7%). Grants were an important source of revenue in 2020 in eight economies (Bhutan, Cambodia, the Cook Islands, Lao PDR, Papua New Guinea,

[2] The Africa (30) average refers to the unweighted average of the 30 African countries participating in *Revenue Statistics in Africa 2021*.

Samoa, Tokelau and Vanuatu), exceeding 30% of total non-tax revenues. Property-related income accounted for the largest share of non-tax revenues in Singapore (78.8%), Kazakhstan (75.2%), Pakistan (74.9%), Tokelau (59.6%), the Philippines (58.0%), Nauru (54.7%) and Thailand (53.2%), and also contributed more than 30% of non-tax revenues in Mongolia, Papua New Guinea, Bhutan and Lao PDR.

## Special feature: Strengthening tax revenues in Asia

The report includes a special feature exploring potential avenues for Asian countries to increase tax revenues while discussing the constraints and challenges they face in doing so. Policy considerations include the optimisation of key sources of revenues, improving the strategic use of tax expenditures, adapting to the growth of the digital economy and supporting multilateral initiatives to increase revenues from CIT. Recent estimates suggest that developing countries in Asia have the potential to increase tax revenues by 3.6% of GDP on average.

# 1 Tax revenue trends in Asia and the Pacific

Chapter 1 provides information on trends in tax and non-tax revenues in 28 Asian and Pacific economies, including changes in tax-to-GDP ratios, tax structures, taxes by level of government and non-tax revenue levels and structures. It includes data for 2020, the first year of the COVID-19 pandemic, and tracks trends in tax revenues across the region since 2010.

Achieving the Sustainable Development Goals in the 2030 Agenda for Sustainable Development requires mobilising additional resources – in particular government revenues – to fund public goods and services in developing countries. Taxation provides the largest share of government revenues in almost all countries and is relatively predictable and sustainable, in contrast with non-tax revenues such as official development assistance and royalties.

This edition of *Revenue Statistics in Asia and the Pacific* provides comprehensive data on public revenues in 2020, the first year of the COVID-19 pandemic. Like other regions of the world, the pandemic had far-reaching social and economic consequences for Asia and the Pacific, although not all economies were affected in the same way. The report shows how the majority of economies in the region experienced declines in tax revenues both in nominal terms and as a percentage of GDP, thereby placing major stress on their public finances. It also demonstrates which tax types were particularly affected by the pandemic in different parts of the region. Chapter 2 discusses opportunities for mobilising higher revenues in developing Asia in the wake of the pandemic in order to repair countries' fiscal systems and promote investment while also fostering equality and enhancing the region's resilience.

This report presents detailed and internationally comparable data on tax revenues in 28 Asian and Pacific economies: Australia, Bangladesh, Bhutan, Cambodia, People's Republic of China (hereafter "China"), the Cook Islands, Fiji, Indonesia, Japan, Kazakhstan, Korea, Kyrgyzstan[1], Lao People's Democratic Republic (hereafter Lao PDR), Malaysia, the Maldives, Mongolia, Nauru, New Zealand, Pakistan, Papua New Guinea, the Philippines, Samoa, Singapore, the Solomon Islands, Thailand, Tokelau, Vanuatu and Viet Nam. It also provides information on non-tax revenues for Bhutan, Cambodia, the Cook Islands, Fiji, Kazakhstan, Kyrgyzstan, Lao PDR, the Maldives, Mongolia, Nauru, Pakistan, Papua New Guinea, the Philippines, Samoa, Singapore, Thailand, Tokelau, Vanuatu and Viet Nam.

Chapter 1 discusses key tax indicators for these 28 economies: the tax-to-GDP ratio; the tax structure and the share of tax revenue by level of government. It also analyses non-tax revenues for selected economies. The discussion is supplemented by the comparative tables in Chapter 3 and detailed information for each economy in Chapters 4 and 5.

## The impact of COVID-19 on tax revenues

This section analyses the impact of COVID-19 on nominal tax revenues and nominal gross domestic product (GDP) in the Asia-Pacific region between 2019 and 2020 as well as changes in the tax-to-GDP ratio over this period. The value of the tax-to-GDP ratio depends on two components: the numerator (tax revenues) and the denominator (GDP) (Box 1.1). Changes in tax-to-GDP ratios between 2019 and 2020 reflect changes in both components over this period.

The COVID-19 pandemic resulted in historic falls in nominal tax revenues and nominal GDP. Twenty out of 26 economies for which data are available for 2020 (excluding Australia and Japan) recorded falls in nominal tax revenues between 2019 and 2020, which fell by 8.8% on average over the period. Nominal GDP fell in 15 economies and decreased by -2.6% on average between 2019 and 2020.

Figure 1.1 shows the falls in nominal tax revenues and GDP between 2019 and 2020 across the 26 economies. Decreases in nominal tax revenues larger than 15% were observed in Indonesia (-15.2%), Vanuatu (-19.3%), the Maldives (-33.5%), Fiji (-39.1%) and the Cook Islands (-40.0%). Nominal GDP decreased by less than tax revenues in most of these economies: by -2.5% in Indonesia, -3.7% in Vanuatu, -18.0% in Fiji and -14.6% in the Cook Islands, the exception being the Maldives, where nominal GDP decreased by -33.7%, almost the same amount as tax revenue. As a result, tax-to-GDP ratios decreased in Indonesia, Vanuatu, Fiji and the Cook Islands, while there was a small increase in the tax-to-GDP ratio in the Maldives as tax revenues fell by slightly less than GDP. A similar effect can be observed for Nauru:

nominal GDP increased by more than nominal tax revenue, which translated into a decrease in the tax-to-GDP ratio of -0.8 p.p. between 2019 and 2020.

### Figure 1.1. Changes in nominal tax and nominal GDP, 2019-20

Year-on-year, percentage change

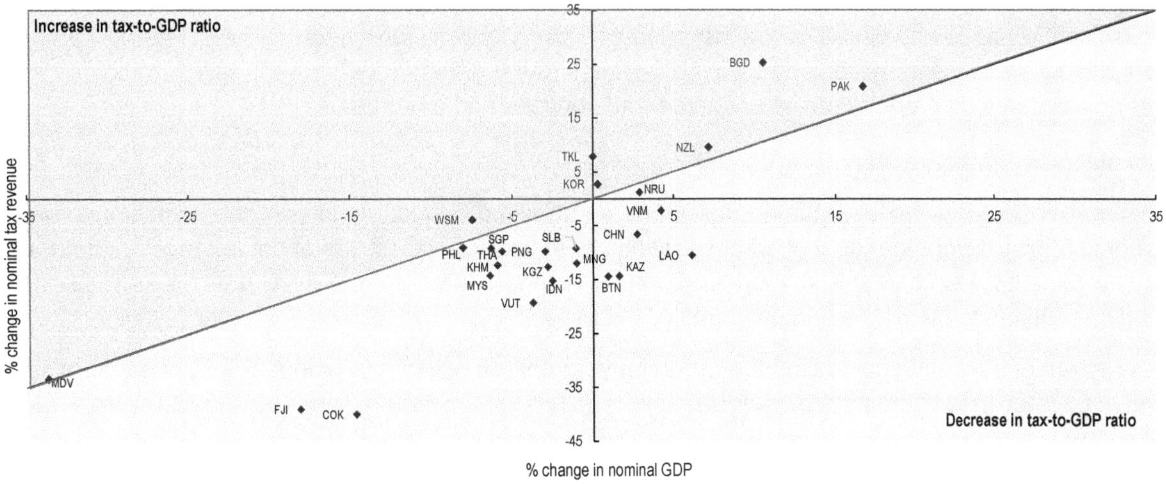


Note: Australia, Japan, Korea and New Zealand are part of the OECD (38) group. Data for Australia, Japan, Korea and New Zealand are taken from *Revenue Statistics 2021* (OECD, 2021[1]).
Australia and Japan are excluded from the graph as data for 2020 were not available.
Source: Author's calculation based on (OECD, 2022[2]).

StatLink https://stat.link/gzutnj

**Box 1.1. The tax-to-GDP ratio methodology**

The tax-to-GDP ratios shown in *Revenue Statistics in Asia and the Pacific 2022* express aggregate tax revenues as a percentage of GDP. The value of this ratio depends on its denominator (GDP) and its numerator (tax revenues). Both the numerator and the denominator may be subject to historical revision.

Taxes are defined as compulsory, unrequited payments to general government. In the OECD classification, taxes are classified by the base of the tax and include taxes on incomes and profits, compulsory social security contributions (SSCs) paid to the general government, taxes on payroll and workforce, taxes on property, taxes on goods and services and other taxes.

***The numerator (tax revenues)***

This publication uses tax revenue figures that are submitted by focal points or published annually by national Ministries of Finance, tax administrations or statistical offices. Historical tax revenue data are subject to revision each year, with more important revisions in later years. Past figures may also change from one edition to the next when new data are obtained.

In 16 Asian and Pacific economies, the reporting year coincides with the calendar year. The remaining twelve countries report on a fiscal year basis:

- The fiscal year in Australia, Bangladesh, Bhutan, the Cook Islands, Nauru, New Zealand, Pakistan, Samoa and Tokelau runs from July to June. This means that reporting year 2020 corresponds to Q3/2020-Q2/2021.
- The fiscal year in Singapore and Japan covers April to March while in Thailand it covers October to September. The reporting year 2020 spans Q2/2020-Q1/2021 and Q4/2019-Q3/2020, respectively.

***The denominator (GDP)***

The GDP figures used in this publication are sourced from OECD National Accounts data for Australia, Indonesia, Japan, Korea and New Zealand; National Statistical Offices for Cambodia, China, Cook Islands, Fiji, Kazakhstan, Kyrgyzstan, Lao PDR, Malaysia, Maldives, Mongolia, Philippines, Singapore, Thailand, Tokelau and Viet Nam; the Asian Development Bank's Key Indicators Database for Papua New Guinea, Solomon Islands and Vanuatu; and World Economic Outlook data published by the IMF for Bangladesh, Bhutan and Pakistan.

Using these GDP figures ensures maximum consistency across countries, as well as international comparability. GDP figures are also revised and updated to reflect better data sources and improved estimation procedures, or to move towards new internationally-agreed guidelines for measuring the value of GDP.

Between 2019 and 2020, almost three-quarters of the economies in this publication for which data are available experienced decreases in their tax-to-GDP ratios (Figure 1.2). Nineteen economies had lower tax-to-GDP ratios in 2020 relative to 2019, whereas seven recorded higher ratios than in 2019 (data for 2020 are not available for Australia and Japan). The largest increases were seen in Tokelau and Bangladesh at 1.5 percentage points (p.p.) and 1.2 p.p., respectively. The increases in the remaining economies were smaller than 1 p.p.

By contrast, fourteen economies experienced decreases in their tax-to-GDP ratio larger than or equal to 1 p.p. Tax-to-GDP ratios declined by between -1.0 p.p. and -2.0 p.p. in Malaysia, Viet Nam, Cambodia, Indonesia, Bhutan, Lao PDR, the Solomon Islands, Kyrgyzstan and China between 2019 and 2020. Five economies reported decreases larger than 2.0 p.p.: Kazakhstan and Mongolia (both by -2.6 p.p.), Vanuatu

(-2.8 p.p.), Fiji (-5.7 p.p.) and the Cook Islands (-8.3 p.p.). In the remaining five countries, the decreases were smaller than 1 p.p.

On average, the tax-to-GDP ratio for the Asia-Pacific region fell by -1.2 p.p. between 2019 and 2020. This was larger than the decline in Latin America and the Caribbean (LAC), where the regional average declined by -0.8 p.p. between 2019 and 2020 (OECD et al., 2022[3]). Meanwhile, the OECD average increased by 0.1 p.p. over the same period (OECD, 2021[1]). Tax-to-GDP ratios increased in 20 of the 36 OECD countries for which 2020 data are available, while they decreased in 20 of the 26 LAC countries and increased in six between 2019 and 2020.

### Figure 1.2. Annual changes in tax-to-GDP ratios (2019-20)

Percentage point (p.p.) change

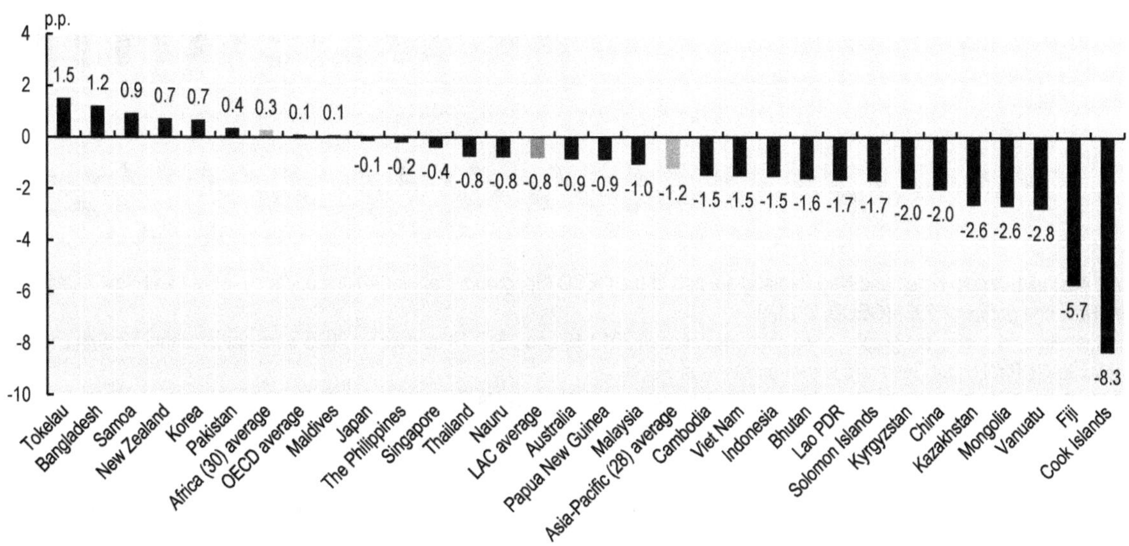


Note: Australia, Japan, Korea and New Zealand are part of the OECD (38) group. Data for Australia, Japan, Korea and New Zealand are taken from *Revenue Statistics 2021* (OECD, 2021[1]).
Data for the change between 2018 and 2019 are used for Australia and Japan.
Source: Author's calculations based on Table 3.1 in Chapter 3.

StatLink https://stat.link/jsl3gf

## *Evolution of tax-to-GDP ratios since 2010*

Across a longer time horizon, tax-to-GDP ratios declined in 15 of the 28 economies in this publication between 2010 and 2020 while 13 economies observed an increase over this period (Figure 1.3).[2] The largest decreases between 2010 and 2020 were observed in Fiji (-5.1 p.p.), Bhutan (-5.2 p.p.), Papua New Guinea (-5.3 p.p.), the Cook Islands (-7.2 p.p.) and Kazakhstan (-9.7 p.p.). While tax-to-GDP ratios in Kazakhstan, Papua New Guinea and Bhutan were affected by falls in natural resource prices between 2010 and 2020, decreases in Fiji and the Cook Islands over this period were attributable to the COVID-19 pandemic: between 2010 and 2019, their tax-to-GDP ratios increased by 0.6 p.p. (Fiji) and 1.1 p.p. (the Cook Islands) (Figure 1.3).

Between 2010 and 2020, the tax-to-GDP ratio increased most in the Maldives (10.1 p.p.), Cambodia (12.9 p.p.) and Nauru (39.2 p.p., since 2014). Samoa, Korea and Japan also reported increases larger than 5.0 p.p. since 2010. Of the 13 economies whose tax-to-GDP ratios increased since 2010, only Bangladesh, Tokelau and Cambodia reported changes larger than 1 p.p. between 2019 and 2020. By contrast, most economies whose tax-to-GDP ratio has decreased since 2010 reported changes larger than 1 p.p. between 2019 and 2020, the exceptions being Thailand (-0.8 p.p.), China (-0.8 p.p., exclusive of SSCs) and Papua New Guinea (-0.9 p.p.).

### Figure 1.3. Changes in tax-to-GDP ratios (2010-2020 and 2019-2020)

Percentage point (p.p.) change

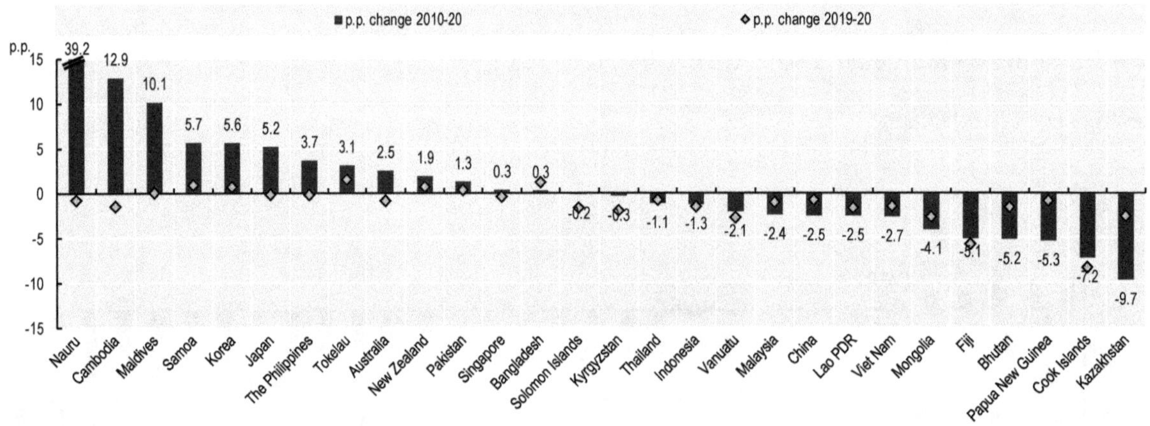


Note: Australia, Japan, Korea and New Zealand are part of the OECD (38) group. Data for Australia, Japan, Korea and New Zealand are taken from *Revenue Statistics 2021* (OECD, 2021[1]).
For Australia and Japan, the graph shows changes between 2010-19 and 2018-19 as data for 2020 were not available for both countries.
The tax-to-GDP ratios for China are shown exclusive of SSCs.
Data for Nauru is only available from 2014 and for Pakistan from 2011 onwards.
Source: Authors' calculations based on Table 3.1 in Chapter 3.

StatLink https://stat.link/mndt0v

## *Tax-to-GDP ratios during the COVID-19 pandemic*

In 2020, tax-to-GDP ratios in Asia and the Pacific ranged from 8.9% in Bhutan and Lao PDR to 47.5% in Nauru (Figure 1.4). Twelve of the 28 economies had tax-to-GDP ratios above the Asia-Pacific (28) average of 19.1% in 2020, and all economies in the publication had lower ratios than the OECD average of 33.5%, with the exception of Nauru. Most of the Asian countries covered in this report had a tax-to-GDP ratio below the regional average of 19.1%, with the exceptions of Japan (31.4%, 2019 figure), Korea (28.0%), Viet Nam (22.7%), Mongolia (21.2%), Cambodia (20.2%), China (20.1%) and the Maldives (19.1%). By contrast, tax-to-GDP ratios observed in the Pacific islands were more evenly distributed, with four economies recording tax-to-GDP ratios above the regional average (the Cook Islands, Tokelau, Samoa and Nauru) and four below (Papua New Guinea, Vanuatu, Fiji and the Solomon Islands).

Tax-to-GDP ratios in Asian and Pacific economies, inclusive and exclusive of SSCs, are shown in Figure 1.4. In countries that levy SSCs, tax-to-GDP ratios exclusive of SSCs ranged from 9.5% of GDP in Indonesia to 20.1% of GDP in Korea in 2020 (Lao PDR and Kyrgyzstan are not included as data are not available). For all countries with SSC data, six countries in Asia had tax-to-GDP ratios exclusive of SSCs between 15% and 20% of GDP: the Philippines (15.0%), China (15.2%), Thailand (15.5%), Viet Nam (15.8%), Japan (18.5%, 2019 figure) and Mongolia (17.3%), while three countries had tax-to-GDP ratios exclusive of SSCs below 15%: Indonesia (9.5%), Malaysia (11.1%) and Kazakhstan (13.3%). While excluding SSCs does not impact the tax-to-GDP ratios in Pacific economies, where social protection is funded predominantly from general revenues and not through SSCs, it plays a more significant role in the ratios of most of the Asian economies included in this publication.

**Figure 1.4. Tax-to-GDP ratios in Asian and Pacific economies and regional averages, including and excluding social security contributions (2020)**

Percentage of GDP

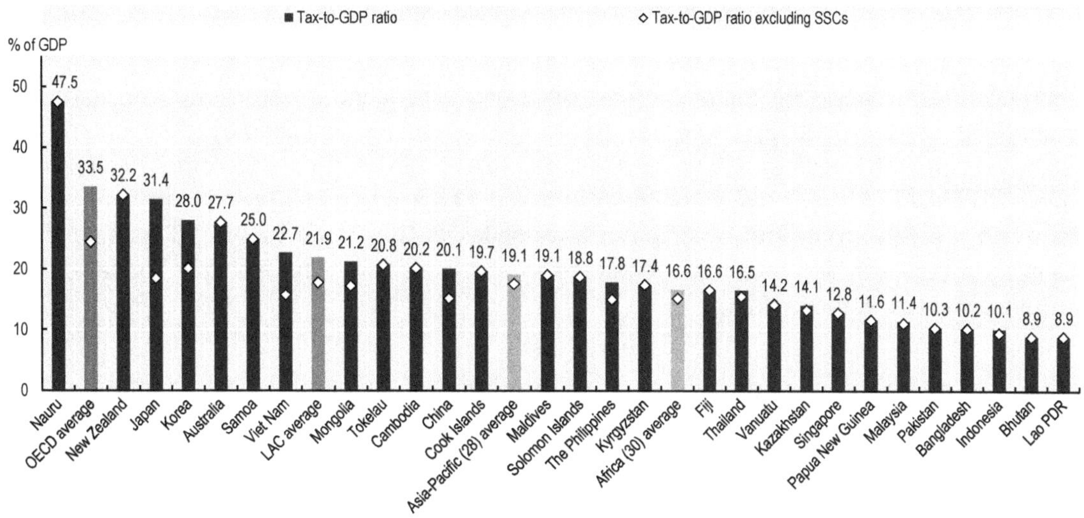

Note: The figures do not include sub-national tax revenue for the Cook Islands, Fiji, Lao PDR, Malaysia, the Maldives, Papua New Guinea, Samoa, the Solomon Islands and Viet Nam as the data are not available.

The averages for Africa (30 countries), for Asia-Pacific (28 economies), for LAC (26 Latin American and Caribbean countries) and the OECD (38 countries) are unweighted.

Australia, Japan, Korea and New Zealand are part of the OECD (38) group. Data for Australia, Japan, Korea, New Zealand and the OECD average are taken from *Revenue Statistics 2021* (OECD, 2021[1]).

2019 data are used for the Africa (30) average, Australia and Japan, as 2020 data are not available.

Source: Authors' calculations based on Table 3.1 in Chapter 3.

StatLink https://stat.link/q9rcts

Structural factors are a key determinant of tax-to-GDP ratios across economies. These include the importance of agriculture in the economy, openness to trade and the size of the informal economy. For example, in many economies with a large agricultural sector, taxation can be particularly challenging as it relates to informality, low incomes and low productivity (Mawejje and Sebudde, 2019[4]). In addition, agriculture benefits from numerous tax exemptions. For example, Malaysia allows an Investment Tax Allowance on capital expenditure and income tax to companies producing certain agricultural products or engaged in certain agricultural activities (Malaysian Investment Development Authority, 2019[5]). The common challenges that Small Island Developing States (SIDS) confront, such as remoteness, exposure to natural disasters and low economic diversification, also influence tax-to-GDP ratios and tax structures in these islands. These factors are discussed in more detail in Box 1.3.

In addition to structural factors, tax policy and tax administration settings also strongly influence the level of tax revenues. These include the size of the tax base, governance and administrative capacity within tax authorities, the level of satisfaction with public service provision and tax morale (i.e. the willingness of people to pay taxes) (OECD, 2019[6]). For example, Aizenman et al. (2019[7]) found that tax-to-GDP ratios in Asia are positively correlated with government effectiveness and institutional quality. Finally, tax-to-GDP ratios tend to be higher in high-income economies, although the relationship is not direct and is less pronounced at lower levels of income due to the influence of other factors (Figure 1.5).

The relationship between GDP per capita and tax levels across the Asian and Pacific economies in this publication is less direct than that observed across LAC or OECD countries. Nine Asian and Pacific economies (China, Fiji, Kazakhstan, the Maldives, Mongolia, the Philippines, Samoa, Thailand and Viet Nam) have broadly similar GDP per capita and tax-to-GDP ratios as the majority of LAC countries. Seven economies (Pakistan, Bangladesh, Kyrgyzstan, Papua New Guinea, Vanuatu, Samoa and the Solomon Islands) have similar per capita levels of income but their tax-to-GDP ratios differ markedly. In contrast, Australia, Japan, Korea and New Zealand have higher per capita income and tax-to-GDP ratios. Finally, Singapore has the highest GDP per capita of the 28 economies considered here and a relatively low tax-to-GDP ratio.

The high GDP per capita in Singapore results from significant inward flows of foreign direct investment (FDI) (UNCTAD, 2012[8]), whereas the tax-to-GDP ratio is explained by lower income tax rates (particularly on corporate income) and value added tax (VAT) rates compared to other Asian and Pacific economies (UNESCAP, 2014[9]). Nauru, on the other hand, has a similar GDP per capita level to Lao PDR, Viet Nam and the Philippines but reports the highest tax-to-GDP ratio of the 28 economies in this publication as a result of high revenues generated in connection with the Refugee Processing Centre (RPC) (Government of Nauru, 2020[10]).

## Figure 1.5. Tax-to-GDP ratios and GDP per capita (in PPP) in Asian and Pacific economies, Latin America and the Caribbean, OECD and African countries (2020)

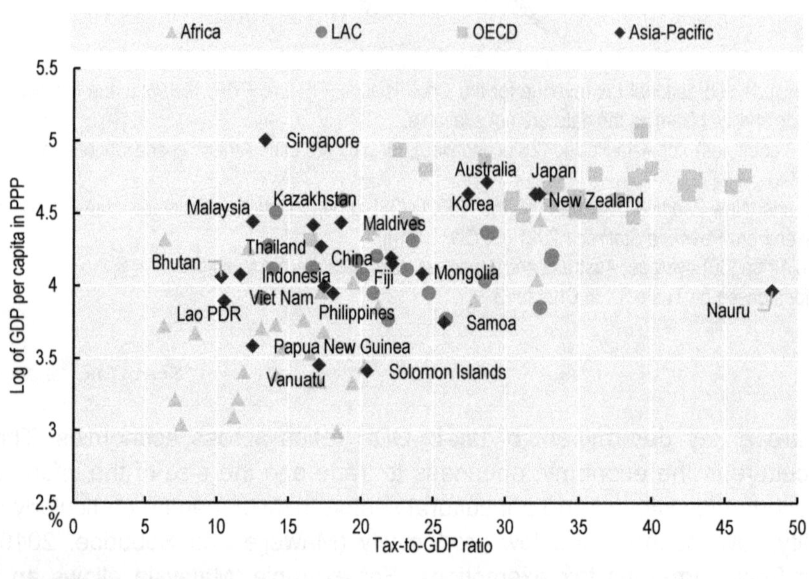


Note: The y-axis is on a logarithmic scale.
Data for 2019 are used for Australia, Japan and all African countries.
The Cook Islands and Tokelau are excluded as GDP per capita data were unavailable for these countries.
The purchasing power parity (PPP) between two countries is the rate at which the currency of one country needs to be converted into that of a second country to ensure that a given amount of the first country's currency will purchase the same volume of goods and services in the second country as it does in the first. The implied PPP conversion rate is expressed as national currency per current international dollar. An international dollar has the same purchasing power as the US dollar has in the United States. An international dollar is a hypothetical currency that is used as a means of translating and comparing costs from one country to the other using a common reference point, the US dollar [definitions derived from (IMF, 2019[11]) and (WHO, 2015[12])].
Source: GDP per capita from *World Economic Outlook, April 2022* (IMF, 2022[13]).

StatLink https://stat.link/9ys1fg

**Box 1.2. Tax revenue trends in the ASEAN (8) and in Pacific Island economies since 2010**

Among the 28 economies included in this publication, two distinct subgroups can be identified: one group of eight Pacific Island economies and another comprising eight members of the Association of Southeast Asian Nations (ASEAN).

The eight Pacific Island economies included in this publication are the Cook Islands, Fiji, Nauru, Papua New Guinea, Samoa, the Solomon Islands, Tokelau and Vanuatu, which together comprise the Pacific Islands (8) average. Despite their diversity, the Pacific Island economies share common characteristics such as remoteness, small populations, limited economic diversification, and exposure to natural disasters and climate change (ADB, 2016[14]).

The second sub-regional group includes the eight ASEAN member states in this publication. Founded in 1967, ASEAN is a regional organisation that promotes economic, political and social collaboration amongst its ten member states and within the region (ASEAN, 2021[15]). The eight ASEAN members included in this publication are Cambodia, Indonesia, Lao PDR, Malaysia, the Philippines, Singapore, Thailand and Viet Nam; they comprise the ASEAN (8) average.[3]

The Pacific Islands generally had higher tax-to-GDP ratios than the ASEAN (8) countries (Figure 1.6). Tax-to-GDP ratios in the former grouping ranged from 11.6% of GDP in Papua New Guinea to 47.5% in Nauru in 2020, with an average of 21.8%. Across the ASEAN (8) economies, tax-to-GDP ratios ranged from 8.9% in Lao PDR to 22.7% in Viet Nam in the same year, with an average of 15.0%.

Since 2010, tax-to-GDP ratios in both groups increased, with a more moderate growth for the ASEAN (8) economies. However, most of the Pacific Island and ASEAN (8) economies registered a decrease in their tax-to-GDP ratios between 2019 and 2020, with the exception of Samoa (increased by 0.9 p.p.) and Tokelau (increased by 1.5 p.p.). The Cook Islands (-8.3 p.p.), Fiji (-5.7 p.p.) and Vanuatu (-2.8 p.p.) experienced the largest decreases in tax-to-GDP ratios among the 16 economies.

Changes in tax-to-GDP ratios between 2010 and 2020 ranged from -7.2 p.p. in the Cook Islands to 39.2 p.p. in Nauru (since 2014) in the Pacific Island economies, while changes in the tax-to-GDP ratio in ASEAN countries ranged between -2.7 p.p. in Viet Nam to 12.9 p.p. in Cambodia.

**Figure 1.6. Tax-to-GDP ratios in ASEAN and Pacific Island economies, 2010-20**

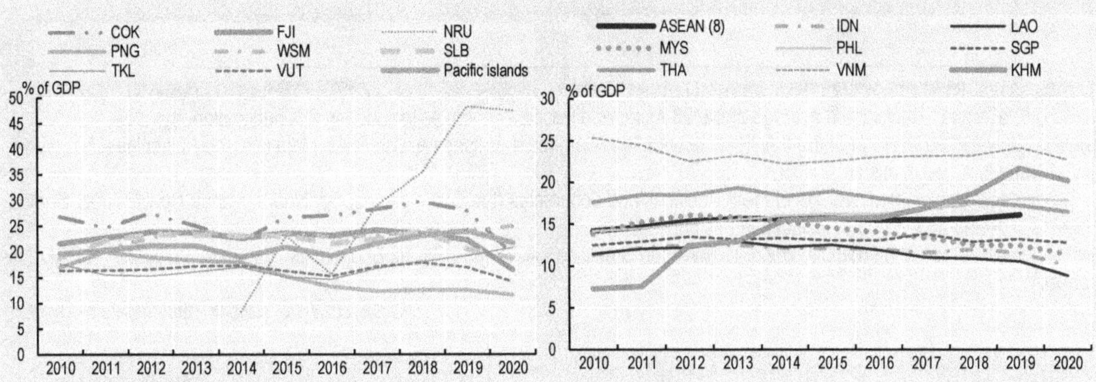


Note: Data for Nauru are only available from 2014 onwards.
Source: Author's calculation based on (OECD, 2022[2]).

StatLink https://stat.link/nv3ewu

Regional differences are also reflected in the average tax structures, as displayed in Figure 1.7. While revenues from taxes on goods and services play an important role in both regions (48.1% of total taxes in the ASEAN (8) economies and 57.5% in the Pacific Island economies), the composition of the taxes on goods and services differs. Revenues from VAT contributed 21.6% of total taxation in the ASEAN (8) economies on average in 2020, which is lower than the Asia-Pacific (28) average (23.1%) and the Pacific Islands (8) average (22.3%). Revenues from other taxes on goods and services accounted for the largest share of total taxes in both the ASEAN (8) and the Pacific Island economies. However, the share of these taxes was 35.2% in the Pacific Island economies, 8.7 p.p. larger than the average share in the ASEAN (8) countries in 2020 (of 26.5%).

Another difference between the averages is the relative importance of revenues from PIT and CIT. CIT revenues played a relatively small role in the tax structures of Pacific Island economies and contributed only 11.0% on average to total tax revenues in 2020, whereas revenues from CIT accounted for 24.1% of total taxes for the ASEAN (8) average and 18.8% of total taxes of the Asia-Pacific (28) average. Revenues from PIT accounted for an average of 13.2% of total taxes in the ASEAN (8) countries, 16.0% in the Asia-Pacific region and 21.2% in Pacific Island economies in 2020.

## Figure 1.7. Tax structure in Asia-Pacific, ASEAN (8) and Pacific Island economies in 2020

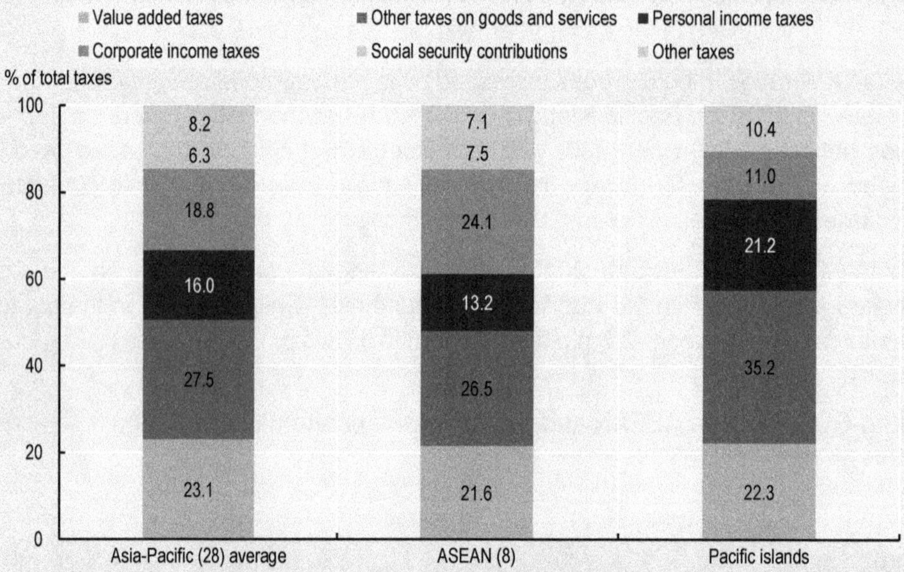


Note: Asia-Pacific (28) average: Unweighted average of the 28 Asian and Pacific economies included in this publication.
ASEAN (8) average: Unweighted average of the 8 ASEAN economies (Cambodia, Indonesia, Lao PDR, Malaysia, the Philippines, Singapore, Thailand, and Viet Nam) included in this publication.
Pacific Islands (8) average: Unweighted average of the 8 Pacific Island economies (the Cook Islands, Fiji, Nauru, Papua New Guinea, Samoa, the Solomon Islands, Tokelau and Vanuatu) included in this publication.
Source: Author's calculations based on (OECD, 2022[2]), "Revenue Statistics - Asian and Pacific Economies: Comparative tables", OECD Tax Statistics (database).

StatLink https://stat.link/0ye2om

## Tax structures in Asia and the Pacific

The tax structure, measured as the composition of tax revenues from different tax types, is the second key indicator in the *Revenue Statistics* publications. Considering the structure of taxation is useful for policy analysis as different taxes have different economic and social effects. Across the 28 economies in this publication, the composition of taxes varies widely, reflecting economies' different policy choices, economic structures and conditions, tax administration capabilities and historical factors.

### *Revenues by tax category in 2020*

Australia, New Zealand and Tokelau recorded the highest levels of personal income tax (PIT) revenues as a percentage of GDP in 2020 (Figure 1.8). Revenue from PIT equated 12.4% of GDP in New Zealand, 11.6% of GDP in Australia (2019 figure) and 10.6% of GDP in Tokelau. In the other Pacific economies covered in this publication, revenue from PIT was above 3.0% of GDP and closer to the Asia-Pacific (28) average of 3.2%, except in Fiji (1.9%) and Vanuatu (which does not have a PIT). For Nauru, it is not possible to distinguish between revenues from PIT and CIT. However, Nauru has the highest level of revenue from income taxes of all economies included in the publication, at 37.2% of GDP.

In the Asian countries in this publication (excluding Japan and Korea), revenue from PIT in 2020 ranged from 0.1% in the Maldives, which introduced PIT in 2020, to 2.7% of GDP in Malaysia. Japan and Korea both had higher revenues from PIT than the rest of the Asian countries included in this publication, at 5.9% (2019 figure) and 5.3% respectively.

#### Figure 1.8. Tax structures as a percentage of GDP (2020)

Percentage of GDP

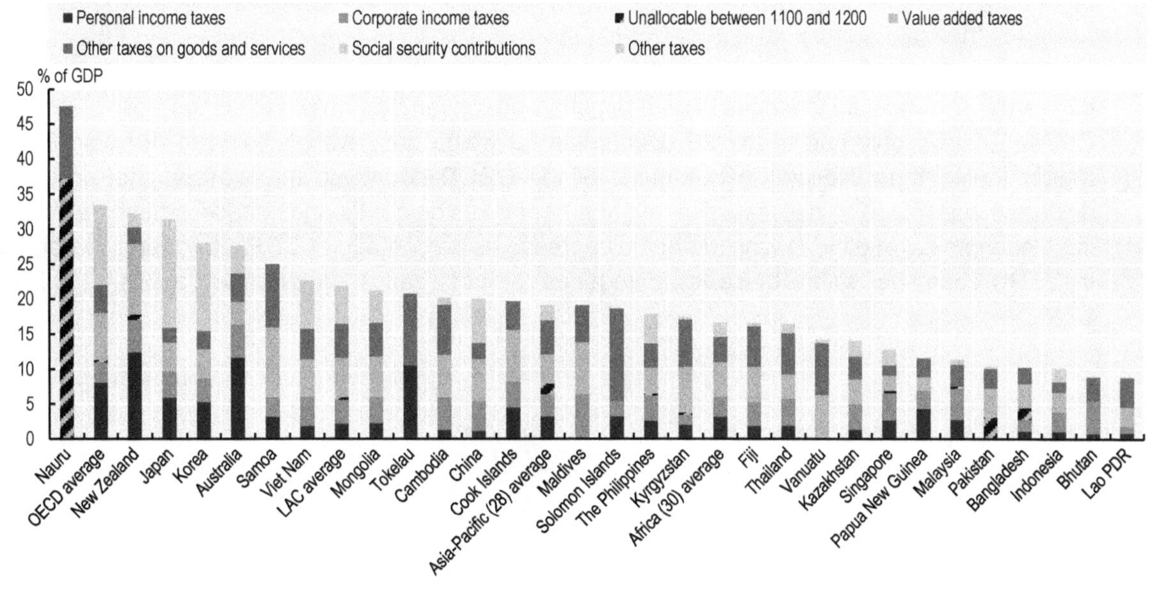


Note: The averages for Africa (30 countries), for Asia-Pacific (28 economies), for LAC (26 Latin American and Caribbean countries) and the OECD (38 countries) are unweighted.
Australia, Japan, Korea and New Zealand are part of the OECD (38) group. Data for Australia, Japan, Korea, New Zealand and the OECD average are taken from *Revenue Statistics 2021* (OECD, 2021[1]).
2019 data are used for the Africa (30) average, Australia, Japan and the OECD average.
Source: (OECD, 2022[2]).

StatLink https://stat.link/qaj48o

Revenues from CIT were equivalent to 3.1% of GDP on average across the Asia-Pacific region. They were higher than revenues from PIT in 15 of the 24 economies considered here (excluding Tokelau and Vanuatu, which do not have a CIT, and Nauru and Pakistan, for which it is not possible to distinguish between PIT and CIT revenues). Revenues from CIT ranged from 1.0% of GDP in the Lao PDR to 6.2% in the Maldives, the only country in which CIT revenues exceeded 5% of GDP.

SSCs account for a relatively small proportion of tax revenues of Asian and Pacific economies. Sixteen economies in this publication, including all the Pacific economies, do not levy SSCs. In most of the other economies, revenues from SSCs were relatively low in 2020, including Malaysia (0.3% of GDP), Indonesia (0.6% of GDP), Kazakhstan (0.7% of GDP), Thailand (1.0% of GDP) and the Philippines (2.8% of GDP). These were significantly below the averages of LAC (4.0% of GDP) and the OECD (8.9% of GDP in 2019). Five Asian economies reported relatively high revenues from SSCs: Mongolia (4.0% of GDP), China (4.9% of GDP), Viet Nam (6.9% of GDP), Korea (7.8% of GDP) and Japan (12.9% of GDP, 2019 figure).[4]

Revenues from taxes on goods and services amounted to 9.0% of GDP on average across the 28 Asian and Pacific economies. In Asian economies, revenues from taxes on goods and services amounted to less than 10% in 2020, with the exception of Mongolia (10.7%), the Maldives (12.7%), Cambodia and Kyrgyzstan (both 13.3%). In contrast, the majority of the Pacific economies in this publication generated revenues from taxes on goods and services that exceeded 10% of GDP, ranging from 10.2% of GDP in Tokelau to 19.1% in Samoa in 2020. The exceptions in the Pacific were Papua New Guinea (4.6% of GDP) and Australia (7.3% of GDP, 2019 figure).

### *Revenue impact of COVID-19 by tax category*

While the majority of the economies included in this publication experienced a decrease in tax revenues as a result of the COVID-19 crisis, the channels through which revenues were impacted by the pandemic varied:

- Figure 1.9 presents the overall distribution of changes in tax types as percentage of GDP between 2019 and 2020 in the OECD and in the Asia-Pacific region. On average, the tax-to-GDP ratio in Asia-Pacific decreased by -1.2 p.p. while in the OECD it increased by 0.1 p.p.. Besides the difference in magnitude, changes in both regions were driven by different tax types. Revenues from CIT declined in only half of the 26 economies for which data are available in the Asia-Pacific region,[5] while they declined in two thirds of the OECD countries. In Asia and thePacific, the decrease was driven by decreases in revenue from taxes on goods and services: these decreased in 21 economies, and the magnitude of the decrease as percentage of GDP was overall larger than in OECD countries, where these tax categories did not change on average between 2019 and 2020.

**Figure 1.9. Changes in tax revenues by category as a share of GDP, OECD and Asia Pacific, 2019-20**

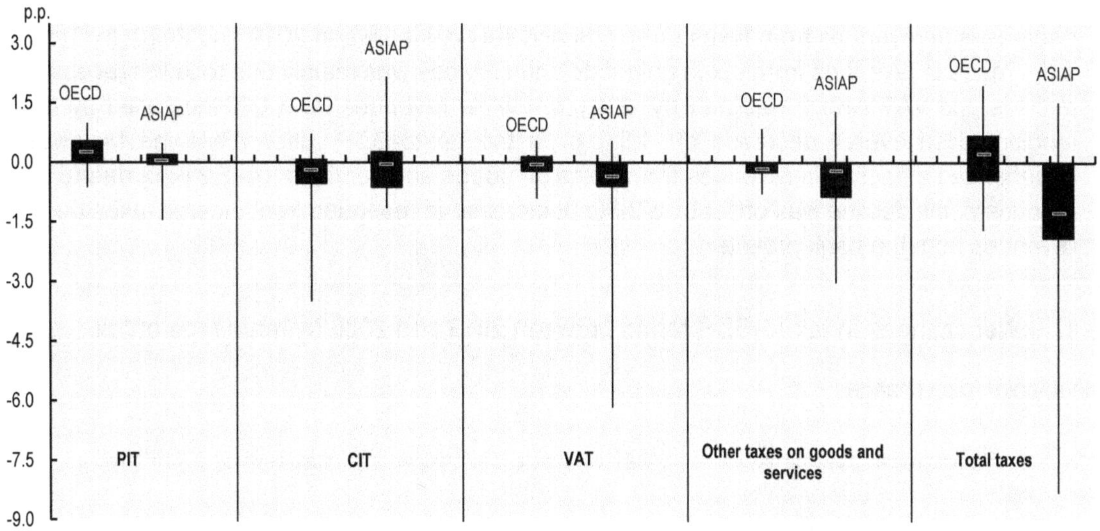


Note: The category SSCs is excluded from the graph as SSCs are less relevant in the Asia-Pacific region.
Source: Author's calculations based on (OECD, 2022[16]), "Revenue Statistics - Asian and Pacific Economies: Comparative tables", *OECD Tax Statistics* (database) and (OECD, 2021[1]).

StatLink https://stat.link/d2h9p6

- Tax-to-GDP ratios across the Pacific Islands decreased primarily because of lower revenues from taxes on goods and services resulting from a sharp fall in tourism. The number of tourist arrivals declined by 99% to 100% between April and December 2020 (ADB, 2020[17]). Vanuatu, Fiji and the Cook Islands, three Pacific Island economies heavily reliant on tourism, experienced the largest decreases among the 28 economies due to border closures: the tax-to-GDP ratio decreased by -2.8 p.p. in Vanuatu, by -5.7 p.p. in Fiji and by -8.3 p.p. in the Cook Islands between 2019 and 2020. Declines in revenues from taxes on goods and services were the main driver of the decreases in all three economies. In Vanuatu, revenues from VAT and other taxes on goods and services contributed equally to the decline, both decreasing by -1.3 p.p. In Fiji, revenues from other taxes on goods and services accounted for the bulk of the decrease (-3.0 p.p.), mostly due to a decline of over 70% in revenues from the airport departure tax (FRCS, 2020[18]) and lower revenues from excises, while VAT revenues declined by -1.7 p.p. between 2019 and 2020. In the Cook Islands, revenues from VAT declined by -6.2 p.p., while revenues from taxes from other goods and services declined by -0.9 p.p. and income tax revenues decreased by -1.2 p.p. over the same period.
- In Asia, the largest decreases in tax-to-GDP ratios occurred in Kyrgyzstan and China (both by -2.0 p.p.), and Kazakhstan and Mongolia (both by -2.6 p.p.). In Kyrgyzstan, revenues from VAT declined by -1.7 p.p., mainly due to lower revenue from VAT on imports. In China, lower revenues from SSCs and VAT were the main drivers of the decrease of the tax-to-GDP ratio between 2019 and 2020. In Kazakhstan, lower revenues from taxes on the production of minerals and from taxes on exports contributed most to a -1.5 p.p. decline in revenues from other taxes on goods and services between 2019 and 2020. Additionally, revenues from taxes on oil companies (to the National Fund) decreased by over 60% in nominal terms, leading to a -1.1 p.p. decline in revenues from income taxes. In Mongolia, declines in revenues from income taxes, VAT revenue and other

tax revenues, including social security contributions, contributed almost equally to the overall decline of -2.6 p.p. (income tax revenue decreased by -0.8 p.p. while the latter both decreased by -0.7 p.p.). Revenue from other taxes on goods and services decreased by -0.4 p.p.

- In Cambodia and the Maldives, increases in revenues from income taxes (partially) offset decreases in revenues from taxes on goods and services between 2019 and 2020. In Cambodia, a decrease in revenues from taxes on goods and services was mainly due to lower revenues from excises and VAT (which declined by -2.4 p.p.), while revenues from CIT increased by 0.9 p.p., leading to an overall decrease of -1.5 p.p. in the tax-to-GDP ratio. While the Maldives also experienced a decline in revenues from taxes on goods and services (of -2.2 p.p.) due to the lack of tourism, the decline was offset by a 2.3 p.p. increase in revenues from income taxes due higher revenues from the bank profit tax.

### Figure 1.10. Net changes in tax-to-GDP ratios between 2019 and 2020 by main type of tax

Percentage point (p.p.) change

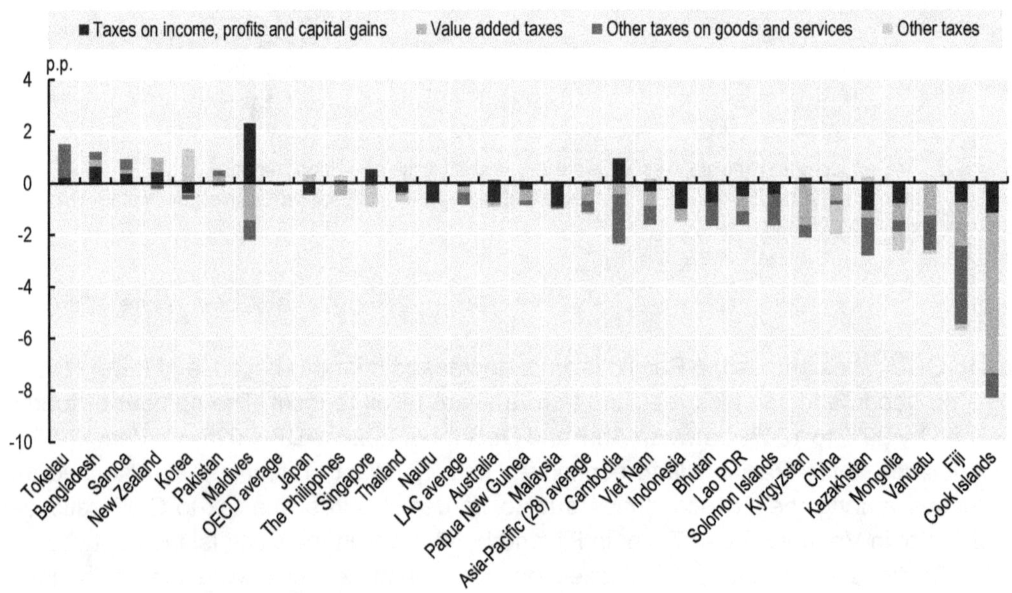


Note: Australia, Japan, Korea and New Zealand are part of the OECD (38) group. Data for Australia, Japan, Korea and New Zealand are taken from *Revenue Statistics 2021* (OECD, 2021[11])

Data for the change between 2018 and 2019 are used for Australia and Japan.

Source: Authors' calculations based on (OECD, 2022[16]), "Revenue Statistics - Asian and Pacific Economies: Comparative tables", *OECD Tax Statistics* (database).

StatLink https://stat.link/72fkz4

### *Tax structures in 2020 and evolution since 2010*

Within the Asia-Pacific region, tax structures varied greatly in 2020. In 18 economies, the main source of tax revenue was taxes on goods and services, while nine economies obtained the largest share of tax revenues from income taxes. Japan is the only country where the greatest share of revenues was derived from SSCs. There were also notable differences between the ASEAN countries and the Pacific Islands in the publication, discussed in Box 1.2.

In 2020, income taxes were the largest source of revenue for Australia (2019 figure), Bhutan, Korea, Malaysia, Nauru, New Zealand, Papua New Guinea, Singapore and Tokelau. Among these economies, the share of income tax revenue in total tax revenue varied from 30.9% in Korea to 78.3% in Nauru. CIT revenues exceeded PIT revenues in three Asian countries (Bhutan, Malaysia and Singapore), while all Pacific economies in this group except Nauru (Australia, New Zealand, Papua New Guinea and Tokelau), as well as Korea, generated higher shares of revenue from PIT than from CIT. [6]

Taxes on goods and services were the main source of tax revenue in Bangladesh, Cambodia, China, the Cook Islands, Fiji, Indonesia, Kazakhstan, Kyrgyzstan, Lao PDR, the Maldives, Mongolia, Pakistan, Philippines, Samoa, the Solomon Islands, Thailand, Vanuatu and Viet Nam in 2020, contributing between 41.7% (China) and 96.6% (Vanuatu) of total tax revenue. In six of these economies, taxes on goods and services other than VAT, such as excises and import duties, contributed a larger share than VAT revenues to total tax revenues. Revenues from other taxes on goods and services in these economies ranged from 34.9% of total tax revenues in Fiji to 70.5% in the Solomon Islands, while eleven economies received a larger share of revenue from VAT, ranging from 21.1% in the Philippines to 40.2% in Samoa.

As discussed earlier, SSCs generated a relatively small proportion of revenues for most Asian and Pacific economies, with a few exceptions among the Asian countries. Japan derives the largest share of total tax revenues from SSCs (41.1% in 2019) while these also generated a significant proportion of revenues in the Philippines (15.7%), Mongolia (18.7%), China (24.2%), Korea (28.0%) and Viet Nam (30.4%).

### Figure 1.11. Tax structures as a percentage of total taxation in 2020

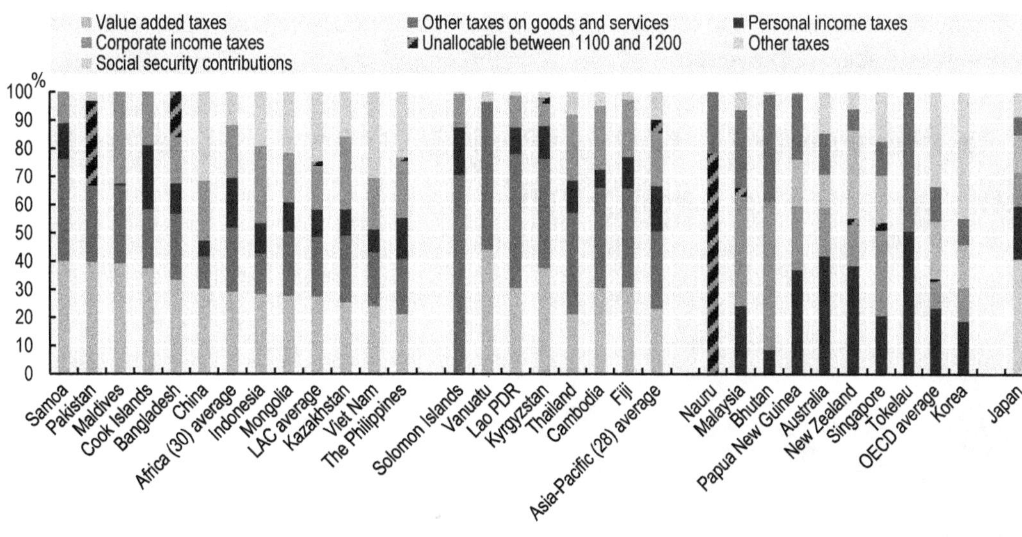


Note: The averages for Africa (30 countries), for Asia-Pacific (28 economies), for LAC (26 Latin American and Caribbean countries) and the OECD (38 countries) are unweighted.

Australia, Japan, Korea and New Zealand are part of the OECD (38) group. Data for Australia, Japan, Korea, New Zealand and the OECD average are taken from *Revenue Statistics 2021* (OECD, 2021[1]).

2019 data are used for the Africa (30) average, Australia, Japan and the OECD average.

Source: (OECD, 2022[16]), "Revenue Statistics - Asian and Pacific Economies: Comparative tables", *OECD Tax Statistics* (database).

StatLink https://stat.link/qrahn5

VAT is an increasingly important source of revenues for most economies in this publication, particularly in the Pacific. Excluding Nauru, Malaysia, Bhutan, Tokelau and the Solomon Islands, which do not have value added taxes, VAT revenues in 2020 ranged from 11.7% of total tax revenue in Australia (2019 figure) to 44.1% in the Vanuatu.

In ten of the 16 Asian economies that levy VAT, it generated more than 25% of total taxes (Kazakhstan, Mongolia, Indonesia, China, Lao PDR, Cambodia, Bangladesh, Kyrgyzstan, the Maldives and Pakistan). In six countries, the share of revenues from VAT was below 25%, ranging from 13.2% in Japan to 24.0% in Viet Nam. The share of revenues from VAT in total taxes was generally higher across Pacific economies, with only two economies (Australia at 11.7% of total taxes [2019 figure] and Papua New Guinea at 16.4%) reporting shares below 30%, while the share in the rest of the economies ranged from 30.9% in Fiji to 44.1% in Vanuatu in 2020. On average, the share of VAT in total tax revenues in Asia-Pacific (28) in 2020 (23.1%) was similar to the OECD average of 20.3% (2019 figure) and lower than the LAC (27.5%) and Africa (30) averages (29.3%, 2019 figure).

In 2020, revenues from other goods and services contributed between 6.5% of total tax revenue in Japan (2019 figure) and 70.5% in the Solomon Islands (Figure 1.11). The high share in the Solomon Islands was derived from general taxes on goods and services, such as the goods tax and the sales tax and export duties on various products, particularly logging (the Solomon Islands does not apply a VAT). The share of other taxes on goods and services in total revenues is also comparatively high in Cambodia, Thailand, Samoa, Bhutan, Kyrgyzstan, Lao PDR, Tokelau and Vanuatu, where they exceed 35% of total tax revenues.

In 2020, revenues from other taxes on goods and services played a more prominent role in the Pacific economies than in the Asian countries covered in this publication. Seven of the ten Pacific economies generated more revenue from other taxes on goods and services than from VAT, whereas 12 of the 18 Asian countries received more revenue from VAT. For the Africa, LAC and OECD averages, revenue from VAT contributed a larger share to total tax revenue than other goods and services while the opposite was true for the Asia-Pacific (28) average.

## Figure 1.12. Tax structure for the Africa (30), Asia-Pacific (28), LAC and OECD averages, 2020

Percentage of total tax revenues and as a percentage of GDP

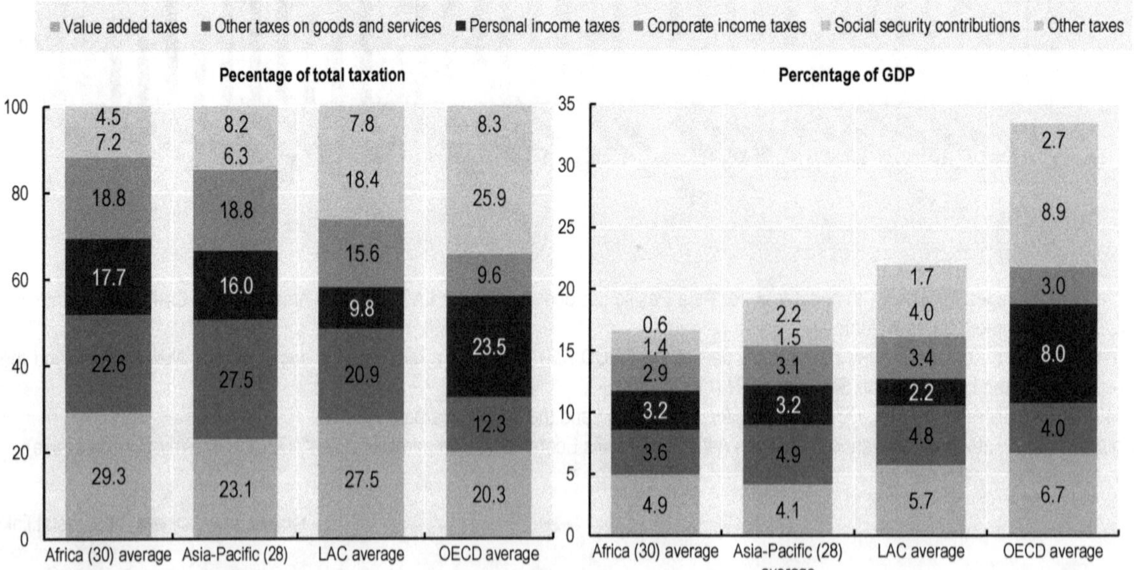


Note: 2019 data are used for the Africa (30) average and the OECD average.
Source: (OECD, 2022[16]), "Revenue Statistics - Asian and Pacific Economies: Comparative tables", *OECD Tax Statistics* (database).

StatLink https://stat.link/qnst8d

Average tax structures across Asia-Pacific, Africa and LAC shared some similarities in 2020. Revenues from goods and services accounted for a similar share of total tax revenues in Africa, Asia-Pacific and LAC, at 51.9% (2019 figure), 50.6% and 48.4% respectively – much higher than the OECD average of 32.6% (2019 figure). Taxes from other goods and services generated the largest share of total tax revenue (27.5%) in the Asia-Pacific region in 2020 (Figure 1.12), which was significantly higher than the share in Africa (22.6%, 2019 figure) and the LAC average (20.9%), and more than twice the OECD average (12.3%, 2019 figure). Revenues from VAT were equivalent to 4.1% of GDP in Asia-Pacific; at 23.1% of total taxation, these revenues were closer to the OECD average of 20.3% (2019 figure) than to the average share of VAT in Africa (29.3%, 2019 figure) and LAC (27.5%).

On average, income tax revenues in the Asia-Pacific region accounted for the same share of total taxation as in Africa (38.4%). In the Asia-Pacific region, revenues from PIT accounted for 16.0% of total taxes, similar to the Africa average of 17.7% (2019 figure), above the LAC average (9.8%) and below the OECD average (23.5%, 2019 figure). CIT revenues accounted for a larger share of total tax revenues in the Asia-Pacific region, on average, at 18.8%, which was the same as the Africa (30) average (also 18.8%, 2019 figure) and above the shares in LAC (15.6%) and the OECD (9.6%, 2019 figure). The Asia-Pacific region had the lowest share of SSCs among the four averages: they contributed 6.3% of total taxes in Asia Pacific, 7.2% in Africa (2019 figure), 18.4% in LAC and 25.9% of total taxes in OECD countries (2019 figure).

### *Changes in tax-to-GDP ratios between 2010 and 2020 by tax category*

Between 2010 and 2020, declines in CIT revenues were the major driver of decreases in tax-to-GDP ratios observed in many economies, whereas a range of tax types accounted for the increases (Figure 1.13). These changes reflect the diverse range of policy measures and economic developments in the 28 Asian and Pacific economies over this period.

Of the fifteen economies where tax-to-GDP ratios declined between 2010 and 2020, lower CIT revenues contributed to the declines in ten. The largest declines in the tax-to-GDP ratios over this period were in Fiji (-5.1 p.p.), Bhutan (-5.2 p.p.), Papua New Guinea (-5.3 p.p.), the Cook Islands (-7.2 p.p.) and Kazakhstan (-9.7 p.p.). As already mentioned, the decreases in the Cook Islands and Fiji were mainly due to the impact of the COVID-19 pandemic. In the remaining economies, decreases reflected a longer-term trend and resulted primarily from declines in CIT revenues, amplified by the COVID-19 pandemic:

- The decrease in Bhutan was mainly driven by decreases in revenue from CIT (-3.4 p.p.) and excises (-1.9 p.p.) due to lower revenues from the business income tax and lower economic activity prior to the COVID-19 pandemic (World Bank, 2021[19]). The removal of the excise duty refund from India due to the introduction of Goods and Service Tax caused a decrease in revenues from excises in 2019 (IMF, 2018[20]).
- Papua New Guinea and Kazakhstan were affected by declines in natural resource prices:
    - Between 2010 and 2020, CIT revenues in Papua New Guinea decreased by -4.8 p.p. due to lower revenues from the mining and petroleum tax, which accounted for half as much tax revenue in nominal terms in 2019 and for only around 12% in nominal terms in 2020 due to the COVID-19 pandemic as it did in 2010. Other factors such as slower economic growth and an earthquake in 2018 also contributed to the decline in the tax-to-GDP ratio in Papua New Guinea (IMF, 2020[21]).
    - The decline in tax-to-GDP ratio for Kazakhstan was mainly driven by decreases in CIT (-4.4 p.p.) and other taxes on goods and services (-5.5 p.p.), which include revenues from customs and import duties and from taxes on the production of useful minerals. Kazakhstan was particularly affected by the commodity price shock in 2014, as more than one-third of budgetary revenues are generated through the oil sector (OECD, 2019[22]).

- Thirteen economies recorded increases in their tax-to-GDP ratios between 2010 and 2020. The largest increases were observed in the Maldives, Cambodia and Nauru (since 2014), which all recorded increases larger than 10 p.p. Tax policy and administrative reforms were the main driver of the increases in tax-to-GDP in all three economies:
  - Since 2014, Nauru has introduced an employment and services tax and a business tax, and has improved revenue collection (IMF, 2020[23]).
  - Cambodia has implemented various administrative and regulatory reforms under the long-term Public Financial Management Reform Programme to improve the government's finance system (Royal Government of Cambodia, 2019[24]). Reforms aimed at making tax administrations more efficient have included the digitalisation of taxpayer services, simplification of procedures, improvements of audits and training for staff, as well as the revision of some tax rates to ease compliance (Royal Government of Cambodia, 2018[25]), (OECD, 2018[26]), (World Bank, 2019[27]).
  - The Maldives have undertaken major tax policy reforms since 2011 to increase tax revenue. Key policy changes have included the introduction of a goods and services tax in 2011, a business tax, and a corporate profit tax (ADB, 2017[28]). The tax-to-GDP ratio increased by 2 p.p. between 2010 and 2011, mainly due to the introduction of VAT. Subsequent rate increases in these three taxes have also contributed to higher tax revenues (ADB, 2017[28]). The Maldives also introduced a personal income tax in 2020 (Maldives Inland Revenue Authority, 2020[29]).

### Figure 1.13. Net changes in tax-to-GDP ratios between 2010 and 2020, by main type of taxes

Percentage point (p.p.) change

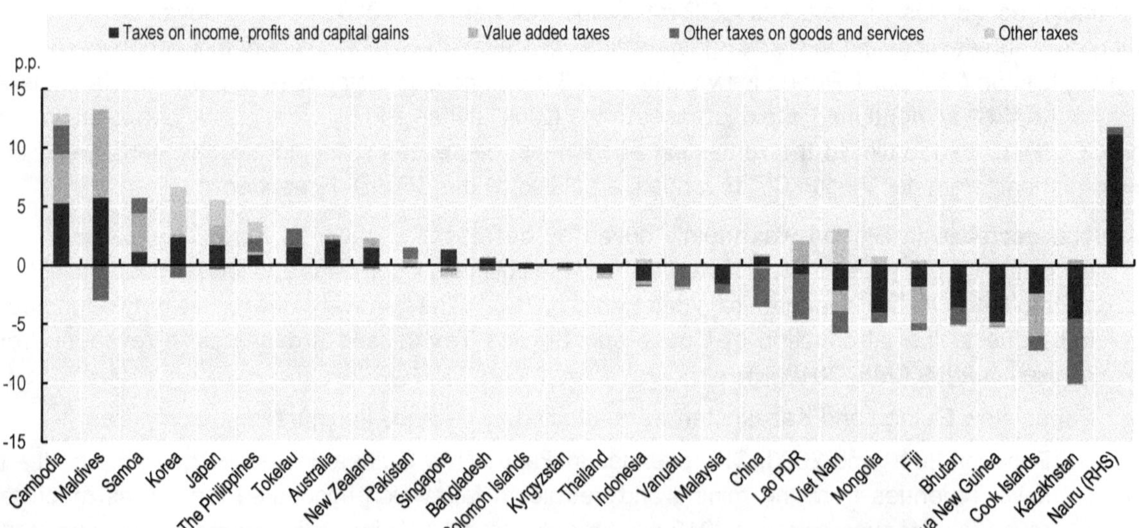


Note: Australia, Japan, Korea and New Zealand are part of the OECD (38) group. Data for Australia, Japan, Korea and New Zealand are taken from *Revenue Statistics 2021* (OECD, 2021[1]).
2019 data are used for Australia and Japan.
Data for Nauru are only available from 2014 and Pakistan from 2011 onwards. The tax-to-GDP ratios for China are shown exclusive of SSCs. Nauru recorded the largest increase among Asian and Pacific economies and uses the axis on the right hand side (RHS).
Source: Authors' calculations based on (OECD, 2022[16]), "Revenue Statistics - Asian and Pacific Economies: Comparative tables", *OECD Tax Statistics* (database).

StatLink https://stat.link/jkufna

Between 2010 and 2020, the share of revenue from VAT increased most in the Maldives (by 39.2 p.p.), Lao PDR (25.0 p.p.) and Kazakhstan (12.4 p.p.). Both the Maldives and Lao PDR introduced a VAT within this timeframe (in 2011 and 2010, respectively). While Lao PDR replaced the earlier turnover tax with a VAT (Keomixay, 2010[30]), the Maldives introduced a goods and sales tax, which is a value added tax, for the first time to raise revenue (ADB, 2017[28]). Increases in the share of VAT in total taxation in Kazakhstan were mainly the result of improved VAT administration (IMF, 2020[31]).

Seven economies experienced a decline in the share of VAT revenues over this period: Australia, Fiji, Korea, the Cook Islands, the Philippines, Singapore and Viet Nam. In Fiji, the share of VAT revenue declined by -7.2 p.p. in 2020 to 30.9% of total tax revenues, following a decrease of the VAT rate from 15% to 9% in 2016. In Viet Nam, the share of VAT decreased by -4.4 p.p. due to the increase in other tax revenues, such as PIT and SSCs. The decrease of -3.4 p.p. in the Cook Islands was a result of lower VAT revenues during the COVID-19 pandemic. Decreases in Australia (2010 to 2019), Korea and Singapore ranged from -1.5 p.p. to -2.7 p.p. over the same period.

### Figure 1.14. Revenues from VAT and other taxes on goods and services and revenues from PIT and CIT, 2020

Percentage of total taxation

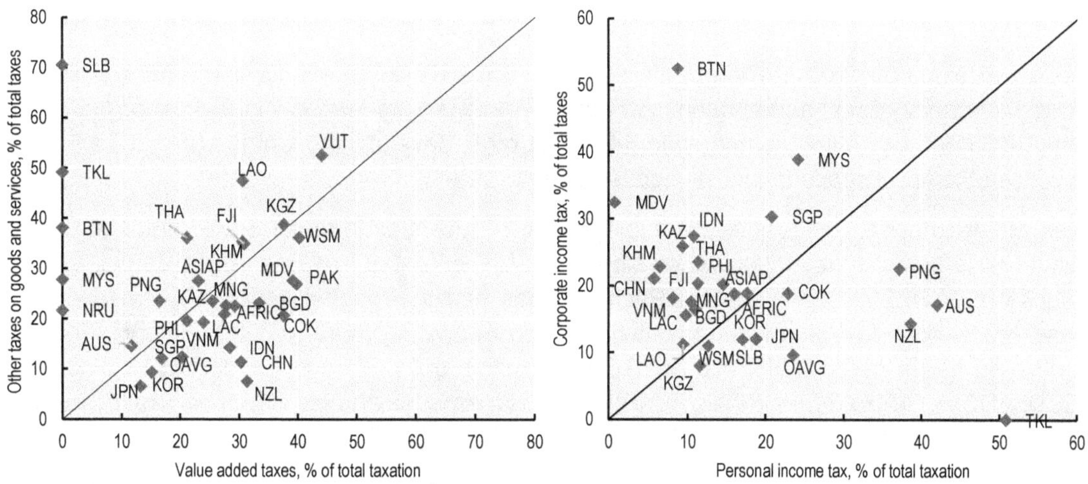


Source: (OECD, 2022[16]), "Revenue Statistics - Asian and Pacific Economies: Comparative tables", *OECD Tax Statistics* (database).

StatLink https://stat.link/xb2dzc

The relative importance of CIT and PIT in income tax revenues also varied between Asian and Pacific economies (Figure 1.14). In most Asian economies included in this publication, the share of revenues from CIT as a percentage of total taxation was higher than the share of revenues from PIT in 2020, except for Japan, Kyrgyzstan and Korea. In contrast, all Pacific economies, with the exception of Fiji, reported higher shares of revenues from PIT than CIT (see Box 1.2).

In 2020, revenues from CIT contributed between 8.0% of total tax revenue in Kyrgyzstan and 52.5% of total tax revenue in Bhutan. In six economies, the share of CIT revenues in total tax revenues exceeded 25% (Bhutan, Indonesia, Kazakhstan, Malaysia, Maldives and Singapore). By contrast, revenue from PIT as a percentage of total tax revenues ranged from 0.8% in the Maldives, which introduced personal income taxes in 2020, to 50.8% in Tokelau (which does not have a CIT).

The share of CIT revenues was lower in 2020 than in 2010 in thirteen economies, by between 0.2 p.p. of total tax revenues in Samoa and 23.2 p.p. in Papua New Guinea. The share of revenues from PIT decreased in five Asian and Pacific economies between 2010 and 2020, with the size of the decrease ranging from 0.3 p.p. in Tokelau to 6.0 p.p. in the Cook Islands. Revenue from PIT increased as a share of total taxation for 20 economies (excluding China, Pakistan, Nauru and Vanuatu which have no PIT data), with the increases ranging from 0.1 p.p. in Bangladesh to 13.4 p.p. in Papua New Guinea.

**Box 1.3. Enhancing domestic resource mobilisation in Small Island Developing States through revenue statistics**

Small Island Developing States (SIDS) comprise a diverse group of the smallest and most remote economies in the world located across Africa, Asia and the Pacific, and Latin America and the Caribbean. They share a common and unique set of development challenges owing to their small populations and landmasses, spatial dispersion and remoteness from major markets, and exposure to severe climate-related events and natural disasters. With small and undiversified economies, SIDS are highly vulnerable to external shocks, as they rely strongly on the global economy for financial services, tourism, remittances and concessional finance.

Two common challenges faced by SIDS are the achievement of adequate domestic resource mobilisation and debt sustainability. Domestic revenues are often erratic due to narrow economic productive bases that are often concentrated in sectors exposed to external fluctuations, such as natural resources or tourism. At the same time, SIDS typically have large current expenditures as the high unit cost of providing services to small and scattered populations increases public sector expenditures above the average levels of other developing countries (31.7% of GDP in SIDS, compared to 21.3% in other developing countries) (World Bank, 2020[32]). Severe climate events and natural disasters also tend to have heavy fiscal and economic impacts. These factors lead to high levels of public debt for many SIDS [59.5% of GDP, compared to 44.6% for other developing countries (World Bank, 2020[33])] and reduce the fiscal space to invest in development.

Taxes are an important and relatively stable source of revenues in many SIDS, although economies' ability to raise domestic revenues varies significantly. The *Global Revenue Statistics* publications and database (OECD, 2022[34]) show that Pacific Islands had the biggest variation of tax-to-GDP ratios among SIDS, from 11.6% in Papua New Guinea to 47.5% in Nauru in 2020. Among African SIDS, Cabo Verde had a tax-to-GDP ratio of 20.6%, Mauritius of 21.1% and Seychelles of 34.3% in 2019 (OECD, AUC, ATAF, 2021[35]). Finally, for SIDS in Latin America and the Caribbean, ratios ranged from 12.6% in the Dominican Republic to 37.5% in Cuba in 2020 (OECD et al., 2022[3]).

The COVID-19 pandemic is hampering SIDS' ability to mobilise and improve the stability of domestic revenues. Public revenues in SIDS have been affected by the crisis via a variety of channels, most notably the sharp fall in tourism, the decline in overall economic activity, and fluctuations in commodity and natural resource prices. To recover from the COVID-19 crisis, enhanced management of key sectors, including fisheries, tourism and natural resource extraction, may provide opportunities to enhance domestic revenue mobilisation in SIDS. Policies to reduce "leakages" from these sectors – especially tourism – and to support backward and forward linkages with other domestic sectors (e.g. food and agriculture, consumer goods and construction) could expand the taxable production base.

Improving the efficiency of revenue collection, enlarging the tax base and employing efficient tax policies are also essential to increase the resources required to sustain development. The *Global Revenue Statistics* project supports 21 SIDS in these efforts by providing accurate, comparable and detailed data on their tax revenues. This information is essential for tax policymaking and administrative reforms, and forms a common evidence base for mutual learning across SIDS on how to scale up domestic resource mobilisation.

Source: Piera Tortora and Talita Yamashiro Fordelone, based on OECD (OECD, 2018[36]), (World Bank, 2020[33]), (World Bank, 2020[32]) and on the Global Revenue Statistics database (OECD, 2022[34]).

## Environmental taxes in Asia and the Pacific

Environmentally related taxes,[7] and price-based policy instruments more generally, play an increasingly significant role in many countries to support a transition to sustainable and low-carbon economic growth. By incorporating a price signal into consumer and producer decisions, these taxes give effect to the polluter-pays principle and encourage businesses and households to consider the environmental costs of their behaviour. Although environmentally related tax revenues[8] (ERTR) are not separately identified in the standard OECD tax classification, they can be identified through the detailed list of specific taxes included for most countries within this overarching classification. It is on this basis that they are included in the *OECD Policy Instruments for the Environment* (PINE) database (OECD, 2022[37]).[9]

A detailed examination of taxes for the Asian and Pacific economies for which information is available demonstrates that revenue from environmentally related taxes in 2020 ranged from no (or very close to zero) environmentally related taxes in Australia and Bangladesh, to 3.8% of GDP in the Solomon Islands.[10] The case of the Solomon Islands is notable as their environmentally related tax revenue is particularly high compared to other Asian and Pacific economies or the OECD average, due in large part to higher export duties, particularly on timber. The next highest revenues from environmentally related taxes in the region in 2020 were observed in Mongolia (1.6%), Japan (1.2%), Pakistan (1.2%), New Zealand (1.1%), and Philippines and Viet Nam (both 1.0%). On average, environmentally related taxes amounted to 0.8% of GDP in the Asia-Pacific region.

### Figure 1.15. Environmentally related tax revenue in Asian and Pacific economies, by main tax base, 2020

Percentage of GDP

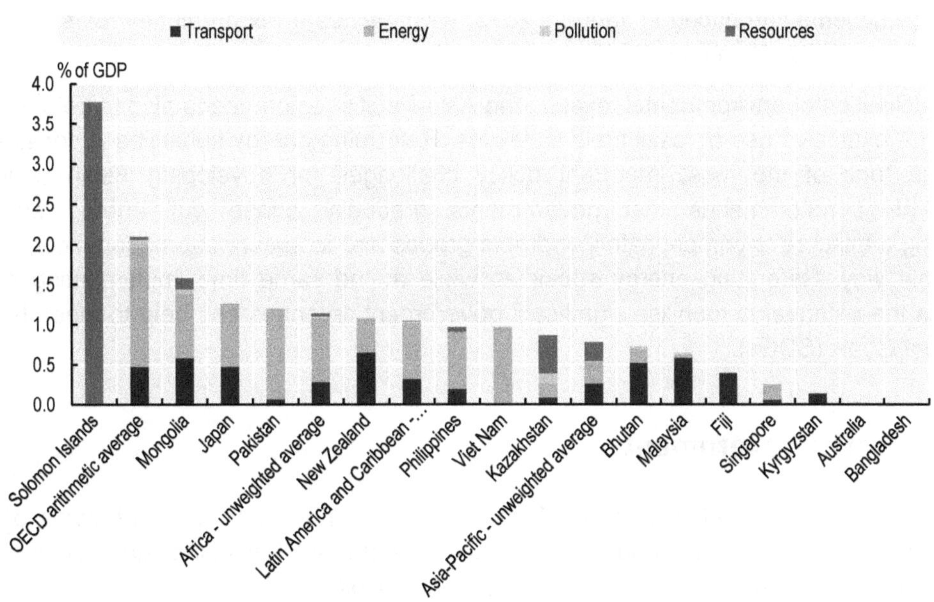


Note: It has not been possible to identify environmentally related tax revenues for Cambodia, China, the Cook Islands, Indonesia, Korea, Lao PDR, Maldives, Nauru, Papua New Guinea, Samoa, Thailand, Tokelau and Vanuatu due to data availability issues. 2019 data are used for the Africa (30) average.
Sources: Restricted ERTR database based on PINE database; (OECD, 2022[37]).

StatLink https://stat.link/f8peav

Asian and Pacific economies rely on a range of bases for their ERTR:

- In New Zealand, Bhutan, Malaysia, Fiji, Kyrgyzstan and Bangladesh, the majority of ERTR comes from transport taxes (registration or road use of motor vehicles or departure taxes). They represent the totality for Fiji, Kyrgyzstan and Bangladesh, and 90% of total ERTR in Malaysia, 72% in Bhutan and 61% in New Zealand.
- In other Asian and Pacific economies, ERTR are principally raised via taxes on energy (most commonly from diesel and petrol excises). They represent the totality of ERTR in Viet Nam, 95% in Pakistan, 76% Singapore, 74% in the Philippines, 61% in Japan and 51% in Mongolia. Other ERTR are levied from pollution and resources taxes. In almost all of these countries, a combination of these two types of taxes is used. Australia and the Solomon Islands are exceptions as they rely entirely on pollution taxes and resource taxes respectively.
- The composition of ERTR is markedly different in Asian and Pacific economies than in African, LAC and OECD countries. In 2020, revenues from energy taxes and transport taxes generated the highest share of total ERTR in the Asia-Pacific region (0.26% of GDP and 34% of the total ERTR for both) whereas resources taxes amounted to 0.23% of GDP on average and pollution taxes 0.01% (29% and 2% of total ERTR in Asia-Pacific respectively). In other regions, energy taxes accounted for 69.8% in Africa [2019 figure] of the total ERTR, 71.2% in the OECD and 67.6% in LAC.

In general, the use of taxation to address environmental issues is low in the region and there is scope to increase use of such instruments, as recently shown by Singapore. In 2019, Singapore became the first country in Southeast Asia to impose a carbon tax. Its payment was first levied in 2020, based on greenhouse gas (GHG) emissions in 2019. The tax is applied on facilities that emit 25 000 tonnes of GHG emissions ($tCO_2e$) or more annually and it is set at a rate of S$5 ($tCO_2e$) from 2019 to 2023, covering six greenhouse gases, and will be progressively raised to S$25/$tCO_2e$ in 2024 and 2025, S$45/$tCO_2e$ in 2026 and 2027 and S$50-80/$tCO_2e$ by 2030 (NCCS, 2020[38]). This tax complements the carbon emissions-based vehicle scheme introduced in January 2013, which levies a tax on all new cars, taxis and newly-imported used cars, based on their $CO_2$/km performance.

The under-utilisation of environmental taxes in the Asia-Pacific region needs also to be understood in the context of the extensive use of fossil fuels subsidies. Reforming energy subsidies is considered by ADB (2016[39]) as "one of the most important policy challenges for developing Asian economies". UN ESCAP (2016[40]) recommends that governments gradually phase out energy subsidies while implementing measures to compensate vulnerable groups and to ensure international competitiveness in a sustainable way. Reforming energy subsidies while at the same time implementing environmental taxation has the potential to mobilise significant government revenues and help to meet the Sustainable Development Goals (SDGs).

## Taxes by level of government

This section discusses the relative share of tax revenues attributed to different levels of government in 2020: central government, regional or provincial government (including state government, where relevant), and local government as well as social security funds.

Sub-national taxes as a share of total tax revenues are highly variable across the region (Table 1.1). In 2020, the share of sub-national government tax revenue in the Asian countries ranged from 0.8% of total revenues in Bhutan to 36.7% in China. In Indonesia, revenues attributed to sub-national governments rose to over 11.5% in 2020, following the shift of property taxation to the local level in 2014. Revenue collected by sub-national governments accounted for 15.4% of total taxes in Mongolia in 2020, 6.5% in New Zealand and 19.2% in Australia (including both state and local tax revenues, 2019 figure).

The types of taxes levied by local governments vary between countries. Local governments in the Philippines have a narrow range of taxes under their jurisdiction, relying on property taxes and taxes on income and profits. Sub-national governments in Japan and Korea raise revenue from taxes on income and profits, property taxes, taxes on goods and services, payroll (Korea only) and other taxes. The share of sub-national government revenue also depends on the range of services that local governments are expected to provide. For example, the two types of local governments in Japan, prefectures and municipalities, participate in a wide range of responsibilities such as economic development plans, education, urban planning, public health and other social assistance expenditures (OECD/UCLG, 2019[41]) Between 2000 and 2020, the share of revenues collected by sub-national governments was stable across the region, with the exception of Indonesia and Kazakhstan. In Indonesia, the share of revenues attributed to sub-national governments increased by 8.4 p.p., whereas in Kazakhstan decreased by -20.1 p.p.

With SSCs generating a smaller proportion of total revenues in Asia and the Pacific than in other regions, the share of revenues attributed to social security funds was also low. Australia, Bhutan, Cambodia, New Zealand, Pakistan and Singapore do not have social security funds and the proportion of total tax revenues collected by social security funds was zero in 2020, and was under 6% of total revenues in Indonesia, Kazakhstan, Malaysia and Thailand. By contrast, countries that source a greater share of their revenues from SSCs also had higher shares of revenues attributed to social security funds: at 41.1% of tax revenues in Japan in 2019, 28.0% in Korea, 24.2% in China, 18.7% in Mongolia, and 15.7% in the Philippines in 2020. The share of tax revenues attributed to social security funds has increased in Japan (by 5.8 p.p.) and Korea (by 11.3 p.p.) since 2000, and in Mongolia since 2006 (by 8.6. p.p.).

## Table 1.1. Attribution of tax revenues to sub-sectors of general government

| | Federal or central government | | | | Sub-national government | | | | Social security funds | | | |
|---|---|---|---|---|---|---|---|---|---|---|---|---|
| | 2000 | 2010 | 2015 | 2020 | 2000 | 2010 | 2015 | 2020 | 2000 | 2010 | 2015 | 2020 |
| Australia | 81.8 | 80.2 | 79.3 | 80.8 | 18.2 | 19.8 | 20.7 | 19.2 | 0.0 | 0.0 | 0.0 | 0.0 |
| Bhutan | 99.7 | 99.9 | 99.6 | 99.2 | 0.3 | 0.1 | 0.4 | 0.8 | 0.0 | 0.0 | 0.0 | 0.0 |
| China | .. | 54.7 | 50.3 | 39.1 | .. | 45.3 | 49.7 | 36.7 | .. | .. | .. | 24.2 |
| Indonesia | 96.8 | 92.8 | 88.9 | 82.6 | 3.2 | 7.2 | 10.6 | 11.5 | .. | .. | 0.6 | 5.9 |
| Japan | 38.7 | 33.0 | 36.7 | 35.5 | 26.1 | 25.9 | 23.9 | 23.5 | 35.2 | 41.1 | 39.4 | 41.1 |
| Kazakhstan | 50.3 | 81.3 | 72.2 | 65.0 | 49.7 | 16.2 | 24.0 | 29.7 | .. | 2.5 | 3.8 | 5.3 |
| Cambodia | .. | 100.0 | 93.4 | 90.7 | .. | .. | 6.6 | 9.3 | .. | 0.0 | 0.0 | 0.0 |
| Korea | 68.2 | 60.0 | 55.4 | 53.0 | 15.1 | 16.6 | 18.0 | 19.0 | 16.7 | 23.3 | 26.6 | 28.0 |
| Mongolia | .. | 75.5 | 61.5 | 65.9 | .. | 11.4 | 16.5 | 15.4 | .. | 13.1 | 22.0 | 18.7 |
| Malaysia | 98.0 | 98.2 | 98.3 | 97.4 | .. | .. | .. | .. | 2.0 | 1.8 | 1.7 | 2.6 |
| New Zealand | 94.3 | 92.8 | 93.2 | 93.5 | 5.7 | 7.2 | 6.8 | 6.5 | 0.0 | 0.0 | 0.0 | 0.0 |
| Pakistan | .. | .. | 92.4 | 91.1 | .. | .. | 7.6 | 8.9 | .. | .. | 0.0 | 0.0 |
| The Philippines | 81.5 | 82.0 | 80.6 | 78.3 | 5.3 | 5.3 | 5.3 | 5.9 | 13.1 | 12.6 | 14.1 | 15.7 |
| Singapore | 100.0 | 100.0 | 100.0 | 100.0 | .. | .. | .. | .. | 0.0 | 0.0 | 0.0 | 0.0 |
| Thailand | 88.9 | 86.3 | 86.4 | 86.6 | 7.5 | 6.6 | 8.0 | 7.6 | 3.7 | 7.1 | 5.6 | 5.8 |

Note: Australia, Japan, Korea and New Zealand are part of the OECD (38) group. Data for Australia, Japan, Korea and New Zealand are taken from (OECD, 2020[42]) (OECD, 2021[1]).
2019 data are used for Australia and Japan.
Australia: Sub-national figures include data of state and local government.
Data for China are included for 2020. Detailed data on revenue from social security contributions were not available in previous years.
Source: (OECD, 2022[16]), "Revenue Statistics - Asian and Pacific Economies: Comparative tables", *OECD Tax Statistics* (database).

StatLink https://stat.link/ehy6c9

## Non-tax revenues in selected economies

This publication includes information on non-tax revenues for selected economies for which data are available. Non-tax revenues are defined as all revenues received by general government that do not meet the OECD definition of taxes, as set out in the Interpretative Guide (Annex A). They are further divided into five categories according to the definitions set out in Annex B: grants; property income; sales of goods and services; fines, penalties and forfeits; and miscellaneous and unidentified revenues.

### *Non-tax revenues as a percentage of GDP*

Non-tax revenues were equivalent to a significant share of GDP in 2020 for six of the 19 economies for which data are available. In 2020, non-tax revenues amounted to 11.6% of GDP in Samoa, 19.8% in Bhutan, 24.0% in Vanuatu and 27.4% in the Cook Islands, whereas they amounted to 67.5% in Nauru and 218.7% in Tokelau. The very high level of non-tax revenues in Tokelau, measured as a share of GDP, is due to the fact that non-tax revenues are derived primarily from payments by foreign vessels for access to fishing waters under the Exclusive Economic Zone (EEZ) of Tokelau. In the 2008 System of National Accounts, these revenues are recorded as part of GNI but they do not add to GDP. By contrast, non-tax revenues are below 8.5% of GDP in the remaining economies. Similarly, fishing activities represent a significant source of revenue for the Nauru government and accounts for more than 50% of the total non-tax revenue in 2020, collected mainly from access fees paid by foreign fishing vessels.

Between 2019 and 2020, non-tax revenues declined in 12 economies as a percentage of GDP while they increased in seven. The declines exceeded 1 p.p. in five economies: Pakistan (-1.1 p.p.), Lao PDR and Tokelau (both -1.4 p.p.), Singapore (-2.4 p.p.) and Nauru (-17.8 p.p.). The decline in non-tax revenues in Nauru was mostly attributable to lower fishing and visa fee revenues, which were heavily affected by the COVID-19 crisis. In contrast, the Cook Islands reported an increase of 11.4 p.p. in non-tax revenue due to an increase in other revenue earned on behalf of the crown (classified under miscellaneous non-tax revenue), while the remaining economies reported increases smaller than one percentage point.

Non-tax revenues have been increasing since 2010 (or earliest available year) as a share of GDP in the majority of the economies but declining for Bhutan, Cambodia, Kyrgyzstan, Lao PDR, Maldives, Mongolia, Pakistan and Papua New Guinea. The largest increases occurred in Tokelau (64.1 p.p.), Nauru (38.9 p.p., since 2014), Vanuatu (15.7 p.p.), and the Cook Islands (13.9 p.p.). The upward trend for Tokelau and Nauru has been driven by higher revenues from property income, which is mostly sourced from fishery income. Tokelau receives support from New Zealand to strengthen the management of its Exclusive Economic Zone to maximise Tokelau's revenue collection from its international fisheries (New Zealand Foreign Affairs & Trade, 2018[43]). Fisheries income also increased for Tokelau and Nauru after they became partners to the Parties to the Nauru Agreement (PNA), which administers the fishing vessel-day scheme (VDS). The VDS is the system to sustainably manage the world's largest tuna fishery in the Western and Central Pacific Ocean, and has increased revenue to the PNA by over 700% in the past seven years (Parties to the Nauru Agreement, 2016[44]). The increase in non-tax revenue for Vanuatu is mainly due to development project grants from Australia, the World Bank, New Zealand and China, and the government's Honorary Citizenship Programme (Department of Finance and Treasury of Vanuatu, 2018[45]). For the Cook Islands, grants have constituted an increasing share of non-tax revenue. Official Development Assistance (ODA) from New Zealand to support education, health and tourism initiatives in the Cook Islands accounts for the largest source of grants revenues (Ministry of Finance and Economic Management, 2020[46]).

While tax revenue increased in economies such as Cambodia, Nauru, Maldives and Samoa as a percentage of GDP since 2010 (or earliest available year), non-tax revenues have been a more volatile source of revenue. In Bhutan, Lao PDR, and Samoa, the volatility of grants contributed most to the overall volatility of non-tax revenues. In Pakistan, revenues from property income were notably volatile.

**Table 1.2. Non-tax revenue of main headings in selected Asia Pacific economies, 2010-20**

Percentage of GDP

| | 2010 | 2011 | 2012 | 2013 | 2014 | 2015 | 2016 | 2017 | 2018 | 2019 | 2020 |
|---|---|---|---|---|---|---|---|---|---|---|---|
| Bhutan | 22.1 | 21.5 | 16.6 | 20.6 | 14.8 | 17.7 | 15.0 | 16.4 | 13.1 | 19.5 | 19.8 |
| Cambodia | 6.4 | 4.6 | 4.4 | 5.7 | 4.4 | 4.0 | 5.1 | 4.7 | 5.1 | 5.1 | 4.3 |
| Cook Islands | 13.5 | 8.2 | 8.4 | 14.3 | 16.2 | 13.9 | 16.4 | 14.3 | 12.9 | 16.0 | 27.4 |
| Fiji | 2.9 | 3.6 | 3.0 | 2.9 | 2.9 | 2.9 | 3.2 | 3.5 | 3.6 | 3.4 | 4.1 |
| Kazakhstan | 1.0 | 1.4 | 1.8 | 1.0 | 1.5 | 1.3 | 1.2 | 1.1 | 1.7 | 1.5 | 1.2 |
| Kyrgyzstan | 8.3 | 8.7 | 7.6 | 8.4 | 9.4 | 10.7 | 7.9 | 8.5 | 6.3 | 7.6 | 7.8 |
| Lao PDR | 9.5 | 6.7 | 10.2 | 7.3 | 9.6 | 7.7 | 4.5 | 5.3 | 5.4 | 5.1 | 3.7 |
| Maldives | 10.2 | 9.0 | 6.3 | 5.1 | 7.0 | 6.7 | 7.2 | 6.8 | 6.8 | 6.4 | 5.7 |
| Mongolia | 6.5 | 7.4 | 6.9 | 7.2 | 7.8 | 6.4 | 5.1 | 4.3 | 4.6 | 4.3 | 3.6 |
| Nauru | .. | .. | .. | .. | 28.6 | 65.2 | 63.7 | 70.8 | 92.7 | 85.3 | 67.5 |
| Pakistan | .. | 2.5 | 3.0 | 3.6 | 3.5 | 2.5 | 2.8 | 2.0 | 1.1 | 3.3 | 2.2 |
| Papua New Guinea | 4.7 | 3.3 | 3.1 | 2.4 | 3.1 | 3.2 | 3.2 | 3.3 | 3.7 | 2.8 | 2.7 |
| The Philippines | .. | .. | .. | .. | 1.8 | 2.0 | 1.8 | 1.7 | 1.8 | 2.0 | 2.3 |
| Samoa | 8.9 | 6.0 | 4.8 | 7.1 | 4.8 | 4.7 | 4.5 | 5.3 | 5.6 | 10.9 | 11.6 |
| Singapore | 3.5 | 3.5 | 3.4 | 3.5 | 3.9 | 4.4 | 4.4 | 5.3 | 4.3 | 7.2 | 4.7 |
| Thailand | 3.3 | 2.7 | 2.9 | 2.9 | 3.1 | 3.6 | 3.7 | 3.6 | 3.8 | 3.7 | 4.0 |
| Tokelau | 154.6 | 196.4 | 192.6 | 246.6 | 173.4 | 230.4 | 236.5 | 210.0 | 236.4 | 220.1 | 218.7 |
| Vanuatu | 8.3 | 5.9 | 5.2 | 4.2 | 5.8 | 14.8 | 9.6 | 14.2 | 19.8 | 24.3 | 24.0 |
| Viet Nam | 5.7 | 5.1 | 4.9 | 5.1 | 5.1 | 6.5 | 7.2 | 8.4 | 8.6 | 8.3 | 8.2 |

Note: Tokelau receives significant revenues from foreign vessels for access to Tokelau fishing waters. In the 2008 SNA, these revenues are recorded as part of GNI, but they do not add to GDP.
Source: (OECD, 2022[16]), "Revenue Statistics in Asian and Pacific Economies: Comparative tables", *OECD Tax Statistics* (database).

StatLink https://stat.link/p7j41n

### *Structure of non-tax revenues*

Non-tax revenues are divided into different categories: grants; property income; sales of goods and services; fines, penalties and forfeits; and miscellaneous and unidentified revenues. In 2020, the shares of each of these categories in total non-tax revenues varied across the 19 economies for which data are available (Figure 1.16). Notable trends include:

- Grants were an important source of revenues for half of the economies in 2020, exceeding 30% of total non-tax revenues in eight economies: Vanuatu (32.8%), Tokelau (36.2%), Lao PDR (39.7%), Bhutan (42.6%), Cambodia (45.8%), the Cook Islands (49.9%), Samoa (59.0%) and Papua New Guinea (65.4%). In 2020, they accounted for the majority of non-tax revenues for the Samoa and Papua New Guinea
- Property income accounted for over 30% of total non-tax revenue in more than half the economies for which non-tax revenue data are available. There were only five economies in which property income accounted for less than 20% of total non-tax revenue: Vanuatu, which does not generate revenues from property income, Viet Nam (5.9%), Cook Islands (9.2%), Cambodia (12.7%) and Samoa (13.3%). Property income accounted for more than half of total non-tax revenues in seven economies in 2020: Thailand (53.2%), Nauru (54.7%), the Philippines (58.0%), Tokelau (59.6%), Pakistan (74.9%), Kazakhstan (75.2%) and Singapore (78.8%).
- Property income in Tokelau and Nauru was derived predominantly from fisheries (i.e. fishing rents, fishing days, support vessels, etc.), which represented more than 90% of total property income in both economies. Rents and royalties accounted for 56.4% of total non-tax revenue in Kazakhstan

in 2020, mainly from oil revenues. Interests and dividends represented the majority of non-tax revenues for Pakistan (67.8%) and Singapore (73.7%). Other property income for the Philippines made up 57.6% of non-tax revenues.

- Finally, sales of goods and services accounted for more than half of non-tax revenues for Viet Nam (55.5%, composed by fees and charges, land rents, and revenues from land user right assignment) and Maldives (64.4%, mainly from leasing, fees and charges).

## Figure 1.16. Structure of non-tax revenues, 2020

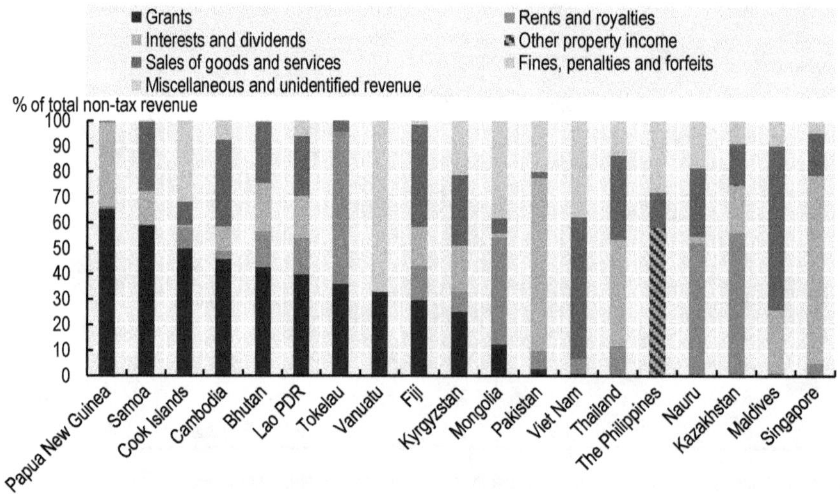


Source: (OECD, 2022[16]), "Revenue Statistics - Asian and Pacific Economies: Comparative tables", *OECD Tax Statistics* (database).

StatLink https://stat.link/tixwpm

## References


ADB (2020), *Pacific Economic Monitor, December 2020*, https://www.adb.org/sites/default/files/publication/662406/pem-december-2020.pdf (accessed on 14 June 2022). [17]

ADB (2017), "Fast-Track Tax Reform Lessons from Maldives", https://doi.org/10.22617/TIM178673-2. [28]

ADB (2016), *Fossil Fuel Subsidies in Asia: Trends, Impacts, and Reforms*, https://www.adb.org/sites/default/files/publication/182255/fossil-fuel-subsidies-asia.pdf. [39]

ADB (2016), *Pacific Approach 2016-2020*, https://www.adb.org/documents/pacific-approach-2016-2020 (accessed on 4 June 2021). [14]

Aizenman, J. et al. (2019), "Tax Revenue Trends in Latin America and Asia: A Comparative Analysis", *Emerging Markets Finance and Trade*, pp. 427–449. [7]

ASEAN (2021), *History - ASEAN | One Vision One Identity One Community*, https://asean.org/asean/about-asean/history/ (accessed on 4 June 2021). [15]

Department of Finance and Treasury of Vanuatu (2018), *Treasury Monthly Budget Report-November 2018*, https://doft.gov.vu/images/2019/November_Monthly_Report_FINAL.pdf (accessed on 10 June 2020). [45]

FRCS (2020), *Airport departure tax 1986*, https://www.frcs.org.fj/wp-content/uploads/2020/08/Airport-Departur-Tax-Act-1986-Revised-31-July-2020.pdf (accessed on 14 June 2022). [18]

Government of Nauru (2020), *GON 2019-20 Final Budget Outcome*, https://naurufinance.info/wp-content/uploads/2020/10/GON-Final-Budget-Outcome-2019-20-20201018.pdf (accessed on 3 June 2021). [10]

IMF (2022), *World Economic Outlook, April 2022: War Sets Back The Global Recovery*, International Monetary Fund, Washington, DC, https://www.imf.org/en/Publications/WEO/Issues/2022/04/19/world-economic-outlook-april-2022 (accessed on 13 June 2022). [13]

IMF (2020), *Papua New Guinea : 2019 Article IV Consultation and Request for Staff Monitored Program-Press Release; Staff Report; and Statement by the Executive Director for Papua New Guinea*, https://www.imf.org/en/Publications/CR/Issues/2020/04/06/Papua-New-Guinea-2019-Article-IV-Consultation-and-Request-for-Staff-Monitored-Program-Press-49307 (accessed on 17 May 2021). [21]

IMF (2020), *Republic of Kazakhstan : 2019 Article IV Consultation-Press Release; and Staff Report*, https://www.imf.org/en/Publications/CR/Issues/2020/01/29/Republic-of-Kazakhstan-2019-Article-IV-Consultation-Press-Release-and-Staff-Report-49002 (accessed on 10 May 2021). [31]

IMF (2020), *Republic of Nauru : 2019 Article IV Consultation*, https://www.imf.org/en/Publications/CR/Issues/2020/01/29/Republic-of-Nauru-2019-Article-IV-Consultation-Press-Release-Staff-Report-and-Statement-by-49001 (accessed on 30 June 2020). [23]

IMF (2019), *World Economic Outlook - Frequently Asked Questions*, https://www.imf.org/external/pubs/ft/weo/faq.htm#q4d (accessed on 6 September 2019). [11]

IMF (2018), "Bhutan: 2018 Article IV Consultation—Press Release; Staff Report; and Statement by the Executive Director for Bhutan", *IMF Staff Country Reports*, Vol. 2018/300, https://doi.org/10.5089/9781484382073.002.A001. [20]

Keomixay, D. (2010), *Value Added Tax in Lao PDR: Agenda for the Future.* [30]

Malaysian Investment Development Authority (2019), *Incentives*, https://www.mida.gov.my/wp-content/uploads/2020/07/20200603104248_MIDA_Booklet_FINAL-as-at-03062020.pdf. [5]

Maldives Inland Revenue Authority (2020), *Annual Report 2020*, https://www.mira.gov.mv/reports/Annual_Report_English_2020.pdf (accessed on 14 June 2022). [29]

Mawejje, J. and R. Sebudde (2019), "Tax revenue potential and effort: Worldwide estimates using a new dataset", *Economic Analysis and Policy*, pp. 119–129. [4]

Ministry of Finance and Economic Management (2020), *Quarterly Financial Results*, http://www.mfem.gov.ck/images/treasury/Crown_Accounting/Reports/Quarterly_Financial_Rpts/2021/December_2020_Quarterly_Financial_Report.pdf. [46]

NCCS (2020), *Carbon Tax*, https://www.nccs.gov.sg/faqs/carbon-tax/ (accessed on 22 June 2020). [38]

New Zealand Foreign Affairs & Trade (2018), "Aid partnership with Tokelau", https://www.mfat.govt.nz/en/aid-and-development/our-work-in-the-pacific/tokelau/. [43]

OECD (2022), *"Revenue Statistics in Asian and Pacific Economies: Comparative tables", OECD Tax statistics (database).* [16]

OECD (2022), *Database on Policy Instruments for the Environment*, https://pinedatabase.oecd.org/ (accessed on 15 June 2020). [37]

OECD (2022), *Global Revenue Statistics Database*, OECD Publishing, http://www.oecd.org/tax/tax-policy/global-revenue-statistics-database.htm. [34]

OECD (2022), *Revenue Statistics - Asian and Pacific Economies: Country tables, OECD Tax statistics (database).* [2]

OECD (2021), *ERTR restricted database.* [48]

OECD (2021), *Revenue Statistics*, OECD Publishing, Paris, https://doi.org/10.1787/2522770x. [1]

OECD (2020), *Revenue Statistics 2020*, OECD Publishing, Paris, https://doi.org/10.1787/8625f8e5-en. [42]

OECD (2019), *Application of the Going for Growth Framework to Kazakhstan.* [22]

OECD (2019), *Tax Morale: What Drives People and Businesses to Pay Tax?*, OECD Publishing, Paris, https://doi.org/10.1787/f3d8ea10-en. [6]

OECD (2018), *Good Regulatory Practices to Support Small and Medium Enterprises in Southeast Asia*, OECD Publishing, Paris, https://doi.org/10.1787/9789264305434-en. [26]

OECD (2018), *Making Development Co-operation Work for Small Island Developing States*, OECD Publishing, Paris, https://doi.org/10.1787/9789264287648-en. [36]

OECD (2017), *Policy INstruments Environment*, http://oe.cd/pine (accessed on 15 June 2020). [47]

OECD (2005), *OECD Glossary of Statistical Terms - Environmental taxes Definition*, https://stats.oecd.org/glossary/detail.asp?ID=6437 (accessed on 12 July 2022). [49]

OECD, AUC, ATAF (2021), *Revenue Statistics in Africa*, OECD Publishing, Paris, https://doi.org/10.1787/2617653x. [35]

OECD et al. (2022), *Revenue Statistics in Latin America and the Caribbean 2022*, OECD Publishing, Paris, https://doi.org/10.1787/58a2dc35-en-es. [3]

OECD/UCLG (2019), *Report World Observatory on Subnational Government Finance and Investment – Country Profiles.* [41]

Parties to the Nauru Agreement (2016), "PNA members confirm: Vessel Day Scheme is here to stay", https://www.pnatuna.com/node/340. [44]

Royal Government of Cambodia (2019), *Progress Report on Public Management Stage 3 3rd Quater 2019 (GDAP3)*, http://www.pfm.gov.kh/index.php/en/reports-en/progress-reports-en. [24]

Royal Government of Cambodia (2018), "Final Draft of Progress Report of Public Financial Management Reform Program Implementation for 2018", http://www.pfm.gov.kh/document/report/2018/Annual%20Progress%20Report%202018%20En.pdf (accessed on 16 June 2022). [25]

UNCTAD (2012), *World Investment Report 2012, Towards a new Generation of Investment Policies, New York*, http://unctad.org/en/PublicationsLibrary/wir2012_embargoed_en.pdf. [8]

UNESCAP (2016), *Environmental Tax Reform in Asia and the Pacific*, https://www.unescap.org/sites/default/files/S2_Environmental-Tax-Reform.pdf (accessed on 25 June 2020). [40]

UNESCAP (2014), *Economic and Social Survey of Asia and the Pacific 2014, Regional Connectivity for Shared Prosperity*, UN, https://www.unescap.org/sites/default/files/Economic20and%20Social%20Survey%20of%20Asia%20and%20the%20Pacific%202014.pdf. [9]

WHO (2015), *Purchasing Power Parity 2005*, http://www.who.int/choice/costs/ppp/en/. [12]

World Bank (2021), *GDP growth (annual %) - Bhutan, World Development Indicators*, https://data.worldbank.org/indicator/NY.GDP.MKTP.KD.ZG?locations=BT. [19]

World Bank (2020), *"Central government debt, total (% of GDP)", World Development Indicators (database)*, https://data.worldbank.org/indicator/GC.DOD.TOTL.GD.ZS. [33]

World Bank (2020), *"Expense (% of GDP)", World Development Indicators (database)*, https://data.worldbank.org/indicator/GC.XPN.TOTL.GD.ZS. [32]

World Bank (2019), "Cambodia Public Expenditure Review: Improving the effectiveness of public finance", http://www.worldbank.org (accessed on 15 June 2022). [27]

## Notes

[1] Note by the ADB: The ADB recognises "Kyrgyzstan" as the "Kyrgyz Republic".

[2] Data for Pakistan are available from 2011 and data for Nauru are available from 2014. In addition, 2020 data for Australia and Japan are not available in (OECD, 2021[48]), so 2019 data are used instead.

[3] The ASEAN members not included in this publication are Myanmar and Brunei Darussalam.

[4] Data on SSCs were not available for Cambodia and Lao PDR.

[5] For Nauru and Pakistan, it is not possible to distinguish between revenues from PIT and CIT.

[6] For Nauru and Pakistan, it is not possible to distinguish between revenues from PIT and CIT.

[7] An environmentally related tax is a tax whose base is a physical unit (or a proxy of a physical unit) of something that has a proven, specific harmful impact on the environment regardless of whether the tax is intended to change behaviours or is levied for another purpose (OECD, 2005[49]).

[8] The figures in this report do not include revenues (that may be significant) from other policies addressing environmental issues such as fees and charges or revenues from emissions trading schemes. However the PINE database provides additional data on fees and charges, subsidies, voluntary approaches, tradable permits, deposit-refund systems for more than 80 countries (OECD, 2017[47]).

[9] Data on environmentally related tax revenue are presented for four tax-base categories: energy (including all $CO_2$ related taxes); transport (mostly motor vehicle taxes); pollution (e.g. discharges of waste or pollutants, taxes on waste or packaging); and resources (e.g. water extraction, hunting and fishing, mining) (OECD, 2017[47]).

[10] These figures need to be treated with caution as some environmentally related taxes may not be captured if the data are not sufficiently disaggregated.

# 2 Strengthening tax revenues in developing Asia

This special feature explores the potential for Asian countries to increase tax revenue in the wake of the COVID-19 pandemic while discussing the constraints and challenges they face in doing so. It examines the use of tax expenditures in the region and identifies opportunities to generate additional revenues through value-added tax, income taxes and international co-operation on taxation.

Tackling developing Asia's[1] varied challenges will require substantial public investments. To meet these challenges and to restore the health of public finances after COVID-19 passes, the region's economies urgently need to mobilise additional fiscal resources, especially tax revenues. Drawing on the *Asian Development Outlook 2022* theme chapter (ADB, 2022[1]), this special feature[2] examines the challenges and opportunities for developing Asia to increase tax revenues. It first presents estimates of tax potential and outlines some of the key constraints to tax revenue mobilisation in the region. Next, it examines the challenge of optimising tax expenditures, which can cause significant revenue losses. Finally, it analyses options for increasing revenue from the key sources of value added, personal income and corporate income taxes.

## Developing Asia has the potential to increase tax revenues

The scope to increase tax revenue in developing Asia can be broadly assessed by estimating tax capacity and comparing this to current tax collection. Tax capacity is the theoretical maximum tax revenues an economy can mobilise given its structural characteristics. General underdevelopment, low education levels and large agriculture sectors have been found to reduce tax capacity (Mawejje and Sebudde, 2019[2]). Tax effort is the ratio of actual tax revenues to tax capacity. High tax effort implies actual tax collection is close to tax capacity and the scope to increase revenues may be more limited. In contrast, low effort implies tax collection falls far short of tax capacity, possibly reflecting low tax rates, narrow tax bases or poor compliance.

**Figure 2.1. Tax potential in Asia: tax capacity and tax revenue, latest available year**

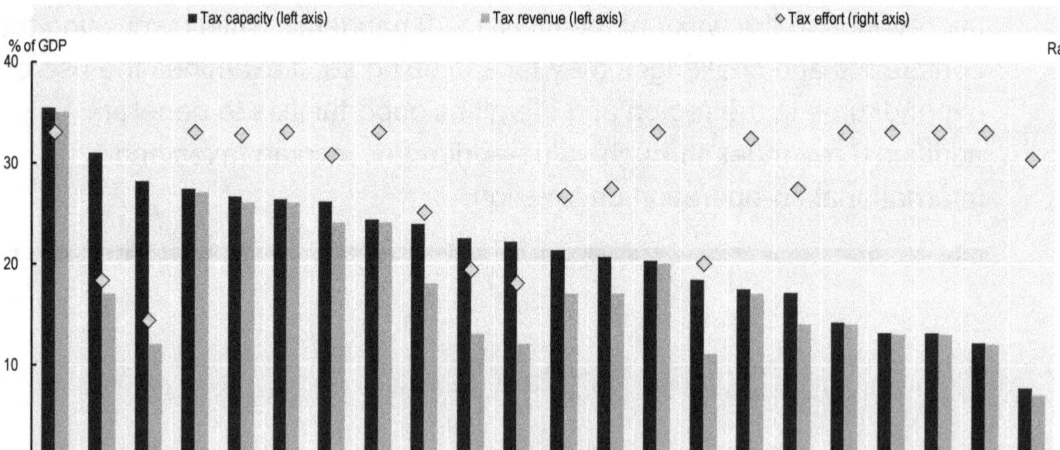


Note: CAM = Cambodia, FIJ = Fiji, FSM = Federated States of Micronesia, HKG = Hong Kong, China, IND = India, INO = Indonesia, KOR = Korea, Republic of, LAO = Lao People's Democratic Republic, MAL = Malaysia, MYA = Myanmar, PAK = Pakistan, PHI = Philippines, PNG = Papua New Guinea, PRC = People's Republic of China, SAM = Samoa, SIN = Singapore, SOL = Solomon Islands, THA = Thailand, TIM = Timor-Leste, TON = Tonga, VAN = Vanuatu, VIE = Viet Nam.
Source: Gupta, and Jalles (2022[3]).

StatLink https://stat.link/al5kus

New indicative tax capacity estimates using stochastic frontier analysis techniques suggest that developing Asia can increase tax revenues by 3.6% of GDP on average, which is significant given current tax levels (Gupta and Jalles, 2022[3]). These estimates benchmark tax revenues across countries controlling for key characteristics including GDP per capita, the size of the agricultural sector, education spending and trade openness. There is substantial sub-regional variation in tax capacity and tax effort (Figure 2.1). Tax effort is lower and tax potential correspondingly greater in South and Southeast Asia, particularly in Malaysia, Pakistan and Thailand. By contrast, tax effort and actual revenue are relatively high in the People's Republic of China (PRC), Korea and some Pacific Island economies. In a few countries, notably Lao People's Democratic Republic (Lao PDR), Papua New Guinea and Timor Leste, tax effort is high despite actual taxes being low. This regional variation underscores the need for country-specific approaches to increasing revenues while avoiding excessive tax burdens that stifle economic growth.

## Tax policy challenges and priorities

Raising tax revenues across developing Asia requires governments to make the most of their key sources of revenue, consistent with local priorities and capacity. These include value-added tax (VAT), personal and corporate income taxes, and property taxes. Some countries have very narrow tax bases and base broadening is therefore an important objective for efficiently increasing revenues. However, particularly in small island economies, narrow tax bases reflect undiversified economies, which can limit their options. In many developing countries, enforcement capacity can be weak and hamstrung by limited third party information on taxpayers from sources such as large employers and financial intermediaries, which plays a key role in developed countries (Kleven, H. et al., 2011[4]; Kleven, Kreiner and Saez, 2016[5]; Pomeranz and Vila-Belda, 2019[6]). The acceleration of the digital economy during the COVID-19 pandemic is creating new economic opportunities but also significant tax challenges, especially on cross-border transactions.

While growth-friendly tax systems are essential, strengthening the equity of tax systems may also be important in countries with high inequality and weak transfer systems. In developing Asia, market income inequality (before government taxes and social benefits) is lower than in Latin American and high-income countries, as indicated by the lower pre-tax and benefit Gini coefficient (Table 2.1). However, taxes and social benefits achieve relatively modest redistribution due to the limited progressivity of taxes and the modest size and poor targeting of social benefits (Clements, Gupta and Jalles, 2022[7]). Fiscal policies can help promote economic growth without exacerbating income inequality. Empirically, such inclusive growth episodes are more likely to occur in developing Asia when the population is better educated, spending on health and social benefits is higher, and tax-benefit systems are more redistributive (Clements, Gupta and Jalles, 2022[7]).

### Table 2.1. Redistributive effects of fiscal policy, latest available data

| | Gini coefficient, pre-tax and benefits | Gini coefficient, post-tax and benefits |
|---|---|---|
| Developing Asia | 42.7 | 38.4 |
| Latin America and the Caribbean | 48.1 | 45.4 |
| Advanced Economies | 48.3 | 30.4 |

Note: Calculations based on latest available data for each country over the years 2010-2020. Developing Asia comprises 38 countries, Latin America and the Caribbean comprises 26 countries and Advanced Economies comprises 30 countries. The redistributive effect of fiscal policy is the difference between the market income Gini coefficient and the net Gini coefficient.
Source: Clements, Gupta and Jalles (2022[7]).

Therefore, in weighing options for enhancing equity, tax and spending policies need to be considered together. Often the primary contribution of tax revenues to inclusive development is providing the resources for equity-promoting public spending. Indeed, even in OECD countries, which rely heavily on progressive personal income taxes, transfers account for around three-quarters of the combined reduction in income inequality achieved by taxes and transfers (Causa and Hermansen, 2017[8]).

A further consideration is fiscal decentralisation, with sub-national governments (SNG) generating their own revenues and accounting for sizeable spending in many developing Asian economies (Figure 2.2). Well-designed fiscal decentralisation, and prudent SNG fiscal policy, can contribute to overall fiscal stability and efficient government. Notably, SNG proximity to residents can help improve the design and implementation of public spending.

#### Figure 2.2. Sub-national governments' share of total government revenues and spending

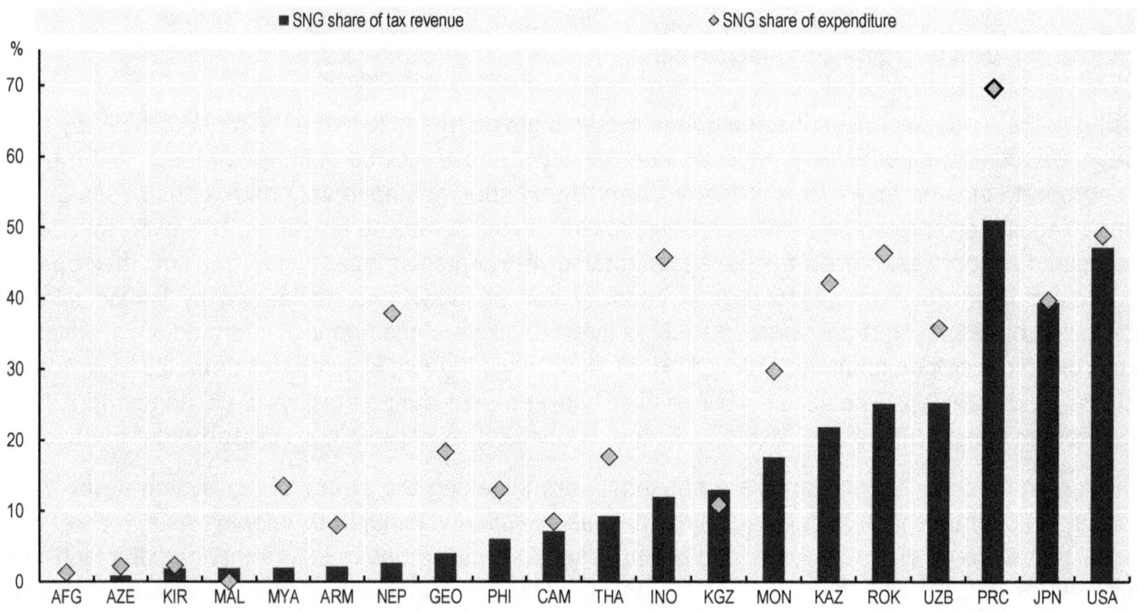


Note: (1) For Malaysia and the Philippines, subnational figures represent the difference between general and central government revenues. (2) Figure shows the most recent year with non-missing entries for both revenue and expenditure. Economies with 2015 data – Republic of Korea; with 2017 data – Afghanistan and Cambodia; with 2018 data – Kiribati, Philippines, Mongolia, Uzbekistan, PRC, and USA. All other economies are presented with 2019 data.
Source: ADB estimates based on IMF GFS Revenue and Expenditure by Function of Government, https://data.imf.org (accessed 31 January 2022); and the Bureau of Local Government Finance for Philippine SNG expenditure data, https://blgf.gov.ph (accessed 16 February 2022).

StatLink https://stat.link/4qb2m9

However, the effectiveness of fiscal decentralisation is constrained by imbalances between SNG expenditure obligations and their own fiscal resources. Except for in the PRC, SNGs' share of tax collection in total tax revenues remains far lower in developing Asia than in advanced economies. Such imbalances leave SNGs vulnerable to inadequate financial support from central governments, which would constrain their ability to provide adequate public goods and services. Such risks can be mitigated by strengthening SNG own revenues. Certain taxes, notably on property as discussed below, are especially attractive for SNGs. However, there is no one-size-fits-all approach to strengthening SNG tax revenue mobilisation.

## Tax expenditures need to be used strategically and transparently

Optimising taxes and ensuring tax system integrity in developing Asia require carefully managing special exemptions. Tax expenditures are preferential tax treatments granted to specific sectors, activities or groups, and they imply a loss of revenues. They include exemptions, deductions, credits, deferrals and lower tax rates, and they are intended to enhance social welfare, promote development, and support other policy goals (Haldenwang, Redonda and Aliu, 2021[9]). Tax incentives, a type of tax expenditure, are often designed to encourage investment in specific sectors or activities, including foreign direct investment (FDI) (IMF et al., 2015[10]; Celani, Dressler and Wermelinger, 2022[11]).

Unlike direct expenditures, tax expenditures are typically not reported in a reliable, comparable and open manner (CBO, 2012[12]; CRS, 2019[13]). Moreover, the cost and benefits of tax expenditures are infrequently assessed and often unknown. In a survey of 43 G20 and OECD countries, only a small minority, including Australia and Korea, published regular, comprehensive and rigorous tax expenditure reports (Redonda and Neubig, 2018[14]). Thus, tax expenditures are characterised by a lack of transparency and accountability and could be conducive to "spending" outside the budget (Burman and Phaup, 2011[15]; Celani, Dressler and Wermelinger, 2022[11]).

Aside from reducing revenue, tax expenditures reduce the efficiency and, depending on their incidence, the equity of the tax system by narrowing the tax base and distorting the rate structure (Bird, 2008[16]). Concessions favouring certain taxpayers require governments to offset revenue losses by imposing a higher tax burden elsewhere or reducing expenditure. Tax incentives that focus on certain businesses can create an unlevel playing field, undermine competition, and reduce tax burdens on investments that would have occurred without the incentive. While it is often claimed that tax incentives create new investment that ultimately boosts revenues, tax incentives are empirically associated with lower overall corporate tax revenues (Kronfol and Steenbergen, 2020[17]). Finally, tax expenditures are likely to increase enforcement costs, give rise to fraud, and encourage rent-seeking behaviour that leads to further tax base erosion.

## Figure 2.3. Foregone revenue due to tax expenditures, selected DMCs

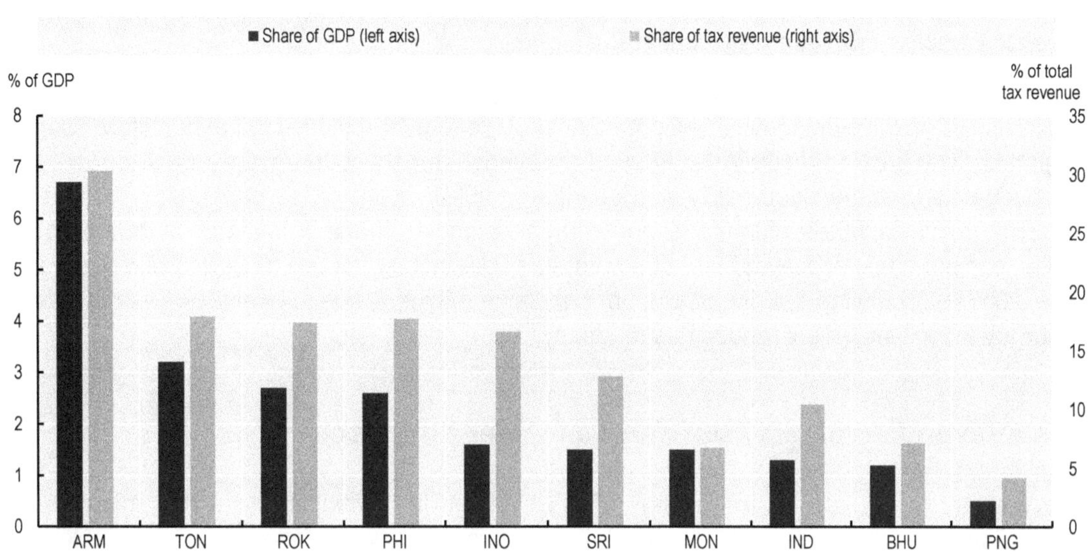


Note: ARM = Armenia; BHU = Bhutan; IND = India; INO = Indonesia; KOR = Korea, Rep. of; MON = Mongolia; PHI = Philippines; PNG = Papua New Guinea; SRI = Sri Lanka; TON = Tonga. The figure reflects the latest reference year with available data: 2019 (ARM, KOR, PHI, INO, SRI); 2018 (MON, IND, BHU, PNG); 2014 (TON).
Source: Global Tax Expenditure Database. https://gted.net (accessed 1 Dec 2021); Asian Development Bank staff estimates.

StatLink https://stat.link/0icldy

Available data suggest tax expenditures are widely used in developing Asia and cause significant revenue losses. Surveys of regional tax authorities indicate tax incentives are used in almost every country in the region, with tax holidays and tax rate reductions particularly prevalent (ADB, 2022[18]). Available data from the Global Tax Expenditure Database indicate tax expenditures in the region typically include exemptions, deductions, and reduced rates granted for taxes on income and consumption. While lower than the global average (possibly due to lower average tax rates), forgone revenue in a sample of ADB developing member countries (DMCs) was nevertheless substantial, averaging around 2% of GDP, or 14% of total tax revenue, and was highest in Armenia, Tonga and the Philippines (Figure 2.3). It should be noted that comparing the value of tax expenditures across countries poses challenges due to differences in approaches to reporting, and these figures represent a lower bound since costs are unavailable for some tax expenditures (Haldenwang, Redonda and Aliu, 2021[9]).

As with direct expenditures, tax expenditures should have clear policy objectives and justifications, including meeting goals in an efficient, cost-effective manner superior to policy alternatives. Well-designed tax expenditures can advance social policy objectives; for example, a long-standing earned income tax credit scheme in the United States effectively supports poorer households (Hoynes and Patel, 2018[19]). Tax expenditures can also be used to promote gender inclusion. However, as discussed below, exemptions and other special arrangements for income and consumption taxes are often poorly targeted and harm equity.

While a lower overall corporate income tax burden can help attract FDI and increase investment overall, evidence casts doubt on the effectiveness of tax incentives, particularly in attracting greenfield investment (Kinda, 2014[20]; Klemm and Van Parys, 2012[21]; Appiah-Kubi et al., 2021[22]). Investor surveys consistently report that tax is only one of many factors that influence investment location and is less important than factors such as political stability and the regulatory environment (World Bank, 2018[23]). Surveys also indicate that many investments would proceed even in the absence of incentives, meaning that existing incentives result in windfall gains for investors (James, 2013[24]). Incentives for FDI motivated by access to large markets or resources are likely to be particularly ineffective and wasteful (Andersen, Kett and Von Uexkull, 2018[25]). Hence broader, less costly reforms to improve the business environment may be more effective for attracting FDI than tax incentives.

Improved reporting, including cost estimates, and stronger governance are essential for ensuring effective tax expenditures. In developing Asia, few countries provide regular, detailed tax expenditure assessments, although headway is being made. A tax incentives revenue impact statement is published with the Indian annual budget[3] and some Southeast Asian countries publish sporadic tax expenditure estimates (ADB, 2021[26]). In many countries, numerous government agencies, notably investment boards and sector ministries, can grant tax incentives. This can create a proliferation of poorly designed and costly incentives (James, 2016[27]).Codifying tax incentives in law, with only the finance minister authorised to grant discretionary incentives, might reduce this tendency.

## VAT is a revenue mainstay but can be further optimised

VAT revenue will likely remain a mainstay of tax systems in developing Asia and must therefore be optimised. The self-enforcement property of VAT, which is a relatively efficient tax, is valuable. The tax is paid by firms only on the value-added portion of their sales, with a tax deduction for inputs. To receive the deduction, firms require their suppliers to provide a receipt, creating an auditable paper trail and an incentive for firms to correctly report their activities to tax authorities (Pomeranz, 2015[28]). This self-enforcement can be further strengthened. For example, a new digital invoice system in the PRC reduced the scope for misreporting of input costs and substantially boosted VAT revenues (Fan et al., 2021[29]).

VAT is often considered regressive since poorer households spend more of their income. However, this depends on consumption patterns and tax design. Exemptions and lower rates often apply to food and other necessities, and evidence on equity is mixed (Alavuotunki, Haapanen and Pirttila, 2019[30]; IMF, 2019[31]). Further, many poor households grow their own food and purchase goods and services from small vendors, leaving much of their consumption beyond the VAT net. After accounting for consumption patterns, VAT may even be progressive in developing countries (Bachas, Gadenne and Jensen, 2021[32]).

VAT revenue performance indicators indicate scope to increase VAT collection in developing Asia. C-efficiency is the ratio of actual to potential revenues assuming a single VAT rate without exemptions across all consumption with perfect compliance. High C-efficiency values therefore imply strong revenue performance. C-efficiency has gradually increased in developing Asia and is comparable to OECD countries (Figure 2.4). However, C-efficiency is much lower in some DMCs.

### Figure 2.4. Value-added tax C-efficiency for select DMCs (latest available year) and regional averages (2000-2018)

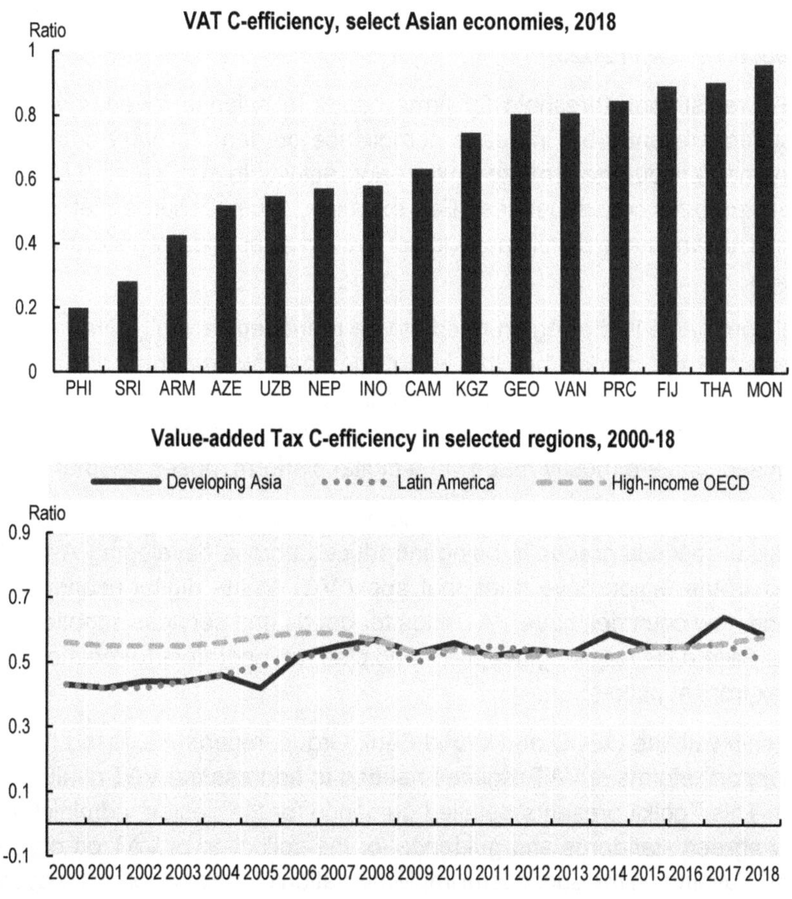


Note: ARM = Armenia, AZE = Azerbaijan, CAM = Cambodia, DMC = developing member country, FIJ = Fiji, GEO = Georgia, INO = Indonesia, KGZ = Kyrgyz Republic, MON = Mongolia, NEP = Nepal, OECD = Organisation for Economic Co-operation and Development, PHI = Philippines, PRC = People's Republic of China, SRI = Sri Lanka, THA = Thailand, UZB = Uzbekistan, VAN = Vanuatu, VAT = value-added tax. Figures for individual DMC represent the latest available data: 2017 (MON, NEP, PRC, VAN); 2018 (ARM, AZE, CAM, FIJ, GEO, INO, KGZ, PHI, SRI, THA, UZB). Figures for each region represent simple annual average for countries with available data and exclude observations where estimated VAT C-efficiency>1.

Source: Gupta and Jalles (2022[3]).

StatLink https://stat.link/lm1r6t

To increase VAT revenues, exemptions and reduced rates should be reviewed and tightened to broaden the tax base, which is more conducive to economic growth than increasing tax rates (Acosta-Ormaechea and Morozumi, 2021[33]). VAT exemptions are generally an inefficient way to improve equity; while they may benefit the poor, they often benefit the wealthy – who consume more – by a greater amount. Adverse impacts on the poor from removing exemptions can be offset by higher pro-poor spending financed by higher revenues. Simplifications including removing exemptions and adopting a streamlined rate structure can also improve compliance. Complexity was a factor motivating Malaysia to abolish its GST in 2018 (Nutman, Isa and Yussof, 2021[34]).

Across developing Asia, VAT tax rates average 12.7%, lower than in Latin America (14.9%) and high-income OECD countries (19.8%). At 10% or less, VAT rates are especially low in Fiji, Sri Lanka, Thailand and Viet Nam. While less efficient than base broadening, there is scope to increase VAT rates to lift revenues, particularly in DMCs where existing rates are very low (Gunter et al., 2021[35]). Indeed, as part of major tax reforms to increase revenues, Indonesia hiked its VAT rate from 10% to 11% in 2022 and plans a further increase to 12% in 2025.

The appropriate VAT registration threshold for firms needs to balance revenue with compliance costs. Lower thresholds support revenue but increase compliance burdens for very small businesses and tax authorities, and they may encourage firms to underreport activity to stay small (Liu et al., 2021[36]). Such behaviour can have adverse consequences. For example, Muthitacharoen et al. (2021[37]) find that unregistered firms in Thailand have significantly lower growth rates than registered firms, especially near registration thresholds.

Finally, rising digital commerce in the region needs to be managed carefully. Normally, VAT on imported goods can be collected at the border, but this is not the case for imported digital products, which are provided directly to the consumer. Foreign suppliers of those services are often not required to register for and pay VAT. Imports may also be tax exempt due to VAT exemptions for low value imports. The sharing economy, where transactions are mostly made via a digital platform, poses another challenge to VAT.

Applying VAT on digital imports bolsters revenues and ensures a level playing field for domestic suppliers. VAT on imported digital goods is gradually being introduced across developing Asia. Around half of the countries with a VAT in the region have rules that apply VAT to the digital economy (Mullins, 2022[38]). However, at this stage, few countries have VAT rules for goods and services supplied via domestic digital platforms. India does have rules requiring suppliers and platform operators to register for the GST, and the operator to collect tax from suppliers.

The ADB, in partnership with the OECD and World Bank Group, recently released the VAT Digital Toolkit for Asia-Pacific to support reforms of VAT regimes needed to address the VAT challenges of e-commerce growth in the region. This Toolkit presents detailed guidance for the design, administration and operation of the internationally agreed standards and guidance for the collection of VAT on digital trade developed by the OECD, notably building on the successful implementation of these reforms by countries in the region and in other parts of the world.

## Personal income taxes can raise more revenue and improve progressivity

Personal income taxes with rising marginal tax rates (imposing proportionately higher tax liabilities on higher earners) are central to a progressive tax system. They are a key source of revenue in OECD countries but much less prominent in developing countries (ADB, 2022[18]). For example, in developing Asia, personal income tax revenue amounts to around 2.0% of GDP compared with around 8.6% in high-income OECD countries. Moreover, their redistributive capacity is relatively weak (Vellutini and Benitez, 2021[39]).

Revenue productivity for personal income tax (the amount of revenue generated by an incremental increase in the tax rate) across developing Asia is similar to other regions but varies enormously within the region (Gupta and Jalles, 2022[3]). In some DMCs, including Bangladesh, it is very low, suggesting significant policy design and enforcement challenges. Therefore, there may be scope for personal income taxes to generate more revenue and become more progressive.

Developing economies characteristically have a large informal sector, which presents several development challenges, notably widespread tax avoidance and weaker fiscal capacity (ADB, 2022[18]). A key challenge to increasing personal income tax revenue in developing countries is prevalent self-employment, which reduces access to third-party information on taxable income, hinders enforcement and shrinks the tax base (Jensen, 2022[40]). Indeed, personal income taxes are often only paid by high-income earners. However, a gradual transition from self-employment to paid employee jobs allows governments to expand the personal income tax base.

Typically, self-employment recedes with development as countries transition from agriculture to manufacturing and services (Gindling and Newhouse, 2014[41]). Developing Asia is no exception, with self-employment on average falling from 56% of total employment in 2000 to around 46% by 2019, still significantly higher than the OECD average but converging towards levels in Latin America (Figure 2.5). However, within developing Asia there is substantial variation, ranging from very high levels in Afghanistan, India and Lao PDR, to less than one quarter of total employment in Kazakhstan and Korea (Figure 2.6).

### Figure 2.5. Self-employment in selected regions, 2000 to 2019

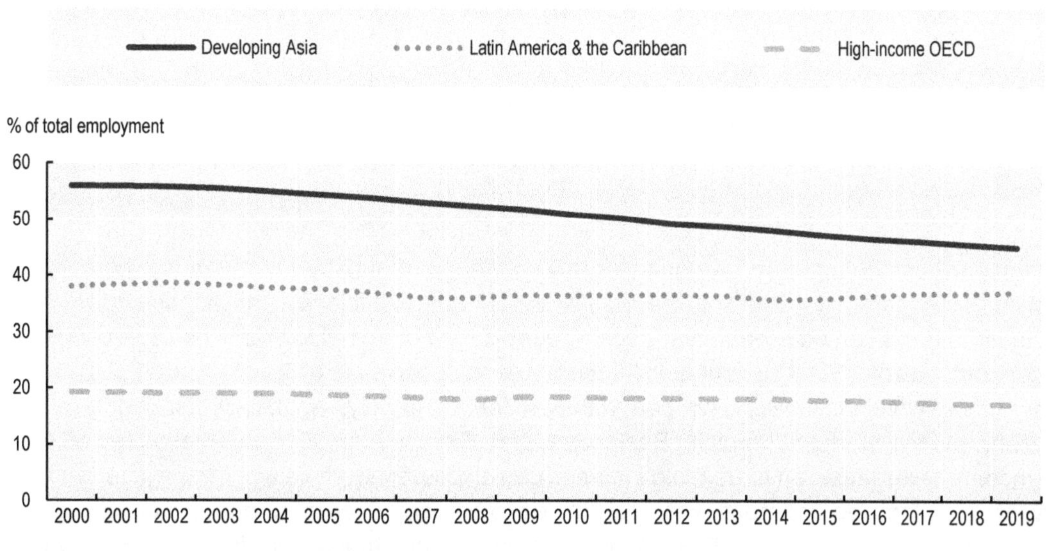


Source: World Bank World Development Indicators. https://databank.worldbank.org/source/world-development-indicators (accessed 1 Dec. 2021); Asian Development Bank staff estimates.

StatLink https://stat.link/q6b9c7

**Figure 2.6. Self-employment in selected DMCs, 2000 and 2019**

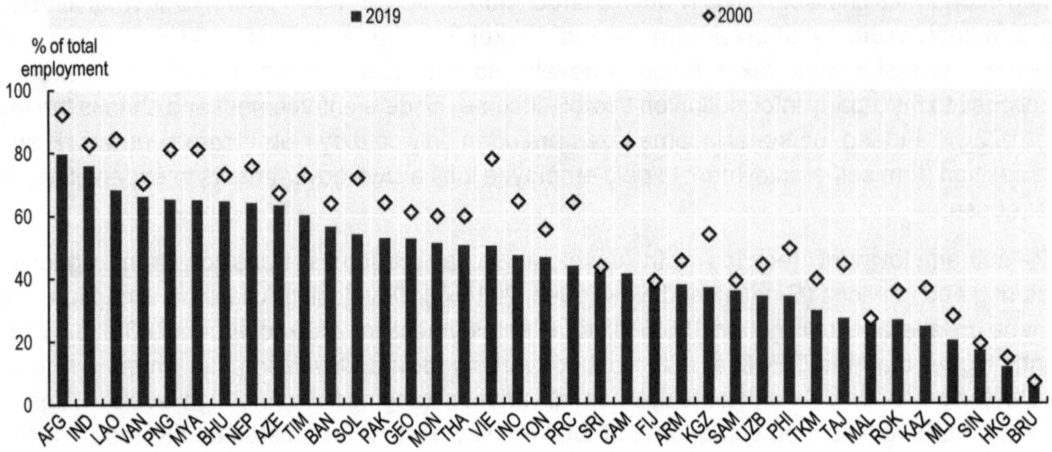


Note: AFG = Afghanistan, ARM = Armenia, AZE = Azerbaijan, BAN = Bangladesh, BHU = Bhutan, BRU = Brunei, CAM = Cambodia, FIJ = Fiji, GEO = Georgia, HKG = Hong Kong, China, IND = India, INO = Indonesia, KAZ = Kazakhstan, KGZ = Kyrgyz Republic, KOR = Korea, Republic of, LAO = Lao People's Democratic Republic, MAL = Malaysia, MLD = Maldives, MON = Mongolia, MYA = Myanmar, NEP = Nepal, PAK = Pakistan, PHI = Philippines, PNG = Papua New Guinea, PRC = People's Republic of China, SAM = Samoa, SIN = Singapore, SOL = Solomon Islands, SRI = Sri Lanka, TAJ = Tajikistan, THA = Thailand, TIM = Timor-Leste, TKM = Turkmenistan, TON = Tonga, UZB = Uzbekistan, VAN = Vanuatu, VIE = Viet Nam.

Source: World Bank World Development Indicators. https://databank.worldbank.org/source/world-development-indicators (accessed 1 Dec. 2021); Asian Development Bank staff estimates.

StatLink https://stat.link/mtgb91

While potentially contributing to more equitable tax systems and substantial revenues, personal income tax design requires carefully balancing the objectives of equity, efficiency and administrative simplicity. Personal income taxes can be economically costly, especially if marginal tax rates rise steeply (Heathcote, Storesletten and Violante, 2014[42]; Blundell, 2016[43]; Keane and Wasi, 2016[44]; Wheaton, 2022[45]). Higher tax rates reduce work incentives and can dampen labour supply, especially for highly skilled and internationally mobile workers (Akcigit, Baslandze and Stantcheva, 2016[46]; Kleven et al., 2020[47]). Personal income taxes levied on household incomes can discourage female workers, exacerbating gender inequality. Married females are more likely than males to be second earners and evidence suggests that joint taxation arrangements disincentivise married female labour market participation (Bick and Fuchs-Schündeln, 2018[48]). By reducing life-time earnings, progressive income taxes may weaken incentives to invest in human capital, compounding efficiency and output losses (Guvenen, Kuruscu and Ozkan, 2014[49]).

The top personal income tax rate on labour income has generally declined across developing Asia (Figure 2.7). Although the average rate of around 27% is much lower than the 40% in OECD countries, there is enormous variation within the region. In countries including the PRC, India and Papua New Guinea, the rate is comparable to the OECD average or even higher. Meanwhile, many Central Asian economies apply a flat tax rate of around 10% to 13%.

**Figure 2.7. Personal income tax top marginal rates in Developing Asia**

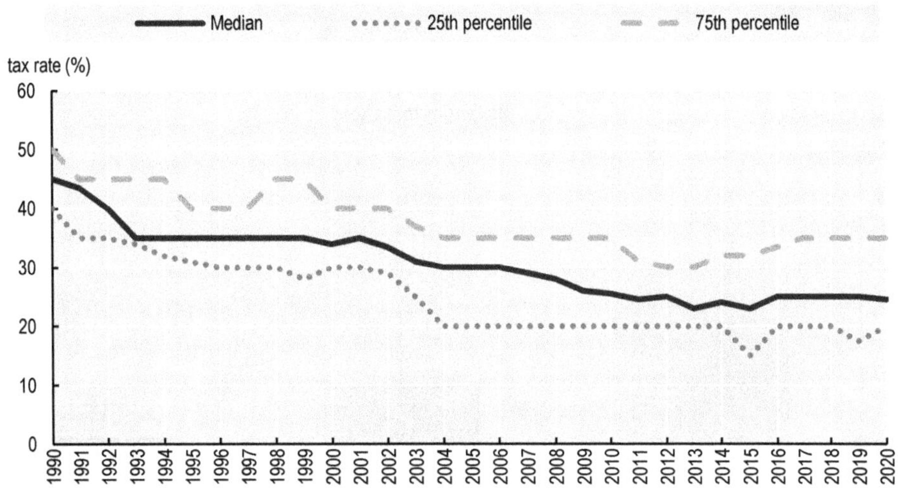


Note: Figure comprises 22 DMCs.
Source: Gupta and Jalles (2022[3]).

StatLink https://stat.link/1wjp3z

Except where flat taxes apply, the top marginal rate also often applies at relatively high income levels. On average in developing Asia, the top marginal rate applies to income of more than 12 times the level of GDP per capita, much higher than 6.6 times GDP per capita in Latin America and 4.1 times GDP per capita in OECD countries (Figure 2.8). In DMCs, where this threshold is high relative to average incomes, it could be lowered to boost personal income tax revenue.

## Figure 2.8. Personal income tax maximum and minimum rate thresholds in select regions

Multiples of GDP per capita

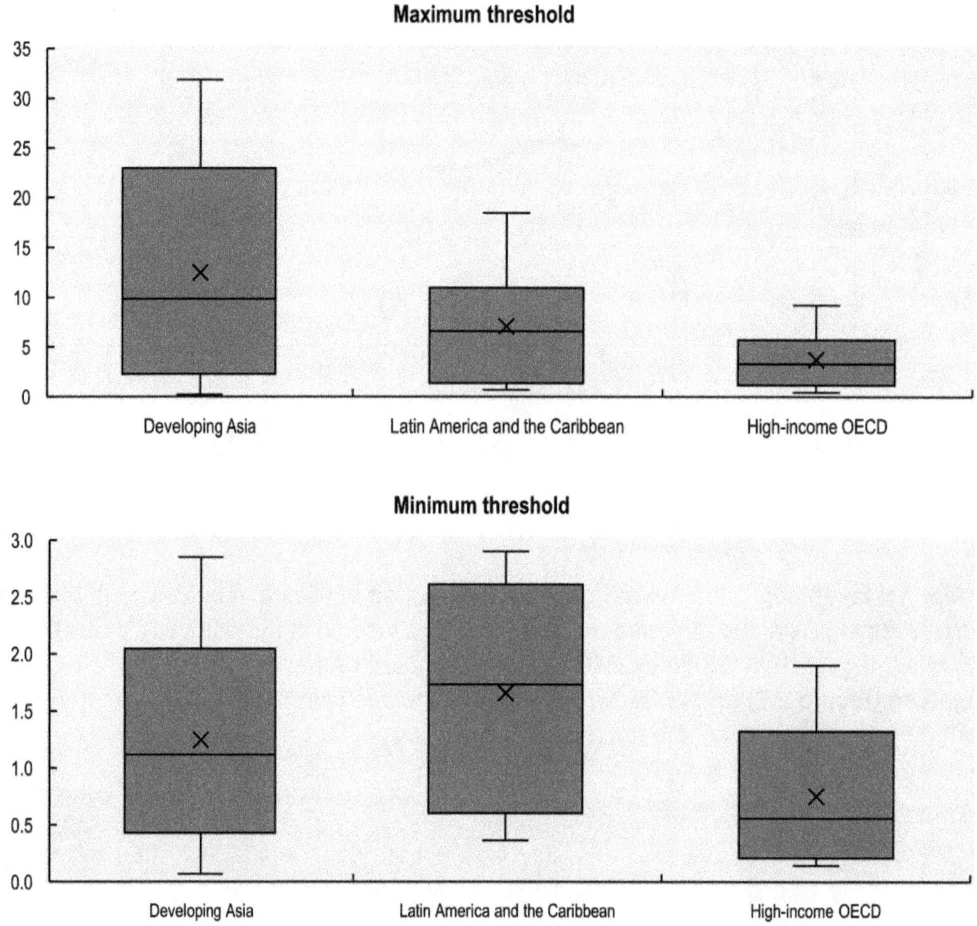


Note: The maximum threshold is the income threshold above which the top marginal personal income tax rate applies. Comprise 23 DMCs, 18 Latin America and the Caribbean and 26 OECD countries. For each box plot, X marks the mean and the middle line the median; its height is from 75th percentile (top) to 25th percentile (bottom); and the extended whiskers cover the maximum and the minimum in the sample, excluding the following outliers: Developing Asia (Philippines = 46.3); High-income OECD (Austria = 22.2).
The minimum threshold is the income level at which personal income taxes start being levied. Comprise 24 DMCs, 16 Latin America and the Caribbean and 27 OECD countries. For each box plot, X marks the mean and the middle line the median; its height is from 75th percentile (top) to 25th percentile (bottom); and the extended whiskers cover the maximum and the minimum in the sample, excluding the following outliers: Latin America and the Caribbean (Guatemala = 8.3, Trinidad and Tobago = 9.2); High-income OECD (Slovak Republic = 3.0).
Source: Gupta and Jalles (2022[3]).

StatLink https://stat.link/rm9wue

Many developing Asian economies apply a tax-free threshold, or zero tax bracket. By exempting the lowest earners, this threshold promotes progressivity and can reduce potentially high compliance costs. On average in DMCs, the threshold applies above the level of GDP per capita, lower than in Latin America but much higher than in OECD countries (Figure 2.8). To expand the tax base, the zero-tax bracket could be lowered, particularly where it is comparatively high and where enforcement capacity and access to third-party information on earnings is stronger. Where it is not currently applied, including in countries with flat taxes, a zero-tax bracket could be added to strengthen progressivity. In some DMCs, there is also potential to expand personal income tax collected through withholding arrangements (ADB, 2021[26])

Taxing capital income can promote progressivity since wealthy individuals earn a disproportionate share of capital income. It can also help ensure self-employed entrepreneurs, who can shift their income from labour to capital, are appropriately taxed. For this reason, the gap between personal, capital and labour income taxation should be minimised. However, in developing countries, poor access to third-party information and the highly mobile nature of capital complicate the taxation of capital income. The wealthy often locate their assets offshore, especially in tax havens, hindering tax enforcement. For example, a voluntary disclosure scheme in Colombia revealed hidden wealth worth around 1.7% of GDP, of which 87% had been concealed offshore (Londoño-Vélez and Ávila-Mahecha, 2021[50]). Initiatives to improve the exchange of information between tax authorities, notably the Exchange of Information on Request and the Automatic Exchange of Information, in which many developing Asian economies participate, can help.

While many countries apply preferential tax rates to certain types of capital income, this practice can create investment distortions and reduce progressivity. For example, tax breaks to encourage retirement savings may encourage a shift into lower tax accounts, resulting in revenue losses that worsen inequality (Chetty et al., 2014[51]).

## Multilateral initiatives can help address corporate income tax challenges

Corporate income taxes represent an important revenue source in developing Asia but are under pressure. Motivated by a desire to attract internationally mobile capital and maintain competitiveness, corporate income tax rates have steadily declined across the region over the past few decades, following a global trend. They now average 20% across DMCs, down from 30% in 2000, a little lower than the Latin American and OECD country average (Figure 2.9). As noted above, tax incentives for business are widespread in developing Asia, reducing the effective tax rate.

**Figure 2.9. Statutory corporate income tax rates in developing Asia**

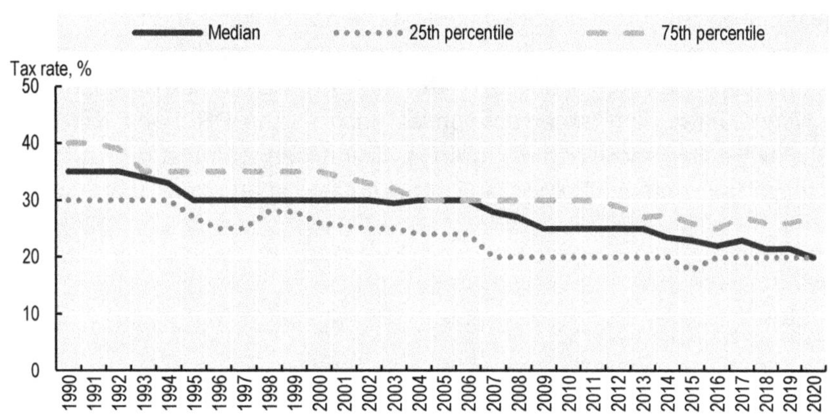


Note: Comprise 36 DMCs.
Source: Gupta and Jalles (2022[3]).

StatLink https://stat.link/m53r2y

Corporate tax revenues are also reduced by tax avoidance. Weaknesses in the international tax framework and differences in tax policies – especially tax rates and corporate tax incentives – across countries can be exploited by Multinational Enterprises (MNEs) to reduce their tax liabilities. For example, firms can engage in transfer pricing – mispricing transactions between firm subsidiaries – and can also route income through countries with the most advantageous tax treaties. This allows incomes and profits to be shifted to lower tax jurisdictions, reducing tax liabilities. Global revenue losses from tax avoidance have been estimated at around 4% to 10% of corporate income tax revenue but losses are larger for developing countries (IMF, 2014[52]; OECD, 2015[53]; Crivelli, De Mooij and Keen, 2016[54]). Within Asia, Cobham and Jansky (2018[55]) estimate revenue losses for South Asia at 1.7% to 1.9% of GDP and for East Asia and the Pacific 0.6% to 0.7% of GDP. MNE tax avoidance distorts the location of FDI and mobile assets, and it gives MNEs an unfair competitive advantage.

The rise of the digital economy in developing Asia exacerbates challenges with respect to international taxation (Mullins, 2022[38]). While the international tax system is based on a concept of physical presence, digitalisation means that it is possible to do business in a country without being physically present there. For example, software might be sold from a platform in one country but downloaded by a user in another country. Further, intangible assets such as licenses, trademarks and data, which are easy to shift to lower tax jurisdictions, are prevalent in the digital economy, meaning digitally-intensive firms may be able to shift assets and profits more easily than other firms. The difficulty of determining arm's length prices for digital intangibles increases firms' ability to exploit transfer pricing. It is likely that MNEs in digital sectors benefit significantly from tax planning and enjoy lower effective tax rates (OECD, 2018[56]; Mullins, 2022[38]).

Widespread attention to the issue of tax avoidance, especially by MNEs, has fueled concerns that firms do not always pay their fair share of tax. The need to address international tax challenges related to digitalisation has led a growing number of governments, including in developing Asia, to introduce discrete digital service taxes. However, these have generated little revenue and provoked retaliatory trade measures (ADB, 2022[18]; Mullins, 2022[38]). Attempts to address the tax challenges related to digitalisation have also spurred efforts to secure multilateral solutions, notably the G20-OECD project on base erosion and profit shifting (BEPS) and the subsequent work of the Inclusive Framework (IF), which includes 20 DMCs.

In 2021, the IF endorsed a new international tax framework featuring two pillars. Under Pillar 1, profits and taxing rights are reallocated to market jurisdictions, while Pillar 2 proposes a global minimum corporate income tax rate of 15%. Together, Pillars 1 and 2 aim to increase fairness and provide limitations to the 'race to the bottom' competition on corporate income tax rates and provide greater certainty for taxpayers and tax administrations.

Estimates suggest that Asian countries may benefit more from Pillar 2 than from Pillar 1. For developing Asia, the revenue impact from the reallocation of taxable profits under Pillar 1 is estimated to be small, with gains or losses of no more than 0.01% of GDP (IMF, 2021[57]). Resource-rich countries which host MNEs, such as Papua New Guinea, and larger economies such as the PRC and Korea gain the most as a percentage of GDP while Singapore and Hong Kong, China lose the most due to their role as investment hubs. Additional global tax revenues from Pillar 2 are estimated at around USD 150 billion per year (OECD, 2021[58]).

## References

Acosta-Ormaechea, S. and A. Morozumi (2021), *The Value-Added Tax and Growth: Design Matters*, International Tax and Public Finance 28. [33]

ADB (2022), *A Comparative Analysis of Tax Administration in Asia and the Pacific (5th edition)*, Asian Development Bank. [18]

ADB (2022), *Asian Development Outlook 2022: Mobilizing Taxes for Development*, Asian Development Bank, Manila. [1]

ADB (2021), *A Comprehensive Assessment of Tax Capacity in Southeast Asia*, Asian Development Bank. [26]

Akcigit, U., S. Baslandze and S. Stantcheva (2016), *Taxation and the International Mobility of Inventors*, American Economic Review 106(10). [46]

Alavuotunki, K., M. Haapanen and J. Pirttila (2019), *The Effects of the Value Added Tax on Revenue and Inequality*, The Journal of Development Studies 55(4). [30]

Andersen, M., B. Kett and E. Von Uexkull (2018), *Corporate Tax Incentives and FDI in Developing Countries*, Global Investment Competitiveness Report 2017/2018, World Bank. [25]

Appiah-Kubi et al. (2021), *Impact of Tax Incentives on Foreign Direct Investment: Evidence from Africa*, Sustainability 13(8661). [22]

Bachas, P., L. Gadenne and A. Jensen (2021), *Informality, Consumption Taxes and Redistribution*, Faculty Research Working Paper RWP21-026, Harvard Kennedy School. [32]

Bick, A. and N. Fuchs-Schündeln (2018), *Taxation and labour supply of married couples across countries: A macroeconomic analysis*, The Review of Economic Studies, 85(3), 1543-1576. [48]

Bird, R. (2008), *Tax Challenges Facing Developing Countries*, Inaugural Lecture of the Annual Public Lecture Series of the National Institute of Public Finance and Policy. [16]

Blundell, R. (2016), *Labor Supply and Taxation*, Oxford University Press. [43]

Burman, L. and M. Phaup (2011), *Tax Expenditures: The Big Government Behind the Curtain*, VoxEU.org. [15]

Causa, O. and M. Hermansen (2017), *Income Redistribution through Taxes and Transfers across OCED Countries*, OECD Economics Department Working Papers No. 1453, OECD Publishing, Paris, https://www.oecd.org/officialdocuments/publicdisplaydocumentpdf/?cote=ECO/WKP(2017)85&docLanguage=En. [8]

CBO (2012), *Tax Expenditures Have a Major Impact on the Federal Budget*, Web Blog Post, Congressional Budget Office. [12]

Celani, A., L. Dressler and M. Wermelinger (2022), *Building an Investment Tax Incentives database: Methodology and initial findings for 36 developing countries*, OECD Working Papers on International Investment, No. 2022/01, OECD Publishing, Paris, https://doi.org/10.1787/62e075a9-en. [11]

Chetty et al. (2014), *Active vs. Passive Decisions and Crowd-Out in Retirement Savings Accounts: Evidence from Denmark*, The Quarterly Journal of Economics 129. [51]

Clements, B., S. Gupta and J. Jalles (2022), *Fiscal Policy for Inclusive Growth in Asia*, Asian Development Bank. [7]

Cobham, A. and P. Janský (2018), *Global distribution of revenue loss from corporate tax avoidance: re-estimation and country results*, Journal of International Development, https://doi.org/10.1002/jid.3348. [55]

Crivelli, E., R. De Mooij and M. Keen (2016), *Base Erosion, Profit Shifting and Developing Countries*, FinanzArchiv 72. [54]

CRS (2019), *Spending and Tax Expenditures: Distinctions and Major Programs*, Congressional Research Service. [13]

Fan et al. (2021), *The Dynamic Effects of Computerized Invoices on Chinese Manufacturing Firms*, NBER Working Paper No. 24414, National Bureau of Economic Research. [29]

Gindling, T. and D. Newhouse (2014), *Self-Employment in the Developing World*, World Development 56. [41]

Gunter et al. (2021), *Non-Linear Effects of Tax Changes on Output: The Role of the Initial Level of Taxation*, Journal of International Economics 131. [35]

Gupta, S. and J. Jalles (2022), *Priorities for Strengthening Key Revenue Sources in Asia*, Asian Development Bank. [3]

Guvenen, F., B. Kuruscu and S. Ozkan (2014), *Taxation of Human Capital and Wage Inequality: A Cross-Country Analysis*, Review of Economic Studies 81. [49]

Haldenwang, C., A. Redonda and F. Aliu (2021), *Shedding Light on Worldwide Tax Expenditures: GTED Flagship Report 2021*, German Development Institute. [9]

Heathcote, J., K. Storesletten and G. Violante (2014), *Optimal Tax Progressivity: An Analytical Framework*, NBER Working Paper No. 19899, National Bureau of Economic Research. [42]

Hoynes, H. and A. Patel (2018), *Effective Policy for Reducing Poverty and Inequality? The Earned Income Tax Credit and Distribution of Income*, Journal of Human Resources 53(4). [19]

IMF (2021), *Fiscal Monitor: A Fair Shot*, International Monetary Fund. [57]

IMF (2019), *Macroeconomic Developments and Prospects in Low-Income Developing Countries 2019*, IMF Policy Paper, International Monetary Fund. [31]

IMF (2014), *Spillovers in International Corporate Taxation*, IMF Policy Paper Volume 2014: Issue 071, International Monetary Fund. [52]

IMF et al. (2015), *Options for Low Income Countries' Effective and Efficient Use of Tax Incentives for Investment*, https://www.oecd.org/tax/tax-global/options-for-low-income-countries-effective-and-efficient-use-of-tax-incentives-for-investment.pdf. [10]

James, S. (2016), *Tax Incentives around the World*, Columbia University Press. [27]

James, S. (2013), *Tax and Non-tax Incentives and Investments: Evidence and Policy Implications*, World Bank. [24]

Jensen, A. (2022), *Employment Structure and the Rise of Modern Tax System*, CID Faculty Working Paper 371, Center for International Development at Harvard University. [40]

Keane, M. and N. Wasi (2016), *Labour Supply: The Roles of Human Capital and the Extensive Margin*, Economic Journal 126. [44]

Kinda, T. (2014), *The Question for Non-Resource-Based FDI: Do Taxes Matter?*, IMF Working Paper WP/14/15, International Monetary Fund. [20]

Klemm, A. and S. Van Parys (2012), *Empirical Evidence on the Effects of Tax Incentives*, International Tax and Public Finance 19. [21]

Kleven et al. (2020), *Taxation and Migration: Evidence and Policy Implications*, Journal of Economic Perspectives 34. [47]

Kleven, H. et al. (2011), *Unwilling or Unable to Cheat? Evidence from a Tax Audit Experiment in Denmark*, Econometrica 79(3). [4]

Kleven, H., C. Kreiner and E. Saez (2016), *Why Can Modern Governments Tax So Much? An Agency Model of Firms as Fiscal Intermediaries*, Economica 83(1). [5]

Kronfol, H. and V. Steenbergen (2020), *Evaluating the Costs and Benefits of Corporate Tax Incentives: Methodological Approaches and Policy Considerations*, World Bank. [17]

Liu et al. (2021), *VAT Notches, Voluntary Registration, and Bunching: Theory and UK Evidence*, Review of Economics and Statistics 103(1). [36]

Londoño-Vélez, J. and J. Ávila-Mahecha (2021), *Enforcing Wealth Taxes in the Developing World: Quasi-Experimental Evidence from Colombia*, American Economic Review: Insights 3. [50]

Mawejje, J. and R. Sebudde (2019), *Tax Revenue Potential and Effort: Worldwide Estimates Using a New Dataset*, Economic Analysis and Policy 63. [2]

Mullins, P. (2022), *Taxing Developing Asia's Digital Economy*, Asian Development Bank. [38]

Muthitacharoen, A., W. Wanichthaworn and T. Burong (2021), *VAT Threshold and Small Business Behavior: Evidence from Thai Tax Returns*, International Tax and Public Finance 28. [37]

Nutman, N., K. Isa and S. Yussof (2021), *GST Complexities in Malaysia: Views from Tax Experts*, International Journal of Law and Management 64(2). [34]

OECD (2021), *Two-Pillar Solution to Address the Tax Challenges Arising from the Digitalisation of the Economy*, OECD Publishing, Paris, https://www.oecd.org/tax/beps/statement-on-a-two-pillar-solution-to-address-the-tax-challenges-arising-from-the-digitalisation-of-the-economy-october-2021.htm. [58]

OECD (2018), *The Role and Design of Net Wealth Taxes in the OECD*, Tax Policy Studies No. 26, OECD Publishing, Paris, http://dx.doi.org/10.1787/9789264290303-en. [56]

OECD (2015), *Examples of Successful DRM Reforms and the Role of International Co-operation*, OECD Discussion Paper, OECD Publishing, Paris, https://www.oecd.org/ctp/tax-global/examples-of-successful-DRM-reforms-and-the-role-of-international-co-operation.pdf. [53]

Pomeranz, D. (2015), *No Taxation without Information: Deterrence and Self-Enforcement in the Value-Added Tax*, American Economic Review 105(8). [28]

Pomeranz, D. and J. Vila-Belda (2019), *Taking State-Capacity Research to the Field: Insights from Collaborations with Tax Authorities*, Annual Review of Economics 11. [6]

Redonda, A. and T. Neubig (2018), *Assessing Tax Expenditure Reporting in G20 and OECD Economies*, Discussion Note 2018/3, Council on Economic Policies. [14]

Vellutini, C. and J. Benitez (2021), *Measuring the Redistributive Capacity of Tax Policies*, IMF Working Paper WP/21/252, International Monetary Fund. [39]

Wheaton, B. (2022), *The Macroeconomic Effects of Flat Taxation: Evidence from a Panel of Transition Economies.* [45]

World Bank (2018), *Global Development Report.* [23]

## Notes

[1] Developing Asia is broadly defined as the developing members of the Asian Development Bank. This includes: Developing members: Afghanistan, Armenia, Azerbaijan, Bangladesh, Bhutan, Brunei Darussalam, Cambodia, Cook Islands, People's Republic of China, Georgia, India, Indonesia, Fiji, Hong Kong, China, Kazakhstan, Kiribati, the Republic of Korea, Kyrgyz Republic, Lao People's Democratic Republic, Malaysia, Maldives, Marshall Islands, Federated States of Micronesia, Mongolia, Myanmar, Nauru, Nepal, Niue, Pakistan, Palau, Papua New Guinea, Philippines, Samoa, Singapore, Solomon Islands, Sri Lanka, Taipei,China, Tajikistan, Thailand, Timor-Leste, Tonga, Turkmenistan, Tuvalu, Uzbekistan, Vanuatu, Viet Nam.

[2] This special feature was written by Sam Hill (World Bank), Yothin Jinjarak (Asian Development Bank), Donghyun Park (Asian Development Bank), and Shu Tian (Asian Development Bank). Sam Hill undertook this work while he was a staff of the Asian Development Bank.

[3] https://www.indiabudget.gov.in/doc/rec/annex7.pdf

# 3 Tax levels and tax structure, 1990-2020

## Comparative tables, 1990-2020

In all of the following tables a ("..") indicates not available. The main series in this volume cover the years 1990 to 2020.

Figures referring to 1991-99, 2011-12 in Table 3.1 and Table 3.2 and figures relating to 1998-99, 2001-06, 2008-09 and 2011-14 in Tables 3.5 to 3.20 have been omitted because of lack of space. Complete series are, however, available on line at OECD (2022), "Revenue Statistics - Asian and Pacific Economies: Comparative tables", OECD Tax statistics (database).

# Table 3.1. Total tax revenue as percentage of GDP, 1990-2020

| | 1990 | 2000 | 2001 | 2002 | 2003 | 2004 | 2005 | 2006 | 2007 | 2008 |
|---|---|---|---|---|---|---|---|---|---|---|
| Australia[1] | 28.1 | 30.5 | 28.9 | 29.8 | 29.9 | 30.2 | 29.9 | 29.3 | 29.5 | 26.8 |
| Bangladesh | .. | 7.1 | 7.1 | 7.5 | 7.5 | 7.7 | 7.8 | 7.7 | 8.5 | 8.4 |
| Bhutan | 5.1 | 9.0 | 10.1 | 10.1 | 8.2 | 9.2 | 9.9 | 8.5 | 9.1 | 10.0 |
| Cambodia | .. | .. | .. | .. | .. | .. | 7.9 | 8.2 | 9.7 | 10.6 |
| China[2] | .. | .. | .. | .. | .. | .. | .. | .. | 16.9 | 17.0 |
| Cook Islands | .. | .. | .. | .. | .. | .. | .. | 25.9 | 24.9 | 24.0 |
| Fiji | .. | .. | .. | .. | .. | .. | .. | .. | .. | 22.2 |
| Indonesia[3] | .. | 7.9 | 10.9 | 11.3 | 11.8 | 12.1 | 12.4 | 11.9 | 12.2 | 13.0 |
| Japan[1] | 27.7 | 25.3 | 25.5 | 24.5 | 24.1 | 24.8 | 25.8 | 26.6 | 27.2 | 27.0 |
| Kazakhstan | .. | 19.9 | 22.2 | 20.5 | 22.7 | 21.7 | 25.5 | 26.1 | 26.1 | 27.6 |
| Kyrgyzstan | 25.6 | 11.7 | 12.4 | 13.6 | 13.7 | 14.2 | 15.7 | 17.2 | 18.4 | 18.6 |
| Korea[1] | 18.6 | 20.9 | 21.2 | 21.3 | 22.0 | 21.2 | 21.7 | 22.6 | 23.7 | 23.6 |
| Lao PDR | .. | .. | .. | .. | .. | .. | .. | .. | .. | .. |
| Malaysia | 18.5 | 14.1 | 18.3 | 18.3 | 16.3 | 15.9 | 15.5 | 15.1 | 14.8 | 15.1 |
| Maldives | .. | .. | .. | .. | .. | .. | .. | .. | 11.9 | 11.5 |
| Mongolia | .. | .. | .. | .. | .. | .. | .. | 26.8 | 28.4 | 26.7 |
| Nauru | .. | .. | .. | .. | .. | .. | .. | .. | .. | .. |
| New Zealand[1] | 36.2 | 32.5 | 31.9 | 33.3 | 33.2 | 34.2 | 36.1 | 35.3 | 33.9 | 32.9 |
| Pakistan | .. | .. | .. | .. | .. | .. | .. | .. | .. | .. |
| Papua New Guinea[4] | .. | 13.4 | 17.4 | 20.0 | 20.2 | 24.2 | 25.6 | 20.0 | 20.8 | 18.6 |
| Philippines | .. | 15.3 | 15.1 | 14.5 | 14.5 | 14.0 | 14.6 | 15.8 | 15.6 | 15.6 |
| Samoa | .. | .. | .. | .. | .. | .. | 21.1 | 24.0 | 22.0 | 19.1 |
| Singapore | .. | 15.2 | 15.1 | 12.9 | 12.3 | 12.0 | 11.8 | 11.8 | 13.2 | 14.0 |
| Solomon Islands | .. | .. | .. | .. | .. | .. | .. | .. | 15.3 | 16.6 |
| Thailand | .. | 14.8 | 14.9 | 15.6 | 16.9 | 17.6 | 18.8 | 17.9 | 17.6 | 17.1 |
| Tokelau | .. | .. | .. | .. | .. | .. | .. | 13.3 | 14.3 | 16.1 |
| Vanuatu | .. | 16.2 | 16.3 | 16.4 | 16.3 | 16.9 | 17.1 | 17.5 | 19.0 | 19.2 |
| Viet Nam[3] | .. | .. | .. | .. | 19.6 | 19.6 | 18.9 | 19.9 | 19.9 | 20.9 |
| Africa (30) average[5] | .. | .. | .. | .. | .. | .. | .. | .. | .. | .. |
| Asia-Pacific (28) average[6, 7] | .. | .. | .. | .. | .. | .. | .. | .. | .. | .. |
| LAC average[8] | 15.6 | 18.0 | 18.3 | 18.4 | 18.7 | 19.1 | 19.9 | 20.5 | 21.2 | 21.2 |
| OECD average[1, 9, 10] | 30.8 | 33.0 | 32.5 | 32.3 | 32.2 | 32.2 | 32.7 | 32.8 | 32.9 | 32.3 |

| | 2009 | 2010 | 2013 | 2014 | 2015 | 2016 | 2017 | 2018 | 2019 | 2020 |
|---|---|---|---|---|---|---|---|---|---|---|
| Australia[1] | 25.5 | 25.2 | 27.0 | 27.2 | 27.7 | 27.5 | 28.5 | 28.5 | 27.7 | .. |
| Bangladesh | 8.8 | 9.9 | 10.8 | 10.7 | 10.6 | 10.2 | 10.4 | 9.8 | 9.0 | 10.2 |
| Bhutan | 13.7 | 14.1 | 13.4 | 13.6 | 13.5 | 12.9 | 13.7 | 12.6 | 10.5 | 8.9 |
| Cambodia | 6.9 | 7.3 | 12.9 | 15.5 | 15.6 | 15.8 | 16.9 | 18.6 | 21.7 | 20.2 |
| China[2] | 17.1 | 17.8 | 18.6 | 18.5 | 18.1 | 17.5 | 17.4 | 17.0 | 22.1 | 20.1 |
| Cook Islands | 26.7 | 26.9 | 25.1 | 22.1 | 26.7 | 27.1 | 28.3 | 29.8 | 28.0 | 19.7 |
| Fiji | 21.6 | 21.6 | 23.7 | 22.7 | 23.6 | 23.1 | 24.2 | 23.5 | 22.3 | 16.6 |
| Indonesia[3] | 11.0 | 11.4 | 12.5 | 12.2 | 12.1 | 12.0 | 11.6 | 12.0 | 11.6 | 10.1 |
| Japan[1] | 25.7 | 26.2 | 28.6 | 30.0 | 30.2 | 30.3 | 30.9 | 31.6 | 31.4 | .. |
| Kazakhstan | 21.2 | 23.8 | 22.6 | 21.1 | 15.5 | 14.9 | 16.0 | 17.0 | 16.7 | 14.1 |
| Kyrgyzstan | 17.6 | 17.8 | 20.3 | 20.4 | 19.1 | 19.5 | 19.3 | 20.3 | 19.4 | 17.4 |
| Korea[1] | 22.6 | 22.4 | 23.1 | 23.4 | 23.7 | 24.7 | 25.4 | 26.7 | 27.3 | 28.0 |
| Lao PDR | .. | 11.5 | 12.9 | 12.3 | 12.6 | 11.9 | 11.0 | 10.9 | 10.6 | 8.9 |
| Maldives | 8.9 | 8.9 | 17.4 | 19.0 | 19.4 | 19.7 | 20.1 | 19.4 | 19.0 | 19.1 |
| Malaysia | 15.5 | 13.8 | 15.8 | 15.3 | 14.5 | 14.0 | 13.4 | 12.5 | 12.4 | 11.4 |
| Mongolia | 22.3 | 25.3 | 23.5 | 20.2 | 19.3 | 19.1 | 21.4 | 23.9 | 23.9 | 21.2 |
| Nauru | .. | .. | .. | 8.3 | 23.1 | 15.6 | 29.0 | 35.4 | 48.3 | 47.5 |
| New Zealand[1] | 30.2 | 30.3 | 30.5 | 31.2 | 31.5 | 31.4 | 31.3 | 32.2 | 31.5 | 32.2 |
| Pakistan | .. | .. | 9.3 | 9.8 | 11.2 | 11.2 | 11.4 | 10.2 | 10.0 | 10.4 |
| Papua New Guinea[4] | 15.9 | 17.0 | 18.4 | 18.0 | 15.2 | 13.2 | 12.4 | 12.6 | 12.5 | 11.6 |
| Philippines | 14.4 | 14.2 | 15.5 | 16.0 | 16.2 | 16.2 | 16.8 | 17.4 | 18.1 | 17.8 |
| Samoa | 20.7 | 19.3 | 24.2 | 23.0 | 23.7 | 22.9 | 23.2 | 23.9 | 24.0 | 25.0 |
| Singapore | 12.4 | 12.5 | 13.2 | 13.4 | 13.0 | 13.1 | 13.8 | 12.9 | 13.2 | 12.8 |
| Solomon Islands | 16.5 | 18.9 | 23.3 | 23.0 | 23.1 | 21.6 | 22.5 | 24.1 | 20.4 | 18.8 |
| Thailand | 16.6 | 17.6 | 19.3 | 18.4 | 18.9 | 18.1 | 17.5 | 17.7 | 17.2 | 16.5 |
| Tokelau | 15.5 | 17.7 | 16.2 | 17.1 | 15.1 | 14.7 | 16.8 | 18.1 | 19.2 | 20.8 |
| Vanuatu | 17.6 | 16.3 | 17.2 | 17.4 | 16.3 | 15.3 | 17.1 | 17.8 | 17.0 | 14.2 |
| Viet Nam[3] | 20.0 | 25.3 | 23.2 | 22.2 | 22.5 | 23.0 | 23.2 | 23.2 | 24.2 | 22.7 |
| Africa (30) average[5] | 14.8 | 14.8 | 15.8 | 16.0 | 16.1 | 16.0 | 16.1 | 16.3 | 16.6 | .. |
| Asia-Pacific (28) average[6, 7] | .. | 18.2 | 19.2 | 18.6 | 19.0 | 18.4 | 19.4 | 20.0 | 20.3 | 19.1 |
| LAC average[8] | 20.5 | 20.9 | 21.6 | 21.8 | 22.3 | 22.2 | 22.3 | 22.5 | 22.7 | 21.9 |
| OECD average[1, 9, 10] | 31.6 | 31.6 | 32.7 | 32.9 | 32.9 | 33.6 | 33.4 | 33.5 | 33.4 | 33.5 |

.. Not available

1. Australia, Japan, Korea and New Zealand are part of the OECD (38) group. Data for Australia, Japan, Korea, New Zealand and the OECD average are taken from OECD (2021), *Revenue Statistics 2021*.

2. 2007 to 2018: The tax-to-GDP ratio for China does not include revenues from social security contributions (SSCs) in these years as historical data were not available.
3. Social security contributions data for Indonesia are only available for 2015 to 2020 and are deemed negligible in earlier years. Social security data for Viet Nam are not available prior to 2010.
4. Total revenues are not calculated for 2000 and 2001 as the data are incomplete and do not include customs revenues for these two years.
5. Represents an unweighted average for the 30 African countries included in the publication *Revenue Statistics in Africa 2021*.
6. Represents an unweighted average of the 28 Asian and Pacific economies in this publication. The Asia-Pacific (28) average should be interpreted with caution as data for social security contributions (category 2000) are not available or are partial in a few economies, including in Indonesia where SSC data are not available before 2015, in Viet Nam where SSC data are not available before 2010 and in China where SSC data are not available before 2019. The Asia-Pacific (28) average excludes Pakistan prior to 2011 and Nauru prior to 2014 as data were not available. See the country tables in Chapter 4 for further information.
7. 2020: Data for 2019 are used for Australia and Japan in the calculation of the Asia-Pacific average in 2020 as data for 2020 are not available.
8. Represents an unweighted average for the 26 Latin American and Caribbean (LAC) countries included in the publication*Revenue Statistics in Latin America and the Caribbean 2022*.
9. 1990 to 2019: represents an unweighted average for the 38 OECD member countries included in the publication *Revenue Statistics 2021*.
10. 2020: calculated by applying the unweighted average percentage change for 2020 in the 36 countries providing data for that year to the overall average tax-to-GDP ratio in 2019.

StatLink https://stat.link/0725z3

## Table 3.2. Total tax revenue (excluding social security contributions) as percentage of GDP, 1990-2020

| | 1990 | 2000 | 2001 | 2002 | 2003 | 2004 | 2005 | 2006 | 2007 | 2008 |
|---|---|---|---|---|---|---|---|---|---|---|
| Australia[1] | 28.1 | 30.5 | 28.9 | 29.8 | 29.9 | 30.2 | 29.9 | 29.3 | 29.5 | 26.8 |
| Bangladesh | .. | 7.1 | 7.1 | 7.5 | 7.5 | 7.7 | 7.8 | 7.7 | 8.5 | 8.4 |
| Bhutan | 5.1 | 9.0 | 10.1 | 10.1 | 8.2 | 9.2 | 9.9 | 8.5 | 9.1 | 10.0 |
| Cambodia | .. | .. | .. | .. | .. | .. | 7.9 | 8.2 | 9.7 | 10.6 |
| China | .. | .. | .. | .. | .. | .. | .. | .. | 16.9 | 17.0 |
| Cook Islands | .. | .. | .. | .. | .. | .. | .. | 25.9 | 24.9 | 24.0 |
| Fiji | .. | .. | .. | .. | .. | .. | .. | .. | .. | 22.2 |
| Indonesia | .. | 7.9 | 10.9 | 11.3 | 11.8 | 12.1 | 12.4 | 11.9 | 12.2 | 13.0 |
| Japan[1] | 20.4 | 16.4 | 16.2 | 15.1 | 14.8 | 15.4 | 16.3 | 16.9 | 17.3 | 16.5 |
| Kazakhstan | .. | 19.9 | 22.2 | 20.5 | 22.7 | 21.7 | 25.4 | 25.9 | 25.7 | 27.2 |
| Kyrgyzstan | 25.6 | 11.7 | 12.4 | 13.6 | 13.7 | 14.2 | 15.7 | 17.2 | 18.4 | 18.6 |
| Korea[1] | 16.7 | 17.4 | 17.3 | 17.3 | 17.7 | 16.7 | 17.1 | 17.8 | 18.8 | 18.4 |
| Lao PDR | .. | .. | .. | .. | .. | .. | .. | .. | .. | .. |
| Malaysia | 18.5 | 13.8 | 18.0 | 18.0 | 16.0 | 15.7 | 15.2 | 14.8 | 14.6 | 14.9 |
| Maldives | .. | .. | .. | .. | .. | .. | .. | .. | 11.9 | 11.5 |
| Mongolia | .. | .. | .. | .. | .. | .. | .. | 24.1 | 25.1 | 23.2 |
| Nauru | .. | .. | .. | .. | .. | .. | .. | .. | .. | .. |
| New Zealand[1] | 36.2 | 32.5 | 31.9 | 33.3 | 33.2 | 34.2 | 36.1 | 35.3 | 33.9 | 32.9 |
| Pakistan | .. | .. | .. | .. | .. | .. | .. | .. | .. | .. |
| Papua New Guinea[2] | .. | 13.4 | 17.4 | 20.0 | 20.2 | 24.2 | 25.6 | 20.0 | 20.8 | 18.6 |
| Philippines | .. | 13.3 | 13.1 | 12.4 | 12.5 | 12.1 | 12.8 | 14.0 | 13.8 | 13.8 |
| Samoa | .. | .. | .. | .. | .. | .. | 21.1 | 24.0 | 22.0 | 19.1 |
| Singapore | .. | 15.2 | 15.1 | 12.9 | 12.3 | 12.0 | 11.8 | 11.8 | 13.2 | 14.0 |
| Solomon Islands | .. | .. | .. | .. | .. | .. | .. | .. | 15.3 | 16.6 |
| Thailand | .. | 14.3 | 14.4 | 15.0 | 16.2 | 16.7 | 17.9 | 17.1 | 16.7 | 16.3 |
| Tokelau | .. | .. | .. | .. | .. | .. | .. | 13.3 | 14.3 | 16.1 |
| Vanuatu | .. | 16.2 | 16.3 | 16.4 | 16.3 | 16.9 | 17.1 | 17.5 | 19.0 | 19.2 |
| Viet Nam | .. | .. | .. | .. | 19.6 | 19.6 | 18.9 | 19.9 | 19.9 | 20.9 |
| Africa (30) average[3] | .. | .. | .. | .. | .. | .. | .. | .. | .. | .. |
| Asia-Pacific (28) average[4, 5] | .. | .. | .. | .. | .. | .. | .. | .. | .. | .. |
| LAC average[6] | 13.3 | 15.3 | 15.4 | 15.5 | 16.0 | 16.4 | 17.1 | 17.7 | 18.3 | 18.3 |
| OECD average[1, 7, 8] | 23.7 | 24.6 | 24.0 | 23.8 | 23.7 | 23.8 | 24.4 | 24.6 | 24.7 | 23.9 |
| | 2009 | 2010 | 2013 | 2014 | 2015 | 2016 | 2017 | 2018 | 2019 | 2020 |
| Australia[1] | 25.5 | 25.2 | 27.0 | 27.2 | 27.7 | 27.5 | 28.5 | 28.5 | 27.7 | .. |
| Bangladesh | 8.8 | 9.9 | 10.8 | 10.7 | 10.6 | 10.2 | 10.4 | 9.8 | 9.0 | 10.2 |
| Bhutan | 13.7 | 14.1 | 13.4 | 13.6 | 13.5 | 12.9 | 13.7 | 12.6 | 10.5 | 8.9 |
| Cambodia | 6.9 | 7.3 | 12.9 | 15.5 | 15.6 | 15.8 | 16.9 | 18.6 | 21.7 | 20.2 |
| China | 17.1 | 17.8 | 18.6 | 18.5 | 18.1 | 17.5 | 17.4 | 17.0 | 16.0 | 15.2 |
| Cook Islands | 26.7 | 26.9 | 25.1 | 22.1 | 26.7 | 27.1 | 28.3 | 29.8 | 28.0 | 19.7 |
| Fiji | 21.6 | 21.6 | 23.7 | 22.7 | 23.6 | 23.1 | 24.2 | 23.5 | 22.3 | 16.6 |
| Indonesia | 11.0 | 11.4 | 12.5 | 12.2 | 12.0 | 11.6 | 11.2 | 11.5 | 11.1 | 9.5 |
| Japan[1] | 15.2 | 15.5 | 16.9 | 18.1 | 18.3 | 18.1 | 18.6 | 18.9 | 18.5 | .. |
| Kazakhstan | 20.7 | 23.2 | 22.0 | 20.5 | 15.0 | 14.4 | 15.5 | 16.4 | 16.1 | 13.3 |
| Kyrgyzstan | 17.6 | 17.8 | 20.3 | 20.4 | 19.1 | 19.5 | 19.3 | 20.3 | 19.4 | 17.4 |
| Korea[1] | 17.4 | 17.2 | 17.0 | 17.1 | 17.4 | 18.3 | 18.8 | 19.9 | 20.0 | 20.1 |
| Lao PDR | .. | 11.5 | 12.9 | 12.3 | 12.6 | 11.9 | 11.0 | 10.9 | 10.6 | 8.9 |
| Maldives | 8.9 | 8.9 | 17.4 | 19.0 | 19.4 | 19.7 | 20.1 | 19.4 | 19.0 | 19.1 |
| Malaysia | 15.2 | 13.6 | 15.6 | 15.1 | 14.3 | 13.8 | 13.1 | 12.2 | 12.1 | 11.1 |
| Mongolia | 18.4 | 22.0 | 19.2 | 16.2 | 15.1 | 14.7 | 16.9 | 19.1 | 19.2 | 17.3 |
| Nauru | .. | .. | .. | 8.3 | 23.1 | 15.6 | 29.0 | 35.4 | 48.3 | 47.5 |
| New Zealand[1] | 30.2 | 30.3 | 30.5 | 31.2 | 31.5 | 31.4 | 31.3 | 32.2 | 31.5 | 32.2 |
| Pakistan | .. | .. | 9.3 | 9.8 | 11.2 | 11.2 | 11.4 | 10.2 | 10.0 | 10.4 |
| Papua New Guinea[2] | 15.9 | 17.0 | 18.4 | 18.0 | 15.2 | 13.2 | 12.4 | 12.6 | 12.5 | 11.6 |
| Philippines | 12.5 | 12.4 | 13.5 | 13.8 | 13.9 | 14.0 | 14.5 | 15.0 | 15.5 | 15.0 |
| Samoa | 20.7 | 19.3 | 24.2 | 23.0 | 23.7 | 22.9 | 23.2 | 23.9 | 24.0 | 25.0 |
| Singapore | 12.4 | 12.5 | 13.2 | 13.4 | 13.0 | 13.1 | 13.8 | 12.9 | 13.2 | 12.8 |
| Solomon Islands | 16.5 | 18.9 | 23.3 | 23.0 | 23.1 | 21.6 | 22.5 | 24.1 | 20.4 | 18.8 |
| Thailand | 15.7 | 16.4 | 18.5 | 17.4 | 17.8 | 17.1 | 16.5 | 16.7 | 16.2 | 15.5 |
| Tokelau | 15.5 | 17.7 | 16.2 | 17.1 | 15.1 | 14.7 | 16.8 | 18.1 | 19.2 | 20.8 |
| Vanuatu | 17.6 | 16.3 | 17.2 | 17.4 | 16.3 | 15.3 | 17.1 | 17.8 | 17.0 | 14.2 |
| Viet Nam | 20.0 | 21.6 | 18.0 | 17.2 | 17.3 | 17.3 | 17.3 | 17.2 | 17.4 | 15.8 |
| Africa (30) average[3] | .. | 13.5 | 14.6 | 14.7 | 14.7 | 14.7 | 14.8 | 15.0 | 15.2 | .. |
| Asia-Pacific (28) average[4, 5] | .. | 17.2 | 18.1 | 17.5 | 17.9 | 17.3 | 18.2 | 18.7 | 18.8 | 17.6 |
| LAC average[6] | 17.3 | 17.6 | 18.0 | 18.2 | 18.5 | 18.5 | 18.4 | 18.7 | 18.8 | 17.9 |
| OECD average[1, 7, 8] | 22.9 | 23.0 | 23.9 | 24.1 | 24.1 | 24.7 | 24.5 | 24.5 | 24.5 | .. |

.. Not available

1. Australia, Japan, Korea and New Zealand are part of the OECD (38) group. Data for Australia, Japan, Korea, New Zealand and the OECD average are taken from OECD (2021), *Revenue Statistics 2021*.
2. Total revenues are not calculated for 2000 and 2001 as the data are incomplete and do not include customs revenues for these two years.
3. Represents an unweighted average for the 30 African countries included in the publication *Revenue Statistics in Africa 2021*.
4. Represents an unweighted average of the 28 Asian and Pacific economies in this publication. The Asia-Pacific (28) average excludes Pakistan prior to 2011 and Nauru prior to 2014 as data were not available.
5. 2020: Data for 2019 are used for Australia and Japan in the calculation of the Asia-Pacific average in 2020 as data for 2020 are not available.
6. Represents an unweighted average for the 26 Latin American and Caribbean (LAC) countries included in the publication *Revenue Statistics in Latin America and the Caribbean 2022*.
7. 1990 to 2019: represents an unweighted average for the 38 OECD member countries included in the publication *Revenue Statistics 2021*.
8. 2020: calculated by applying the unweighted average percentage change for 2020 in the 36 countries providing data for that year to the overall average tax-to-GDP ratio in 2019.

StatLink https://stat.link/b058jr

## Table 3.3. Tax revenue of main headings as percentage of GDP, 2020

| | 1000 Income & profits | 2000 Social security | 3000 Payroll | 4000 Property | 5000 Goods & services | 6000 Other |
|---|---|---|---|---|---|---|
| Australia[1, 2] | 16.4 | 0.0 | 1.3 | 2.7 | 7.3 | 0.0 |
| Bangladesh | 3.8 | 0.0 | 0.0 | 0.0 | 5.2 | 0.0 |
| Bhutan | 5.5 | 0.0 | 0.0 | 0.1 | 3.4 | 0.0 |
| Cambodia[3] | 5.9 | 0.0 | 0.0 | 0.9 | 13.3 | 0.0 |
| China | 5.4 | 4.9 | 0.0 | 1.5 | 8.4 | 0.0 |
| Cook Islands | 8.2 | 0.0 | 0.0 | 0.0 | 11.5 | 0.0 |
| Fiji | 5.2 | 0.0 | 0.0 | 0.4 | 10.9 | 0.0 |
| Indonesia | 3.8 | 0.6 | 0.0 | 0.2 | 4.3 | 1.2 |
| Japan[1, 2] | 9.7 | 12.9 | 0.0 | 2.6 | 6.2 | 0.1 |
| Kazakhstan | 5.0 | 0.7 | 1.0 | 0.4 | 6.9 | 0.0 |
| Kyrgyzstan[3] | 3.8 | 0.0 | 0.0 | 0.3 | 13.3 | 0.0 |
| Korea[2] | 8.7 | 7.8 | 0.1 | 4.0 | 6.8 | 0.6 |
| Lao PDR[3] | 1.8 | 0.0 | 0.0 | 0.1 | 7.0 | 0.0 |
| Malaysia[4] | 7.5 | 0.3 | 0.0 | 0.0 | 3.2 | 0.4 |
| Maldives | 6.3 | 0.0 | .. | 0.0 | 12.7 | 0.0 |
| Mongolia | 5.9 | 4.0 | 0.0 | 0.6 | 10.7 | 0.0 |
| Nauru | 37.2 | 0.0 | 0.0 | 0.0 | 10.3 | 0.0 |
| New Zealand[2] | 17.8 | 0.0 | 0.0 | 1.9 | 12.5 | 0.0 |
| Pakistan | 3.1 | 0.0 | 0.0 | 0.1 | 6.9 | 0.2 |
| Papua New Guinea | 6.9 | 0.0 | 0.0 | 0.1 | 4.6 | 0.0 |
| Philippines | 6.4 | 2.8 | 0.0 | 0.5 | 7.3 | 0.8 |
| Samoa | 5.9 | 0.0 | 0.0 | 0.0 | 19.1 | 0.0 |
| Singapore | 6.9 | 0.0 | 0.0 | 1.5 | 3.7 | 0.8 |
| Solomon Islands[5] | 5.4 | 0.0 | 0.0 | 0.1 | 13.2 | 0.0 |
| Thailand | 5.8 | 1.0 | 0.0 | 0.2 | 9.4 | 0.1 |
| Tokelau | 10.6 | 0.0 | 0.0 | 0.0 | 10.2 | 0.0 |
| Vanuatu | 0.0 | 0.0 | 0.0 | 0.5 | 13.8 | 0.0 |
| Viet Nam | 6.0 | 6.9 | 0.0 | 0.0 | 9.8 | 0.0 |
| Africa (30) average[1, 6] | 6.3 | 1.4 | 0.1 | 0.4 | 8.6 | 0.1 |
| Asia-Pacific (28) average[7] | 7.7 | 1.5 | 0.1 | 0.7 | 9.0 | 0.2 |
| LAC average[8] | 5.9 | 4.0 | 0.3 | 0.8 | 10.5 | 0.4 |
| OECD average[1, 2, 9] | 11.3 | 8.9 | 0.5 | 1.8 | 10.8 | 0.2 |

.. Not available

1. Data for Australia, Japan, the Africa (30) average and the OECD average are for 2019.
2. Australia, Japan, Korea and New Zealand are part of the OECD (38) group. Data for Australia, Japan, Korea, New Zealand and the OECD average are taken from OECD (2021), *Revenue Statistics 2021*.
3. Heading 2000: SSC data are not available.
4. Heading 2000: Data are estimated.
5. The social security contributions in the Solomon Islands are zero as they do not meet the social security criteria of the OECD classifications set in Annex A of the Interpretative Guide.
6. Represents an unweighted average for the 30 African countries included in the publication *Revenue Statistics in Africa 2021*.
7. Represents an unweighted average of the 28 Asian and Pacific economies in this publication. The Asia-Pacific (28) average should be interpreted with caution as data for social security contributions (category 2000) are not available or are partial in a few economies. Data for 2019 are used for Australia and Japan in the calculation as data for 2020 are not available. See the country tables in Chapter 4 for further information.
8. Represents an unweighted average for the 26 Latin American and Caribbean (LAC) countries included in the publication *Revenue Statistics in Latin America and the Caribbean 2022*.
9. Represents an unweighted average for the 38 OECD member countries included in the publication *Revenue Statistics 2021*. Data for 2019 are used as a complete breakdown in 2020 is not available.

StatLink https://stat.link/elqaxb

## Table 3.4. Tax revenue of main headings as percentage of total taxation, 2020

| | 1000 Income & profits | 2000 Social security | 3000 Payroll | 4000 Property | 5000 Goods & services | 6000 Other |
|---|---|---|---|---|---|---|
| Australia[1, 2] | 59.2 | 0.0 | 4.7 | 9.8 | 26.3 | 0.0 |
| Bangladesh | 42.0 | 0.0 | 0.0 | 0.0 | 58.0 | 0.0 |
| Bhutan | 61.2 | 0.0 | 0.1 | 0.8 | 38.0 | 0.0 |
| Cambodia[3] | 29.3 | 0.0 | 0.0 | 4.7 | 65.9 | 0.1 |
| China | 26.8 | 24.2 | 0.0 | 7.4 | 41.7 | 0.0 |
| Cook Islands | 41.7 | 0.0 | 0.0 | 0.0 | 58.3 | 0.0 |
| Fiji | 31.7 | 0.0 | 0.0 | 2.6 | 65.8 | 0.0 |
| Indonesia | 38.2 | 5.9 | 0.0 | 1.7 | 42.7 | 11.6 |
| Japan[1, 2] | 30.8 | 41.1 | 0.0 | 8.2 | 19.7 | 0.3 |
| Kazakhstan | 35.2 | 5.3 | 7.3 | 3.1 | 49.0 | 0.0 |
| Kyrgyzstan[3] | 21.7 | 0.0 | 0.0 | 1.9 | 76.4 | 0.0 |
| Korea[2] | 30.9 | 28.0 | 0.3 | 14.2 | 24.4 | 2.1 |
| Lao PDR[3] | 20.7 | 0.0 | 0.0 | 1.2 | 78.1 | 0.0 |
| Malaysia[4] | 66.0 | 2.6 | 0.0 | 0.0 | 27.8 | 3.7 |
| Maldives | 33.3 | 0.0 | .. | 0.0 | 66.7 | 0.0 |
| Mongolia | 28.0 | 18.7 | 0.0 | 2.9 | 50.4 | 0.0 |
| Nauru | 78.3 | 0.0 | 0.0 | 0.0 | 21.7 | 0.0 |
| New Zealand[2] | 55.2 | 0.0 | 0.0 | 5.9 | 38.8 | 0.0 |
| Pakistan | 30.2 | 0.0 | 0.0 | 1.0 | 66.7 | 2.2 |
| Papua New Guinea | 59.6 | 0.0 | 0.0 | 0.5 | 39.9 | 0.0 |
| Philippines | 36.1 | 15.7 | 0.0 | 2.7 | 40.8 | 4.7 |
| Samoa | 23.7 | 0.0 | 0.0 | 0.0 | 76.3 | 0.0 |
| Singapore | 53.7 | 0.0 | 0.0 | 11.4 | 29.0 | 5.9 |
| Solomon Islands[5] | 29.0 | 0.0 | 0.0 | 0.5 | 70.5 | 0.0 |
| Thailand | 34.9 | 5.8 | 0.0 | 1.4 | 57.2 | 0.7 |
| Tokelau | 50.8 | 0.0 | 0.0 | 0.0 | 49.2 | 0.0 |
| Vanuatu | 0.0 | 0.0 | 0.0 | 3.4 | 96.6 | 0.0 |
| Viet Nam | 26.2 | 30.4 | 0.0 | 0.1 | 43.3 | 0.0 |
| Africa (30) average[1, 6] | 38.4 | 7.2 | 0.9 | 1.9 | 51.9 | 1.1 |
| Asia-Pacific (28) average[7] | 38.4 | 6.3 | 0.5 | 3.0 | 50.6 | 1.1 |
| LAC average[8] | 26.9 | 18.4 | 1.0 | 3.5 | 48.4 | 1.6 |
| OECD average[1, 2, 9] | 34.0 | 25.9 | 1.3 | 5.5 | 32.6 | 0.5 |

.. Not available

1. Data for Australia, Japan, the Africa (30) average and the OECD average are for 2019.
2. Australia, Japan, Korea and New Zealand are part of the OECD (38) group. Data for Australia, Japan, Korea, New Zealand and the OECD average are taken from OECD (2021), *Revenue Statistics 2021*.
3. Heading 2000: SSC data are not available.
4. Heading 2000: Data are estimated.
5. The social security contributions in the Solomon Islands are zero as they do not meet the social security criteria of the OECD classifications set in Annex A of the Interpretative Guide.
6. Represents an unweighted average for the 30 African countries included in the publication *Revenue Statistics in Africa 2021*.
7. Represents an unweighted average of the 28 Asian and Pacific economies in this publication. The Asia-Pacific (28) average should be interpreted with caution as data for social security contributions (category 2000) are not available or are partial in a few economies. Data for 2019 are used for Australia and Japan in the calculation as data for 2020 are not available. See the country tables in Chapter 4 for further information.
8. Represents an unweighted average for the 26 Latin American and Caribbean (LAC) countries included in the publication *Revenue Statistics in Latin America and the Caribbean 2022*.
9. Represents an unweighted average for the 38 OECD member countries included in the publication *Revenue Statistics 2021*. Data for 2019 are used as a complete breakdown in 2020 is not available.

StatLink https://stat.link/iayg2n

## Table 3.5. Taxes on income and profits (1000) as percentage of GDP

| | 1997 | 2000 | 2007 | 2010 | 2015 | 2016 | 2017 | 2018 | 2019 | 2020 |
|---|---|---|---|---|---|---|---|---|---|---|
| Australia[1] | 16.2 | 17.6 | 17.5 | 14.3 | 15.7 | 15.7 | 16.7 | 17.1 | 16.4 | .. |
| Bangladesh | .. | 2.0 | 2.9 | 3.8 | 4.8 | 4.3 | 4.2 | 4.0 | 3.8 | 4.4 |
| Bhutan | 4.6 | 5.9 | 5.0 | 9.0 | 7.6 | 6.8 | 6.8 | 6.5 | 6.3 | 5.5 |
| Cambodia | .. | .. | 1.4 | 0.6 | 3.4 | 3.6 | 4.2 | 4.4 | 5.0 | 5.9 |
| China | .. | .. | 4.6 | 4.6 | 5.7 | 5.8 | 5.9 | 6.0 | 5.5 | 5.4 |
| Cook Islands | .. | .. | 9.8 | 10.6 | 9.4 | 9.1 | 10.3 | 11.5 | 9.4 | 8.2 |
| Fiji | .. | .. | .. | 7.1 | 6.1 | 7.1 | 7.6 | 6.6 | 6.0 | 5.2 |
| Indonesia | 3.6 | 3.8 | 5.5 | 5.2 | 5.2 | 5.4 | 4.8 | 5.1 | 4.9 | 3.8 |
| Japan[1] | 9.5 | 8.8 | 9.9 | 7.9 | 9.4 | 9.3 | 9.5 | 10.1 | 9.7 | .. |
| Kazakhstan | .. | 8.3 | 14.0 | 9.5 | 6.0 | 5.6 | 5.8 | 6.4 | 6.0 | 5.0 |
| Kyrgyzstan | 2.2 | 2.1 | 3.1 | 4.0 | 3.7 | 3.5 | 3.4 | 3.5 | 3.6 | 3.8 |
| Korea[1] | 5.0 | 6.0 | 7.5 | 6.3 | 7.2 | 7.7 | 8.1 | 9.1 | 9.1 | 8.7 |
| Lao PDR | .. | .. | .. | 2.6 | 2.9 | 2.6 | 2.5 | 2.4 | 2.4 | 1.8 |
| Malaysia | 9.8 | 7.7 | 9.9 | 9.1 | 9.0 | 8.3 | 8.0 | 8.6 | 8.5 | 7.5 |
| Maldives | .. | .. | 0.7 | 0.6 | 5.0 | 4.8 | 4.5 | 4.0 | 4.0 | 6.3 |
| Mongolia | .. | .. | 13.1 | 10.0 | 5.1 | 4.4 | 5.8 | 6.4 | 6.8 | 5.9 |
| Nauru | .. | .. | .. | .. | 12.1 | 9.2 | 18.8 | 24.8 | 38.0 | 37.2 |
| New Zealand[1] | 20.3 | 19.5 | 21.3 | 16.3 | 17.3 | 17.4 | 17.4 | 18.1 | 17.3 | 17.8 |
| Pakistan | .. | .. | .. | .. | 3.6 | 3.8 | 3.9 | 3.3 | 3.2 | 3.1 |
| Papua New Guinea | .. | 9.6 | 15.1 | 11.8 | 9.9 | 8.1 | 7.5 | 7.7 | 7.2 | 6.9 |
| Philippines | 6.4 | 5.9 | 6.3 | 5.6 | 6.5 | 6.5 | 6.7 | 6.2 | 6.4 | 6.4 |
| Samoa | .. | .. | 5.2 | 4.8 | 5.5 | 5.2 | 5.1 | 5.5 | 5.5 | 5.9 |
| Singapore | .. | 8.0 | 6.0 | 5.6 | 5.8 | 5.9 | 6.7 | 6.0 | 6.4 | 6.9 |
| Solomon Islands | .. | .. | 3.5 | 5.7 | 7.0 | 6.3 | 6.7 | 6.3 | 5.9 | 5.4 |
| Thailand | .. | 4.7 | 7.0 | 6.4 | 6.6 | 6.2 | 5.9 | 6.0 | 6.1 | 5.8 |
| Tokelau | .. | .. | 6.8 | 9.0 | 7.7 | 8.0 | 9.4 | 8.6 | 10.3 | 10.6 |
| Vanuatu | .. | 0.0 | 0.0 | 0.0 | 0.0 | 0.0 | 0.0 | 0.0 | 0.0 | 0.0 |
| Viet Nam | .. | .. | 9.0 | 8.1 | 6.1 | 5.7 | 5.9 | 6.2 | 6.3 | 6.0 |
| Africa (30) average[2] | .. | .. | .. | 5.7 | 6.1 | 6.0 | 6.0 | 6.1 | 6.3 | .. |
| Asia-Pacific (28) average[3] | .. | .. | .. | 6.9 | 6.9 | 6.7 | 7.2 | 7.5 | 7.9 | 7.7 |
| LAC average[4] | 3.6 | 4.1 | 5.7 | 5.5 | 5.9 | 5.7 | 5.7 | 6.0 | 6.0 | 5.9 |
| OECD average[1, 5] | 11.0 | 11.5 | 11.7 | 10.2 | 10.9 | 10.9 | 11.2 | 11.3 | 11.3 | .. |

.. Not available

1. Australia, Japan, Korea and New Zealand are part of the OECD (38) group. Data for Australia, Japan, Korea, New Zealand and the OECD average are taken from OECD (2021), *Revenue Statistics 2021*.
2. Represents an unweighted average for the 30 African countries included in the publication *Revenue Statistics in Africa 2021*.
3. Represents an unweighted average of the 28 Asian and Pacific economies in this publication. Data for 2019 are used for Australia and Japan in the calculation as data for 2020 are not available.
4. Represents an unweighted average for the 26 Latin American and Caribbean (LAC) countries included in the publication *Revenue Statistics in Latin America and the Caribbean 2022*.
5. Represents an unweighted average for the 38 OECD member countries included in the publication *Revenue Statistics 2021*.

StatLink https://stat.link/4jb7wl

# Table 3.6. Taxes on income and profits (1000) as percentage of total taxation

| | 1997 | 2000 | 2007 | 2010 | 2015 | 2016 | 2017 | 2018 | 2019 | 2020 |
|---|---|---|---|---|---|---|---|---|---|---|
| Australia[1] | 56.6 | 57.9 | 59.4 | 56.7 | 56.7 | 57.3 | 58.7 | 60.1 | 59.2 | .. |
| Bangladesh | .. | 28.4 | 33.6 | 38.7 | 45.3 | 42.0 | 40.2 | 40.2 | 42.0 | 43.4 |
| Bhutan | 53.6 | 65.7 | 55.2 | 64.0 | 55.8 | 52.7 | 49.8 | 51.7 | 59.5 | 61.2 |
| Cambodia | .. | .. | 14.1 | 8.5 | 21.6 | 23.1 | 25.0 | 23.5 | 23.0 | 29.3 |
| China[2] | .. | .. | .. | .. | .. | .. | .. | .. | 24.9 | 26.8 |
| Cook Islands | .. | .. | 39.2 | 39.4 | 35.0 | 33.5 | 36.6 | 38.6 | 33.6 | 41.7 |
| Fiji | .. | .. | .. | 32.6 | 25.8 | 30.6 | 31.5 | 28.1 | 27.0 | 31.7 |
| Indonesia | 47.2 | 47.7 | 45.1 | 45.8 | 43.1 | 44.7 | 41.0 | 42.2 | 42.1 | 38.2 |
| Japan[1] | 37.0 | 34.8 | 36.4 | 30.2 | 31.2 | 30.6 | 30.7 | 31.9 | 30.8 | .. |
| Kazakhstan | .. | 41.4 | 53.7 | 40.0 | 38.8 | 37.3 | 35.9 | 37.9 | 36.3 | 35.2 |
| Kyrgyzstan | 17.8 | 17.9 | 16.6 | 22.3 | 19.3 | 17.9 | 17.6 | 17.1 | 18.5 | 21.7 |
| Korea[1] | 26.2 | 28.8 | 31.8 | 28.0 | 30.3 | 31.2 | 32.1 | 34.1 | 33.2 | 30.9 |
| Lao PDR | .. | .. | .. | 22.7 | 22.7 | 21.9 | 23.1 | 22.3 | 22.4 | 20.7 |
| Malaysia | 49.8 | 54.6 | 66.6 | 66.1 | 61.9 | 59.3 | 60.1 | 68.5 | 68.1 | 66.0 |
| Maldives | .. | .. | 5.9 | 6.9 | 26.0 | 24.4 | 22.6 | 20.7 | 21.3 | 33.3 |
| Mongolia | .. | .. | 46.1 | 39.5 | 26.5 | 22.8 | 26.9 | 26.8 | 28.3 | 28.0 |
| Nauru | .. | .. | .. | .. | 52.2 | 58.7 | 64.9 | 70.2 | 78.6 | 78.3 |
| New Zealand[1] | 59.8 | 60.0 | 62.9 | 53.8 | 54.9 | 55.6 | 55.6 | 56.3 | 55.1 | 55.2 |
| Pakistan | .. | .. | .. | .. | 32.6 | 33.8 | 34.4 | 32.3 | 32.1 | 30.2 |
| Papua New Guinea | .. | 71.7 | 73.0 | 69.4 | 65.2 | 61.4 | 60.9 | 61.3 | 57.6 | 59.6 |
| Philippines | 37.4 | 38.6 | 40.4 | 39.2 | 40.2 | 40.3 | 39.8 | 35.4 | 35.7 | 36.1 |
| Samoa | .. | .. | 23.6 | 24.7 | 23.1 | 22.8 | 22.1 | 23.0 | 23.0 | 23.7 |
| Singapore | .. | 52.8 | 45.4 | 44.7 | 44.7 | 44.9 | 48.3 | 46.6 | 48.1 | 53.7 |
| Solomon Islands | .. | .. | 23.1 | 30.3 | 30.1 | 29.1 | 29.6 | 26.3 | 28.8 | 29.0 |
| Thailand | .. | 31.8 | 39.6 | 36.5 | 34.9 | 34.4 | 33.4 | 34.1 | 35.6 | 34.9 |
| Tokelau | .. | .. | 47.8 | 51.1 | 51.1 | 54.6 | 55.8 | 47.3 | 53.7 | 50.8 |
| Vanuatu | .. | 0.0 | 0.0 | 0.0 | 0.0 | 0.0 | 0.0 | 0.0 | 0.0 | 0.0 |
| Viet Nam | .. | .. | 45.1 | 32.0 | 27.2 | 24.6 | 25.5 | 26.9 | 26.1 | 26.2 |
| Africa (30) average[3] | .. | .. | .. | 38.9 | 39.0 | 37.9 | 38.0 | 38.0 | 38.4 | .. |
| Asia-Pacific (28) average[4] | .. | .. | .. | 36.9 | 36.9 | 36.7 | 37.1 | 37.2 | 37.3 | 38.4 |
| LAC average[5] | 20.3 | 22.1 | 26.4 | 26.0 | 26.3 | 26.0 | 25.9 | 26.5 | 26.6 | 26.9 |
| OECD average[1, 6] | 33.1 | 33.9 | 35.2 | 32.2 | 33.2 | 32.8 | 33.6 | 34.0 | 34.0 | .. |

.. Not available

1. Australia, Japan, Korea and New Zealand are part of the OECD (38) group. Data for Australia, Japan, Korea, New Zealand and the OECD average are taken from OECD (2021), *Revenue Statistics 2021*.
2. 2007 to 2018: Data for China are not included in this table as historical data on revenues from social security contributions are not available.
3. Represents an unweighted average for the 30 African countries included in the publication *Revenue Statistics in Africa 2021*.
4. Represents an unweighted average of the 28 Asian and Pacific economies in this publication. Data for China are not included in the calculation prior to 2019 as historic data for social security contributions are not available. Data for 2019 are used for Australia and Japan in the calculation of the average in 2020 as data for 2020 are not available.
5. Represents an unweighted average for the 26 Latin American and Caribbean (LAC) countries included in the publication *Revenue Statistics in Latin America and the Caribbean 2022*.
6. Represents an unweighted average for the 38 OECD member countries included in the publication *Revenue Statistics 2021*.

StatLink https://stat.link/hl1kgm

## Table 3.7. Social security contributions (2000) as percentage of GDP

| | 1997 | 2000 | 2007 | 2010 | 2015 | 2016 | 2017 | 2018 | 2019 | 2020 |
|---|---|---|---|---|---|---|---|---|---|---|
| Australia[1] | 0.0 | 0.0 | 0.0 | 0.0 | 0.0 | 0.0 | 0.0 | 0.0 | 0.0 | .. |
| Bangladesh | .. | 0.0 | 0.0 | 0.0 | 0.0 | 0.0 | 0.0 | 0.0 | 0.0 | 0.0 |
| Bhutan | 0.0 | 0.0 | 0.0 | 0.0 | 0.0 | 0.0 | 0.0 | 0.0 | 0.0 | 0.0 |
| Cambodia | .. | .. | 0.0 | 0.0 | 0.0 | 0.0 | 0.0 | 0.0 | 0.0 | 0.0 |
| China[2] | .. | .. | .. | .. | .. | .. | .. | .. | 6.1 | 4.9 |
| Cook Islands | .. | .. | 0.0 | 0.0 | 0.0 | 0.0 | 0.0 | 0.0 | 0.0 | 0.0 |
| Fiji | .. | .. | .. | 0.0 | 0.0 | 0.0 | 0.0 | 0.0 | 0.0 | 0.0 |
| Indonesia[3] | .. | .. | .. | .. | 0.1 | 0.4 | 0.4 | 0.4 | 0.5 | 0.6 |
| Japan[1] | 8.8 | 8.9 | 9.9 | 10.8 | 11.9 | 12.2 | 12.3 | 12.7 | 12.9 | .. |
| Kazakhstan | .. | 0.0 | 0.4 | 0.6 | 0.6 | 0.6 | 0.5 | 0.5 | 0.5 | 0.7 |
| Kyrgyzstan | 0.0 | 0.0 | 0.0 | 0.0 | 0.0 | 0.0 | 0.0 | 0.0 | 0.0 | 0.0 |
| Korea[1] | 2.7 | 3.5 | 4.9 | 5.2 | 6.3 | 6.5 | 6.5 | 6.8 | 7.3 | 7.8 |
| Lao PDR | .. | .. | .. | 0.0 | 0.0 | 0.0 | 0.0 | 0.0 | 0.0 | 0.0 |
| Malaysia[4] | .. | 0.3 | 0.3 | 0.2 | 0.2 | 0.3 | 0.3 | 0.3 | 0.3 | 0.3 |
| Maldives | .. | .. | 0.0 | 0.0 | 0.0 | 0.0 | 0.0 | 0.0 | 0.0 | 0.0 |
| Mongolia | .. | .. | 3.2 | 3.3 | 4.2 | 4.4 | 4.5 | 4.8 | 4.7 | 4.0 |
| Nauru | .. | .. | .. | .. | 0.0 | 0.0 | 0.0 | 0.0 | 0.0 | 0.0 |
| New Zealand[1] | 0.0 | 0.0 | 0.0 | 0.0 | 0.0 | 0.0 | 0.0 | 0.0 | 0.0 | 0.0 |
| Pakistan | .. | .. | .. | .. | 0.0 | 0.0 | 0.0 | 0.0 | 0.0 | 0.0 |
| Papua New Guinea | .. | 0.0 | 0.0 | 0.0 | 0.0 | 0.0 | 0.0 | 0.0 | 0.0 | 0.0 |
| Philippines | 1.3 | 2.0 | 1.8 | 1.8 | 2.3 | 2.3 | 2.2 | 2.4 | 2.6 | 2.8 |
| Samoa | .. | .. | 0.0 | 0.0 | 0.0 | 0.0 | 0.0 | 0.0 | 0.0 | 0.0 |
| Singapore | .. | 0.0 | 0.0 | 0.0 | 0.0 | 0.0 | 0.0 | 0.0 | 0.0 | 0.0 |
| Solomon Islands[5] | .. | .. | 0.0 | 0.0 | 0.0 | 0.0 | 0.0 | 0.0 | 0.0 | 0.0 |
| Thailand | .. | 0.5 | 0.9 | 1.2 | 1.1 | 1.0 | 1.0 | 1.0 | 1.0 | 1.0 |
| Tokelau | .. | .. | 0.0 | 0.0 | 0.0 | 0.0 | 0.0 | 0.0 | 0.0 | 0.0 |
| Vanuatu | .. | 0.0 | 0.0 | 0.0 | 0.0 | 0.0 | 0.0 | 0.0 | 0.0 | 0.0 |
| Viet Nam[6] | .. | .. | .. | 3.7 | 5.2 | 5.7 | 5.8 | 6.0 | 6.7 | 6.9 |
| Africa (30) average[7] | .. | .. | .. | 1.3 | 1.3 | 1.3 | 1.4 | 1.4 | 1.4 | .. |
| Asia-Pacific (28) average[8] | .. | .. | .. | 1.1 | 1.2 | 1.2 | 1.2 | 1.3 | 1.5 | 1.5 |
| LAC average[9] | 2.6 | 2.8 | 2.8 | 3.3 | 3.8 | 3.8 | 3.8 | 3.8 | 3.9 | 4.0 |
| OECD average[1, 10] | 8.5 | 8.4 | 8.2 | 8.6 | 8.8 | 8.9 | 8.9 | 9.0 | 8.9 | .. |

.. Not available

1. Australia, Japan, Korea and New Zealand are part of the OECD (38) group. Data for Australia, Japan, Korea, New Zealand and the OECD average are taken from OECD (2021), *Revenue Statistics 2021*.
2. 2007 to 2018: Data for China are not included in this table as historical data on revenues from social security contributions are not available.
3. Social security contributions data for Indonesia are only available for 2015 to 2020 and are deemed negligible in earlier years. SSCs in Indonesia include contributions from Death Benefit (JK), Work Accident Insurance (JKK), Pension Insurance (JP), and mandatory contributions from BPJS Health for formal workers. Contributions from the BPJS Health since 2018 have been estimated.
4. Heading 2000: Starting from 2015, Social Security Contribution data is given as a lump sum. Data for 2020 is estimated.
5. The social security contributions in the Solomon Islands are zero as they do not meet the social security criteria of the OECD classifications set in Annex A of the Interpretative Guide.
6. Social security data for Viet Nam are not available prior to 2010.
7. Represents an unweighted average for the 30 African countries included in the publication *Revenue Statistics in Africa 2021*.
8. Represents an unweighted average of the 28 Asian and Pacific economies in this publication. The Asia-Pacific (28) average should be interpreted with caution as data for social security contributions (category 2000) are not available or are partial in a few economies, including in Indonesia where SSC data are not available before 2015, in Viet Nam where SSC data are not available before 2010 and in China where SSC data are not available before 2019. The Asia-Pacific (28) average excludes Pakistan prior to 2011 and Nauru prior to 2014 as data were not available. See the country tables in Chapter 4 for further information.
9. Represents an unweighted average for the 26 Latin American and Caribbean (LAC) countries included in the publication *Revenue Statistics in Latin America and the Caribbean 2022*.
10. Represents an unweighted average for the 38 OECD member countries included in the publication *Revenue Statistics 2021*.

StatLink https://stat.link/r9p7kd

## Table 3.8. Social security contributions (2000) as percentage of total taxation

| | 1997 | 2000 | 2007 | 2010 | 2015 | 2016 | 2017 | 2018 | 2019 | 2020 |
|---|---|---|---|---|---|---|---|---|---|---|
| Australia[1] | 0.0 | 0.0 | 0.0 | 0.0 | 0.0 | 0.0 | 0.0 | 0.0 | 0.0 | .. |
| Bangladesh | .. | 0.0 | 0.0 | 0.0 | 0.0 | 0.0 | 0.0 | 0.0 | 0.0 | 0.0 |
| Bhutan | 0.0 | 0.0 | 0.0 | 0.0 | 0.0 | 0.0 | 0.0 | 0.0 | 0.0 | 0.0 |
| Cambodia | .. | .. | 0.0 | 0.0 | 0.0 | 0.0 | 0.0 | 0.0 | 0.0 | 0.0 |
| China[2] | .. | .. | .. | .. | .. | .. | .. | .. | 27.5 | 24.2 |
| Cook Islands | .. | .. | 0.0 | 0.0 | 0.0 | 0.0 | 0.0 | 0.0 | 0.0 | 0.0 |
| Fiji | .. | .. | .. | 0.0 | 0.0 | 0.0 | 0.0 | 0.0 | 0.0 | 0.0 |
| Indonesia[3] | .. | .. | .. | .. | 0.6 | 3.2 | 3.4 | 3.6 | 4.3 | 5.9 |
| Japan[1] | 34.3 | 35.2 | 36.5 | 41.1 | 39.4 | 40.4 | 39.9 | 40.2 | 41.1 | .. |
| Kazakhstan | .. | 0.0 | 1.5 | 2.5 | 3.8 | 3.8 | 3.4 | 3.2 | 3.2 | 5.3 |
| Kyrgyzstan | 0.0 | 0.0 | 0.0 | 0.0 | 0.0 | 0.0 | 0.0 | 0.0 | 0.0 | 0.0 |
| Korea[1] | 14.2 | 16.7 | 20.7 | 23.3 | 26.6 | 26.2 | 25.7 | 25.4 | 26.7 | 28.0 |
| Lao PDR | .. | .. | .. | 0.0 | 0.0 | 0.0 | 0.0 | 0.0 | 0.0 | 0.0 |
| Malaysia[4] | .. | 2.0 | 1.7 | 1.8 | 1.7 | 1.8 | 1.9 | 2.4 | 2.5 | 2.6 |
| Maldives | .. | .. | 0.0 | 0.0 | 0.0 | 0.0 | 0.0 | 0.0 | 0.0 | 0.0 |
| Mongolia | .. | .. | 11.4 | 13.1 | 22.0 | 23.2 | 21.0 | 20.1 | 19.8 | 18.7 |
| Nauru | .. | .. | .. | .. | 0.0 | 0.0 | 0.0 | 0.0 | 0.0 | 0.0 |
| New Zealand[1] | 0.0 | 0.0 | 0.0 | 0.0 | 0.0 | 0.0 | 0.0 | 0.0 | 0.0 | 0.0 |
| Pakistan | .. | .. | .. | .. | 0.0 | 0.0 | 0.0 | 0.0 | 0.0 | 0.0 |
| Papua New Guinea | .. | 0.0 | 0.0 | 0.0 | 0.0 | 0.0 | 0.0 | 0.0 | 0.0 | 0.0 |
| Philippines | 7.7 | 13.1 | 11.8 | 12.6 | 14.1 | 14.0 | 13.4 | 13.6 | 14.3 | 15.7 |
| Samoa | .. | .. | 0.0 | 0.0 | 0.0 | 0.0 | 0.0 | 0.0 | 0.0 | 0.0 |
| Singapore | .. | 0.0 | 0.0 | 0.0 | 0.0 | 0.0 | 0.0 | 0.0 | 0.0 | 0.0 |
| Solomon Islands[5] | .. | .. | 0.0 | 0.0 | 0.0 | 0.0 | 0.0 | 0.0 | 0.0 | 0.0 |
| Thailand | .. | 3.7 | 5.1 | 7.1 | 5.6 | 5.6 | 5.7 | 5.7 | 5.9 | 5.8 |
| Tokelau | .. | .. | 0.0 | 0.0 | 0.0 | 0.0 | 0.0 | 0.0 | 0.0 | 0.0 |
| Vanuatu | .. | 0.0 | 0.0 | 0.0 | 0.0 | 0.0 | 0.0 | 0.0 | 0.0 | 0.0 |
| Viet Nam[6] | .. | .. | .. | 14.8 | 23.1 | 24.8 | 25.1 | 25.8 | 27.9 | 30.4 |
| Africa (30) average[7] | .. | .. | .. | 7.3 | 7.3 | 7.5 | 7.6 | 7.3 | 7.2 | .. |
| Asia-Pacific (28) average[8] | .. | .. | .. | 4.8 | 5.1 | 5.3 | 5.2 | 5.2 | 6.2 | 6.3 |
| LAC average[9] | 14.8 | 15.3 | 13.7 | 15.7 | 16.7 | 16.7 | 17.1 | 16.9 | 17.3 | 18.4 |
| OECD average[1, 10] | 25.2 | 24.9 | 24.5 | 26.6 | 25.9 | 25.9 | 25.8 | 25.9 | 25.9 | .. |

.. Not available

1. Australia, Japan, Korea and New Zealand are part of the OECD (38) group. Data for Australia, Japan, Korea, New Zealand and the OECD average are taken from OECD (2021), *Revenue Statistics 2021*.
2. 2007 to 2018: Data for China are not included in this table as historical data on revenues from social security contributions are not available.
3. Social security contributions data for Indonesia are only available for 2015 to 2020 and are deemed negligible in earlier years. SSCs in Indonesia include contributions from Death Benefit (JK), Work Accident Insurance (JKK), Pension Insurance (JP), and mandatory contributions from BPJS Health for formal workers. Contributions from the BPJS Health since 2018 have been estimated.
4. Heading 2000: Starting from 2015, Social Security Contribution data is given as a lump sum. Data for 2020 is estimated.
5. The social security contributions in the Solomon Islands are zero as they do not meet the social security criteria of the OECD classifications set in Annex A of the Interpretative Guide.
6. Social security data for Viet Nam are not available prior to 2010.
7. Represents an unweighted average for the 30 African countries included in the publication *Revenue Statistics in Africa 2021*.
8. Represents an unweighted average of the 28 Asian and Pacific economies in this publication. The Asia-Pacific (28) average should be interpreted with caution as data for social security contributions (category 2000) are not available or are partial in a few economies, including in Indonesia where SSC data are not available before 2015, in Viet Nam where SSC data are not available before 2010 and in China where SSC data are not available before 2019. The Asia-Pacific (28) average excludes Pakistan prior to 2011 and Nauru prior to 2014 as data were not available. See the country tables in Chapter 4 for further information.
9. Represents an unweighted average for the 26 Latin American and Caribbean (LAC) countries included in the publication *Revenue Statistics in Latin America and the Caribbean 2022*.
10. Represents an unweighted average for the 38 OECD member countries included in the publication *Revenue Statistics 2021*.

StatLink https://stat.link/6jpe8g

## Table 3.9. Taxes on property (4000) as percentage of GDP

| | 1997 | 2000 | 2007 | 2010 | 2015 | 2016 | 2017 | 2018 | 2019 | 2020 |
|---|---|---|---|---|---|---|---|---|---|---|
| Australia[1] | 2.6 | 2.7 | 2.6 | 2.4 | 3.0 | 3.0 | 2.9 | 2.7 | 2.7 | .. |
| Bangladesh | .. | 0.0 | 0.0 | 0.0 | 0.0 | 0.0 | 0.0 | 0.0 | 0.0 | 0.0 |
| Bhutan | 0.0 | 0.0 | 0.1 | 0.0 | 0.0 | 0.0 | 0.0 | 0.0 | 0.0 | 0.1 |
| Cambodia | .. | .. | 0.0 | 0.0 | 0.6 | 0.4 | 0.6 | 0.8 | 1.0 | 0.9 |
| China | .. | .. | 1.6 | 1.3 | 1.7 | 1.5 | 1.5 | 1.4 | 1.4 | 1.5 |
| Cook Islands | .. | .. | 0.0 | 0.0 | 0.0 | 0.0 | 0.0 | 0.0 | 0.0 | 0.0 |
| Fiji | .. | .. | .. | 0.0 | 0.7 | 0.8 | 0.7 | 0.8 | 0.7 | 0.4 |
| Indonesia | 0.3 | 0.3 | 0.7 | 0.6 | 0.3 | 0.2 | 0.2 | 0.2 | 0.2 | 0.2 |
| Japan[1] | 2.9 | 2.7 | 2.4 | 2.6 | 2.5 | 2.5 | 2.5 | 2.6 | 2.6 | .. |
| Kazakhstan | .. | 0.8 | 0.6 | 0.6 | 0.6 | 0.5 | 0.5 | 0.5 | 0.5 | 0.4 |
| Kyrgyzstan | 0.9 | 0.3 | 0.4 | 0.6 | 0.4 | 0.4 | 0.3 | 0.3 | 0.3 | 0.3 |
| Korea[1] | 2.4 | 2.6 | 3.0 | 2.5 | 2.9 | 2.9 | 3.0 | 3.1 | 3.1 | 4.0 |
| Lao PDR | .. | .. | .. | 0.1 | 0.1 | 0.1 | 0.1 | 0.1 | 0.1 | 0.1 |
| Malaysia | 0.0 | 0.0 | .. | .. | 0.0 | 0.0 | 0.0 | 0.0 | 0.0 | 0.0 |
| Maldives | .. | .. | 0.1 | 0.0 | 0.1 | 0.0 | 0.1 | 0.0 | 0.0 | 0.0 |
| Mongolia | .. | .. | 0.6 | 0.5 | 0.5 | 0.5 | 0.6 | 0.5 | 0.6 | 0.6 |
| Nauru | .. | .. | .. | .. | 0.0 | 0.0 | 0.0 | 0.0 | 0.0 | 0.0 |
| New Zealand[1] | 1.8 | 1.7 | 1.8 | 2.0 | 2.0 | 1.9 | 1.9 | 1.9 | 1.9 | 1.9 |
| Pakistan[2] | .. | .. | .. | .. | 0.1 | 0.1 | 0.2 | 0.2 | 0.1 | 0.1 |
| Papua New Guinea | .. | 0.5 | 0.3 | 0.2 | 0.1 | 0.1 | 0.1 | 0.1 | 0.1 | 0.1 |
| Philippines | 0.6 | 0.5 | 0.4 | 0.4 | 0.5 | 0.4 | 0.5 | 0.5 | 0.4 | 0.5 |
| Samoa | .. | .. | 0.1 | 0.0 | 0.0 | 0.0 | 0.0 | 0.0 | 0.0 | 0.0 |
| Singapore | .. | 1.7 | 2.3 | 1.8 | 1.7 | 1.7 | 1.9 | 1.8 | 1.8 | 1.5 |
| Solomon Islands | .. | .. | 0.2 | 0.1 | 0.2 | 0.2 | 0.1 | 0.1 | 0.1 | 0.1 |
| Thailand | .. | 0.3 | 0.2 | 0.2 | 0.5 | 0.4 | 0.5 | 0.5 | 0.5 | 0.2 |
| Tokelau | .. | .. | 0.0 | 0.0 | 0.0 | 0.0 | 0.0 | 0.0 | 0.0 | 0.0 |
| Vanuatu | .. | 0.5 | 0.8 | 0.7 | 0.5 | 0.4 | 0.5 | 0.6 | 0.6 | 0.5 |
| Viet Nam | .. | .. | 0.1 | 0.1 | 0.0 | 0.0 | 0.0 | 0.0 | 0.0 | 0.0 |
| Africa (30) average[3] | .. | .. | .. | 0.4 | 0.4 | 0.4 | 0.3 | 0.3 | 0.4 | .. |
| Asia-Pacific (28) average[4] | .. | .. | .. | 0.7 | 0.7 | 0.6 | 0.7 | 0.7 | 0.7 | 0.7 |
| LAC average[5] | 0.6 | 0.7 | 1.0 | 0.8 | 0.9 | 0.8 | 0.9 | 0.8 | 0.9 | 0.8 |
| OECD average[1, 6] | 1.6 | 1.7 | 1.7 | 1.6 | 1.8 | 2.2 | 1.9 | 1.8 | 1.8 | .. |

.. Not available

1. Australia, Japan, Korea and New Zealand are part of the OECD (38) group. Data for Australia, Japan, Korea, New Zealand and the OECD average are taken from OECD (2021), *Revenue Statistics 2021*.
2. Other taxes on property data are not available separately in 2020. They are included in other local tax revenues classified under heading 6200.
3. Represents an unweighted average for the 30 African countries included in the publication *Revenue Statistics in Africa 2021*.
4. Represents an unweighted average of the 28 Asian and Pacific economies in this publication. Data for 2019 are used for Australia and Japan in the calculation as data for 2020 are not available. See the country tables in Chapter 4 for further information.
5. Represents an unweighted average for the 26 Latin American and Caribbean (LAC) countries included in the publication *Revenue Statistics in Latin America and the Caribbean 2022*.
6. Represents an unweighted average for the 38 OECD member countries included in the publication *Revenue Statistics 2021*.

StatLink https://stat.link/tjhkz8

## Table 3.10. Taxes on property (4000) as percentage of total taxation

| | 1997 | 2000 | 2007 | 2010 | 2015 | 2016 | 2017 | 2018 | 2019 | 2020 |
|---|---|---|---|---|---|---|---|---|---|---|
| Australia[1] | 9.2 | 8.8 | 9.0 | 9.4 | 10.7 | 10.8 | 10.1 | 9.5 | 9.8 | .. |
| Bangladesh | .. | 0.0 | 0.0 | 0.0 | 0.0 | 0.0 | 0.0 | 0.0 | 0.0 | 0.0 |
| Bhutan | 0.4 | 0.3 | 0.6 | 0.1 | 0.4 | 0.3 | 0.2 | 0.2 | 0.1 | 0.8 |
| Cambodia | .. | .. | 0.0 | 0.0 | 3.8 | 2.9 | 3.7 | 4.3 | 4.6 | 4.7 |
| China[2] | .. | .. | .. | .. | .. | .. | .. | .. | 6.4 | 7.4 |
| Cook Islands | .. | .. | 0.0 | 0.0 | 0.0 | 0.0 | 0.0 | 0.0 | 0.0 | 0.0 |
| Fiji | .. | .. | .. | 0.0 | 3.1 | 3.3 | 2.9 | 3.3 | 3.0 | 2.6 |
| Indonesia | 4.2 | 3.7 | 6.1 | 5.2 | 2.4 | 1.6 | 1.4 | 1.4 | 1.5 | 1.7 |
| Japan[1] | 11.2 | 10.5 | 9.0 | 9.7 | 8.2 | 8.3 | 8.2 | 8.1 | 8.2 | .. |
| Kazakhstan | .. | 4.1 | 2.2 | 2.4 | 3.6 | 3.3 | 3.0 | 2.8 | 2.8 | 3.1 |
| Kyrgyzstan | 7.2 | 2.3 | 2.3 | 3.2 | 1.9 | 1.8 | 1.8 | 1.7 | 1.8 | 1.9 |
| Korea[1] | 12.7 | 12.4 | 12.8 | 11.3 | 12.4 | 11.6 | 11.7 | 11.6 | 11.4 | 14.2 |
| Lao PDR | .. | .. | .. | 1.1 | 0.9 | 0.7 | 0.7 | 1.1 | 1.2 | 1.2 |
| Malaysia | 0.0 | 0.0 | .. | .. | 0.0 | 0.0 | 0.0 | 0.0 | 0.0 | 0.0 |
| Maldives | .. | .. | 0.4 | 0.4 | 0.3 | 0.2 | 0.7 | 0.3 | 0.2 | 0.0 |
| Mongolia | .. | .. | 2.0 | 1.9 | 2.6 | 2.7 | 2.6 | 2.2 | 2.5 | 2.9 |
| Nauru | .. | .. | .. | .. | 0.0 | 0.0 | 0.0 | 0.0 | 0.0 | 0.0 |
| New Zealand[1] | 5.4 | 5.3 | 5.3 | 6.6 | 6.2 | 6.1 | 6.0 | 5.8 | 6.2 | 5.9 |
| Pakistan[3] | .. | .. | .. | .. | 1.1 | 1.1 | 1.5 | 1.7 | 1.4 | 1.0 |
| Papua New Guinea | .. | 3.4 | 1.4 | 1.0 | 0.6 | 0.9 | 0.5 | 1.0 | 0.4 | 0.5 |
| Philippines | 3.3 | 3.1 | 2.9 | 3.0 | 2.8 | 2.7 | 2.8 | 2.6 | 2.5 | 2.7 |
| Samoa | .. | .. | 0.5 | 0.0 | 0.0 | 0.0 | 0.0 | 0.0 | 0.0 | 0.0 |
| Singapore | .. | 11.2 | 17.1 | 14.5 | 13.0 | 13.0 | 14.1 | 14.0 | 13.2 | 11.4 |
| Solomon Islands | .. | .. | 1.1 | 0.6 | 0.8 | 0.7 | 0.5 | 0.5 | 0.6 | 0.5 |
| Thailand | .. | 2.2 | 1.2 | 1.3 | 2.7 | 2.3 | 2.8 | 2.7 | 2.7 | 1.4 |
| Tokelau | .. | .. | 0.0 | 0.0 | 0.0 | 0.0 | 0.0 | 0.0 | 0.0 | 0.0 |
| Vanuatu | .. | 3.2 | 4.4 | 4.4 | 3.0 | 2.9 | 3.0 | 3.1 | 3.6 | 3.4 |
| Viet Nam | .. | .. | 0.3 | 0.3 | 0.2 | 0.1 | 0.1 | 0.1 | 0.1 | 0.1 |
| Africa (30) average[4] | .. | .. | .. | 1.9 | 1.9 | 1.8 | 1.7 | 1.7 | 1.9 | .. |
| Asia-Pacific (28) average[5] | .. | .. | .. | 3.2 | 3.0 | 2.9 | 2.9 | 2.9 | 3.0 | 3.0 |
| LAC average[6] | 3.8 | 3.7 | 4.9 | 4.0 | 4.0 | 3.8 | 3.9 | 3.7 | 3.8 | 3.5 |
| OECD average[1,7] | 5.1 | 5.3 | 5.4 | 5.4 | 5.7 | 6.5 | 5.8 | 5.5 | 5.5 | .. |

.. Not available

1. Australia, Japan, Korea and New Zealand are part of the OECD (38) group. Data for Australia, Japan, Korea, New Zealand and the OECD average are taken from OECD (2021), *Revenue Statistics 2021*.
2. 2007 to 2018: Data for China are not included in this table as historical data on revenues from social security contributions are not available.
3. Other taxes on property data are not available separately in 2020. They are included in other local tax revenues classified under heading 6200.
4. Represents an unweighted average for the 30 African countries included in the publication *Revenue Statistics in Africa 2021*.
5. Represents an unweighted average of the 28 Asian and Pacific economies in this publication. The Asia-Pacific (28) average should be interpreted with caution as data for social security contributions (category 2000) are not available or are partial in a few economies. Data for 2019 are used for Australia and Japan in the calculation as data for 2020 are not available. See the country tables in Chapter 4 for further information.
6. Represents an unweighted average for the 26 Latin American and Caribbean (LAC) countries included in the publication *Revenue Statistics in Latin America and the Caribbean 2022*.
7. Represents an unweighted average for the 38 OECD member countries included in the publication *Revenue Statistics 2021*.

StatLink https://stat.link/1ibasg

## Table 3.11. Taxes on goods and services (5000) as percentage of GDP

| | 1997 | 2000 | 2007 | 2010 | 2015 | 2016 | 2017 | 2018 | 2019 | 2020 |
|---|---|---|---|---|---|---|---|---|---|---|
| Australia[1] | 7.9 | 8.8 | 7.9 | 7.2 | 7.6 | 7.4 | 7.5 | 7.3 | 7.3 | .. |
| Bangladesh | .. | 5.1 | 5.6 | 6.1 | 5.8 | 5.9 | 6.2 | 5.9 | 5.2 | 5.8 |
| Bhutan | 3.8 | 2.9 | 3.9 | 4.9 | 5.9 | 6.1 | 6.9 | 6.0 | 4.3 | 3.4 |
| Cambodia | .. | .. | 8.3 | 6.7 | 11.6 | 11.7 | 12.0 | 13.5 | 15.7 | 13.3 |
| China | .. | .. | 10.7 | 11.9 | 10.7 | 10.2 | 10.0 | 9.6 | 9.1 | 8.4 |
| Cook Islands | .. | .. | 15.1 | 16.3 | 17.4 | 18.0 | 17.9 | 18.3 | 18.6 | 11.5 |
| Fiji | .. | .. | .. | 14.6 | 16.8 | 15.3 | 15.9 | 16.1 | 15.6 | 10.9 |
| Indonesia | 3.6 | 3.5 | 5.1 | 4.7 | 5.2 | 4.8 | 5.0 | 5.0 | 4.7 | 4.3 |
| Japan[1] | 4.4 | 4.9 | 4.9 | 4.9 | 6.3 | 6.2 | 6.5 | 6.2 | 6.2 | .. |
| Kazakhstan | .. | 6.9 | 8.8 | 11.9 | 7.2 | 7.2 | 8.2 | 8.5 | 8.6 | 6.9 |
| Kyrgyzstan | 9.2 | 9.3 | 14.9 | 13.2 | 15.0 | 15.7 | 15.5 | 16.5 | 15.5 | 13.3 |
| Korea[1] | 8.1 | 8.0 | 7.4 | 7.5 | 6.7 | 7.0 | 7.0 | 7.0 | 7.0 | 6.8 |
| Lao PDR | .. | .. | .. | 8.7 | 9.6 | 9.2 | 8.4 | 8.3 | 8.1 | 7.0 |
| Malaysia | 8.9 | 5.6 | 4.1 | 3.9 | 4.8 | 5.0 | 4.7 | 3.2 | 3.2 | 3.2 |
| Maldives | .. | .. | 11.2 | 8.3 | 14.3 | 14.9 | 15.4 | 15.3 | 14.9 | 12.7 |
| Mongolia | .. | .. | 11.5 | 11.5 | 9.4 | 9.8 | 10.6 | 12.2 | 11.8 | 10.7 |
| Nauru | .. | .. | .. | .. | 11.0 | 6.5 | 10.2 | 10.5 | 10.3 | 10.3 |
| New Zealand[1] | 11.8 | 11.3 | 10.7 | 12.0 | 12.3 | 12.0 | 12.0 | 12.2 | 12.2 | 12.5 |
| Pakistan | .. | .. | .. | .. | 7.1 | 7.0 | 7.1 | 6.5 | 6.4 | 6.9 |
| Papua New Guinea | .. | 3.3 | 5.3 | 5.0 | 5.2 | 5.0 | 4.8 | 4.7 | 5.2 | 4.6 |
| Philippines | 8.1 | 6.4 | 6.3 | 5.9 | 6.3 | 6.4 | 6.8 | 7.5 | 7.7 | 7.3 |
| Samoa | .. | .. | 16.7 | 14.5 | 18.2 | 17.7 | 18.1 | 18.4 | 18.5 | 19.1 |
| Singapore | .. | 4.7 | 4.3 | 4.3 | 4.1 | 4.1 | 3.9 | 3.8 | 3.8 | 3.7 |
| Solomon Islands | .. | .. | 11.6 | 13.1 | 16.0 | 15.1 | 15.7 | 17.6 | 14.4 | 13.2 |
| Thailand | .. | 9.2 | 9.4 | 9.6 | 10.6 | 10.3 | 10.1 | 10.0 | 9.5 | 9.4 |
| Tokelau | .. | .. | 7.4 | 8.6 | 7.4 | 6.7 | 7.4 | 9.5 | 8.9 | 10.2 |
| Vanuatu | .. | 15.7 | 18.2 | 15.6 | 15.8 | 14.8 | 16.6 | 17.3 | 16.4 | 13.8 |
| Viet Nam | .. | .. | 10.9 | 13.4 | 11.1 | 11.6 | 11.4 | 11.0 | 11.1 | 9.8 |
| Africa (30) average[2] | .. | .. | .. | 7.6 | 8.2 | 8.4 | 8.4 | 8.6 | 8.6 | .. |
| Asia-Pacific (28) average[3] | .. | .. | .. | 9.4 | 10.0 | 9.7 | 10.1 | 10.3 | 10.0 | 9.0 |
| LAC average[4] | 9.8 | 10.1 | 11.0 | 10.5 | 11.1 | 11.2 | 11.3 | 11.3 | 11.2 | 10.5 |
| OECD average[1, 5] | 10.8 | 10.8 | 10.7 | 10.5 | 10.8 | 10.9 | 10.9 | 10.8 | 10.8 | .. |

.. Not available

1. Australia, Japan, Korea and New Zealand are part of the OECD (38) group. Data for Australia, Japan, Korea, New Zealand and the OECD average are taken from OECD (2021), *Revenue Statistics 2021*.
2. Represents an unweighted average for the 30 African countries included in the publication *Revenue Statistics in Africa 2021*.
3. Represents an unweighted average of the 28 Asian and Pacific economies in this publication. Data for 2019 are used for Australia and Japan in the calculation as data for 2020 are not available. See the country tables in Chapter 4 for further information.
4. Represents an unweighted average for the 26 Latin American and Caribbean (LAC) countries included in the publication *Revenue Statistics in Latin America and the Caribbean 2022*.
5. Represents an unweighted average for the 38 OECD member countries included in the publication *Revenue Statistics 2021*.

StatLink https://stat.link/8o1ihz

## Table 3.12. Taxes on goods and services (5000) as percentage of total taxation

| | 1997 | 2000 | 2007 | 2010 | 2015 | 2016 | 2017 | 2018 | 2019 | 2020 |
|---|---|---|---|---|---|---|---|---|---|---|
| Australia[1] | 27.5 | 28.8 | 26.8 | 28.8 | 27.5 | 27.0 | 26.4 | 25.5 | 26.3 | .. |
| Bangladesh | .. | 71.6 | 66.4 | 61.3 | 54.7 | 58.0 | 59.8 | 59.8 | 58.0 | 56.6 |
| Bhutan | 44.9 | 32.2 | 42.7 | 34.8 | 43.5 | 47.4 | 50.0 | 47.8 | 40.6 | 38.0 |
| Cambodia | .. | .. | 85.6 | 91.4 | 74.6 | 74.0 | 71.2 | 72.1 | 72.3 | 65.9 |
| China[2] | .. | .. | .. | .. | .. | .. | .. | .. | 41.3 | 41.7 |
| Cook Islands | .. | .. | 60.8 | 60.6 | 65.0 | 66.5 | 63.4 | 61.4 | 66.4 | 58.3 |
| Fiji | .. | .. | .. | 67.4 | 71.2 | 66.2 | 65.6 | 68.6 | 70.0 | 65.8 |
| Indonesia | 47.6 | 44.7 | 41.7 | 41.8 | 43.3 | 39.8 | 42.7 | 41.8 | 40.6 | 42.7 |
| Japan[1] | 17.2 | 19.3 | 18.0 | 18.7 | 21.0 | 20.4 | 21.0 | 19.5 | 19.7 | .. |
| Kazakhstan | .. | 34.7 | 33.8 | 50.2 | 46.5 | 48.1 | 51.0 | 50.2 | 51.8 | 49.0 |
| Kyrgyzstan | 74.8 | 79.7 | 81.1 | 74.4 | 78.7 | 80.2 | 80.7 | 81.2 | 79.7 | 76.4 |
| Korea[1] | 42.7 | 38.4 | 31.3 | 33.7 | 28.0 | 28.1 | 27.7 | 26.3 | 25.8 | 24.4 |
| Lao PDR | .. | .. | .. | 76.2 | 76.4 | 77.4 | 76.2 | 76.6 | 76.4 | 78.1 |
| Malaysia | 45.2 | 39.8 | 27.9 | 28.4 | 33.0 | 35.6 | 34.8 | 25.8 | 25.9 | 27.8 |
| Maldives | .. | .. | 93.7 | 92.7 | 73.7 | 75.4 | 76.7 | 79.0 | 78.5 | 66.7 |
| Mongolia | .. | .. | 40.4 | 45.5 | 48.9 | 51.3 | 49.6 | 50.8 | 49.5 | 50.4 |
| Nauru | .. | .. | .. | .. | 47.8 | 41.3 | 35.1 | 29.8 | 21.4 | 21.7 |
| New Zealand[1] | 34.8 | 34.7 | 31.7 | 39.6 | 38.9 | 38.4 | 38.4 | 37.9 | 38.7 | 38.8 |
| Pakistan | .. | .. | .. | .. | 63.9 | 63.0 | 62.3 | 63.8 | 64.2 | 66.7 |
| Papua New Guinea | .. | 24.9 | 25.5 | 29.6 | 34.3 | 37.5 | 38.5 | 37.6 | 42.0 | 39.9 |
| Philippines | 47.7 | 42.0 | 40.7 | 41.2 | 39.1 | 39.2 | 40.3 | 43.0 | 42.5 | 40.8 |
| Samoa | .. | .. | 76.0 | 75.3 | 76.9 | 77.2 | 77.9 | 77.0 | 77.0 | 76.3 |
| Singapore | .. | 31.1 | 32.9 | 34.4 | 31.7 | 31.8 | 28.5 | 29.5 | 28.8 | 29.0 |
| Solomon Islands | .. | .. | 75.8 | 69.1 | 69.1 | 70.1 | 69.8 | 73.1 | 70.6 | 70.5 |
| Thailand | .. | 61.9 | 53.4 | 54.4 | 56.2 | 56.9 | 57.4 | 56.7 | 55.1 | 57.2 |
| Tokelau | .. | .. | 52.2 | 48.9 | 48.9 | 45.4 | 44.2 | 52.7 | 46.3 | 49.2 |
| Vanuatu | .. | 96.8 | 95.6 | 95.6 | 97.0 | 97.1 | 97.0 | 96.9 | 96.5 | 96.6 |
| Viet Nam | .. | .. | 54.6 | 53.0 | 49.5 | 50.5 | 49.2 | 47.2 | 45.9 | 43.3 |
| Africa (30) average[3] | .. | .. | .. | 52.0 | 51.1 | 52.3 | 52.2 | 52.3 | 51.9 | .. |
| Asia-Pacific (28) average[4] | .. | .. | .. | 53.9 | 53.3 | 53.5 | 53.2 | 53.0 | 51.8 | 50.6 |
| LAC average[5] | 58.6 | 57.0 | 52.1 | 51.1 | 50.4 | 50.6 | 50.6 | 50.3 | 49.7 | 48.4 |
| OECD average[1, 6] | 34.3 | 33.9 | 33.0 | 34.0 | 33.3 | 33.1 | 33.1 | 32.8 | 32.6 | .. |

.. Not available

1. Australia, Japan, Korea and New Zealand are part of the OECD (38) group. Data for Australia, Japan, Korea, New Zealand and the OECD average are taken from OECD (2021), *Revenue Statistics 2021*.
2. 2007 to 2018: Data for China are not included in this table as historical data on revenues from social security contributions are not available.
3. Represents an unweighted average for the 30 African countries included in the publication *Revenue Statistics in Africa 2021*.
4. Represents an unweighted average of the 28 Asian and Pacific economies in this publication. The Asia-Pacific (28) average should be interpreted with caution as data for social security contributions (category 2000) are not available or are partial in a few economies. Data for 2019 are used for Australia and Japan in the calculation as data for 2020 are not available. See the country tables in Chapter 4 for further information.
5. Represents an unweighted average for the 26 Latin American and Caribbean (LAC) countries included in the publication *Revenue Statistics in Latin America and the Caribbean 2022*.
6. Represents an unweighted average for the 38 OECD member countries included in the publication *Revenue Statistics 2021*.

StatLink https://stat.link/osc8mb

## Table 3.13. Taxes on general consumption (5110) as percentage of GDP

| | 1997 | 2000 | 2007 | 2010 | 2015 | 2016 | 2017 | 2018 | 2019 | 2020 |
|---|---|---|---|---|---|---|---|---|---|---|
| Australia[1] | 2.4 | 3.7 | 3.8 | 3.4 | 3.7 | 3.6 | 3.6 | 3.4 | 3.3 | .. |
| Bangladesh | .. | 2.2 | 2.8 | 3.3 | 3.2 | 3.2 | 3.4 | 3.4 | 3.1 | 3.4 |
| Bhutan | 1.3 | 1.5 | 1.6 | 2.1 | 2.6 | 2.5 | 2.6 | 2.7 | 2.8 | 2.3 |
| Cambodia | .. | .. | 3.3 | 2.0 | 5.0 | 5.1 | 5.3 | 5.6 | 6.6 | 6.2 |
| China[2] | .. | .. | 8.8 | 9.1 | 7.8 | 7.6 | 7.6 | 7.3 | 6.7 | 6.1 |
| Cook Islands | .. | .. | 10.8 | 11.0 | 12.5 | 12.5 | 12.6 | 13.3 | 13.6 | 7.4 |
| Fiji | .. | .. | .. | 8.7 | 9.8 | 7.5 | 7.8 | 7.6 | 7.5 | 5.3 |
| Indonesia | 2.7 | 2.3 | 3.6 | 3.4 | 3.7 | 3.3 | 3.5 | 3.6 | 3.4 | 2.9 |
| Japan[1] | 1.9 | 2.3 | 2.4 | 2.5 | 4.1 | 4.0 | 4.0 | 4.0 | 4.1 | .. |
| Kazakhstan | .. | 4.4 | 4.9 | 3.1 | 2.3 | 3.2 | 3.1 | 3.3 | 3.9 | 3.6 |
| Kyrgyzstan | 6.3 | 5.8 | 11.1 | 10.3 | 10.8 | 10.7 | 10.5 | 11.2 | 10.1 | 8.8 |
| Korea[1] | 3.6 | 3.6 | 3.8 | 3.9 | 3.6 | 3.9 | 4.1 | 4.1 | 4.3 | 4.2 |
| Lao PDR | .. | .. | .. | 3.3 | 4.3 | 3.6 | 3.5 | 3.4 | 3.3 | 2.7 |
| Malaysia[3] | 2.2 | 1.7 | 1.0 | 1.0 | 2.7 | 3.3 | 3.2 | 1.7 | 1.0 | 1.0 |
| Maldives | .. | .. | 0.0 | 0.0 | 9.6 | 9.3 | 9.4 | 9.4 | 8.9 | 7.5 |
| Mongolia | .. | .. | 5.3 | 5.9 | 4.6 | 4.8 | 5.8 | 6.7 | 6.6 | 5.9 |
| Nauru | .. | .. | .. | .. | 0.0 | 0.0 | 0.0 | 0.0 | 0.0 | 0.0 |
| New Zealand[1] | 8.3 | 8.1 | 8.0 | 9.3 | 9.5 | 9.4 | 9.4 | 9.5 | 9.5 | 10.1 |
| Pakistan | .. | .. | .. | .. | 4.4 | 4.2 | 4.4 | 3.8 | 3.9 | 4.1 |
| Papua New Guinea | .. | 3.3 | 2.3 | 2.3 | 2.7 | 2.5 | 2.2 | 2.1 | 2.4 | 1.9 |
| Philippines | 3.2 | 2.6 | 3.8 | 3.5 | 4.0 | 4.1 | 4.2 | 4.3 | 4.3 | 3.8 |
| Samoa | .. | .. | 8.4 | 6.8 | 9.6 | 8.8 | 9.3 | 9.6 | 9.9 | 10.0 |
| Singapore | .. | 1.3 | 2.2 | 2.4 | 2.4 | 2.5 | 2.3 | 2.2 | 2.2 | 2.2 |
| Solomon Islands | .. | .. | 11.6 | 6.3 | 7.0 | 6.2 | 6.6 | 6.9 | 5.8 | 5.5 |
| Thailand | .. | 3.4 | 3.6 | 3.7 | 3.9 | 3.9 | 3.8 | 3.9 | 3.6 | 3.5 |
| Tokelau | .. | .. | 0.0 | 0.0 | 0.0 | 0.0 | 0.0 | 0.0 | 0.0 | 0.0 |
| Vanuatu | .. | 9.1 | 10.9 | 6.3 | 7.0 | 6.4 | 7.3 | 8.2 | 7.6 | 6.3 |
| Viet Nam | .. | .. | 5.6 | 7.2 | 6.0 | 6.0 | 6.3 | 6.2 | 6.0 | 5.4 |
| Africa (30) average[4] | .. | .. | .. | 4.3 | 4.8 | 4.8 | 4.9 | 5.0 | 5.0 | .. |
| Asia-Pacific (28) average[5] | .. | .. | .. | 4.6 | 5.2 | 5.1 | 5.2 | 5.3 | 5.2 | 4.6 |
| LAC average[6] | 5.3 | 5.5 | 6.7 | 6.4 | 7.1 | 7.2 | 7.2 | 7.2 | 7.1 | 6.8 |
| OECD average[1, 7] | 6.6 | 6.6 | 6.7 | 6.6 | 6.8 | 6.9 | 6.9 | 7.0 | 6.9 | .. |

.. Not available

1. Australia, Japan, Korea and New Zealand are part of the OECD (38) group. Data for Australia, Japan, Korea, New Zealand and the OECD average are taken from OECD (2021), *Revenue Statistics 2021*.
2. 2007 to 2018: Revenues from import excise tax and refund of excise tax for export are included under heading 5111 as they cannot be separated from revenues from import VAT and refunds of VAT for export and VAT represents the majority of the revenues.
3. Heading 5111: Starting from 2015, VAT (GST, Goods and Services Tax) is sourced from the IMF's Government Finance Statistics dataset. GST was abolished by the government in 2018 and replaced by sales tax and service tax.
4. Represents an unweighted average for the 30 African countries included in the publication *Revenue Statistics in Africa 2021*.
5. Represents an unweighted average of the 28 Asian and Pacific economies in this publication. Data for 2019 are used for Australia and Japan in the calculation as data for 2020 are not available. See the country tables in Chapter 4 for further information.
6. Represents an unweighted average for the 26 Latin American and Caribbean (LAC) countries included in the publication *Revenue Statistics in Latin America and the Caribbean 2022*.
7. Represents an unweighted average for the 38 OECD member countries included in the publication *Revenue Statistics 2021*.

StatLink https://stat.link/emhg05

## Table 3.14. Taxes on general consumption (5110) as percentage of total taxation

| | 1997 | 2000 | 2007 | 2010 | 2015 | 2016 | 2017 | 2018 | 2019 | 2020 |
|---|---|---|---|---|---|---|---|---|---|---|
| Australia[1] | 8.4 | 12.0 | 12.9 | 13.5 | 13.2 | 13.0 | 12.5 | 12.0 | 12.0 | .. |
| Bangladesh | .. | 30.5 | 33.1 | 33.1 | 30.1 | 31.6 | 32.4 | 35.0 | 34.9 | 33.4 |
| Bhutan | 15.4 | 16.7 | 18.0 | 15.1 | 19.3 | 19.3 | 19.1 | 21.7 | 26.8 | 25.9 |
| Cambodia | .. | .. | 34.1 | 27.3 | 31.7 | 32.4 | 31.2 | 30.1 | 30.5 | 30.6 |
| China[2, 3] | .. | .. | .. | .. | .. | .. | .. | .. | 30.2 | 30.3 |
| Cook Islands | .. | .. | 43.4 | 41.1 | 46.6 | 46.1 | 44.4 | 44.6 | 48.5 | 37.6 |
| Fiji | .. | .. | .. | 40.4 | 41.3 | 32.4 | 32.3 | 32.2 | 33.8 | 32.2 |
| Indonesia | 35.5 | 29.4 | 29.2 | 29.6 | 30.4 | 27.8 | 30.5 | 30.3 | 29.0 | 29.0 |
| Japan[1] | 7.2 | 9.1 | 8.8 | 9.6 | 13.7 | 13.3 | 13.0 | 12.8 | 13.2 | .. |
| Kazakhstan | .. | 22.2 | 18.8 | 13.1 | 14.8 | 21.3 | 19.1 | 19.4 | 23.2 | 25.5 |
| Kyrgyzstan | 51.2 | 49.7 | 60.3 | 58.0 | 56.7 | 54.8 | 54.4 | 55.4 | 52.2 | 50.4 |
| Korea[1] | 18.9 | 17.0 | 15.8 | 17.5 | 15.3 | 15.8 | 16.0 | 15.3 | 15.7 | 15.1 |
| Lao PDR | .. | .. | .. | 28.6 | 33.9 | 30.5 | 31.8 | 31.4 | 31.4 | 30.6 |
| Malaysia[4] | 11.1 | 11.9 | 6.7 | 7.2 | 18.9 | 23.6 | 24.2 | 13.4 | 8.2 | 9.1 |
| Maldives | .. | .. | 0.0 | 0.0 | 49.5 | 47.1 | 46.7 | 48.6 | 46.9 | 39.2 |
| Mongolia | .. | .. | 18.9 | 23.4 | 23.7 | 25.0 | 27.0 | 28.2 | 27.5 | 27.8 |
| Nauru | .. | .. | .. | .. | 0.0 | 0.0 | 0.0 | 0.0 | 0.0 | 0.0 |
| New Zealand[1] | 24.5 | 24.9 | 23.5 | 30.7 | 30.2 | 29.9 | 30.2 | 29.6 | 30.3 | 31.3 |
| Pakistan | .. | .. | .. | .. | 39.7 | 37.6 | 38.4 | 37.3 | 38.5 | 39.8 |
| Papua New Guinea | .. | 24.9 | 11.1 | 13.3 | 17.9 | 19.1 | 18.0 | 16.4 | 18.9 | 16.5 |
| Philippines | 19.1 | 17.0 | 24.4 | 24.8 | 24.9 | 25.2 | 25.3 | 24.7 | 23.6 | 21.1 |
| Samoa | .. | .. | 38.2 | 35.0 | 40.4 | 38.5 | 40.0 | 40.1 | 41.1 | 40.2 |
| Singapore | .. | 8.3 | 16.8 | 19.6 | 18.6 | 18.9 | 16.5 | 16.8 | 16.5 | 16.8 |
| Solomon Islands | .. | .. | 75.8 | 33.3 | 30.1 | 28.8 | 29.4 | 28.8 | 28.6 | 29.5 |
| Thailand | .. | 23.1 | 20.6 | 20.8 | 20.8 | 21.5 | 21.9 | 22.2 | 20.6 | 21.1 |
| Tokelau | .. | .. | 0.0 | 0.0 | 0.0 | 0.0 | 0.0 | 0.0 | 0.0 | 0.0 |
| Vanuatu | .. | 56.4 | 57.1 | 38.8 | 42.8 | 41.6 | 42.5 | 45.8 | 44.6 | 44.1 |
| Viet Nam | .. | .. | 28.1 | 28.4 | 26.7 | 26.0 | 27.1 | 26.8 | 24.9 | 24.0 |
| Africa (30) average[5] | .. | .. | .. | 29.8 | 29.4 | 29.7 | 30.0 | 30.2 | 29.9 | .. |
| Asia-Pacific (28) average[6] | .. | .. | .. | 24.1 | 27.1 | 26.7 | 26.8 | 26.6 | 26.8 | 25.9 |
| LAC average[7] | 29.8 | 28.9 | 30.6 | 30.1 | 31.5 | 32.0 | 31.7 | 31.9 | 31.3 | 31.0 |
| OECD average[1, 8] | 20.7 | 20.4 | 20.8 | 21.3 | 21.0 | 20.8 | 21.1 | 21.1 | 21.0 | .. |

.. Not available

1. Australia, Japan, Korea and New Zealand are part of the OECD (38) group. Data for Australia, Japan, Korea, New Zealand and the OECD average are taken from OECD (2021), *Revenue Statistics 2021*.
2. 2007 to 2018: Data for China are not included in this table as historical data on revenues from social security contributions are not available.
3. 2007 to 2018: Revenues from import excise tax and refund of excise tax for export are included under heading 5111 as they cannot be separated from revenues from import VAT and refunds of VAT for export and VAT represents the majority of the revenues.
4. Heading 5111: Starting from 2015, VAT (GST, Goods and Services Tax) is sourced from the IMF's Government Finance Statistics dataset. GST was abolished by the government in 2018 and replaced by sales tax and service tax.
5. Represents an unweighted average for the 30 African countries included in the publication *Revenue Statistics in Africa 2021*.
6. Represents an unweighted average of the 28 Asian and Pacific economies in this publication. The Asia-Pacific (28) average should be interpreted with caution as data for social security contributions (category 2000) are not available or are partial in a few economies. Data for 2019 are used for Australia and Japan in the calculation as data for 2020 are not available. See the country tables in Chapter 4 for further information.
7. Represents an unweighted average for the 26 Latin American and Caribbean (LAC) countries included in the publication *Revenue Statistics in Latin America and the Caribbean 2022*.
8. Represents an unweighted average for the 38 OECD member countries included in the publication *Revenue Statistics 2021*.

StatLink https://stat.link/xe2yqd

## Table 3.15. Taxes on specific goods and services (5120) as percentage of GDP

| | 1997 | 2000 | 2007 | 2010 | 2015 | 2016 | 2017 | 2018 | 2019 | 2020 |
|---|---|---|---|---|---|---|---|---|---|---|
| Australia[1] | 4.0 | 4.3 | 3.3 | 3.0 | 2.9 | 2.8 | 2.9 | 2.8 | 2.9 | .. |
| Bangladesh | .. | 2.9 | 2.8 | 2.8 | 2.6 | 2.7 | 2.8 | 2.4 | 2.1 | 2.4 |
| Bhutan | 2.5 | 1.4 | 2.2 | 2.8 | 3.1 | 3.4 | 4.0 | 3.0 | 1.3 | 0.8 |
| Cambodia | .. | .. | 5.0 | 2.5 | 6.4 | 6.3 | 6.5 | 7.5 | 8.7 | 6.7 |
| China[2] | .. | .. | 1.8 | 2.5 | 2.5 | 2.2 | 2.2 | 2.0 | 2.2 | 2.0 |
| Cook Islands | .. | .. | 4.1 | 5.0 | 4.7 | 5.3 | 5.1 | 4.8 | 4.8 | 3.8 |
| Fiji | .. | .. | .. | 5.8 | 7.0 | 7.8 | 8.0 | 8.5 | 8.0 | 5.5 |
| Indonesia | 0.9 | 1.2 | 1.5 | 1.4 | 1.6 | 1.4 | 1.4 | 1.4 | 1.3 | 1.4 |
| Japan[1] | 2.0 | 2.0 | 1.9 | 1.9 | 1.8 | 1.7 | 2.0 | 1.7 | 1.6 | .. |
| Kazakhstan | .. | 2.1 | 3.1 | 8.3 | 4.6 | 3.7 | 4.8 | 4.9 | 4.5 | 3.1 |
| Kyrgyzstan | 2.3 | 2.8 | 3.7 | 2.7 | 4.1 | 4.8 | 4.9 | 5.0 | 5.2 | 4.4 |
| Korea[1] | 4.1 | 4.1 | 3.4 | 3.4 | 2.6 | 2.6 | 2.6 | 2.5 | 2.4 | 2.2 |
| Lao PDR | .. | .. | .. | 4.3 | 4.1 | 4.5 | 3.7 | 4.3 | 4.1 | 3.1 |
| Malaysia | 5.4 | 2.9 | 2.5 | 2.4 | 1.6 | 1.3 | 1.0 | 1.2 | 1.8 | 1.8 |
| Maldives | .. | .. | 11.0 | 8.1 | 4.6 | 5.4 | 5.9 | 5.8 | 5.9 | 5.1 |
| Mongolia | .. | .. | 4.9 | 4.8 | 4.1 | 4.1 | 3.8 | 4.5 | 4.5 | 4.2 |
| Nauru | .. | .. | .. | .. | 10.3 | 6.0 | 9.6 | 9.8 | 9.6 | 9.6 |
| New Zealand[1] | 2.8 | 2.5 | 2.0 | 1.9 | 1.9 | 1.8 | 1.8 | 1.9 | 1.8 | 1.6 |
| Pakistan | .. | .. | .. | .. | 2.6 | 2.8 | 2.7 | 2.7 | 2.5 | 2.7 |
| Papua New Guinea | .. | .. | 3.0 | 2.8 | 2.5 | 2.4 | 2.5 | 2.7 | 2.9 | 2.7 |
| Philippines | 4.8 | 3.7 | 2.4 | 2.2 | 2.2 | 2.2 | 2.4 | 3.1 | 3.3 | 3.4 |
| Samoa | .. | .. | 8.3 | 7.8 | 8.7 | 8.9 | 8.8 | 8.8 | 8.6 | 9.0 |
| Singapore | .. | 2.0 | 1.3 | 1.3 | 1.3 | 1.2 | 1.2 | 1.1 | 1.1 | 1.1 |
| Solomon Islands | .. | .. | 6.2 | 6.7 | 8.9 | 8.8 | 8.9 | 10.6 | 8.4 | 7.5 |
| Thailand | .. | 5.5 | 5.5 | 5.7 | 5.4 | 5.3 | 5.3 | 5.1 | 5.1 | 4.9 |
| Tokelau | .. | .. | 7.4 | 8.6 | 7.4 | 6.7 | 7.4 | 9.5 | 8.9 | 10.2 |
| Vanuatu | .. | 6.5 | 7.3 | 6.7 | 6.2 | 5.9 | 6.4 | 6.4 | 6.0 | 5.6 |
| Viet Nam | .. | .. | 4.8 | 5.6 | 4.6 | 5.0 | 4.6 | 4.2 | 4.4 | 3.8 |
| Africa (30) average[3] | .. | .. | .. | 3.1 | 3.2 | 3.4 | 3.4 | 3.3 | 3.4 | .. |
| Asia-Pacific (28) average[4] | .. | .. | .. | 4.3 | 4.3 | 4.2 | 4.4 | 4.6 | 4.4 | 4.0 |
| LAC average[5] | 4.2 | 4.3 | 3.9 | 3.7 | 3.6 | 3.6 | 3.7 | 3.7 | 3.7 | 3.5 |
| OECD average[1, 6] | 3.7 | 3.7 | 3.3 | 3.3 | 3.3 | 3.4 | 3.3 | 3.2 | 3.1 | .. |

.. Not available

1. Australia, Japan, Korea and New Zealand are part of the OECD (38) group. Data for Australia, Japan, Korea, New Zealand and the OECD average are taken from OECD (2021), *Revenue Statistics 2021*.
2. 2007 to 2018: Revenues from import excise tax and refund of excise tax for export are included under heading 5111 as they cannot be separated from revenues from import VAT and refunds of VAT for export and VAT represents the majority of the revenues.
3. Represents an unweighted average for the 30 African countries included in the publication *Revenue Statistics in Africa 2021*.
4. Represents an unweighted average of the 28 Asian and Pacific economies in this publication. Data for 2019 are used for Australia and Japan in the calculation as data for 2020 are not available. See the country tables in Chapter 4 for further information.
5. Represents an unweighted average for the 26 Latin American and Caribbean (LAC) countries included in the publication *Revenue Statistics in Latin America and the Caribbean 2022*.
6. Represents an unweighted average for the 38 OECD member countries included in the publication *Revenue Statistics 2021*.

StatLink https://stat.link/s5ao3p

## Table 3.16. Taxes on specific goods and services (5120) as percentage of total taxation

| | 1997 | 2000 | 2007 | 2010 | 2015 | 2016 | 2017 | 2018 | 2019 | 2020 |
|---|---|---|---|---|---|---|---|---|---|---|
| Australia[1] | 13.8 | 14.1 | 11.4 | 12.0 | 10.5 | 10.1 | 10.1 | 9.9 | 10.5 | .. |
| Bangladesh | .. | 41.1 | 33.3 | 28.2 | 24.6 | 26.4 | 27.4 | 24.8 | 23.1 | 23.2 |
| Bhutan | 29.4 | 15.5 | 24.7 | 19.6 | 22.6 | 26.4 | 29.2 | 24.2 | 11.9 | 9.5 |
| Cambodia | .. | .. | 51.6 | 33.6 | 41.1 | 39.8 | 38.3 | 40.4 | 40.3 | 33.3 |
| China[2, 3] | .. | .. | .. | .. | .. | .. | .. | .. | 9.9 | 10.1 |
| Cook Islands | .. | .. | 16.3 | 18.6 | 17.7 | 19.5 | 18.1 | 16.1 | 17.3 | 19.3 |
| Fiji | .. | .. | .. | 26.9 | 29.8 | 33.7 | 33.2 | 36.3 | 36.1 | 33.5 |
| Indonesia | 12.1 | 15.3 | 12.4 | 12.2 | 12.9 | 12.0 | 12.2 | 11.6 | 11.6 | 13.7 |
| Japan[1] | 7.9 | 7.9 | 7.1 | 7.2 | 5.8 | 5.7 | 6.6 | 5.3 | 5.1 | .. |
| Kazakhstan | .. | 10.3 | 12.1 | 35.1 | 29.5 | 24.9 | 30.1 | 29.1 | 26.8 | 21.8 |
| Kyrgyzstan | 18.4 | 23.7 | 20.3 | 15.4 | 21.2 | 24.6 | 25.4 | 24.8 | 26.6 | 25.1 |
| Korea[1] | 21.6 | 19.7 | 14.5 | 15.1 | 10.9 | 10.5 | 10.1 | 9.4 | 8.7 | 7.8 |
| Lao PDR | .. | .. | .. | 37.8 | 32.9 | 37.9 | 33.7 | 39.3 | 38.8 | 34.4 |
| Malaysia | 27.5 | 20.5 | 17.1 | 17.3 | 11.0 | 9.0 | 7.8 | 9.4 | 14.4 | 15.7 |
| Maldives | .. | .. | 92.2 | 90.8 | 23.5 | 27.6 | 29.3 | 29.8 | 30.9 | 26.5 |
| Mongolia | .. | .. | 17.3 | 19.0 | 21.3 | 21.6 | 17.8 | 18.9 | 18.8 | 19.6 |
| Nauru | .. | .. | .. | .. | 44.6 | 38.2 | 33.3 | 27.8 | 19.9 | 20.3 |
| New Zealand[1] | 8.2 | 7.5 | 5.9 | 6.4 | 6.1 | 5.9 | 5.7 | 5.8 | 5.8 | 5.0 |
| Pakistan | .. | .. | .. | .. | 23.6 | 24.8 | 23.3 | 26.0 | 25.3 | 26.5 |
| Papua New Guinea | .. | .. | 14.4 | 16.3 | 16.4 | 18.4 | 20.5 | 21.2 | 23.0 | 23.4 |
| Philippines | 28.2 | 24.5 | 15.5 | 15.7 | 13.7 | 13.4 | 14.5 | 17.8 | 18.4 | 19.3 |
| Samoa | .. | .. | 37.8 | 40.2 | 36.5 | 38.7 | 38.0 | 36.9 | 35.9 | 36.2 |
| Singapore | .. | 13.0 | 10.1 | 10.3 | 10.0 | 9.2 | 8.8 | 8.7 | 8.7 | 8.3 |
| Solomon Islands | .. | .. | 40.7 | 35.3 | 38.4 | 40.6 | 39.8 | 43.9 | 41.3 | 40.2 |
| Thailand | .. | 37.0 | 31.5 | 32.1 | 28.3 | 29.0 | 30.0 | 28.8 | 29.4 | 30.0 |
| Tokelau | .. | .. | 52.2 | 48.9 | 48.9 | 45.4 | 44.2 | 52.7 | 46.3 | 49.2 |
| Vanuatu | .. | 40.4 | 38.6 | 40.8 | 38.1 | 38.7 | 37.6 | 36.0 | 35.4 | 39.2 |
| Viet Nam | .. | .. | 24.2 | 22.3 | 20.5 | 21.8 | 19.7 | 17.9 | 18.3 | 16.9 |
| Africa (30) average[4] | .. | .. | .. | 20.9 | 20.7 | 21.6 | 21.2 | 21.0 | 20.9 | .. |
| Asia-Pacific (28) average | .. | .. | .. | 26.3 | 23.7 | 24.2 | 23.9 | 24.2 | 22.8 | 22.3 |
| LAC average[5] | 27.3 | 26.5 | 19.9 | 19.2 | 17.0 | 16.8 | 17.1 | 16.7 | 16.7 | 16.0 |
| OECD average[1, 6] | 11.7 | 11.6 | 10.3 | 10.8 | 10.2 | 10.2 | 10.0 | 9.7 | 9.5 | .. |

.. Not available

1. Australia, Japan, Korea and New Zealand are part of the OECD (38) group. Data for Australia, Japan, Korea, New Zealand and the OECD average are taken from OECD (2021), *Revenue Statistics 2021*.
2. 2007 to 2018: Data for China are not included in this table as historical data on revenues from social security contributions are not available.
3. 2007 to 2018: Revenues from import excise tax and refund of excise tax for export are included under heading 5111 as they cannot be separated from revenues from import VAT and refunds of VAT for export and VAT represents the majority of the revenues.
4. Represents an unweighted average for the 30 African countries included in the publication *Revenue Statistics in Africa 2021*.
5. Represents an unweighted average for the 26 Latin American and Caribbean (LAC) countries included in the publication *Revenue Statistics in Latin America and the Caribbean 2022*.
6. Represents an unweighted average for the 38 OECD member countries included in the publication *Revenue Statistics 2021*.

StatLink https://stat.link/z1dwur

# Table 3.17. Gross domestic product for tax reporting years at market prices, in national currency

| | 1997 | 2000 | 2007 | 2010 | 2015 | 2016 | 2017 | 2018 | 2019 | 2020 |
|---|---|---|---|---|---|---|---|---|---|---|
| Australia[1, 2] | 588 | 705 | 1 177 | 1 417 | 1 661 | 1 762 | 1 849 | 1 953 | 1 986 | .. |
| Bangladesh[2] | 2 322 | 2 942 | 6 287 | 9 158 | 17 329 | 19 758 | 22 505 | 25 425 | 27 393 | 30 284 |
| Bhutan[2] | 14 226 | 20 460 | 50 862 | 76 860 | 136 911 | 152 390 | 163 456 | 172 951 | 175 067 | 176 671 |
| Cambodia | .. | .. | 35 042 | 47 048 | 73 423 | 81 242 | 89 831 | 99 544 | 110 014 | 103 512 |
| China | 7 972 | 10 028 | 27 009 | 41 212 | 68 886 | 74 640 | 83 204 | 91 928 | 98 652 | 101 357 |
| Cook Islands[2] | .. | .. | 314 585 | 339 219 | 439 214 | 465 766 | 504 258 | 548 693 | 505 541 | 431 795 |
| Fiji | 3 275 | 3 572 | 5 440 | 6 024 | 9 822 | 10 327 | 11 065 | 11 651 | 11 843 | 9 707 |
| Indonesia | 754 614 | 1 520 683 | 4 323 057 | 6 864 133 | 11 526 333 | 12 401 729 | 13 589 826 | 14 838 756 | 15 832 657 | 15 438 018 |
| Japan[1,4] | 542 500 | 537 616 | 538 484 | 504 872 | 540 739 | 544 827 | 555 687 | 556 419 | 558 313 | .. |
| Kazakhstan | 1 672 | 2 600 | 12 850 | 21 816 | 40 884 | 46 971 | 54 379 | 61 820 | 69 533 | 70 649 |
| Kyrgyzstan | 31 | 65 | 142 | 220 | 430 | 476 | 530 | 569 | 619 | 602 |
| Lao PDR | 4 399 | 14 132 | 45 648 | 61 997 | 117 252 | 129 279 | 140 698 | 152 414 | 162 657 | 172 612 |
| Korea | 542 002 | 651 634 | 1 089 660 | 1 322 611 | 1 658 020 | 1 740 780 | 1 835 698 | 1 898 193 | 1 919 040 | 1 924 453 |
| Maldives | .. | .. | 23 915 | 33 129 | 63 147 | 67 300 | 73 155 | 81 568 | 86 788 | 57 569 |
| Malaysia | 282 | 356 | 665 | 821 | 1 177 | 1 250 | 1 372 | 1 448 | 1 513 | 1 417 |
| Mongolia | 933 | 1 224 | 4 957 | 9 757 | 22 895 | 23 931 | 28 011 | 32 583 | 37 839 | 37 453 |
| Nauru[2] | .. | .. | 29 090 | 53 762 | 104 318 | 137 494 | 145 347 | 159 999 | 165 701 | 170 500 |
| New Zealand[1, 2] | 105 | 122 | 189 | 206 | 259 | 276 | 296 | 310 | 317 | 340 |
| Pakistan[2] | 3 949 | 5 107 | 11 973 | 20 570 | 32 725 | 35 553 | 39 190 | 43 798 | 47 522 | 55 488 |
| Papua New Guinea | 10 701 | 9 736 | 28 304 | 38 752 | 60 139 | 65 038 | 72 522 | 79 405 | 84 109 | 81 627 |
| Philippines | 2 773 | 3 698 | 7 198 | 9 399 | 13 944 | 15 132 | 16 557 | 18 265 | 19 518 | 17 952 |
| Samoa[2, 3] | 733 | 822 | 1 501 | 1 768 | 2 089 | 2 244 | 2 254 | 2 390 | 2 344 | 2 169 |
| Singapore[4] | 150 | 169 | 278 | 336 | 426 | 450 | 480 | 513 | 512 | 480 |
| Solomon Islands | .. | .. | 5 347 | 7 279 | 10 345 | 10 957 | 11 703 | 12 522 | 12 834 | 12 697 |
| Thailand[5] | 4 695 | 4 989 | 8 846 | 10 621 | 13 589 | 14 345 | 15 246 | 16 168 | 16 810 | 15 863 |
| Tokelau[2, 6] | .. | .. | 8 399 | 9 597 | 14 222 | 14 838 | 15 000 | 15 739 | 15 800 | 15 800 |
| Vanuatu | 31 606 | 37 627 | 53 926 | 67 912 | 82 798 | 87 250 | 94 887 | 100 771 | 107 449 | 103 475 |
| Viet Nam | 313 623 | 441 646 | 1 246 769 | 2 157 828 | 4 192 862 | 4 502 733 | 5 005 975 | 5 542 332 | 6 037 348 | 6 293 145 |

.. Not available

Note: All units are in billions except for Bhutan, Cook Islands, Fiji, Maldives, Nauru, Papua New Guinea, Samoa, Solomon Islands, Tokelau, Vanuatu and Viet Nam. Due to the size of their economies, the GDP figures for Cook Islands, Nauru and Tokelau are expressed in thousands while they are in millions for Bhutan, Fiji, Maldives, Papua New Guinea, Samoa, Solomon Islands and Vanuatu.

1. The year Y is calculated as the sum of: Q2(Y) to Q1(Y+1) for Japan; and Q3(Y) to Q2(Y+1) for Australia and New Zealand.
2. Data are reported on a fiscal year basis beginning 1st July. For example, the data for 2020 represent the period from July 2020 to June 2021. Data for 2020 are provisional.
3. The year Y is calculated using the formula GDP(Y)/2+GDP(Y-1)/2. This is done in order to make the value of the GDP correspond more closely to a July(Y-1)-to-June(Y) fiscal year.
4. Data are on a fiscal year basis ending 31st March. For example, the data for 2020 represent 1 April 2020 to 31 March 2021.
5. Data are on a fiscal year basis ending 30th September. For example, the data for 2020 represent 1 October 2019 to 30 September 2020.
6. 2020: Data are provisional.

Source: OECD National Accounts data for Australia, Indonesia, Japan, Korea and New Zealand; National Statistical Offices for Cambodia, China, Cook Islands, Fiji, Kazakhstan, Kyrgyzstan, Lao PDR, Malaysia, Maldives, Mongolia, Philippines, Singapore, Thailand, Tokelau and Viet Nam; Asian Development Bank's Key Indicators Database for Papua New Guinea, Solomon Islands and Vanuatu; IMF *World Economic Outlook* (WEO) April 2021 data for Bangladesh, Bhutan and Pakistan. Data for 2018 and 2019 were estimated for the Solomon Islands and Vanuatu, using the GDP growth rates of the IMF's *World Economic Outlook* (WEO) April 2022 edition.

StatLink https://stat.link/4rapo8

## Table 3.18. Gross domestic product for tax reporting years at market prices, in millions of US dollars at market exchange rates

| | 1997 | 2000 | 2007 | 2010 | 2015 | 2016 | 2017 | 2018 | 2019 | 2020 |
|---|---|---|---|---|---|---|---|---|---|---|
| Australia[1, 2] | 400 022 | 385 083 | 984 095 | 1 375 786 | 1 241 090 | 1 329 981 | 1 398 551 | 1 406 159 | 1 373 224 | .. |
| Bangladesh[2] | 54 209 | 58 121 | 91 040 | 132 377 | 223 014 | 252 458 | 284 424 | 309 596 | 325 998 | 357 150 |
| Bhutan[2] | 398 | 469 | 1 151 | 1 648 | 2 207 | 2 297 | 2 460 | 2 654 | 2 482 | 2 438 |
| Cambodia | .. | .. | 8 630 | 11 232 | 18 083 | 20 043 | 22 208 | 24 599 | 27 088 | 25 192 |
| China | 961 600 | 1 211 344 | 3 550 304 | 6 087 209 | 11 061 553 | 11 233 136 | 12 310 500 | 13 894 818 | 14 279 903 | 14 687 780 |
| Cook Islands[2] | .. | .. | 226 | 256 | 306 | 328 | 353 | 370 | 330 | 280 |
| Fiji | .. | 1 678 | 3 378 | 3 140 | 4 682 | 4 930 | 5 353 | 5 581 | 5 482 | 4 476 |
| Indonesia | 259 373 | 180 566 | 472 983 | 755 256 | 860 741 | 932 066 | 1 015 488 | 1 042 711 | 1 120 050 | 1 059 903 |
| Japan[1,4] | 4 393 745 | 4 832 637 | 4 716 784 | 5 887 915 | 4 584 386 | 4 968 883 | 4 972 738 | 5 054 227 | 5 146 928 | .. |
| Kazakhstan | 22 166 | 18 292 | 104 850 | 148 047 | 184 388 | 137 289 | 166 806 | 179 340 | 181 667 | 171 082 |
| Kyrgyzstan | 1 767 | 1 368 | 3 807 | 4 794 | 6 678 | 6 813 | 7 703 | 8 271 | 8 872 | 7 792 |
| Lao PDR | 3 515 | 1 720 | 4 757 | 7 506 | 14 418 | 15 905 | 17 055 | 18 131 | 18 722 | 19 056 |
| Korea | 570 224 | 576 341 | 1 172 370 | 1 144 691 | 1 465 577 | 1 499 910 | 1 623 599 | 1 725 338 | 1 646 829 | 1 630 715 |
| Maldives | .. | .. | 1 868 | 2 588 | 4 098 | 4 367 | 4 747 | 5 293 | 5 632 | 3 736 |
| Malaysia | 99 877 | 93 790 | 193 679 | 255 018 | 301 360 | 301 918 | 319 249 | 358 994 | 365 385 | 337 280 |
| Mongolia | 1 181 | 1 137 | 4 235 | 7 185 | 11 620 | 11 154 | 11 481 | 13 207 | 14 206 | 13 313 |
| Nauru[2] | .. | .. | 24 | 52 | 78 | 104 | 110 | 115 | 115 | 117 |
| New Zealand[1,2] | 61 991 | 53 293 | 135 540 | 154 989 | 180 257 | 194 007 | 207 502 | 209 409 | 207 401 | 220 517 |
| Pakistan[2] | 101 270 | 98 643 | 197 478 | 244 540 | 322 171 | 339 959 | 373 949 | 396 117 | 345 550 | 349 470 |
| Papua New Guinea | .. | 3 499 | 9 545 | 14 251 | 21 723 | 20 759 | 22 743 | 24 110 | 24 829 | 23 592 |
| Philippines | 94 106 | 83 667 | 155 980 | 208 369 | 306 446 | 318 627 | 328 481 | 346 842 | 376 823 | 361 751 |
| Samoa[2, 3] | .. | 264 | 554 | 697 | 862 | 858 | 889 | 949 | 895 | 804 |
| Singapore[4] | 100 936 | 97 930 | 184 360 | 246 140 | 310 174 | 325 490 | 347 555 | 380 434 | 375 244 | 347 603 |
| Solomon Islands | .. | .. | 699 | 903 | 1 307 | 1 379 | 1 484 | 1 575 | 1 570 | 1 546 |
| Thailand[5] | 149 701 | 124 127 | 256 347 | 335 010 | 396 635 | 406 545 | 449 365 | 500 192 | 541 373 | 506 988 |
| Tokelau[2, 6] | .. | .. | 6 | 7 | 10 | 10 | 11 | 11 | 10 | 10 |
| Vanuatu | .. | 273 | 527 | 681 | 774 | 798 | 880 | 928 | 930 | 994 |
| Viet Nam | 26 892 | 31 176 | 77 518 | 112 790 | 191 252 | 201 324 | 220 374 | 240 757 | 259 926 | 270 920 |

.. Not available

Note: This table is produced based on GDP data in national currency from Table 3.17 and exchange rate data from Table 3.20.

1. The year Y is calculated as the sum of: Q2(Y) to Q1(Y+1) for Japan; and Q3(Y) to Q2(Y+1) for Australia and New Zealand.
2. Data are reported on a fiscal year basis beginning 1st July. For example, the data for 2020 represent the period from July 2020 to June 2021. Data for 2020 are provisional.
3. The year Y is calculated using the formula GDP(Y)/2+GDP(Y-1)/2. This is done in order to make the value of the GDP correspond more closely to a July(Y-1)-to-June(Y) fiscal year.
4. Data are on a fiscal year basis ending 31st March. For example, the data for 2020 represent 1 April 2020 to 31 March 2021.
5. Data are on a fiscal year basis ending 30th September. For example, the data for 2020 represents 1 October 2019 to 30 September 2020.
6. 2020: Data are provisional.

StatLink https://stat.link/beomw4

## Table 3.19. Total tax revenue in millions of US dollars at market exchange rates

| | 1997 | 2000 | 2007 | 2010 | 2015 | 2016 | 2017 | 2018 | 2019 | 2020 |
|---|---|---|---|---|---|---|---|---|---|---|
| Australia | 115 | 117 | 290 | 346 | 344 | 365 | 398 | 401 | 380 | .. |
| Bangladesh | .. | 4 | 8 | 13 | 24 | 26 | 30 | 30 | 29 | 36 |
| Bhutan | 34 | 42 | 104 | 232 | 298 | 296 | 337 | 334 | 261 | 217 |
| Cambodia | .. | .. | 1 | 1 | 3 | 3 | 4 | 5 | 6 | 5 |
| China[1] | .. | .. | 599 674 | 1 081 334 | 2 005 970 | 1 961 783 | 2 135 984 | 2 364 009 | 3 154 303 | 2 948 831 |
| Cook Islands | .. | .. | 56 | 69 | 82 | 89 | 100 | 110 | 92 | 55 |
| Fiji | .. | .. | .. | 680 | 1 105 | 1 140 | 1 296 | 1 312 | 1 221 | 741 |
| Indonesia | 19 709 | 14 213 | 57 818 | 85 766 | 104 245 | 111 934 | 117 917 | 124 842 | 129 793 | 106 782 |
| Japan | 1 131 | 1 225 | 1 281 | 1 545 | 1 386 | 1 505 | 1 537 | 1 595 | 1 617 | .. |
| Kazakhstan | .. | 3 643 | 27 329 | 35 169 | 28 652 | 20 478 | 26 711 | 30 416 | 30 294 | 24 057 |
| Kyrgyzstan | 0 | 0 | 1 | 1 | 1 | 1 | 1 | 2 | 2 | 1 |
| Lao PDR | .. | .. | .. | 860 | 1 810 | 1 894 | 1 883 | 1 970 | 1 978 | 1 698 |
| Korea | 108 | 121 | 278 | 256 | 348 | 371 | 412 | 460 | 450 | 456 |
| Maldives | .. | .. | 223 | 231 | 794 | 861 | 955 | 1 026 | 1 072 | 713 |
| Malaysia | 19 668 | 13 180 | 28 693 | 35 259 | 43 776 | 42 357 | 42 697 | 44 898 | 45 476 | 38 441 |
| Mongolia | .. | .. | 1 201 | 1 819 | 2 244 | 2 129 | 2 461 | 3 157 | 3 391 | 2 826 |
| Nauru | .. | .. | .. | .. | 18 | 16 | 32 | 41 | 55 | 56 |
| New Zealand | 21 | 17 | 46 | 47 | 57 | 61 | 65 | 67 | 65 | 71 |
| Pakistan | .. | .. | .. | .. | 36 | 38 | 43 | 40 | 35 | 36 |
| Papua New Guinea | .. | 469 | 1 981 | 2 417 | 3 302 | 2 747 | 2 818 | 3 031 | 3 105 | 2 743 |
| Philippines | 16 019 | 12 769 | 24 304 | 29 555 | 49 723 | 51 717 | 55 129 | 60 328 | 68 058 | 64 562 |
| Samoa | .. | .. | 122 | 134 | 204 | 197 | 206 | 227 | 215 | 201 |
| Singapore | .. | 14 865 | 24 305 | 30 691 | 40 476 | 42 488 | 48 057 | 49 081 | 49 587 | 44 507 |
| Solomon Islands | .. | .. | 107 | 171 | 302 | 298 | 334 | 379 | 321 | 290 |
| Thailand | .. | 18 414 | 45 006 | 59 001 | 74 959 | 73 563 | 78 798 | 88 385 | 93 324 | 83 547 |
| Tokelau | .. | .. | 1 | 1 | 1 | 2 | 2 | 2 | 2 | 2 |
| Vanuatu | .. | 44 | 100 | 111 | 126 | 122 | 151 | 166 | 158 | 142 |
| Viet Nam | .. | .. | 15 443 | 28 580 | 43 023 | 46 297 | 51 020 | 55 847 | 62 800 | 61 436 |

.. Not available

Note: This table is produced based on total tax revenues from Chapter 4 and exchange rate data from Table 3.20.

1. 2007 to 2018: The figures for China do not include revenue from social security contributions as detailed data were not available.

StatLink https://stat.link/p08yc9

## Table 3.20. Exchange rates used, national currency per US dollar

| | 1997 | 2000 | 2007 | 2010 | 2015 | 2016 | 2017 | 2018 | 2019 | 2020 |
|---|---|---|---|---|---|---|---|---|---|---|
| Australia | 1.47 | 1.83 | 1.20 | 1.03 | 1.34 | 1.33 | 1.32 | 1.39 | 1.45 | .. |
| Bangladesh | 42.84 | 50.61 | 69.06 | 69.18 | 77.70 | 78.26 | 79.12 | 82.12 | 84.03 | 84.79 |
| Bhutan | 35.77 | 43.64 | 44.19 | 46.65 | 62.04 | 66.35 | 66.43 | 65.16 | 70.53 | 72.47 |
| Cambodia | 2 946.25 | 3 840.75 | 4 060.38 | 4 188.70 | 4 060.34 | 4 053.32 | 4 045.05 | 4 046.70 | 4 061.33 | 4 108.98 |
| China | 8.29 | 8.28 | 7.61 | 6.77 | 6.23 | 6.65 | 6.76 | 6.62 | 6.91 | 6.90 |
| Cook Islands | 1.69 | 2.29 | 1.39 | 1.33 | 1.44 | 1.42 | 1.43 | 1.48 | 1.53 | 1.54 |
| Fiji | 1.44 | 2.13 | 1.61 | 1.92 | 2.10 | 2.10 | 2.07 | 2.09 | 2.16 | 2.17 |
| Indonesia | 2 909.38 | 8 421.78 | 9 139.99 | 9 088.49 | 13 391.17 | 13 305.63 | 13 382.56 | 14 230.93 | 14 135.67 | 14 565.50 |
| Japan | 123.47 | 111.25 | 114.16 | 85.75 | 117.95 | 109.65 | 111.75 | 110.09 | 108.48 | .. |
| Kazakhstan | 75.44 | 142.13 | 122.55 | 147.36 | 221.73 | 342.13 | 326.00 | 344.71 | 382.75 | 412.95 |
| Kyrgyzstan | 17.37 | 47.78 | 37.27 | 45.96 | 64.46 | 69.91 | 68.87 | 68.84 | 69.78 | 77.23 |
| Lao PDR | 1 251.52 | 8 217.50 | 9 596.19 | 8 259.59 | 8 132.19 | 8 128.29 | 8 249.74 | 8 406.38 | 8 688.24 | 9 057.93 |
| Korea | 950.51 | 1 130.64 | 929.45 | 1 155.43 | 1 131.31 | 1 160.59 | 1 130.64 | 1 100.19 | 1 165.29 | 1 180.13 |
| Maldives | 11.77 | 11.77 | 12.80 | 12.80 | 15.41 | 15.41 | 15.41 | 15.41 | 15.41 | 15.41 |
| Malaysia | 2.82 | 3.80 | 3.44 | 3.22 | 3.91 | 4.14 | 4.30 | 4.03 | 4.14 | 4.20 |
| Mongolia | 789.73 | 1 076.44 | 1 170.40 | 1 357.90 | 1 970.31 | 2 145.53 | 2 439.78 | 2 467.05 | 2 663.54 | 2 813.29 |
| Nauru | 1.47 | 1.83 | 1.20 | 1.03 | 1.34 | 1.33 | 1.32 | 1.39 | 1.45 | 1.45 |
| New Zealand | 1.69 | 2.29 | 1.39 | 1.33 | 1.44 | 1.42 | 1.43 | 1.48 | 1.53 | 1.54 |
| Pakistan | 38.99 | 51.77 | 60.63 | 84.12 | 101.58 | 104.58 | 104.80 | 110.57 | 137.52 | 158.78 |
| Papua New Guinea | 1.44 | 2.78 | 2.97 | 2.72 | 2.77 | 3.13 | 3.19 | 3.29 | 3.39 | 3.46 |
| Philippines | 29.47 | 44.19 | 46.15 | 45.11 | 45.50 | 47.49 | 50.40 | 52.66 | 51.80 | 49.62 |
| Samoa | 2.56 | 3.12 | 2.71 | 2.54 | 2.42 | 2.61 | 2.54 | 2.52 | 2.62 | 2.70 |
| Singapore | 1.49 | 1.72 | 1.51 | 1.36 | 1.38 | 1.38 | 1.38 | 1.35 | 1.36 | 1.38 |
| Solomon Islands | 3.72 | 5.09 | 7.65 | 8.07 | 7.92 | 7.95 | 7.89 | 7.95 | 8.17 | 8.21 |
| Thailand | 31.36 | 40.19 | 34.51 | 31.70 | 34.26 | 35.29 | 33.93 | 32.32 | 31.05 | 31.29 |
| Tokelau | 1.69 | 2.29 | 1.39 | 1.33 | 1.44 | 1.42 | 1.43 | 1.48 | 1.53 | 1.54 |
| Vanuatu | 115.87 | 137.87 | 102.33 | 99.70 | 107.00 | 109.31 | 107.77 | 108.53 | 115.57 | 104.10 |
| Viet Nam | 11 662.21 | 14 166.28 | 16 083.64 | 19 131.32 | 21 923.26 | 22 365.60 | 22 715.85 | 23 020.47 | 23 227.17 | 23 228.83 |

.. Not available

Source: OECD National Accounts data for Australia, the Cook Islands, Indonesia, Japan, Korea, Nauru and New Zealand; IMF's World Economic Outlook (April 2022) for the Bangladesh, Bhutan, Cambodia, China, Fiji, Kazakhstan, Kyrgysztan, Lao PDR, Malaysia, Maldives, Mongolia, Nauru, Pakistan, Papua New Guinea, Philippines, Samoa, Singapore, Solomon Islands, Thailand, Viet Nam and Vanuatu.

StatLink https://stat.link/ty7bxq

# 4 Country tables, tax revenues, 1990-2020

## Country tax revenue tables, 1990-2020

In all of the following tables a ("..") indicates not available. The main series in this volume cover the years 1990 to 2020.

Figures referring to 1998-99, 2001-06, 2008-09 and 2011-14 in Tables 4.1 to 4.24 have been omitted because of lack of space. Full time series can be accessed at https://stats.oecd.org/ within the theme Public Sector, Taxation and Market Regulation/Taxation/Revenue Statistics Asian and Pacific Economies.

## Table 4.1. Australia: Details of tax revenue

Million AUD

| | 1997 | 2000 | 2007 | 2010 | 2015 | 2016 | 2017 | 2018 | 2019 | 2020 |
|---|---|---|---|---|---|---|---|---|---|---|
| **Total tax revenue** | **168 582** | **214 753** | **346 772** | **356 747** | **460 729** | **484 020** | **526 002** | **557 175** | **549 536** | .. |
| **1000 Taxes on income, profits and capital gains** | **95 367** | **124 427** | **206 134** | **202 184** | **261 345** | **277 446** | **308 732** | **334 856** | **325 116** | .. |
| 1100 Of individuals | 70 782 | 80 991 | 127 587 | 138 163 | 191 720 | 198 479 | 212 463 | 229 439 | 230 932 | .. |
| 1110 On income and profits | 69 212 | 80 991 | 127 587 | 138 163 | 191 720 | 198 479 | 212 463 | 229 439 | 230 932 | .. |
| 1120 On capital gains | 1 570 | 0 | 0 | 0 | 0 | 0 | 0 | 0 | 0 | .. |
| 1200 Corporate | 24 585 | 43 436 | 78 547 | 64 021 | 69 625 | 78 967 | 96 269 | 105 417 | 94 184 | .. |
| 1210 On profits | 22 253 | 43 436 | 78 547 | 64 021 | 69 625 | 78 967 | 96 269 | 105 417 | 94 184 | .. |
| Income tax on companies | 21 242 | 42 221 | 76 655 | 62 549 | 67 794 | 76 991 | 94 287 | 103 318 | 92 191 | .. |
| Dividend and interest taxes | 693 | 846 | 1 892 | 1 472 | 1 831 | 1 976 | 1 982 | 2 099 | 1 993 | .. |
| Other withholding taxes | 318 | 369 | 0 | 0 | 0 | 0 | 0 | 0 | 0 | .. |
| 1220 On capital gains | 2 332 | 0 | 0 | 0 | 0 | 0 | 0 | 0 | 0 | .. |
| 1300 Unallocable between 1100 and 1200 | 0 | 0 | 0 | 0 | 0 | 0 | 0 | 0 | 0 | .. |
| **2000 Social security contributions** | **0** | **0** | **0** | **0** | **0** | **0** | **0** | **0** | **0** | .. |
| 2100 Employees | 0 | 0 | 0 | 0 | 0 | 0 | 0 | 0 | 0 | .. |
| 2110 On a payroll basis | .. | .. | .. | .. | .. | .. | .. | .. | .. | .. |
| 2120 On an income tax basis | .. | .. | .. | .. | .. | .. | .. | .. | .. | .. |
| 2200 Employers | 0 | 0 | 0 | 0 | 0 | 0 | 0 | 0 | 0 | .. |
| 2210 On a payroll basis | .. | .. | .. | .. | .. | .. | .. | .. | .. | .. |
| 2220 On an income tax basis | .. | .. | .. | .. | .. | .. | .. | .. | .. | .. |
| 2300 Self-employed or non-employed | 0 | 0 | 0 | 0 | 0 | 0 | 0 | 0 | 0 | .. |
| 2310 On a payroll basis | .. | .. | .. | .. | .. | .. | .. | .. | .. | .. |
| 2320 On an income tax basis | .. | .. | .. | .. | .. | .. | .. | .. | .. | .. |
| 2400 Unallocable between 2100, 2200 and 2300 | 0 | 0 | 0 | 0 | 0 | 0 | 0 | 0 | 0 | .. |
| 2410 On a payroll basis | .. | .. | .. | .. | .. | .. | .. | .. | .. | .. |
| 2420 On an income tax basis | .. | .. | .. | .. | .. | .. | .. | .. | .. | .. |
| **3000 Taxes on payroll and workforce** | **11 277** | **9 624** | **16 407** | **18 492** | **23 354** | **23 799** | **25 520** | **26 923** | **26 027** | .. |
| **4000 Taxes on property** | **15 505** | **18 825** | **31 130** | **33 498** | **49 168** | **52 066** | **52 942** | **53 114** | **53 982** | .. |
| 4100 Recurrent taxes on immovable property | 7 739 | 9 067 | 15 615 | 19 907 | 26 649 | 28 745 | 30 305 | 32 694 | 33 803 | .. |
| 4110 Households | .. | .. | .. | .. | .. | .. | .. | .. | .. | .. |
| 4120 Others | .. | .. | .. | .. | .. | .. | .. | .. | .. | .. |
| 4200 Recurrent taxes on net wealth | 0 | 0 | 0 | 0 | 0 | 0 | 0 | 0 | 0 | .. |
| 4210 Individual | .. | .. | .. | .. | .. | .. | .. | .. | .. | .. |
| 4220 Corporate | .. | .. | .. | .. | .. | .. | .. | .. | .. | .. |
| 4300 Estate, inheritance and gift taxes | 0 | 0 | 0 | 0 | 0 | 0 | 0 | 0 | 0 | .. |
| 4310 Estate and inheritance taxes | .. | .. | .. | .. | .. | .. | .. | .. | .. | .. |
| Estate duty central government | .. | .. | .. | .. | .. | .. | .. | .. | .. | .. |
| St. and loc. estate probate and succession | .. | .. | .. | .. | .. | .. | .. | .. | .. | .. |
| 4320 Gift taxes | .. | .. | .. | .. | .. | .. | .. | .. | .. | .. |
| 4400 Taxes on financial and capital transactions | 7 766 | 9 758 | 15 515 | 13 591 | 22 519 | 23 321 | 22 637 | 20 420 | 20 179 | .. |
| 4500 Non-recurrent taxes | 0 | 0 | 0 | 0 | 0 | 0 | 0 | 0 | 0 | .. |
| 4510 On net wealth | .. | .. | .. | .. | .. | .. | .. | .. | .. | .. |
| 4520 Other non-recurrent taxes | .. | .. | .. | .. | .. | .. | .. | .. | .. | .. |
| 4600 Other recurrent taxes on property | 0 | 0 | 0 | 0 | 0 | 0 | 0 | 0 | 0 | .. |
| **5000 Taxes on goods and services** | **46 433** | **61 877** | **93 101** | **102 573** | **126 862** | **130 709** | **138 808** | **142 282** | **144 411** | .. |
| 5100 Taxes on production, sale, transfer, etc. | 37 359 | 56 179 | 84 104 | 90 824 | 109 050 | 111 934 | 118 867 | 122 053 | 123 639 | .. |
| 5110 General taxes | 14 085 | 25 830 | 44 739 | 48 146 | 60 680 | 63 029 | 65 700 | 66 829 | 65 720 | .. |
| 5111 Value added taxes | 0 | 23 854 | 43 634 | 46 910 | 59 177 | 61 505 | 64 062 | 65 147 | 64 048 | .. |
| 5112 Sales tax | 14 085 | 1 976 | 1 105 | 1 236 | 1 503 | 1 524 | 1 638 | 1 682 | 1 672 | .. |
| 5113 Other | 0 | 0 | 0 | 0 | 0 | 0 | 0 | 0 | 0 | .. |
| 5120 Taxes on specific goods and services | 23 274 | 30 349 | 39 365 | 42 678 | 48 370 | 48 905 | 53 167 | 55 224 | 57 919 | .. |
| 5121 Excise duties | 14 449 | 19 768 | 24 357 | 26 689 | 22 541 | 22 773 | 23 673 | 24 486 | 24 065 | .. |
| Excises central government | 13 573 | 19 019 | 23 526 | 25 803 | 21 625 | 21 895 | 22 763 | 23 488 | 23 116 | .. |
| Statutory corporate payments | 258 | 295 | 231 | 452 | 405 | 335 | 346 | 435 | 480 | .. |
| Primary production charges | 618 | 454 | 600 | 434 | 511 | 543 | 564 | 563 | 469 | .. |
| 5122 Profits of fiscal monopolies | 0 | 0 | 0 | 0 | 0 | 0 | 0 | 0 | 0 | .. |
| 5123 Customs and import duties | 3 637 | 4 606 | 6 070 | 5 828 | 14 046 | 14 196 | 15 690 | 15 944 | 19 507 | .. |
| Customs duties central government | 3 637 | 4 606 | 6 070 | 5 828 | 14 046 | 14 196 | 15 690 | 15 944 | 19 507 | .. |
| 5124 Taxes on exports | 6 | 0 | 10 | 11 | 11 | 11 | 0 | 0 | 0 | .. |
| Customs duties on coal exports | 0 | .. | 0 | 0 | 0 | 0 | .. | .. | .. | .. |
| Other | 6 | .. | 10 | 11 | 11 | 11 | .. | .. | .. | .. |
| 5125 Taxes on investment goods | 0 | 0 | 0 | 0 | 0 | 0 | 0 | 0 | 0 | .. |
| 5126 Taxes on specific services | 5 182 | 5 975 | 8 928 | 10 150 | 11 772 | 11 925 | 13 804 | 14 794 | 14 347 | .. |
| Taxes race meetings | 601 | 301 | 359 | 373 | 265 | 233 | 265 | 411 | 596 | .. |
| Poker machines | 1 760 | 2 074 | 3 009 | 3 125 | 3 684 | 3 717 | 3 881 | 3 986 | 3 202 | .. |
| Lotteries | 330 | 890 | 1 118 | 1 141 | 1 362 | 1 286 | 1 330 | 1 632 | 1 676 | .. |
| Levies on fire insurance companies | 521 | 574 | 937 | 1 232 | 786 | 803 | 812 | 806 | 932 | .. |
| Other | 1 970 | 2 136 | 3 505 | 4 279 | 5 675 | 5 886 | 7 516 | 7 959 | 7 941 | .. |
| 5127 Other taxes on internat. trade and transactions | 0 | 0 | 0 | 0 | 0 | 0 | 0 | 0 | 0 | .. |
| 5128 Other taxes | 0 | 0 | 0 | 0 | 0 | 0 | 0 | 0 | 0 | .. |

| | 1997 | 2000 | 2007 | 2010 | 2015 | 2016 | 2017 | 2018 | 2019 | 2020 |
|---|---|---|---|---|---|---|---|---|---|---|
| 5130 Unallocable between 5110 and 5120 | 0 | 0 | 0 | 0 | 0 | 0 | 0 | 0 | 0 | .. |
| 5200 Taxes on use of goods and perform activities | 9 074 | 5 698 | 8 997 | 11 749 | 17 812 | 18 775 | 19 941 | 20 229 | 20 772 | .. |
| 5210 Recurrent taxes | 8 956 | 5 698 | 8 997 | 11 749 | 15 898 | 16 730 | 17 915 | 17 899 | 18 615 | .. |
| 5211 Paid by households: motor vehicles | 2 188 | 2 748 | 4 381 | 5 064 | 7 253 | 7 519 | 7 709 | 7 914 | 8 128 | .. |
| 5212 Paid by others: motor vehicles | 1 350 | 1 285 | 2 005 | 2 397 | 2 649 | 2 755 | 3 077 | 3 072 | 3 174 | .. |
| Fees on motor vehicle registry | 1 287 | 778 | 1 165 | 1 499 | 1 530 | 1 596 | 1 838 | 1 864 | 1 975 | .. |
| Drivers licences | 0 | 0 | 0 | 0 | 0 | 0 | 0 | 0 | 0 | .. |
| Stamp duty on vehicle registry | 63 | 506 | 839 | 898 | 1 119 | 1 159 | 1 239 | 1 208 | 1 199 | .. |
| 5213 Paid in respect of other goods | 5 418 | 1 665 | 2 611 | 4 288 | 5 996 | 6 456 | 7 129 | 6 913 | 7 313 | .. |
| Broadcasting tv licences | 329 | 210 | 288 | 150 | 128 | 0 | 52 | 52 | 37 | .. |
| Business franchise lic. tobac. fuel | 3 992 | 227 | 0 | 0 | 1 | 0 | 1 | 0 | 0 | .. |
| Other taxes | 565 | 1 129 | 2 321 | 4 136 | 5 846 | 6 433 | 7 040 | 6 816 | 7 271 | .. |
| Liquor taxes | 532 | 97 | 2 | 1 | 22 | 23 | 36 | 45 | 5 | .. |
| Dog licenses | 0 | 0 | 0 | 0 | 0 | 0 | 0 | 0 | 0 | .. |
| 5220 Non-recurrent taxes | 118 | 0 | 0 | 0 | 1 914 | 2 046 | 2 026 | 2 330 | 2 157 | .. |
| 5300 Unallocable between 5100 and 5200 | 0 | 0 | 0 | 0 | 0 | 0 | 0 | 0 | 0 | .. |
| **6000 Other taxes** | **0** | **0** | **0** | **0** | **0** | **0** | **0** | **0** | **0** | **..** |
| 6100 Paid solely by business | .. | .. | .. | .. | .. | .. | .. | .. | .. | .. |
| 6200 Other | .. | .. | .. | .. | .. | .. | .. | .. | .. | .. |

.. Not available

Note: Data are on a fiscal year basis beginning 1st July.

From 1998 taxes are recorded on an accrual basis; prior to that they were on a cash basis.

Direct taxes paid by public trading enterprises are excluded from receipts.

The figures for total tax revenue do not match the published totals in Taxation Revenue Australia. The latter is based on an accrual IMF GFS methodology and there are some differences between that and the OECD equivalent.

Heading 5213 includes radio and television licenses fees, though these are usually not regarded as a tax revenue in the OECD list.

Headings for non-wastable tax credits 1110 and 1210 include the private health insurance tax offset, family benefit, baby bonus tax offsets (paid during the 2003-04 budget year), film tax offset, and research and development tax offsets. The estimation of non-wastable credits into the expenditure and transfer components is in accordance with the OECD guidelines on the treatment and the data for this memorandum item has been provided by the Australian Taxation Office.

Source: Australian Bureau of Statistics.

StatLink https://stat.link/nt4gdi

## Table 4.2. Bangladesh: Details of tax revenue

Million BDT

| | 1997 | 2000 | 2007 | 2010 | 2015 | 2016 | 2017 | 2018 | 2019 | 2020 |
|---|---|---|---|---|---|---|---|---|---|---|
| **Total tax revenue** | .. | **209 490** | **533 918** | **911 182** | **1 839 968** | **2 018 284** | **2 339 088** | **2 497 270** | **2 467 352** | **3 093 116** |
| **1000 Taxes on income, profits and capital gains** | .. | **59 506** | **179 203** | **352 411** | **833 254** | **847 425** | **940 510** | **1 004 792** | **1 037 012** | **1 343 180** |
| 1100 Of individuals | .. | 19 638 | 48 024 | 98 932 | 253 798 | 209 198 | 206 378 | 247 706 | 248 090 | 339 550 |
| 1110 On income and profits | .. | 19 638 | 48 024 | 98 932 | 253 798 | 209 198 | 206 378 | 247 706 | 248 090 | 339 550 |
| 1120 On capital gains | .. | .. | .. | .. | .. | .. | .. | .. | .. | .. |
| 1200 Corporate | .. | 15 371 | 69 423 | 131 143 | 259 491 | 318 351 | 360 581 | 336 180 | 370 870 | 509 330 |
| 1210 On profits | .. | 15 371 | 69 423 | 131 143 | 259 491 | 318 351 | 360 581 | 336 180 | 370 870 | 509 330 |
| 1220 On capital gains of corporates | .. | .. | .. | .. | .. | .. | .. | .. | .. | .. |
| 1300 Unallocable between 1100 and 1200 | .. | 24 498 | 61 756 | 122 336 | 319 964 | 319 876 | 373 551 | 420 906 | 418 052 | 494 300 |
| **2000 Social security contributions** | .. | **0** | **0** | **0** | **0** | **0** | **0** | **0** | **0** | **0** |
| 2100 Employees | .. | .. | .. | .. | .. | .. | .. | .. | .. | .. |
| 2110 On a payroll basis | .. | .. | .. | .. | .. | .. | .. | .. | .. | .. |
| 2120 On an income tax basis | .. | .. | .. | .. | .. | .. | .. | .. | .. | .. |
| 2200 Employers | .. | .. | .. | .. | .. | .. | .. | .. | .. | .. |
| 2210 On a payroll basis | .. | .. | .. | .. | .. | .. | .. | .. | .. | .. |
| 2220 On an income tax basis | .. | .. | .. | .. | .. | .. | .. | .. | .. | .. |
| 2300 Self-employed or non-employed | .. | .. | .. | .. | .. | .. | .. | .. | .. | .. |
| 2310 On a payroll basis | .. | .. | .. | .. | .. | .. | .. | .. | .. | .. |
| 2320 On an income tax basis | .. | .. | .. | .. | .. | .. | .. | .. | .. | .. |
| 2400 Unallocable between 2100, 2200 and 2300 | .. | .. | .. | .. | .. | .. | .. | .. | .. | .. |
| 2410 On a payroll basis | .. | .. | .. | .. | .. | .. | .. | .. | .. | .. |
| 2420 On an income tax basis | .. | .. | .. | .. | .. | .. | .. | .. | .. | .. |
| **3000 Taxes on payroll and workforce** | .. | **0** | **0** | **0** | **0** | **0** | **0** | **0** | **0** | **0** |
| **4000 Taxes on property** | .. | **0** | **0** | **0** | **0** | **0** | **0** | **0** | **0** | **0** |
| 4100 Recurrent taxes on immovable property | .. | .. | .. | .. | .. | .. | .. | .. | .. | .. |
| 4110 Households | .. | .. | .. | .. | .. | .. | .. | .. | .. | .. |
| 4120 Others | .. | .. | .. | .. | .. | .. | .. | .. | .. | .. |
| 4200 Recurrent taxes on net wealth | .. | .. | .. | .. | .. | .. | .. | .. | .. | .. |
| 4210 Individual | .. | .. | .. | .. | .. | .. | .. | .. | .. | .. |
| 4220 Corporate | .. | .. | .. | .. | .. | .. | .. | .. | .. | .. |
| 4300 Estate, inheritance and gift taxes | .. | .. | .. | .. | .. | .. | .. | .. | .. | .. |
| 4310 Estate and inheritance taxes | .. | .. | .. | .. | .. | .. | .. | .. | .. | .. |
| 4320 Gift taxes | .. | .. | .. | .. | .. | .. | .. | .. | .. | .. |
| 4400 Taxes on financial and capital transactions | .. | .. | .. | .. | .. | .. | .. | .. | .. | .. |
| 4500 Other non-reccurrent taxes on property | .. | .. | .. | .. | .. | .. | .. | .. | .. | .. |
| 4510 On net wealth | .. | .. | .. | .. | .. | .. | .. | .. | .. | .. |
| 4520 Other non-recurrent taxes | .. | .. | .. | .. | .. | .. | .. | .. | .. | .. |
| 4600 Other recurrent taxes on property | .. | .. | .. | .. | .. | .. | .. | .. | .. | .. |
| **5000 Taxes on goods and services** | .. | **149 984** | **354 716** | **558 771** | **1 006 714** | **1 170 859** | **1 398 578** | **1 492 478** | **1 430 341** | **1 749 936** |
| 5100 Taxes on production, sale, transfer, etc | .. | 149 984 | 354 716 | 558 771 | 1 006 714 | 1 170 859 | 1 398 578 | 1 492 478 | 1 430 341 | 1 749 936 |
| 5110 General taxes on goods and services | .. | 63 798 | 176 714 | 301 907 | 554 500 | 638 489 | 757 662 | 873 720 | 860 973 | 1 033 131 |
| 5111 Value added taxes | .. | 63 798 | 176 714 | 301 907 | 554 500 | 638 489 | 757 662 | 873 720 | 860 973 | 1 033 131 |
| 5112 Sales tax | .. | 0 | 0 | 0 | 0 | 0 | 0 | 0 | 0 | 0 |
| 5113 Other | .. | 0 | 0 | 0 | 0 | 0 | 0 | 0 | 0 | 0 |
| 5120 Taxes on specific goods and services | .. | 86 186 | 178 002 | 256 864 | 452 215 | 532 370 | 640 916 | 618 757 | 569 367 | 716 805 |
| 5121 Excises | .. | 33 694 | 77 552 | 136 974 | 261 913 | 311 106 | 377 759 | 364 795 | 324 463 | 408 880 |
| Supplementary duty (SD) | .. | 33 694 | 77 552 | 136 974 | 261 913 | 311 106 | 377 759 | 364 795 | 324 463 | 408 880 |
| 5122 Profits of fiscal monopolies | .. | 0 | 0 | 0 | 0 | 0 | 0 | 0 | 0 | 0 |
| 5123 Customs and import duties | .. | 51 007 | 96 014 | 115 769 | 180 118 | 210 692 | 243 198 | 242 695 | 235 595 | 304 565 |
| 5124 Taxes on exports | .. | 0 | 0 | 0 | 0 | 0 | 0 | 0 | 0 | 0 |
| 5125 Taxes on investment goods | .. | 0 | 0 | 0 | 0 | 0 | 0 | 0 | 0 | 0 |
| 5126 Taxes on specific services | .. | 1 485 | 4 436 | 4 120 | 10 184 | 10 572 | 19 959 | 11 267 | 9 310 | 3 359 |
| Travel tax | .. | 1 485 | 4 436 | 4 120 | 10 184 | 10 572 | 19 959 | 11 267 | 9 310 | 3 359 |
| 5127 Other taxes on internat. trade and transactions | .. | 0 | 0 | 0 | 0 | 0 | 0 | 0 | 0 | 0 |
| 5128 Other taxes | .. | 0 | 0 | 0 | 0 | 0 | 0 | 0 | 0 | 0 |
| 5130 Unallocable between 5110 and 5120 | .. | 0 | 0 | 0 | 0 | 0 | 0 | 0 | 0 | 0 |
| 5200 Taxes on use of goods and to perform activities | .. | 0 | 0 | 0 | 0 | 0 | 0 | 0 | 0 | 0 |
| 5210 Recurrent taxes | .. | .. | .. | .. | .. | .. | .. | .. | .. | .. |
| 5211 Paid by households: motor vehicles | .. | .. | .. | .. | .. | .. | .. | .. | .. | .. |
| 5212 Paid by others: motor vehicles | .. | .. | .. | .. | .. | .. | .. | .. | .. | .. |
| 5213 Paid in respect of other goods | .. | .. | .. | .. | .. | .. | .. | .. | .. | .. |
| 5220 Non-recurrent taxes | .. | .. | .. | .. | .. | .. | .. | .. | .. | .. |
| 5300 Unallocable between 5100 and 5200 | .. | 0 | 0 | 0 | 0 | 0 | 0 | 0 | 0 | 0 |

| | 1997 | 2000 | 2007 | 2010 | 2015 | 2016 | 2017 | 2018 | 2019 | 2020 |
|---|---|---|---|---|---|---|---|---|---|---|
| **6000 Other taxes** | **..** | **0** | **0** | **0** | **0** | **0** | **0** | **0** | **0** | **0** |
| 6100 Paid solely by business | .. | .. | .. | .. | .. | .. | .. | .. | .. | .. |
| 6200 Other | .. | .. | .. | .. | .. | .. | .. | .. | .. | .. |

.. Not available

Note: Data are on a fiscal year basis ending 31st June. For example, the data for 2020 represent 1 July 2020 to 31 June 2021.
The data are on a cash basis.

Source: National Board of Revenue of Bangladesh.

StatLink https://stat.link/45y8t1

## Table 4.3. Bhutan: Details of tax revenue

Million BTN

| | 1997 | 2000 | 2007 | 2010 | 2015 | 2016 | 2017 | 2018 | 2019 | 2020 |
|---|---|---|---|---|---|---|---|---|---|---|
| **Total tax revenue** | **1 209** | **1 851** | **4 613** | **10 816** | **18 518** | **19 649** | **22 404** | **21 746** | **18 398** | **15 744** |
| **1000 Taxes on income, profits and capital gains** | **648** | **1 217** | **2 547** | **6 925** | **10 337** | **10 355** | **11 167** | **11 240** | **10 941** | **9 632** |
| 1100 Of individuals | 24 | 66 | 265 | 705 | 1 764 | 953 | 1 335 | 1 543 | 2 291 | 1 367 |
| 1110 On income and profits | 24 | 66 | 265 | 705 | 1 764 | 953 | 1 335 | 1 543 | 2 291 | 1 367 |
| Salary income | .. | .. | .. | .. | 1 617 | 696 | 1 111 | 1 270 | .. | .. |
| Rental income | .. | .. | .. | .. | 32 | 34 | 37 | 43 | .. | .. |
| Dividends and interest | .. | .. | .. | .. | 92 | 125 | 106 | 122 | .. | .. |
| Other income | .. | .. | .. | .. | 23 | 97 | 80 | 108 | .. | .. |
| 1120 On capital gains | .. | .. | .. | .. | .. | .. | .. | .. | .. | .. |
| 1200 Corporate | 624 | 1 151 | 2 283 | 6 220 | 8 573 | 9 402 | 9 832 | 9 697 | 8 651 | 8 265 |
| 1210 On profits | 624 | 1 151 | 2 283 | 6 220 | 8 573 | 9 402 | 9 832 | 9 697 | 8 651 | 8 265 |
| Corporate income tax | 559 | 920 | 1 818 | 5 110 | 7 430 | 8 149 | 9 014 | 9 022 | .. | 7 225 |
| Druk Holdings and Investments (DHI) | 0 | 0 | 0 | 1 372 | .. | .. | .. | .. | .. | .. |
| Druk Green Power Corporation Limited (DGPC) | 0 | 0 | 878 | 1 953 | .. | .. | .. | .. | .. | .. |
| Bhutan Power Corporation Limited (BPC) | 0 | 0 | 109 | 346 | .. | .. | .. | .. | .. | .. |
| Others | 559 | 920 | 831 | 1 439 | .. | .. | .. | .. | .. | .. |
| Business income tax | 65 | 232 | 465 | 1 110 | 1 143 | 1 254 | 818 | 674 | .. | 1 040 |
| 1220 On capital gains of corporates | .. | .. | .. | .. | .. | .. | .. | .. | .. | .. |
| 1300 Unallocable between 1100 and 1200 | 0 | 0 | 0 | 0 | 0 | 0 | 0 | 0 | 0 | 0 |
| **2000 Social security contributions** | **0** | **0** | **0** | **0** | **0** | **0** | **0** | **0** | **0** | **0** |
| 2100 Employees | .. | .. | .. | .. | .. | .. | .. | .. | .. | .. |
| 2110 On a payroll basis | .. | .. | .. | .. | .. | .. | .. | .. | .. | .. |
| 2120 On an income tax basis | .. | .. | .. | .. | .. | .. | .. | .. | .. | .. |
| 2200 Employers | .. | .. | .. | .. | .. | .. | .. | .. | .. | .. |
| 2210 On a payroll basis | .. | .. | .. | .. | .. | .. | .. | .. | .. | .. |
| 2220 On an income tax basis | .. | .. | .. | .. | .. | .. | .. | .. | .. | .. |
| 2300 Self-employed or non-employed | .. | .. | .. | .. | .. | .. | .. | .. | .. | .. |
| 2310 On a payroll basis | .. | .. | .. | .. | .. | .. | .. | .. | .. | .. |
| 2320 On an income tax basis | .. | .. | .. | .. | .. | .. | .. | .. | .. | .. |
| 2400 Unallocable between 2100, 2200 and 2300 | .. | .. | .. | .. | .. | .. | .. | .. | .. | .. |
| 2410 On a payroll basis | .. | .. | .. | .. | .. | .. | .. | .. | .. | .. |
| 2420 On an income tax basis | .. | .. | .. | .. | .. | .. | .. | .. | .. | .. |
| **3000 Taxes on payroll and workforce** | **13** | **22** | **58** | **105** | **57** | **-80** | **-9** | **74** | **-32** | **14** |
| Health contribution | 13 | 22 | 58 | 105 | 57 | -80 | -9 | 74 | -32 | 14 |
| **4000 Taxes on property** | **4** | **5** | **25** | **6** | **67** | **55** | **34** | **33** | **27** | **119** |
| 4100 Recurrent taxes on immovable property | 4 | 5 | 25 | 6 | 4 | 3 | 7 | 7 | 5 | 9 |
| 4110 Households | 4 | 5 | 25 | 6 | 4 | 3 | 7 | 7 | 5 | 9 |
| 4120 Others | 0 | 0 | 0 | 0 | 0 | 0 | 0 | 0 | 0 | 0 |
| 4200 Recurrent taxes on net wealth | 0 | 0 | 0 | 0 | 0 | 0 | 0 | 0 | 0 | 0 |
| 4210 Individual | .. | .. | .. | .. | .. | .. | .. | .. | .. | .. |
| 4220 Corporate | .. | .. | .. | .. | .. | .. | .. | .. | .. | .. |
| 4300 Estate, inheritance and gift taxes | 0 | 0 | 0 | 0 | 0 | 0 | 0 | 0 | 0 | 0 |
| 4310 Estate and inheritance taxes | .. | .. | .. | .. | .. | .. | .. | .. | .. | .. |
| 4320 Gift taxes | .. | .. | .. | .. | .. | .. | .. | .. | .. | .. |
| 4400 Taxes on financial and capital transactions | 0 | 0 | 0 | 0 | 63 | 52 | 28 | 25 | 22 | 110 |
| 4500 Other non-reccurrent taxes on property | 0 | 0 | 0 | 0 | 0 | 0 | 0 | 0 | 0 | 0 |
| 4510 On net wealth | .. | .. | .. | .. | .. | .. | .. | .. | .. | .. |
| 4520 Other non-recurrent taxes | .. | .. | .. | .. | .. | .. | .. | .. | .. | .. |
| 4600 Other recurrent taxes on property | 0 | 0 | 0 | 0 | 0 | 0 | 0 | 0 | 0 | 0 |
| **5000 Taxes on goods and services** | **542** | **596** | **1 969** | **3 760** | **8 056** | **9 318** | **11 212** | **10 399** | **7 462** | **5 980** |
| 5100 Taxes on production, sale, transfer, etc | 542 | 596 | 1 969 | 3 760 | 7 765 | 8 974 | 10 816 | 9 978 | 7 117 | 5 575 |
| 5110 General taxes on goods and services | 186 | 309 | 831 | 1 636 | 3 575 | 3 796 | 4 270 | 4 714 | 4 922 | 4 085 |
| 5111 Value added taxes | 0 | 0 | 0 | 0 | 0 | 0 | 0 | 0 | 0 | 0 |
| 5112 Sales tax | 186 | 309 | 831 | 1 636 | 3 575 | 3 796 | 4 270 | 4 714 | 4 922 | 4 085 |
| Goods and commodities | .. | .. | .. | .. | 1 979 | 1 710 | 1 315 | 1 370 | 1 486 | 2 468 |
| Beer | .. | .. | .. | .. | 767 | 952 | 1 137 | 1 212 | 1 438 | 1 024 |
| Vehicles | .. | .. | .. | .. | 0 | 0 | 540 | 643 | 757 | 321 |
| Petroleum products | .. | .. | .. | .. | 234 | 434 | 414 | 522 | 296 | 0 |
| Hotels and restaurants | .. | .. | .. | .. | 318 | 393 | 448 | 500 | 440 | 55 |
| Telecom services | .. | .. | .. | .. | 178 | 179 | 223 | 252 | 323 | 3 |
| Cement | .. | .. | .. | .. | 50 | 70 | 92 | 97 | 97 | 59 |
| Aerated water | .. | .. | .. | .. | 26 | 35 | 76 | 94 | 85 | 121 |
| Entertainment services | .. | .. | .. | .. | 23 | 23 | 26 | 25 | 0 | 34 |
| 5113 Other | 0 | 0 | 0 | 0 | 0 | 0 | 0 | 0 | 0 | 0 |
| 5120 Taxes on specific goods and services | 356 | 287 | 1 138 | 2 124 | 4 190 | 5 178 | 6 546 | 5 264 | 2 196 | 1 490 |
| 5121 Excises | 266 | 130 | 878 | 1 605 | 2 483 | 3 580 | 4 834 | 3 406 | 803 | 342 |
| Distillery products | 104 | 130 | 153 | 321 | 539 | 663 | 885 | 906 | 680 | 342 |
| Excise duty refund from India | 162 | 0 | 725 | 1 284 | 1 944 | 2 917 | 3 949 | 2 500 | 123 | 0 |
| 5122 Profits of fiscal monopolies | 0 | 0 | 0 | 0 | 0 | 0 | 0 | 0 | 0 | 0 |

| | 1997 | 2000 | 2007 | 2010 | 2015 | 2016 | 2017 | 2018 | 2019 | 2020 |
|---|---|---|---|---|---|---|---|---|---|---|
| 5123 Customs and import duties | 65 | 139 | 237 | 483 | 1 605 | 1 472 | 1 712 | 1 704 | 1 280 | 1 149 |
| Customs duty on goods and commodities and customs service charge | .. | .. | .. | .. | 597 | 563 | 773 | 678 | 468 | 555 |
| Fuel | .. | .. | .. | .. | 348 | 411 | 405 | 525 | 401 | 293 |
| Motor vehicles | .. | .. | .. | .. | 659 | 499 | 534 | 501 | 411 | 301 |
| 5124 Taxes on exports | 19 | 13 | 0 | 0 | 0 | 0 | 0 | 0 | 0 | 0 |
| 5125 Taxes on investment goods | 0 | 0 | 0 | 0 | 0 | 0 | 0 | 0 | 0 | 0 |
| 5126 Taxes on specific services | 5 | 5 | 23 | 35 | 103 | 126 | 0 | 154 | 112 | 0 |
| 5127 Other taxes on internat. trade and transactions | 0 | 0 | 0 | 0 | 0 | 0 | 0 | 0 | 0 | 0 |
| 5128 Other taxes | 0 | 0 | 0 | 0 | 0 | 0 | 0 | 0 | 0 | 0 |
| 5130 Unallocable between 5110 and 5120 | 0 | 0 | 0 | 0 | 0 | 0 | 0 | 0 | 0 | 0 |
| 5200 Taxes on use of goods and to perform activities | 0 | 0 | 0 | 0 | 291 | 344 | 395 | 422 | 345 | 404 |
| 5210 Recurrent taxes | .. | .. | .. | .. | 259 | 303 | 323 | 351 | 290 | 331 |
| 5211 Paid by households: motor vehicles | .. | .. | .. | .. | 172 | 198 | 214 | 238 | 193 | 196 |
| 5212 Paid by others: motor vehicles | .. | .. | .. | .. | 0 | 0 | 0 | 0 | 0 | 0 |
| 5213 Paid in respect of other goods | .. | .. | .. | .. | 87 | 105 | 110 | 114 | 97 | 135 |
| 5220 Non-recurrent taxes | .. | .. | .. | .. | 32 | 41 | 72 | 70 | 54 | 74 |
| 5300 Unallocable between 5100 and 5200 | 0 | 0 | 0 | 0 | 0 | 0 | 0 | 0 | 0 | 0 |
| **6000 Other taxes** | **1** | **11** | **13** | **20** | **0** | **0** | **0** | **0** | **0** | **0** |
| 6100 Paid solely by business | .. | .. | .. | .. | .. | .. | .. | .. | .. | .. |
| 6200 Other | .. | .. | .. | .. | .. | .. | .. | .. | .. | .. |

.. Not available

Note: Data are reported on a fiscal year basis beginning 1st July. For example, the data for 2020 represent the period from July 2020 to June 2021.

The data are on a cash basis.

Heading 1000: Detailed breakdown of corporate income tax is not available for 2019 and for personal income taxes it is not available for 2020 at the time of publication. The numbers may include fines and penalties which are not considered tax revenues by the OECD.

Source: Ministry of Finance, Bhutan.

StatLink https://stat.link/pyxezh

# Table 4.4. Cambodia: Details of tax revenue

Million KHR

| | 1997 | 2000 | 2007 | 2010 | 2015 | 2016 | 2017 | 2018 | 2019 | 2020 |
|---|---|---|---|---|---|---|---|---|---|---|
| **Total tax revenue** | .. | .. | **3 398 035** | **3 440 971** | **11 468 515** | **12 800 088** | **15 192 684** | **18 560 887** | **23 821 776** | **20 881 713** |
| **1000 Taxes on income, profits and capital gains** | .. | .. | **480 287** | **290 876** | **2 472 094** | **2 952 788** | **3 798 294** | **4 367 432** | **5 467 480** | **6 110 374** |
| 1100 Of individuals | .. | .. | 89 587 | 197 724 | 753 929 | 835 720 | 1 031 691 | 1 106 117 | 1 296 595 | 1 343 255 |
| 1110 On income and profits | .. | .. | 89 587 | 197 724 | 753 929 | 835 720 | 1 031 691 | 1 106 117 | 1 296 595 | 1 343 255 |
| 1120 On capital gains | .. | .. | .. | .. | .. | .. | .. | .. | .. | .. |
| 1200 Corporate | .. | .. | 390 700 | 93 153 | 1 718 165 | 2 117 068 | 2 766 603 | 3 261 315 | 4 170 885 | 4 767 119 |
| 1210 On profits | .. | .. | 390 700 | 93 153 | 1 718 165 | 2 117 068 | 2 766 603 | 3 261 315 | 4 170 885 | 4 767 119 |
| 1220 On capital gains of corporates | .. | .. | .. | .. | .. | .. | .. | .. | .. | .. |
| 1300 Unallocable between 1100 and 1200 | .. | .. | 0 | 0 | 0 | 0 | 0 | 0 | 0 | 0 |
| **2000 Social security contributions** | .. | .. | **0** | **0** | **0** | **0** | **0** | **0** | **0** | **0** |
| 2100 Employees | .. | .. | .. | .. | .. | .. | .. | .. | .. | .. |
| 2110 On a payroll basis | .. | .. | .. | .. | .. | .. | .. | .. | .. | .. |
| 2120 On an income tax basis | .. | .. | .. | .. | .. | .. | .. | .. | .. | .. |
| 2200 Employers | .. | .. | .. | .. | .. | .. | .. | .. | .. | .. |
| 2210 On a payroll basis | .. | .. | .. | .. | .. | .. | .. | .. | .. | .. |
| 2220 On an income tax basis | .. | .. | .. | .. | .. | .. | .. | .. | .. | .. |
| 2300 Self-employed or non-employed | .. | .. | .. | .. | .. | .. | .. | .. | .. | .. |
| 2310 On a payroll basis | .. | .. | .. | .. | .. | .. | .. | .. | .. | .. |
| 2320 On an income tax basis | .. | .. | .. | .. | .. | .. | .. | .. | .. | .. |
| 2400 Unallocable between 2100, 2200 and 2300 | .. | .. | .. | .. | .. | .. | .. | .. | .. | .. |
| 2410 On a payroll basis | .. | .. | .. | .. | .. | .. | .. | .. | .. | .. |
| 2420 On an income tax basis | .. | .. | .. | .. | .. | .. | .. | .. | .. | .. |
| **3000 Taxes on payroll and workforce** | .. | .. | **0** | **0** | **0** | **0** | **0** | **0** | **0** | **0** |
| **4000 Taxes on property** | .. | .. | **0** | **0** | **437 990** | **365 151** | **563 393** | **794 284** | **1 103 579** | **981 380** |
| 4100 Recurrent taxes on immovable property | .. | .. | .. | .. | 95 025 | 91 568 | 108 472 | 134 017 | 161 581 | 153 965 |
| 4110 Households | .. | .. | .. | .. | .. | .. | .. | .. | .. | .. |
| 4120 Others | .. | .. | .. | .. | .. | .. | .. | .. | .. | .. |
| 4200 Recurrent taxes on net wealth | .. | .. | .. | .. | 0 | 0 | 0 | 0 | 0 | 0 |
| 4210 Individual | .. | .. | .. | .. | .. | .. | .. | .. | .. | .. |
| 4220 Corporate | .. | .. | .. | .. | .. | .. | .. | .. | .. | .. |
| 4300 Estate, inheritance and gift taxes | .. | .. | .. | .. | 0 | 0 | 0 | 0 | 0 | 0 |
| 4310 Estate and inheritance taxes | .. | .. | .. | .. | .. | .. | .. | .. | .. | .. |
| 4320 Gift taxes | .. | .. | .. | .. | .. | .. | .. | .. | .. | .. |
| 4400 Taxes on financial and capital transactions | .. | .. | .. | .. | 342 964 | 273 583 | 454 921 | 660 267 | 941 997 | 827 415 |
| 4500 Other non-reccurrent taxes on property | .. | .. | .. | .. | 0 | 0 | 0 | 0 | 0 | 0 |
| 4510 On net wealth | .. | .. | .. | .. | .. | .. | .. | .. | .. | .. |
| 4520 Other non-recurrent taxes | .. | .. | .. | .. | .. | .. | .. | .. | .. | .. |
| 4600 Other recurrent taxes on property | .. | .. | .. | .. | 0 | 0 | 0 | 0 | 0 | 0 |
| **5000 Taxes on goods and services** | .. | .. | **2 910 331** | **3 146 690** | **8 550 924** | **9 476 106** | **10 823 127** | **13 388 678** | **17 234 748** | **13 769 113** |
| 5100 Taxes on production, sale, transfer, etc | .. | .. | 2 910 331 | 2 095 323 | 8 353 361 | 9 242 602 | 10 552 076 | 13 083 945 | 16 866 195 | 13 337 004 |
| 5110 General taxes on goods and services | .. | .. | 1 157 545 | 940 348 | 3 639 882 | 4 142 807 | 4 734 680 | 5 581 051 | 7 272 114 | 6 380 770 |
| 5111 Value added taxes | .. | .. | 1 142 787 | 940 348 | 3 612 478 | 4 142 115 | 4 734 640 | 5 580 970 | 7 272 100 | 6 380 768 |
| 5112 Sales tax | .. | .. | 0 | 0 | 0 | 0 | 0 | 0 | 0 | 0 |
| 5113 Other | .. | .. | 14 758 | 0 | 27 403 | 692 | 40 | 81 | 14 | 2 |
| 5120 Taxes on specific goods and services | .. | .. | 1 752 786 | 1 154 975 | 4 713 480 | 5 099 795 | 5 817 395 | 7 502 894 | 9 594 081 | 6 956 234 |
| 5121 Excises | .. | .. | 616 660 | 902 367 | 2 568 103 | 3 095 077 | 3 832 780 | 5 128 519 | 6 674 530 | 4 750 955 |
| 5122 Profits of fiscal monopolies | .. | .. | 0 | 261 | 0 | 0 | 0 | 0 | 0 | 0 |
| 5123 Customs and import duties | .. | .. | 880 055 | 0 | 1 808 836 | 1 957 120 | 1 920 676 | 2 303 136 | 2 848 269 | 2 174 133 |
| 5124 Taxes on exports | .. | .. | 141 118 | 118 637 | 180 241 | 31 364 | 45 512 | 51 473 | 48 779 | 23 807 |
| 5125 Taxes on investment goods | .. | .. | 0 | 0 | 0 | 0 | 0 | 0 | 0 | 0 |
| 5126 Taxes on specific services | .. | .. | 114 953 | 132 307 | 156 300 | 16 233 | 18 427 | 19 767 | 22 504 | 7 339 |
| 5127 Other taxes on internat. trade and transactions | .. | .. | 0 | 1 404 | 0 | 0 | 0 | 0 | 0 | 0 |
| 5128 Other taxes | .. | .. | 0 | 0 | 0 | 0 | 0 | 0 | 0 | 0 |
| 5130 Unallocable between 5110 and 5120 | .. | .. | 0 | 0 | 0 | 0 | 0 | 0 | 0 | 0 |
| 5200 Taxes on use of goods and to perform activities | .. | .. | 0 | 1 051 366 | 197 563 | 233 504 | 271 052 | 304 733 | 368 553 | 432 110 |
| 5210 Recurrent taxes | .. | .. | .. | 1 051 366 | 197 563 | 233 504 | 271 052 | 304 733 | 368 553 | 432 110 |
| 5211 Paid by households: motor vehicles | .. | .. | .. | 1 032 930 | 0 | 0 | 0 | 0 | 0 | 0 |
| 5212 Paid by others: motor vehicles | .. | .. | .. | 0 | 0 | 0 | 0 | 0 | 0 | 0 |
| 5213 Paid in respect of other goods | .. | .. | .. | 18 436 | 197 563 | 233 504 | 271 052 | 304 733 | 368 553 | 432 110 |
| 5220 Non-recurrent taxes | .. | .. | .. | 0 | 0 | 0 | 0 | 0 | 0 | 0 |
| 5300 Unallocable between 5100 and 5200 | .. | .. | 0 | 0 | 0 | 0 | 0 | 0 | 0 | 0 |

| | 1997 | 2000 | 2007 | 2010 | 2015 | 2016 | 2017 | 2018 | 2019 | 2020 |
|---|---|---|---|---|---|---|---|---|---|---|
| **6000 Other taxes** | .. | .. | **7 417** | **3 405** | **7 508** | **6 044** | **7 870** | **10 494** | **15 970** | **20 845** |
| 6100 Paid solely by business | .. | .. | 0 | 0 | 0 | 0 | 0 | 0 | 0 | 0 |
| 6200 Other | .. | .. | 7 417 | 3 405 | 7 508 | 6 044 | 7 870 | 10 494 | 15 970 | 20 845 |

.. Not available

Note: Year ending 31st December.

The data are on an accrual basis.

Local government revenue data are not available before 2012.

Heading 2000: Social security contribution data are not available.

Source: Ministry of Economy and Finance of Cambodia.

StatLink https://stat.link/5rj9fe

## Table 4.5. China: Details of tax revenue

Billion CNY

| | 1997 | 2000 | 2007 | 2010 | 2015 | 2016 | 2017 | 2018 | 2019 | 2020 |
|---|---|---|---|---|---|---|---|---|---|---|
| **Total tax revenue** | .. | .. | **4 562** | **7 321** | **12 492** | **13 035** | **14 437** | **15 640** | **21 791** | **20 349** |
| **1000 Taxes on income, profits and capital gains** | .. | .. | **1 237** | **1 896** | **3 958** | **4 315** | **4 899** | **5 484** | **5 416** | **5 446** |
| 1100 Of individuals | .. | .. | 319 | 484 | 862 | 1 009 | 1 197 | 1 387 | 1 039 | 1 157 |
| 1110 On income and profits | .. | .. | .. | .. | .. | .. | .. | .. | .. | .. |
| 1120 On capital gains | .. | .. | .. | .. | .. | .. | .. | .. | .. | .. |
| 1200 Corporate | .. | .. | 918 | 1 412 | 3 097 | 3 306 | 3 703 | 4 097 | 4 377 | 4 289 |
| Enterprise income tax | .. | .. | 878 | 1 284 | 2 713 | 2 885 | 3 212 | 3 532 | 3 730 | 3 643 |
| Land appreciation tax | .. | .. | 40 | 128 | 383 | 421 | 491 | 564 | 647 | 647 |
| 1210 On profits | .. | .. | .. | .. | .. | .. | .. | .. | .. | .. |
| 1220 On capital gains of corporates | .. | .. | .. | .. | .. | .. | .. | .. | .. | .. |
| 1300 Unallocable between 1100 and 1200 | .. | .. | 0 | 0 | 0 | 0 | 0 | 0 | 0 | 0 |
| **2000 Social security contributions** | .. | .. | .. | .. | .. | .. | .. | .. | **5 999** | **4 922** |
| 2100 Employees | .. | .. | .. | .. | .. | .. | .. | .. | .. | .. |
| 2110 On a payroll basis | .. | .. | .. | .. | .. | .. | .. | .. | .. | .. |
| 2120 On an income tax basis | .. | .. | .. | .. | .. | .. | .. | .. | .. | .. |
| 2200 Employers | .. | .. | .. | .. | .. | .. | .. | .. | .. | .. |
| 2210 On a payroll basis | .. | .. | .. | .. | .. | .. | .. | .. | .. | .. |
| 2220 On an income tax basis | .. | .. | .. | .. | .. | .. | .. | .. | .. | .. |
| 2300 Self-employed or non-employed | .. | .. | .. | .. | .. | .. | .. | .. | .. | .. |
| 2310 On a payroll basis | .. | .. | .. | .. | .. | .. | .. | .. | .. | .. |
| 2320 On an income tax basis | .. | .. | .. | .. | .. | .. | .. | .. | .. | .. |
| 2400 Unallocable between 2100, 2200 and 2300 | .. | .. | .. | .. | .. | .. | .. | .. | 5 999 | 4 922 |
| 2410 On a payroll basis | .. | .. | .. | .. | .. | .. | .. | .. | .. | .. |
| 2420 On an income tax basis | .. | .. | .. | .. | .. | .. | .. | .. | .. | .. |
| **3000 Taxes on payroll and workforce** | .. | .. | **0** | **0** | **0** | **0** | **0** | **0** | **0** | **0** |
| **4000 Taxes on property** | .. | .. | **443** | **540** | **1 153** | **1 099** | **1 208** | **1 321** | **1 386** | **1 505** |
| 4100 Recurrent taxes on immovable property | .. | .. | 96 | 190 | 419 | 448 | 496 | 528 | 518 | 490 |
| 4110 Households | .. | .. | 0 | 0 | 0 | 0 | 0 | 0 | 0 | 0 |
| 4120 Others | .. | .. | 96 | 190 | 419 | 448 | 496 | 528 | 518 | 490 |
| House property tax | .. | .. | 58 | 89 | 205 | 222 | 260 | 289 | 299 | 284 |
| Urban and town land use tax | .. | .. | 39 | 100 | 214 | 226 | 236 | 239 | 220 | 206 |
| 4200 Recurrent taxes on net wealth | .. | .. | 0 | 0 | 0 | 0 | 0 | 0 | 0 | 0 |
| 4210 Individual | .. | .. | .. | .. | .. | .. | .. | .. | .. | .. |
| 4220 Corporate | .. | .. | .. | .. | .. | .. | .. | .. | .. | .. |
| 4300 Estate, inheritance and gift taxes | .. | .. | 0 | 0 | 0 | 0 | 0 | 0 | 0 | 0 |
| 4310 Estate and inheritance taxes | .. | .. | .. | .. | .. | .. | .. | .. | .. | .. |
| 4320 Gift taxes | .. | .. | .. | .. | .. | .. | .. | .. | .. | .. |
| 4400 Taxes on financial and capital transactions | .. | .. | 347 | 351 | 734 | 651 | 712 | 793 | 868 | 1 015 |
| Stamp tax on securities transactions | .. | .. | 201 | 54 | 255 | 125 | 107 | 98 | 123 | 177 |
| Other stamp duties | .. | .. | 26 | 50 | 89 | 96 | 114 | 122 | 123 | 131 |
| Deed tax | .. | .. | 121 | 246 | 390 | 430 | 491 | 573 | 621 | 706 |
| 4500 Other non-reccurrent taxes on property | .. | .. | 0 | 0 | 0 | 0 | 0 | 0 | 0 | 0 |
| 4510 On net wealth | .. | .. | .. | .. | .. | .. | .. | .. | .. | .. |
| 4520 Other non-recurrent taxes | .. | .. | .. | .. | .. | .. | .. | .. | .. | .. |
| 4600 Other recurrent taxes on property | .. | .. | 0 | 0 | 0 | 0 | 0 | 0 | 0 | 0 |
| **5000 Taxes on goods and services** | .. | .. | **2 882** | **4 885** | **7 381** | **7 621** | **8 329** | **8 836** | **8 990** | **8 476** |
| 5100 Taxes on production, sale, transfer, etc | .. | .. | 2 855 | 4 769 | 7 105 | 7 345 | 8 081 | 8 601 | 8 736 | 8 229 |
| 5110 General taxes on goods and services | .. | .. | 2 373 | 3 730 | 5 397 | 5 688 | 6 284 | 6 734 | 6 581 | 6 170 |
| 5111 Value added taxes | .. | .. | 1 715 | 2 614 | 3 466 | 4 538 | 6 284 | 6 734 | 6 581 | 6 170 |
| Domestic VAT | .. | .. | 1 547 | 2 109 | 3 111 | 4 071 | 5 638 | 6 153 | 6 235 | 5 679 |
| Import VAT | .. | .. | 615 | 1 049 | 1 253 | 1 278 | 1 597 | 1 688 | 1 512 | 1 391 |
| Urban maintenance and construction tax | .. | .. | 116 | 189 | 389 | 403 | 436 | 484 | 482 | 461 |
| Refund of VAT for export | .. | .. | -563 | -733 | -1 287 | -1 215 | -1 387 | -1 591 | -1 648 | -1 361 |
| 5112 Sales tax | .. | .. | 0 | 0 | 0 | 0 | 0 | 0 | 0 | 0 |
| 5113 Other | .. | .. | 658 | 1 116 | 1 931 | 1 150 | 0 | 0 | 0 | 0 |
| Business tax | .. | .. | 658 | 1 116 | 1 931 | 1 150 | 0 | 0 | 0 | 0 |
| 5120 Taxes on specific goods and services | .. | .. | 483 | 1 039 | 1 707 | 1 658 | 1 797 | 1 867 | 2 155 | 2 059 |
| 5121 Excises | .. | .. | 313 | 794 | 1 348 | 1 302 | 1 362 | 1 420 | 1 684 | 1 627 |
| Domestic excise tax | .. | .. | 221 | 607 | 1 054 | 1 022 | 1 023 | 1 063 | 1 256 | 1 203 |
| Import excise tax | .. | .. | 0 | 0 | 0 | 0 | 0 | 0 | 69 | 62 |
| Motor vehicles purchase tax | .. | .. | 88 | 179 | 279 | 267 | 328 | 345 | 350 | 353 |
| Leaf tobacco tax | .. | .. | 5 | 8 | 14 | 13 | 12 | 11 | 11 | 11 |
| Refund of excise tax for export | .. | .. | 0 | 0 | 0 | 0 | 0 | 0 | -2 | -2 |
| 5122 Profits of fiscal monopolies | .. | .. | 0 | 0 | 0 | 0 | 0 | 0 | 0 | 0 |
| 5123 Customs and import duties | .. | .. | 143 | 203 | 256 | 260 | 300 | 285 | 289 | 256 |
| 5124 Taxes on exports | .. | .. | 0 | 0 | 0 | 0 | 0 | 0 | 0 | 0 |
| 5125 Taxes on investment goods | .. | .. | 0 | 0 | 0 | 0 | 0 | 0 | 0 | 0 |
| 5126 Taxes on specific services | .. | .. | 0 | 0 | 0 | 0 | 0 | 0 | 0 | 0 |
| 5127 Other taxes on internat. trade and transactions | .. | .. | 0 | 0 | 0 | 0 | 0 | 0 | 0 | 0 |

| | 1997 | 2000 | 2007 | 2010 | 2015 | 2016 | 2017 | 2018 | 2019 | 2020 |
|---|---|---|---|---|---|---|---|---|---|---|
| 5128 Other taxes | .. | .. | 26 | 42 | 103 | 95 | 135 | 163 | 182 | 175 |
| Resources tax | .. | .. | 26 | 42 | 103 | 95 | 135 | 163 | 182 | 175 |
| 5130 Unallocable between 5110 and 5120 | .. | .. | 0 | 0 | 0 | 0 | 0 | 0 | 0 | 0 |
| 5200 Taxes on use of goods and to perform activities | .. | .. | 27 | 116 | 276 | 276 | 248 | 235 | 254 | 246 |
| 5210 Recurrent taxes | .. | .. | 7 | 24 | 61 | 68 | 77 | 83 | 88 | 95 |
| Vehicle and vessel tax | .. | .. | 7 | 24 | 61 | 68 | 77 | 83 | 88 | 95 |
| 5211 Paid by households: motor vehicles | .. | .. | .. | .. | .. | .. | .. | .. | .. | .. |
| 5212 Paid by others: motor vehicles | .. | .. | .. | .. | .. | .. | .. | .. | .. | .. |
| 5213 Paid in respect of other goods | .. | .. | .. | .. | .. | .. | .. | .. | .. | .. |
| 5220 Non-recurrent taxes | .. | .. | 20 | 92 | 214 | 208 | 170 | 152 | 166 | 152 |
| Cultivated land use tax | .. | .. | 19 | 89 | 210 | 203 | 165 | 132 | 139 | 126 |
| Vessel tonnage tax | .. | .. | 2 | 3 | 5 | 5 | 5 | 5 | 5 | 5 |
| Environmental protection tax | .. | .. | 0 | 0 | 0 | 0 | 0 | 15 | 22 | 21 |
| 5300 Unallocable between 5100 and 5200 | .. | .. | 0 | 0 | 0 | 0 | 0 | 0 | 0 | 0 |
| **6000 Other taxes** | **..** | **..** | **0** | **0** | **0** | **0** | **0** | **0** | **0** | **0** |
| 6100 Paid solely by business | .. | .. | .. | .. | .. | .. | .. | .. | .. | .. |
| 6200 Other | .. | .. | .. | .. | .. | .. | .. | .. | .. | .. |

.. Not available

Note: Year ending 31st December.

The data are on a cash basis

Heading 2000: Social security contribution data for China include contributions from old-age insurance, medical insurance, unemployment insurance and employment injury insurance. The figures also include contributions to individual accounts, which are not considered as tax revenues by the OECD, as disaggregation is not available. Data are not available before 2019.

Heading 5111: In years prior to 2019, import VAT also includes import excise tax as they cannot be distinguished. Similarly, before 2019, refund of VAT for export also includes refund of excise tax for export as they cannot be distinguished. In both cases, the VAT portion accounts for the majority of combined revenues. The heading "Urban maintenance and construction tax" is a surtax of both VAT and excises, but it is not possible to distinguish revenues between the two sources. It is classified under heading 5111 as VAT is the main source of these revenues. A small portion of urban maintenance and construction tax should be attributed to the central government. This portion has been identified since 2019 but it is not possible to separate the central and local portions in previous years.

Heading 5128: A small portion of resources tax should be attributed to the central government. This portion has been identified since 2019 but it is not possible to separate the central and local portions in previous years.

Source: Ministry of Finance of China.

StatLink https://stat.link/1ml8eu

## Table 4.6. Cook Islands: Details of tax revenue

Thousand NZD

| | 1997 | 2000 | 2007 | 2010 | 2015 | 2016 | 2017 | 2018 | 2019 | 2020 |
|---|---|---|---|---|---|---|---|---|---|---|
| **Total tax revenue** | .. | .. | **78 330** | **91 161** | **117 445** | **126 010** | **142 539** | **163 423** | **141 406** | **84 902** |
| **1000 Taxes on income, profits and capital gains** | .. | .. | **30 685** | **35 916** | **41 090** | **42 210** | **52 127** | **63 029** | **47 495** | **35 414** |
| 1100 Of individuals | .. | .. | 22 163 | 26 277 | 27 696 | 26 055 | 30 039 | 38 432 | 30 025 | 19 395 |
| 1110 On income and profits | .. | .. | 22 163 | 26 277 | 27 696 | 26 055 | 30 039 | 38 432 | 30 025 | 19 395 |
| Net Income Tax | .. | .. | 22 163 | 26 361 | 24 768 | 24 298 | 28 197 | 36 929 | 28 757 | 17 842 |
| Withholding Tax | .. | .. | 0 | -84 | 2 928 | 1 757 | 1 842 | 1 504 | 1 268 | 1 554 |
| 1120 On capital gains | .. | .. | 0 | 0 | 0 | 0 | 0 | 0 | 0 | 0 |
| 1200 Corporate | .. | .. | 8 523 | 9 638 | 13 394 | 16 155 | 22 089 | 24 596 | 17 470 | 16 019 |
| 1210 On profits | .. | .. | 8 523 | 9 638 | 13 394 | 16 155 | 22 089 | 24 596 | 17 470 | 16 019 |
| 1220 On capital gains of corporates | .. | .. | 0 | 0 | 0 | 0 | 0 | 0 | 0 | 0 |
| 1300 Unallocable between 1100 and 1200 | .. | .. | 0 | 0 | 0 | 0 | 0 | 0 | 0 | 0 |
| **2000 Social security contributions** | .. | .. | **0** | **0** | **0** | **0** | **0** | **0** | **0** | **0** |
| 2100 Employees | .. | .. | .. | .. | .. | .. | .. | .. | .. | .. |
| 2110 On a payroll basis | .. | .. | .. | .. | .. | .. | .. | .. | .. | .. |
| 2120 On an income tax basis | .. | .. | .. | .. | .. | .. | .. | .. | .. | .. |
| 2200 Employers | .. | .. | .. | .. | .. | .. | .. | .. | .. | .. |
| 2210 On a payroll basis | .. | .. | .. | .. | .. | .. | .. | .. | .. | .. |
| 2220 On an income tax basis | .. | .. | .. | .. | .. | .. | .. | .. | .. | .. |
| 2300 Self-employed or non-employed | .. | .. | .. | .. | .. | .. | .. | .. | .. | .. |
| 2310 On a payroll basis | .. | .. | .. | .. | .. | .. | .. | .. | .. | .. |
| 2320 On an income tax basis | .. | .. | .. | .. | .. | .. | .. | .. | .. | .. |
| 2400 Unallocable between 2100, 2200 and 2300 | .. | .. | .. | .. | .. | .. | .. | .. | .. | .. |
| 2410 On a payroll basis | .. | .. | .. | .. | .. | .. | .. | .. | .. | .. |
| 2420 On an income tax basis | .. | .. | .. | .. | .. | .. | .. | .. | .. | .. |
| **3000 Taxes on payroll and workforce** | .. | .. | **0** | **0** | **0** | **0** | **0** | **0** | **0** | **0** |
| **4000 Taxes on property** | .. | .. | **0** | **0** | **0** | **0** | **0** | **0** | **0** | **0** |
| 4100 Recurrent taxes on immovable property | .. | .. | .. | .. | .. | .. | .. | .. | .. | .. |
| 4110 Households | .. | .. | .. | .. | .. | .. | .. | .. | .. | .. |
| 4120 Others | .. | .. | .. | .. | .. | .. | .. | .. | .. | .. |
| 4200 Recurrent taxes on net wealth | .. | .. | .. | .. | .. | .. | .. | .. | .. | .. |
| 4210 Individual | .. | .. | .. | .. | .. | .. | .. | .. | .. | .. |
| 4220 Corporate | .. | .. | .. | .. | .. | .. | .. | .. | .. | .. |
| 4300 Estate, inheritance and gift taxes | .. | .. | .. | .. | .. | .. | .. | .. | .. | .. |
| 4310 Estate and inheritance taxes | .. | .. | .. | .. | .. | .. | .. | .. | .. | .. |
| 4320 Gift taxes | .. | .. | .. | .. | .. | .. | .. | .. | .. | .. |
| 4400 Taxes on financial and capital transactions | .. | .. | .. | .. | .. | .. | .. | .. | .. | .. |
| 4500 Other non-reccurrent taxes on property | .. | .. | .. | .. | .. | .. | .. | .. | .. | .. |
| 4510 On net wealth | .. | .. | .. | .. | .. | .. | .. | .. | .. | .. |
| 4520 Other non-recurrent taxes | .. | .. | .. | .. | .. | .. | .. | .. | .. | .. |
| 4600 Other recurrent taxes on property | .. | .. | .. | .. | .. | .. | .. | .. | .. | .. |
| **5000 Taxes on goods and services** | .. | .. | **47 645** | **55 246** | **76 355** | **83 800** | **90 411** | **100 394** | **93 911** | **49 489** |
| 5100 Taxes on production, sale, transfer, etc | .. | .. | 46 772 | 54 398 | 75 495 | 82 703 | 89 199 | 99 252 | 93 095 | 48 283 |
| 5110 General taxes on goods and services | .. | .. | 33 973 | 37 444 | 54 708 | 58 140 | 63 330 | 72 958 | 68 579 | 31 918 |
| 5111 Value added taxes | .. | .. | 33 955 | 37 381 | 54 659 | 58 124 | 63 330 | 72 958 | 68 579 | 31 918 |
| VAT revenues (gross) | .. | .. | 41 689 | 45 454 | 67 855 | 70 574 | 82 054 | 86 189 | 82 242 | 49 989 |
| VAT refunds | .. | .. | -5 043 | -4 365 | -7 433 | -7 796 | -9 965 | -3 697 | -3 959 | -8 571 |
| VAT on Crown Appropriations | .. | .. | -2 692 | -3 707 | -5 763 | -4 653 | -8 759 | -9 535 | -9 704 | -9 499 |
| 5112 Sales tax | .. | .. | 0 | 0 | 0 | 0 | 0 | 0 | 0 | 0 |
| 5113 Other | .. | .. | 18 | 63 | 49 | 16 | 0 | 0 | 0 | 0 |
| 5120 Taxes on specific goods and services | .. | .. | 12 799 | 16 955 | 20 787 | 24 564 | 25 869 | 26 294 | 24 516 | 16 365 |
| 5121 Excises | .. | .. | 0 | 0 | 0 | 0 | 0 | 0 | 0 | 0 |
| 5122 Profits of fiscal monopolies | .. | .. | 0 | 0 | 0 | 0 | 0 | 0 | 0 | 0 |
| 5123 Customs and import duties | .. | .. | 9 810 | 11 052 | 12 320 | 14 330 | 15 098 | 14 566 | 15 407 | 13 408 |
| 5124 Taxes on exports | .. | .. | 0 | 0 | 0 | 0 | 0 | 0 | 0 | 0 |
| 5125 Taxes on investment goods | .. | .. | 0 | 0 | 0 | 0 | 0 | 0 | 0 | 0 |
| 5126 Taxes on specific services | .. | .. | 2 989 | 5 903 | 8 468 | 10 234 | 10 771 | 11 729 | 9 109 | 431 |
| 5127 Other taxes on internat. trade and transactions | .. | .. | 0 | 0 | 0 | 0 | 0 | 0 | 0 | 2 527 |
| 5128 Other taxes | .. | .. | 0 | 0 | 0 | 0 | 0 | 0 | 0 | 0 |
| 5130 Unallocable between 5110 and 5120 | .. | .. | 0 | 0 | 0 | 0 | 0 | 0 | 0 | 0 |
| 5200 Taxes on use of goods and to perform activities | .. | .. | 873 | 847 | 860 | 1 097 | 1 212 | 1 142 | 816 | 1 205 |
| 5210 Recurrent taxes | .. | .. | 218 | 207 | 229 | 209 | 291 | 271 | 323 | 282 |
| 5211 Paid by households: motor vehicles | .. | .. | 0 | 0 | 0 | 0 | 0 | 0 | 0 | 0 |
| 5212 Paid by others: motor vehicles | .. | .. | 0 | 0 | 0 | 0 | 0 | 0 | 0 | 0 |
| 5213 Paid in respect of other goods | .. | .. | 218 | 207 | 229 | 209 | 291 | 271 | 323 | 282 |
| 5220 Non-recurrent taxes | .. | .. | 655 | 640 | 631 | 888 | 922 | 871 | 493 | 924 |
| 5300 Unallocable between 5100 and 5200 | .. | .. | 0 | 0 | 0 | 0 | 0 | 0 | 0 | 0 |

| | 1997 | 2000 | 2007 | 2010 | 2015 | 2016 | 2017 | 2018 | 2019 | 2020 |
|---|---|---|---|---|---|---|---|---|---|---|
| **6000 Other taxes** | .. | .. | 0 | 0 | 0 | 0 | 0 | 0 | 0 | 0 |
| 6100 Paid solely by business | .. | .. | .. | .. | .. | .. | .. | .. | .. | .. |
| 6200 Other | .. | .. | .. | .. | .. | .. | .. | .. | .. | .. |

.. Not available

Note: Data are reported on a fiscal year basis beginning 1st July. For example, the data for 2020 represent the period from July 2020 to June 2021.

The data are on a cash basis.

Figures exclude tax revenues collected by sub-national governments as the data are not available.

Source: Ministry of Finance and Economic Management of the Cook Islands.

StatLink https://stat.link/k8tfpi

## Table 4.7. Fiji: Details of tax revenue

Million FJD

| | 1997 | 2000 | 2007 | 2010 | 2015 | 2016 | 2017 | 2018 | 2019 | 2020 |
|---|---|---|---|---|---|---|---|---|---|---|
| **Total tax revenue** | .. | .. | .. | **1 304** | **2 318** | **2 387** | **2 679** | **2 739** | **2 637** | **1 607** |
| **1000 Taxes on income, profits and capital gains** | .. | .. | .. | **426** | **598** | **730** | **845** | **769** | **712** | **509** |
| 1100 Of individuals | .. | .. | .. | 184 | 211 | 222 | 231 | 224 | 202 | 182 |
| 1110 On income and profits | .. | .. | .. | 184 | 187 | 198 | 200 | 177 | 182 | 163 |
| PAYE | .. | .. | .. | 184 | 159 | 167 | 167 | 146 | 152 | 137 |
| Social responsibility tax | .. | .. | .. | 0 | 8 | 11 | 10 | 8 | 7 | 6 |
| Fringe benefit tax | .. | .. | .. | 0 | 20 | 21 | 24 | 22 | 23 | 19 |
| 1120 On capital gains | .. | .. | .. | 0 | 24 | 23 | 31 | 47 | 20 | 20 |
| 1200 Corporate | .. | .. | .. | 242 | 386 | 508 | 614 | 545 | 510 | 326 |
| 1210 On profits | .. | .. | .. | 242 | 386 | 508 | 614 | 545 | 510 | 326 |
| Company Tax | .. | .. | .. | 161 | 291 | 348 | 445 | 385 | 358 | 232 |
| Dividend and Withholding | .. | .. | .. | 73 | 85 | 105 | 121 | 120 | 119 | 93 |
| Provisional tax | .. | .. | .. | 11 | 10 | 49 | 59 | 61 | 68 | 32 |
| Other income taxes | .. | .. | .. | 30 | 45 | 44 | 49 | 57 | 49 | 33 |
| Income tax refunds | .. | .. | .. | -34 | -45 | -38 | -60 | -78 | -83 | -63 |
| 1220 On capital gains of corporates | .. | .. | .. | 0 | 0 | 0 | 0 | 0 | 0 | 0 |
| 1300 Unallocable between 1100 and 1200 | .. | .. | .. | 0 | 0 | 0 | 0 | 0 | 0 | 0 |
| **2000 Social security contributions** | .. | .. | .. | **0** | **0** | **0** | **0** | **0** | **0** | **0** |
| 2100 Employees | .. | .. | .. | .. | .. | .. | .. | .. | .. | .. |
| 2110 On a payroll basis | .. | .. | .. | .. | .. | .. | .. | .. | .. | .. |
| 2120 On an income tax basis | .. | .. | .. | .. | .. | .. | .. | .. | .. | .. |
| 2200 Employers | .. | .. | .. | .. | .. | .. | .. | .. | .. | .. |
| 2210 On a payroll basis | .. | .. | .. | .. | .. | .. | .. | .. | .. | .. |
| 2220 On an income tax basis | .. | .. | .. | .. | .. | .. | .. | .. | .. | .. |
| 2300 Self-employed or non-employed | .. | .. | .. | .. | .. | .. | .. | .. | .. | .. |
| 2310 On a payroll basis | .. | .. | .. | .. | .. | .. | .. | .. | .. | .. |
| 2320 On an income tax basis | .. | .. | .. | .. | .. | .. | .. | .. | .. | .. |
| 2400 Unallocable between 2100, 2200 and 2300 | .. | .. | .. | .. | .. | .. | .. | .. | .. | .. |
| 2410 On a payroll basis | .. | .. | .. | .. | .. | .. | .. | .. | .. | .. |
| 2420 On an income tax basis | .. | .. | .. | .. | .. | .. | .. | .. | .. | .. |
| **3000 Taxes on payroll and workforce** | .. | .. | .. | **0** | **0** | **0** | **0** | **0** | **0** | **0** |
| **4000 Taxes on property** | .. | .. | .. | **0** | **71** | **78** | **78** | **92** | **79** | **42** |
| 4100 Recurrent taxes on immovable property | .. | .. | .. | .. | 0 | 0 | 0 | 0 | 0 | 0 |
| 4110 Households | .. | .. | .. | .. | .. | .. | .. | .. | .. | .. |
| 4120 Others | .. | .. | .. | .. | .. | .. | .. | .. | .. | .. |
| 4200 Recurrent taxes on net wealth | .. | .. | .. | .. | 0 | 0 | 0 | 0 | 0 | 0 |
| 4210 Individual | .. | .. | .. | .. | .. | .. | .. | .. | .. | .. |
| 4220 Corporate | .. | .. | .. | .. | .. | .. | .. | .. | .. | .. |
| 4300 Estate, inheritance and gift taxes | .. | .. | .. | .. | 0 | 0 | 0 | 0 | 0 | 0 |
| 4310 Estate and inheritance taxes | .. | .. | .. | .. | .. | .. | .. | .. | .. | .. |
| 4320 Gift taxes | .. | .. | .. | .. | .. | .. | .. | .. | .. | .. |
| 4400 Taxes on financial and capital transactions | .. | .. | .. | .. | 71 | 78 | 78 | 92 | 79 | 42 |
| 4500 Other non-reccurrent taxes on property | .. | .. | .. | .. | 0 | 0 | 0 | 0 | 0 | 0 |
| 4510 On net wealth | .. | .. | .. | .. | .. | .. | .. | .. | .. | .. |
| 4520 Other non-recurrent taxes | .. | .. | .. | .. | .. | .. | .. | .. | .. | .. |
| 4600 Other recurrent taxes on property | .. | .. | .. | .. | 0 | 0 | 0 | 0 | 0 | 0 |
| **5000 Taxes on goods and services** | .. | .. | .. | **878** | **1 650** | **1 580** | **1 757** | **1 879** | **1 846** | **1 057** |
| 5100 Taxes on production, sale, transfer, etc | .. | .. | .. | 877 | 1 648 | 1 578 | 1 755 | 1 877 | 1 844 | 1 056 |
| 5110 General taxes on goods and services | .. | .. | .. | 526 | 958 | 774 | 864 | 882 | 892 | 518 |
| 5111 Value added taxes | .. | .. | .. | 496 | 893 | 653 | 744 | 789 | 804 | 496 |
| VAT revenues (gross) | .. | .. | .. | 646 | 1 204 | 943 | 987 | 1 049 | 1 014 | 733 |
| VAT refunds | .. | .. | .. | -150 | -311 | -290 | -243 | -259 | -210 | -237 |
| 5112 Sales tax | .. | .. | .. | 0 | 0 | 0 | 0 | 0 | 0 | 0 |
| 5113 Other | .. | .. | .. | 31 | 65 | 121 | 121 | 93 | 88 | 22 |
| 5120 Taxes on specific goods and services | .. | .. | .. | 350 | 690 | 804 | 890 | 995 | 952 | 538 |
| 5121 Excises | .. | .. | .. | 88 | 145 | 246 | 313 | 394 | 370 | 185 |
| Environmental levy | .. | .. | .. | 0 | 0 | 67 | 108 | 161 | 166 | 55 |
| Import excises | .. | .. | .. | 20 | 43 | 47 | 54 | 61 | 41 | 13 |
| Domestic excises | .. | .. | .. | 81 | 106 | 134 | 154 | 174 | 167 | 125 |
| Other excises | .. | .. | .. | 5 | 2 | 2 | 2 | 2 | 2 | 1 |
| Rebates | .. | .. | .. | -17 | -6 | -5 | -5 | -4 | -6 | -9 |
| 5122 Profits of fiscal monopolies | .. | .. | .. | 0 | 0 | 0 | 0 | 0 | 0 | 0 |
| 5123 Customs and import duties | .. | .. | .. | 252 | 392 | 398 | 419 | 441 | 420 | 305 |
| 5124 Taxes on exports | .. | .. | .. | 9 | 10 | 10 | 10 | 9 | 8 | 8 |
| 5125 Taxes on investment goods | .. | .. | .. | 0 | 0 | 0 | 0 | 0 | 0 | 0 |
| 5126 Taxes on specific services | .. | .. | .. | 0 | 143 | 150 | 148 | 150 | 154 | 39 |
| 5127 Other taxes on internat. trade and transactions | .. | .. | .. | 0 | 0 | 0 | 0 | 0 | 0 | 0 |
| 5128 Other taxes | .. | .. | .. | 0 | 0 | 0 | 0 | 0 | 0 | 0 |
| 5130 Unallocable between 5110 and 5120 | .. | .. | .. | 0 | 0 | 0 | 0 | 0 | 0 | 0 |

| | 1997 | 2000 | 2007 | 2010 | 2015 | 2016 | 2017 | 2018 | 2019 | 2020 |
|---|---|---|---|---|---|---|---|---|---|---|
| 5200 Taxes on use of goods and to perform activities | .. | .. | .. | 2 | 2 | 2 | 2 | 2 | 2 | 1 |
| 5210 Recurrent taxes | .. | .. | .. | 2 | 1 | 1 | 2 | 2 | 2 | 1 |
| 5211 Paid by households: motor vehicles | .. | .. | .. | 0 | 0 | 0 | 0 | 0 | 0 | 0 |
| 5212 Paid by others: motor vehicles | .. | .. | .. | 0 | 0 | 0 | 0 | 0 | 0 | 0 |
| 5213 Paid in respect of other goods | .. | .. | .. | 2 | 1 | 1 | 2 | 2 | 2 | 1 |
| 5220 Non-recurrent taxes | .. | .. | .. | 0 | 0 | 0 | 0 | 0 | 0 | 0 |
| 5300 Unallocable between 5100 and 5200 | .. | .. | .. | 0 | 0 | 0 | 0 | 0 | 0 | 0 |
| **6000 Other taxes** | **..** | **..** | **..** | **0** | **0** | **0** | **0** | **0** | **0** | **0** |
| 6100 Paid solely by business | .. | .. | .. | .. | .. | .. | .. | .. | .. | .. |
| 6200 Other | .. | .. | .. | .. | .. | .. | .. | .. | .. | .. |

.. Not available

Note: Year ending 31st December.

The data are on a cash basis.

Figures exclude tax revenues collected by sub-national governments as the data are not available.

The resource tax and the tourist VAT refund registration fee (about 0.5% of GDP in 2020) are not included in tax revenues. These revenues are considered as non-tax revenue in accordance with the OECD classification, as set out in the Interpretative Guide in Annex A.

Source: Revenue and Customs Service of Fiji.

StatLink https://stat.link/1c0u7h

## Table 4.8. Indonesia: Details of tax revenue

Billion IDR

| | 1997 | 2000 | 2007 | 2010 | 2015 | 2016 | 2017 | 2018 | 2019 | 2020 |
|---|---|---|---|---|---|---|---|---|---|---|
| **Total tax revenue** | **57 340** | **119 697** | **528 453** | **779 484** | **1 395 962** | **1 489 357** | **1 578 033** | **1 776 622** | **1 834 711** | **1 555 331** |
| **1000 Taxes on income, profits and capital gains** | **27 062** | **57 073** | **238 431** | **357 046** | **602 308** | **666 212** | **646 793** | **749 977** | **772 266** | **594 033** |
| 1100 Of individuals | .. | .. | 77 250 | 62 221 | 132 761 | 209 879 | 149 726 | 163 346 | 179 370 | 168 150 |
| 1110 On income and profits | .. | .. | .. | 59 540 | 128 550 | 205 754 | 145 606 | 156 783 | 172 444 | 162 111 |
| 1120 On capital gains | .. | .. | .. | 2 682 | 4 211 | 4 124 | 4 120 | 6 563 | 6 927 | 6 039 |
| 1200 Corporate | .. | .. | 161 181 | 294 824 | 469 547 | 456 334 | 497 067 | 586 631 | 592 895 | 425 883 |
| 1210 On profits | .. | .. | .. | 287 843 | 434 471 | 426 922 | 486 885 | 577 541 | 585 031 | 419 083 |
| 1220 On capital gains | .. | .. | .. | 6 981 | 35 076 | 29 412 | 10 182 | 9 090 | 7 865 | 6 800 |
| 1300 Unallocable between 1100 and 1200 | 27 062 | 57 073 | 0 | 0 | 0 | 0 | 0 | 0 | 0 | 0 |
| **2000 Social security contributions** | **..** | **..** | **..** | **..** | **7 715** | **47 220** | **54 401** | **63 643** | **79 631** | **91 024** |
| 2100 Employees | .. | .. | .. | .. | 1 590 | 1 829 | 2 121 | 2 494 | 2 814 | 1 825 |
| 2110 On a payroll basis | .. | .. | .. | .. | .. | .. | .. | .. | .. | .. |
| 2120 On an income tax basis | .. | .. | .. | .. | .. | .. | .. | .. | .. | .. |
| 2200 Employers | .. | .. | .. | .. | 3 505 | 4 108 | 4 650 | 5 322 | 5 926 | 3 791 |
| 2210 On a payroll basis | .. | .. | .. | .. | .. | .. | .. | .. | .. | .. |
| 2220 On an income tax basis | .. | .. | .. | .. | .. | .. | .. | .. | .. | .. |
| 2300 Self-employed or non-employed | .. | .. | .. | .. | .. | .. | .. | .. | .. | .. |
| 2310 On a payroll basis | .. | .. | .. | .. | .. | .. | .. | .. | .. | .. |
| 2320 On an income tax basis | .. | .. | .. | .. | .. | .. | .. | .. | .. | .. |
| 2400 Unallocable between 2100, 2200 and 2300 | .. | .. | .. | .. | 2 620 | 41 283 | 47 630 | 55 827 | 70 891 | 85 409 |
| 2410 On a payroll basis | .. | .. | .. | .. | .. | .. | .. | .. | .. | .. |
| 2420 On an income tax basis | .. | .. | .. | .. | .. | .. | .. | .. | .. | .. |
| **3000 Taxes on payroll and workforce** | **0** | **0** | **0** | **0** | **0** | **0** | **0** | **0** | **0** | **0** |
| **4000 Taxes on property** | **2 413** | **4 456** | **32 161** | **40 537** | **33 826** | **24 253** | **21 854** | **24 901** | **26 744** | **26 038** |
| 4100 Recurrent taxes on immovable property | 2 413 | 3 525 | 23 724 | 28 581 | 29 250 | 19 443 | 16 770 | 19 445 | 21 146 | 20 954 |
| 4110 Households | .. | .. | .. | .. | .. | .. | .. | .. | .. | .. |
| 4120 Others | .. | .. | .. | .. | .. | .. | .. | .. | .. | .. |
| 4200 Recurrent taxes on net wealth | 0 | 0 | 0 | 0 | 0 | 0 | 0 | 0 | 0 | 0 |
| 4210 Individual | .. | .. | .. | .. | .. | .. | .. | .. | .. | .. |
| 4220 Corporate | .. | .. | .. | .. | .. | .. | .. | .. | .. | .. |
| 4300 Estate, inheritance and gift taxes | 0 | 0 | 0 | 0 | 0 | 0 | 0 | 0 | 0 | 0 |
| 4310 Estate and inheritance taxes | .. | .. | .. | .. | .. | .. | .. | .. | .. | .. |
| 4320 Gift taxes | .. | .. | .. | .. | .. | .. | .. | .. | .. | .. |
| 4400 Taxes on financial and capital transactions | 0 | 931 | 8 438 | 11 956 | 4 576 | 4 809 | 5 083 | 5 456 | 5 598 | 5 085 |
| Tax on acquisition of land and buildings | .. | 931 | 8 438 | 11 956 | 4 576 | 4 809 | 5 083 | 5 456 | 5 598 | 5 085 |
| 4500 Non-recurrent taxes | 0 | 0 | 0 | 0 | 0 | 0 | 0 | 0 | 0 | 0 |
| 4510 On net wealth | .. | .. | .. | .. | .. | .. | .. | .. | .. | .. |
| 4520 Other non-recurrent taxes | .. | .. | .. | .. | .. | .. | .. | .. | .. | .. |
| 4600 Other recurrent taxes on property | 0 | 0 | 0 | 0 | 0 | 0 | 0 | 0 | 0 | 0 |
| **5000 Taxes on goods and services** | **27 274** | **53 547** | **220 143** | **325 685** | **603 869** | **592 291** | **674 209** | **743 395** | **745 592** | **663 844** |
| 5100 Taxes on production, sale, transfer, etc | 27 274 | 53 547 | 220 143 | 325 685 | 603 869 | 592 291 | 674 209 | 743 395 | 745 592 | 663 844 |
| 5110 General taxes | 20 351 | 35 232 | 154 527 | 230 605 | 424 288 | 413 295 | 481 707 | 537 924 | 532 116 | 450 813 |
| 5111 Value added taxes | 20 351 | 35 232 | 154 527 | 218 133 | 410 391 | 396 042 | 463 528 | 520 390 | 515 972 | 441 773 |
| 5112 Sales tax | 0 | 0 | 0 | 12 472 | 13 897 | 17 253 | 18 179 | 17 534 | 16 144 | 9 041 |
| 5113 Other | 0 | 0 | 0 | 0 | 0 | 0 | 0 | 0 | 0 | 0 |
| 5120 Taxes on specific goods and services | 6 923 | 18 315 | 65 616 | 95 080 | 179 581 | 178 996 | 192 502 | 205 470 | 213 476 | 213 031 |
| 5121 Excises | 4 263 | 11 287 | 44 679 | 66 166 | 144 641 | 143 525 | 153 288 | 159 589 | 172 422 | 176 309 |
| 5122 Profits of fiscal monopolies | 0 | 0 | 0 | 0 | 0 | 0 | 0 | 0 | 0 | 0 |
| 5123 Customs and import duties | 2 579 | 6 697 | 16 699 | 20 017 | 31 213 | 32 472 | 35 066 | 39 117 | 37 527 | 32 443 |
| 5124 Taxes on exports | 81 | 331 | 4 237 | 8 898 | 3 727 | 2 999 | 4 147 | 6 765 | 3 527 | 4 278 |
| 5125 Taxes on investment goods | 0 | 0 | 0 | 0 | 0 | 0 | 0 | 0 | 0 | 0 |
| 5126 Taxes on specific services | 0 | 0 | 0 | 0 | 0 | 0 | 0 | 0 | 0 | 0 |
| 5127 Other taxes on internat. trade and transactions | 0 | 0 | 0 | 0 | 0 | 0 | 0 | 0 | 0 | 0 |
| 5128 Other taxes | 0 | 0 | 0 | 0 | 0 | 0 | 0 | 0 | 0 | 0 |
| 5130 Unallocable between 5110 and 5120 | 0 | 0 | 0 | 0 | 0 | 0 | 0 | 0 | 0 | 0 |
| 5200 Taxes on use of goods and to perform activities | 0 | 0 | 0 | 0 | 0 | 0 | 0 | 0 | 0 | 0 |
| 5210 Recurrent taxes | .. | .. | .. | .. | .. | .. | .. | .. | .. | .. |
| 5211 Paid by households: motor vehicles | .. | .. | .. | .. | .. | .. | .. | .. | .. | .. |
| 5212 Paid by others: motor vehicles | .. | .. | .. | .. | .. | .. | .. | .. | .. | .. |
| 5213 Paid in respect of other goods | .. | .. | .. | .. | .. | .. | .. | .. | .. | .. |
| 5220 Non-recurrent taxes | .. | .. | .. | .. | .. | .. | .. | .. | .. | .. |
| 5300 Unallocable between 5100 and 5200 | 0 | 0 | 0 | 0 | 0 | 0 | 0 | 0 | 0 | 0 |
| **6000 Other taxes** | **591** | **4 621** | **37 718** | **56 216** | **148 244** | **159 380** | **180 775** | **194 707** | **210 479** | **180 392** |
| 6100 Paid solely by business | 0 | 0 | 0 | 0 | 0 | 0 | 0 | 0 | 0 | 0 |
| 6200 Other | 591 | 4 621 | 37 718 | 56 216 | 148 244 | 159 380 | 180 775 | 194 707 | 210 479 | 180 392 |
| Other local level | 0 | 3 784 | 34 981 | 56 177 | 147 829 | 157 166 | 180 101 | 194 190 | 208 938 | 179 170 |
| Other non local level | 591 | 837 | 2 738 | 39 | 416 | 2 214 | 674 | 517 | 1 541 | 1 221 |

.. Not available

Note: Year ending 31st December.
The data are on a cash basis.
Revenue data in 2016 and 2017 include revenues from the "Tax Amnesty" policy which will not be repeated in the following year.
Revenue data since 2008 have been updated based on more detailed classification provided by the government.
Heading 2000: Social security contribution data are obtained from BPJS Kesehatan and BPJS Ketenagakerjaan. The government of Indonesia does not consider social security contributions as part of tax revenues.
Heading 2100: Includes Death Benefit (JK), a life insurance with payment for participants upon the death of their wives/husbands/children or for families upon the death of participants.
Heading 2200: Includes Work Accident Insurance (JKK) which provides protection against the risks of work-related accidents.
Heading 2400: Includes Pension Insurance (JP), and mandatory contributions from BPJS Health for formal workers. Data in 2015 only include Pension Insurance (JP). Contributions from the BPJS Health since 2018 have been estimated.

Source: Fiscal Policy Agency, Ministry of Finance; BPJS Kesehatan (Social Security Administrator for Health); BPJS Ketenagakerjaan (Employees Social Security System).

StatLink https://stat.link/ue015l

## Table 4.9. Japan: Details of tax revenue

Billion JPY

| | 1997 | 2000 | 2007 | 2010 | 2015 | 2016 | 2017 | 2018 | 2019 | 2020 |
|---|---|---|---|---|---|---|---|---|---|---|
| **Total tax revenue** | **139 617** | **136 236** | **146 248** | **132 484** | **163 533** | **164 970** | **171 805** | **175 564** | **175 380** | **98 985** |
| **1000 Taxes on income, profits and capital gains** | **51 673** | **47 398** | **53 174** | **40 034** | **50 969** | **50 448** | **52 658** | **56 083** | **53 994** | **49 150** |
| 1100 Of individuals | 29 809 | 28 677 | 28 600 | 24 663 | 30 847 | 30 670 | 32 325 | 33 492 | 32 947 | 32 321 |
| 1110 On income and profits | 29 809 | 28 677 | 28 600 | 24 663 | 30 847 | 30 670 | 32 325 | 33 492 | 32 947 | 32 321 |
| Income tax | 19 183 | 18 789 | 16 080 | 12 984 | 18 178 | 17 978 | 19 276 | 20 316 | 19 571 | 18 884 |
| Prefectural inhabitants tax | 3 183 | 3 621 | 5 008 | 4 699 | 5 252 | 5 128 | 5 376 | 4 863 | 4 840 | 4 905 |
| Municipal inhabitants tax | 7 172 | 6 044 | 7 294 | 6 795 | 7 224 | 7 365 | 7 471 | 8 106 | 8 325 | 8 319 |
| Enterprise tax | 271 | 223 | 218 | 184 | 194 | 198 | 203 | 207 | 211 | 213 |
| 1120 On capital gains | 0 | 0 | 0 | 0 | 0 | 0 | 0 | 0 | 0 | 0 |
| 1200 Corporate | 21 864 | 18 721 | 24 573 | 15 372 | 20 122 | 19 778 | 20 333 | 22 591 | 21 046 | 16 828 |
| 1210 On profits | 21 864 | 18 721 | 24 573 | 15 372 | 20 122 | 19 778 | 20 333 | 22 591 | 21 046 | 16 828 |
| Corporation tax | 13 477 | 11 747 | 14 744 | 8 968 | 10 832 | 10 332 | 11 995 | 12 318 | 10 797 | 8 041 |
| Prefectural inhabitants tax | 1 026 | 879 | 1 206 | 777 | 859 | 763 | 762 | 835 | 821 | 531 |
| Municipal inhabitants tax | 2 532 | 2 176 | 3 015 | 1 954 | 2 324 | 2 392 | 2 224 | 2 427 | 2 395 | 1 732 |
| Enterprise tax | 4 830 | 3 918 | 5 608 | 2 253 | 3 510 | 4 395 | 3 991 | 4 243 | 4 385 | 3 764 |
| Local special corporate tax | 0 | 0 | 0 | 1 420 | 2 081 | 1 782 | 1 858 | 2 088 | 2 044 | 1 016 |
| Local corporate tax | 0 | 0 | 0 | 0 | 516 | 629 | 654 | 681 | 604 | 1 034 |
| 1220 On capital gains | 0 | 0 | 0 | 0 | 0 | 0 | 0 | 0 | 0 | 0 |
| 1300 Unallocable between 1100 and 1200 | 0 | 0 | 0 | 0 | 0 | 0 | 0 | 0 | 0 | 0 |
| **2000 Social security contributions** | **47 861** | **47 968** | **53 325** | **54 461** | **64 465** | **66 622** | **68 616** | **70 588** | **71 993** | **..** |
| 2100 Employees | 19 682 | 19 830 | 21 975 | 23 593 | 28 224 | 29 312 | 30 348 | 31 243 | 31 954 | .. |
| 2110 On a payroll basis | 19 682 | 19 830 | 21 975 | 23 593 | 28 224 | 29 312 | 30 348 | 31 243 | 31 954 | .. |
| 2120 On an income tax basis | 0 | 0 | 0 | 0 | 0 | 0 | 0 | 0 | 0 | .. |
| 2200 Employers | 22 826 | 22 456 | 24 243 | 24 674 | 29 479 | 30 540 | 31 648 | 32 664 | 33 488 | .. |
| 2210 On a payroll basis | 22 826 | 22 456 | 24 243 | 24 674 | 29 479 | 30 540 | 31 648 | 32 664 | 33 488 | .. |
| 2220 On an income tax basis | 0 | 0 | 0 | 0 | 0 | 0 | 0 | 0 | 0 | .. |
| 2300 Self-employed or non-employed | 5 352 | 5 683 | 7 108 | 6 194 | 6 763 | 6 771 | 6 620 | 6 681 | 6 552 | .. |
| 2310 On a payroll basis | 5 352 | 5 683 | 7 108 | 6 194 | 6 763 | 6 771 | 6 620 | 6 681 | 6 552 | .. |
| 2320 On an income tax basis | 0 | 0 | 0 | 0 | 0 | 0 | 0 | 0 | 0 | .. |
| 2400 Unallocable between 2100, 2200 and 2300 | 0 | 0 | 0 | 0 | 0 | 0 | 0 | 0 | 0 | .. |
| 2410 On a payroll basis | .. | .. | .. | .. | .. | .. | .. | .. | .. | .. |
| 2420 On an income tax basis | .. | .. | .. | .. | .. | .. | .. | .. | .. | .. |
| **3000 Taxes on payroll and workforce** | **0** | **0** | **0** | **0** | **0** | **0** | **0** | **0** | **0** | **0** |
| **4000 Taxes on property** | **15 679** | **14 294** | **13 138** | **12 878** | **13 400** | **13 772** | **14 073** | **14 196** | **14 340** | **14 119** |
| 4100 Recurrent taxes on immovable property | 10 410 | 10 414 | 9 949 | 10 225 | 10 005 | 10 165 | 10 323 | 10 386 | 10 612 | 10 669 |
| Prefectural property tax | 8 | 11 | 14 | 5 | 2 | 3 | 4 | 11 | 8 | 9 |
| Municipal property tax | 8 822 | 9 041 | 8 729 | 8 961 | 8 755 | 9 077 | 9 025 | 9 083 | 9 286 | 9 339 |
| City planning tax | 1 326 | 1 318 | 1 202 | 1 256 | 1 244 | 1 262 | 1 277 | 1 291 | 1 318 | 1 322 |
| Special landholding tax | 94 | 43 | 4 | 3 | 3 | 7 | 1 | 0 | 0 | 0 |
| Water and land utilization tax | 0 | 0 | 0 | 0 | 0 | 0 | 0 | 0 | 0 | 0 |
| Land value tax | 160 | 1 | 0 | 0 | 0 | 0 | 0 | 0 | 0 | 0 |
| 4110 Households | .. | .. | .. | .. | .. | .. | .. | .. | .. | .. |
| 4120 Others | .. | .. | .. | .. | .. | .. | .. | .. | .. | .. |
| 4200 Recurrent taxes on net wealth | 0 | 0 | 0 | 0 | 0 | 0 | 0 | 0 | 0 | 0 |
| 4210 Individual | .. | .. | .. | .. | .. | .. | .. | .. | .. | .. |
| 4220 Corporate | .. | .. | .. | .. | .. | .. | .. | .. | .. | .. |
| 4300 Estate, inheritance and gift taxes | 2 413 | 1 782 | 1 503 | 1 250 | 1 968 | 2 131 | 2 292 | 2 333 | 2 301 | 2 231 |
| 4310 Estate and inheritance taxes | .. | .. | .. | .. | .. | .. | .. | .. | .. | .. |
| Inheritance tax | .. | .. | .. | .. | .. | .. | .. | .. | .. | .. |
| 4320 Gift taxes | .. | .. | .. | .. | .. | .. | .. | .. | .. | .. |
| Tax on gifts | .. | .. | .. | .. | .. | .. | .. | .. | .. | .. |
| 4400 Taxes on financial and capital transactions | 2 856 | 2 099 | 1 686 | 1 403 | 1 426 | 1 476 | 1 458 | 1 477 | 1 427 | 1 219 |
| Bourse tax | 40 | 0 | 0 | 0 | 0 | 0 | 0 | 0 | 0 | 0 |
| Securities transaction | 404 | 0 | 0 | 0 | 0 | 0 | 0 | 0 | 0 | 0 |
| Bank of Japan note issue tax | 0 | 0 | 0 | 0 | 0 | 0 | 0 | 0 | 0 | 0 |
| Stamp revenues | 1 681 | 1 532 | 1 202 | 1 024 | 1 050 | 1 079 | 1 052 | 1 073 | 1 023 | 870 |
| Real property acquisition tax | 731 | 567 | 485 | 379 | 377 | 397 | 407 | 404 | 404 | 349 |
| 4500 Non-recurrent taxes | 0 | 0 | 0 | 0 | 0 | 0 | 0 | 0 | 0 | 0 |
| 4510 On net wealth | .. | .. | .. | .. | .. | .. | .. | .. | .. | .. |
| 4520 Other non-recurrent taxes | .. | .. | .. | .. | .. | .. | .. | .. | .. | .. |
| 4600 Other recurrent taxes on property | 0 | 0 | 0 | 0 | 0 | 0 | 0 | 0 | 0 | 0 |
| **5000 Taxes on goods and services** | **24 058** | **26 227** | **26 256** | **24 730** | **34 286** | **33 711** | **36 031** | **34 252** | **34 599** | **35 279** |
| 5100 Taxes on production, sale, transfer, etc. | 21 132 | 23 180 | 23 241 | 22 160 | 31 871 | 31 254 | 33 582 | 31 754 | 32 046 | 32 694 |
| 5110 General taxes | 10 112 | 12 350 | 12 841 | 12 675 | 22 400 | 21 931 | 22 249 | 22 496 | 23 148 | 24 608 |
| 5111 Value added taxes | 10 112 | 12 350 | 12 841 | 12 675 | 22 400 | 21 931 | 22 249 | 22 496 | 23 148 | 24 608 |
| 5112 Sales tax | 0 | 0 | 0 | 0 | 0 | 0 | 0 | 0 | 0 | 0 |
| 5113 Other | 0 | 0 | 0 | 0 | 0 | 0 | 0 | 0 | 0 | 0 |
| 5120 Taxes on specific goods and services | 11 021 | 10 830 | 10 400 | 9 485 | 9 470 | 9 323 | 11 333 | 9 258 | 8 898 | 8 086 |

| | 1997 | 2000 | 2007 | 2010 | 2015 | 2016 | 2017 | 2018 | 2019 | 2020 |
|---|---|---|---|---|---|---|---|---|---|---|
| 5121 Excise duties | 9 764 | 9 837 | 9 374 | 8 622 | 8 351 | 8 316 | 10 241 | 8 121 | 7 891 | 7 214 |
| Liquor tax | 1 962 | 1 816 | 1 524 | 1 389 | 1 338 | 1 320 | 1 304 | 1 275 | 1 247 | 1 143 |
| Sugar excises | 0 | 0 | 0 | 0 | 0 | 0 | 0 | 0 | 0 | 0 |
| Local gasoline tax | 276 | 296 | 302 | 294 | 264 | 261 | 256 | 251 | 244 | 219 |
| Gasoline tax | 2 583 | 2 769 | 2 820 | 2 750 | 2 465 | 2 434 | 2 396 | 2 348 | 2 281 | 2 047 |
| Liquefied petroleum gas tax | 29 | 28 | 27 | 24 | 18 | 17 | 17 | 15 | 14 | 12 |
| Aviation fuel tax | 104 | 104 | 104 | 89 | 66 | 66 | 67 | 68 | 65 | 14 |
| Commodity tax | 0 | 0 | 0 | 0 | 0 | 0 | 0 | 0 | 0 | 0 |
| Playing-card tax | 0 | 0 | 0 | 0 | 0 | 0 | 0 | 0 | 0 | 0 |
| Prefectural tobacco tax | 248 | 282 | 278 | 256 | 153 | 149 | 141 | 139 | 140 | 137 |
| Municipal tobacco tax | 799 | 865 | 853 | 788 | 936 | 911 | 862 | 850 | 854 | 841 |
| Timber delivery tax | 0 | 0 | 0 | 0 | 0 | 0 | 0 | 0 | 0 | 0 |
| Mineral product tax | 2 | 2 | 2 | 2 | 2 | 2 | 2 | 2 | 2 | 2 |
| Electricity and gas tax | 0 | 0 | 0 | 0 | 0 | 0 | 0 | 0 | 0 | 0 |
| Diesel oil tax | 1 331 | 1 208 | 1 034 | 918 | 925 | 933 | 949 | 958 | 945 | 903 |
| Vehicle acquisition tax | 562 | 464 | 425 | 192 | 137 | 146 | 190 | 198 | 104 | 0 |
| Promotion of power resources development tax | 354 | 375 | 352 | 349 | 316 | 320 | 326 | 322 | 316 | 315 |
| Petroleum and coal tax | 497 | 489 | 513 | 502 | 630 | 702 | 691 | 701 | 638 | 599 |
| Tobacco tax | 1 018 | 876 | 925 | 908 | 954 | 914 | 864 | 861 | 874 | 862 |
| Special tobacco tax | 0 | 264 | 214 | 163 | 148 | 141 | 134 | 125 | 124 | 116 |
| 5122 Profits of fiscal monopolies | 0 | 0 | 0 | 0 | 0 | 0 | 0 | 0 | 0 | 0 |
| Monopoly profits | .. | .. | .. | .. | .. | .. | .. | .. | .. | .. |
| 5123 Customs and import duties | 1 012 | 877 | 941 | 786 | 1 049 | 939 | 1 024 | 1 071 | 941 | 825 |
| Customs duty | 1 012 | 877 | 941 | 786 | 1 049 | 939 | 1 024 | 1 071 | 941 | 825 |
| 5124 Taxes on exports | 0 | 0 | 0 | 0 | 0 | 0 | 0 | 0 | 0 | 0 |
| 5125 Taxes on investment goods | 0 | 0 | 0 | 0 | 0 | 0 | 0 | 0 | 0 | 0 |
| 5126 Taxes on specific services | 245 | 116 | 85 | 77 | 70 | 68 | 67 | 66 | 66 | 47 |
| Travel tax | 0 | 0 | 0 | 0 | 0 | 0 | 0 | 0 | 0 | 0 |
| Admission tax | 0 | 0 | 0 | 0 | 0 | 0 | 0 | 0 | 0 | 0 |
| Local entertainment tax | 0 | 0 | 0 | 0 | 0 | 0 | 0 | 0 | 0 | 0 |
| Golf course utilization tax | 98 | 81 | 60 | 55 | 48 | 46 | 45 | 43 | 43 | 36 |
| Meal and lodging tax | 0 | 0 | 0 | 0 | 0 | 0 | 0 | 0 | 0 | 0 |
| Special local consumption tax | 125 | 12 | 0 | 0 | 0 | 0 | 0 | 0 | 0 | 0 |
| Bathing tax | 22 | 23 | 25 | 22 | 23 | 22 | 23 | 22 | 23 | 12 |
| 5127 Other taxes on internat. trade and transactions | 0 | 0 | 0 | 0 | 0 | 0 | 0 | 0 | 0 | 0 |
| 5128 Other taxes | 0 | 0 | 0 | 0 | 0 | 0 | 0 | 0 | 0 | 0 |
| 5130 Unallocable between 5110 and 5120 | 0 | 0 | 0 | 0 | 0 | 0 | 0 | 0 | 0 | 0 |
| 5200 Taxes on use of goods and perform activities | 2 926 | 3 047 | 3 015 | 2 570 | 2 416 | 2 457 | 2 450 | 2 498 | 2 553 | 2 585 |
| 5210 Recurrent taxes | 2 905 | 3 027 | 2 993 | 2 548 | 2 393 | 2 435 | 2 427 | 2 475 | 2 530 | 2 562 |
| Automobile tax | 1 705 | 1 765 | 1 717 | 1 616 | 1 543 | 1 535 | 1 541 | 1 550 | 1 588 | 1 600 |
| Light vehicle tax | 113 | 125 | 164 | 178 | 200 | 238 | 249 | 258 | 269 | 282 |
| Motor vehicle tonnage tax | 1 084 | 1 134 | 1 110 | 753 | 649 | 660 | 637 | 665 | 671 | 680 |
| Hunter licence tax | 2 | 2 | 0 | 0 | 0 | 0 | 0 | 0 | 0 | 0 |
| Hunting tax | 1 | 1 | 2 | 2 | 1 | 1 | 1 | 1 | 1 | 1 |
| Mine lot tax | 1 | 1 | 0 | 0 | 0 | 0 | 0 | 0 | 0 | 0 |
| 5211 Paid by households: motor vehicles | .. | .. | .. | .. | .. | .. | .. | .. | .. | .. |
| 5212 Paid by others: motor vehicles | .. | .. | .. | .. | .. | .. | .. | .. | .. | .. |
| 5213 Paid in respect of other goods | .. | .. | .. | .. | .. | .. | .. | .. | .. | .. |
| 5220 Non-recurrent taxes | 21 | 20 | 22 | 21 | 22 | 22 | 22 | 23 | 23 | 23 |
| 5300 Unallocable between 5100 and 5200 | 0 | 0 | 0 | 0 | 0 | 0 | 0 | 0 | 0 | 0 |
| **6000 Other taxes** | **346** | **348** | **356** | **381** | **413** | **418** | **427** | **445** | **454** | **437** |
| 6100 Paid solely by business | 325 | 324 | 313 | 330 | 361 | 366 | 371 | 378 | 387 | 377 |
| Business office tax | 325 | 324 | 313 | 330 | 361 | 366 | 371 | 378 | 387 | 377 |
| 6200 Other | 22 | 24 | 43 | 52 | 52 | 52 | 56 | 67 | 68 | 61 |
| Taxes not in local tax law | 21 | 24 | 43 | 52 | 52 | 52 | 56 | 65 | 67 | 61 |
| Other | 0 | 0 | 0 | 0 | 0 | 0 | 0 | 2 | 1 | 0 |

.. Not available

Note: Data are on a fiscal year basis beginning 1st April.

From 1990, data are on accrual basis.

The figures for different groups of taxes are reported on different reporting bases, namely: Social security contributions (heading 2000): in principle accrual basis, Central government taxes: accrual basis (revenues accrued during the fiscal year plus cash receipts collected before the end of May (the end of April until 1977), Local government taxes: accrual basis (due to be paid during the fiscal year and cash receipts collected before the end of May).

The Japanese authorities take the view that the Enterprise tax (classified in 1100 and 1200) and the Mineral product tax (classified in 5121) should be classified in heading 6000 since under articles 72 and 519 of the Local Tax Law these taxes are regarded as levies on the business or mining activity itself.

Heading 2000 includes some unidentifiable voluntary contributions.

Heading 2300: Includes contibutions to the National pension, National Health Insurance and the Farmer's pension fund. Contributions to the Farmer's pension fund are not available for the years before 1999.

Heading 4100: Municipal property tax, includes Prefectural property tax from 1990 to 1994 because data is not available to provide a breakdown.

Heading 5121: Municipal tobacco tax, includes Prefectural tobacco tax from 1990 to 1994 because data is not available to provide a breakdown.

Heading 5121: In sub-item Petroleum and coal tax, the data before 2003 refer to petroleum tax.

Source: Tax Bureau, Ministry of Finance.

StatLink https://stat.link/2eu8c1

## Table 4.10. Kazakhstan: Details of tax revenue

Million KZT

| | 1997 | 2000 | 2007 | 2010 | 2015 | 2016 | 2017 | 2018 | 2019 | 2020 |
|---|---|---|---|---|---|---|---|---|---|---|
| **Total tax revenue** | .. | **517 777** | **3 349 317** | **5 182 379** | **6 352 963** | **7 006 053** | **8 707 756** | **10 484 416** | **11 594 940** | **9 934 305** |
| **1000 Taxes on income, profits and capital gains** | .. | **214 545** | **1 797 785** | **2 072 357** | **2 467 977** | **2 610 413** | **3 128 907** | **3 972 562** | **4 204 258** | **3 500 145** |
| 1100 Of individuals | .. | 51 016 | 221 025 | 312 332 | 598 807 | 691 778 | 750 212 | 838 394 | 876 324 | 929 588 |
| 1110 On income and profits | .. | 51 016 | 221 025 | 312 332 | 598 807 | 691 778 | 750 212 | 838 394 | 876 324 | 929 588 |
| From non-foreign citizens | .. | 51 016 | 221 025 | 276 089 | 566 974 | 688 023 | 744 662 | 831 567 | 869 181 | 923 762 |
| From foreign citizens | .. | 0 | 0 | 36 243 | 31 832 | 3 755 | 5 550 | 6 828 | 7 143 | 5 826 |
| 1120 On capital gains | .. | .. | .. | .. | .. | .. | .. | .. | .. | .. |
| 1200 Corporate | .. | 163 529 | 1 576 760 | 1 760 025 | 1 869 170 | 1 918 635 | 2 378 695 | 3 134 167 | 3 327 934 | 2 570 557 |
| 1210 On profits | .. | 163 529 | 1 576 760 | 1 760 025 | 1 869 170 | 1 918 635 | 2 378 695 | 3 134 167 | 3 327 934 | 2 570 557 |
| From non-oil companies | .. | 163 529 | 766 979 | 847 057 | 1 236 561 | 1 445 066 | 1 545 293 | 1 703 353 | 1 975 134 | 2 045 260 |
| From oil companies | .. | 0 | 0 | 0 | 0 | 0 | 0 | 0 | 0 | 0 |
| From oil companies to National Fund | .. | 0 | 809 782 | 912 968 | 632 609 | 473 569 | 833 402 | 1 430 814 | 1 352 800 | 525 297 |
| 1220 On capital gains | .. | .. | .. | .. | .. | .. | .. | .. | .. | .. |
| 1300 Unallocable between 1100 and 1200 | .. | 0 | 0 | 0 | 0 | 0 | 0 | 0 | 0 | 0 |
| **2000 Social security contributions** | .. | **0** | **49 904** | **131 041** | **240 590** | **264 710** | **297 615** | **330 852** | **369 835** | **526 657** |
| 2100 Employees | .. | .. | .. | .. | .. | .. | .. | .. | .. | .. |
| 2110 On a payroll basis | .. | .. | .. | .. | .. | .. | .. | .. | .. | .. |
| 2120 On an income tax basis | .. | .. | .. | .. | .. | .. | .. | .. | .. | .. |
| 2200 Employers | .. | .. | .. | .. | .. | .. | .. | .. | .. | .. |
| 2210 On a payroll basis | .. | .. | .. | .. | .. | .. | .. | .. | .. | .. |
| 2220 On an income tax basis | .. | .. | .. | .. | .. | .. | .. | .. | .. | .. |
| 2300 Self-employed or non-employed | .. | .. | .. | .. | .. | .. | .. | .. | .. | .. |
| 2310 On a payroll basis | .. | .. | .. | .. | .. | .. | .. | .. | .. | .. |
| 2320 On an income tax basis | .. | .. | .. | .. | .. | .. | .. | .. | .. | .. |
| 2400 Unallocable between 2100, 2200 and 2300 | .. | .. | 49 904 | 131 041 | 240 590 | 264 710 | 297 615 | 330 852 | 369 835 | 526 657 |
| 2410 On a payroll basis | .. | .. | .. | .. | .. | .. | .. | .. | .. | .. |
| 2420 On an income tax basis | .. | .. | .. | .. | .. | .. | .. | .. | .. | .. |
| **3000 Taxes on payroll and workforce** | .. | **99 082** | **295 733** | **253 830** | **464 674** | **530 440** | **576 607** | **618 505** | **696 635** | **727 139** |
| The social tax | .. | 99 082 | 295 733 | 253 830 | 464 674 | 530 440 | 576 607 | 618 505 | 696 635 | 727 139 |
| **4000 Taxes on property** | .. | **21 013** | **73 822** | **124 632** | **226 853** | **227 862** | **257 012** | **298 617** | **322 481** | **309 811** |
| 4100 Recurrent taxes on immovable property | .. | 20 504 | 71 592 | 122 146 | 224 752 | 226 815 | 255 868 | 298 455 | 322 481 | 309 811 |
| 4110 Households | .. | 3 230 | 2 936 | 4 402 | 10 164 | 11 906 | 3 922 | 22 374 | 29 386 | 29 289 |
| 4120 Others | .. | 17 274 | 68 655 | 117 744 | 214 588 | 214 909 | 251 946 | 276 082 | 293 095 | 280 522 |
| Uniform land tax | .. | 235 | 428 | 762 | 833 | 944 | 1 004 | 1 036 | 1 055 | 399 |
| Property tax | .. | 13 699 | 59 140 | 104 745 | 200 710 | 200 685 | 236 542 | 269 534 | 292 040 | 280 122 |
| Land tax | .. | 3 340 | 9 086 | 12 238 | 13 045 | 13 281 | 14 401 | 5 512 | 0 | 0 |
| 4200 Recurrent taxes on net wealth | .. | 0 | 0 | 0 | 0 | 0 | 0 | 0 | 0 | 0 |
| 4210 Individual | .. | .. | .. | .. | .. | .. | .. | .. | .. | .. |
| 4220 Corporate | .. | .. | .. | .. | .. | .. | .. | .. | .. | .. |
| 4300 Estate, inheritance and gift taxes | .. | 0 | 0 | 0 | 0 | 0 | 0 | 0 | 0 | 0 |
| 4310 Estate and inheritance taxes | .. | .. | .. | .. | .. | .. | .. | .. | .. | .. |
| 4320 Gift taxes | .. | .. | .. | .. | .. | .. | .. | .. | .. | .. |
| 4400 Taxes on financial and capital transactions | .. | 509 | 2 231 | 2 486 | 2 101 | 1 047 | 1 143 | 161 | 0 | 0 |
| 4500 Non-recurrent taxes | .. | 0 | 0 | 0 | 0 | 0 | 0 | 0 | 0 | 0 |
| 4510 On net wealth | .. | .. | .. | .. | .. | .. | .. | .. | .. | .. |
| 4520 Other non-recurrent taxes | .. | .. | .. | .. | .. | .. | .. | .. | .. | .. |
| 4600 Other recurrent taxes on property | .. | 0 | 0 | 0 | 0 | 0 | 0 | 0 | 0 | 0 |
| **5000 Taxes on goods and services** | .. | **179 452** | **1 131 164** | **2 600 514** | **2 952 727** | **3 372 218** | **4 437 419** | **5 259 064** | **6 000 743** | **4 868 250** |
| 5100 Taxes on production, sale, transfer, etc | .. | 168 678 | 1 032 930 | 2 497 709 | 2 816 629 | 3 238 137 | 4 285 158 | 5 080 971 | 5 799 325 | 4 698 929 |
| 5110 General taxes | .. | 115 159 | 629 279 | 677 229 | 943 051 | 1 495 682 | 1 664 699 | 2 034 314 | 2 693 127 | 2 532 524 |
| 5111 Value added taxes | .. | 115 159 | 629 279 | 677 229 | 943 051 | 1 495 682 | 1 664 699 | 2 034 314 | 2 693 127 | 2 532 524 |
| Domestic VAT | .. | 75 625 | 137 290 | 197 358 | 203 247 | 525 318 | 532 864 | 800 800 | 1 221 658 | 1 078 752 |
| Domestic VAT to National Fund | .. | 0 | 0 | 0 | 0 | 0 | 0 | 0 | 0 | 0 |
| VAT on imported goods | .. | 39 534 | 464 361 | 435 869 | 667 404 | 860 801 | 1 017 876 | 1 124 959 | 1 338 188 | 1 325 816 |
| Other VAT | .. | 0 | 27 628 | 44 002 | 72 399 | 109 563 | 113 959 | 108 554 | 133 281 | 127 956 |
| 5112 Sales tax | .. | 0 | 0 | 0 | 0 | 0 | 0 | 0 | 0 | 0 |
| 5113 Other | .. | 0 | 0 | 0 | 0 | 0 | 0 | 0 | 0 | 0 |
| 5120 Taxes on specific goods and services | .. | 53 519 | 403 651 | 1 820 480 | 1 873 579 | 1 742 455 | 2 620 458 | 3 046 657 | 3 106 198 | 2 166 406 |
| 5121 Excises | .. | 19 285 | 58 753 | 61 423 | 161 068 | 205 231 | 255 994 | 311 856 | 343 409 | 432 653 |
| Alcohol | .. | 12 939 | 18 189 | 15 691 | 36 345 | 40 712 | 58 793 | 79 874 | 75 013 | 81 047 |
| Tobacco | .. | 5 182 | 10 953 | 22 903 | 98 346 | 121 403 | 137 791 | 163 140 | 195 093 | 218 874 |
| Petroleum product | .. | 1 164 | 20 970 | 20 966 | 26 216 | 42 042 | 58 146 | 67 504 | 71 761 | 127 499 |
| Automobiles | .. | 0 | 8 641 | 1 864 | 931 | 0 | 0 | 0 | 0 | 0 |
| Others | .. | 0 | 0 | 0 | -770 | 1 075 | 1 265 | 1 338 | 1 542 | 5 234 |
| 5122 Profits of fiscal monopolies | .. | 0 | 0 | 0 | 0 | 0 | 0 | 0 | 0 | 0 |
| 5123 Customs and import duties | .. | 18 471 | 150 355 | 354 487 | 189 522 | 266 484 | 296 905 | 331 629 | 372 223 | 344 453 |
| 5124 Taxes on exports | .. | 0 | 611 | 492 870 | 920 175 | 807 011 | 1 154 883 | 1 586 728 | 1 647 138 | 763 976 |
| Taxes on exports | .. | .. | 0 | 22 060 | 692 855 | 688 122 | 904 476 | 1 099 662 | 1 215 970 | 603 666 |
| Taxes on exports to National Fund | .. | .. | 611 | 470 810 | 227 320 | 118 889 | 250 408 | 487 066 | 431 168 | 160 311 |

| | 1997 | 2000 | 2007 | 2010 | 2015 | 2016 | 2017 | 2018 | 2019 | 2020 |
|---|---|---|---|---|---|---|---|---|---|---|
| 5125 Taxes on investment goods | .. | 0 | 0 | 0 | 0 | 0 | 0 | 0 | 0 | 0 |
| 5126 Taxes on specific services | .. | 0 | 6 184 | 14 566 | 24 798 | 25 856 | 27 144 | 43 076 | 38 673 | 27 142 |
| Telecommunication | .. | .. | 3 624 | 5 535 | 8 151 | 8 124 | 8 286 | 8 596 | 9 281 | 10 020 |
| Placement of outdoor advertisements | .. | .. | 2 560 | 3 723 | 6 076 | 5 855 | 5 510 | 5 615 | 6 047 | 5 095 |
| Gambling business | .. | .. | 0 | 3 693 | 9 231 | 10 518 | 11 746 | 26 846 | 21 003 | 11 628 |
| Others | .. | .. | 0 | 1 614 | 1 340 | 1 359 | 1 602 | 2 018 | 2 341 | 399 |
| 5127 Other taxes on internat. trade and transactions | .. | 0 | 0 | 0 | 0 | 0 | 0 | 0 | 0 | 0 |
| 5128 Other taxes | .. | 15 763 | 187 748 | 897 133 | 578 015 | 437 873 | 885 532 | 773 369 | 704 755 | 598 180 |
| Production of useful minerals of non-oil sector companies | .. | 15 763 | 16 510 | 122 128 | 118 073 | 159 276 | 259 183 | 308 717 | 365 225 | 333 013 |
| Production of useful minerals of oil sector companies | .. | 0 | 0 | 0 | 0 | 0 | 0 | 0 | 0 | 0 |
| Production of useful minerals of oil sector co. to National Fund | .. | 0 | 171 238 | 775 005 | 459 942 | 278 597 | 626 350 | 464 652 | 339 530 | 265 167 |
| 5130 Unallocable between 5110 and 5120 | .. | 0 | 0 | 0 | 0 | 0 | 0 | 0 | 0 | 0 |
| 5200 Taxes on use of goods and perform activities | .. | 10 774 | 98 234 | 102 806 | 136 098 | 134 081 | 152 261 | 178 093 | 201 419 | 169 321 |
| 5210 Recurrent taxes | .. | 5 901 | 11 382 | 26 327 | 42 319 | 46 879 | 59 981 | 67 191 | 73 032 | 59 601 |
| 5211 Paid by households: motor vehicles | .. | 3 930 | 8 099 | 21 565 | 34 466 | 38 572 | 51 271 | 57 814 | 63 210 | 49 564 |
| 5212 Paid by others: motor vehicles | .. | 1 971 | 3 241 | 4 697 | 7 812 | 8 307 | 8 710 | 9 377 | 9 823 | 10 037 |
| 5213 Paid in respect of other goods | .. | 0 | 42 | 65 | 41 | 0 | 0 | 0 | 0 | 0 |
| 5220 Non-recurrent taxes | .. | 4 873 | 86 852 | 76 478 | 93 779 | 87 202 | 92 280 | 110 902 | 128 386 | 109 720 |
| Emissions into the environment | .. | 0 | 70 958 | 57 982 | 63 379 | 67 216 | 72 529 | 87 126 | 100 810 | 85 593 |
| Others | .. | 4 873 | 15 894 | 18 497 | 30 399 | 19 985 | 19 752 | 23 776 | 27 577 | 24 127 |
| 5300 Unallocable between 5100 and 5200 | .. | 0 | 0 | 0 | 0 | 0 | 0 | 0 | 0 | 0 |
| **6000 Other taxes** | **..** | **3 684** | **909** | **6** | **141** | **410** | **10 198** | **4 816** | **988** | **2 303** |
| 6100 Paid solely by business | .. | 0 | 0 | 0 | 0 | 0 | 0 | 0 | 0 | 0 |
| 6200 Other | .. | 3 684 | 909 | 6 | 141 | 410 | 10 198 | 4 816 | 988 | 2 303 |

.. Not available

Note: Year ending 31st December.

Data are on a cash basis.

The share of the Republic of Kazakhstan under production sharing contracts of oil companies, the bonuses of oil and non-oil sector companies, the levy for the use of the radio-frequency spectrum, the payment to compensate for historic costs as well as certain other items are classified as non-tax revenues according to the OECD Interpretative Guide, but are considered as tax revenues in Kazakhstan.

Headings 1210, 5124 and 5128: These categories includes revenues that are paid to the National Fund of the Republic of Kazakhstan. This fund was created in 2000 as a stabilisation fund and includes revenues levied from oil and gas companies.

Heading 2000: Social security contribution data since 2017 have also included contributions to compulsory social health insurance in this edition. Social security contribution revenues are not considered as tax revenues in Kazakhstan, but are considered as tax revenues under the OECD Interpretative Guide, subject to certain criteria.

Heading 4120: The uniform land tax is a presumptive tax for farmers and peasants' households. Such payers are not obliged to pay personal income tax, land tax, environmental fees, transport tax, property tax and other mandatory payments to the budget. The uniform land tax is levied on the value of land in use.

Source: Ministry of Finance of the Republic of Kazakhstan.

StatLink https://stat.link/zw3rem

## Table 4.11. Korea: Details of tax revenue

Billion KRW

| | 1997 | 2000 | 2007 | 2010 | 2015 | 2016 | 2017 | 2018 | 2019 | 2020 |
|---|---|---|---|---|---|---|---|---|---|---|
| **Total tax revenue** | **102 916** | **136 295** | **258 571** | **295 968** | **393 559** | **430 752** | **465 470** | **506 548** | **523 985** | **538 450** |
| **1000 Taxes on income, profits and capital gains** | **26 916** | **39 254** | **82 239** | **82 905** | **119 151** | **134 503** | **149 420** | **172 976** | **174 040** | **166 564** |
| 1100 Of individuals | 16 543 | 19 950 | 43 276 | 42 098 | 67 600 | 75 711 | 83 121 | 93 274 | 91 714 | 101 286 |
| 1110 On income and profits | 14 586 | 18 569 | 31 984 | 33 935 | 55 744 | 62 028 | 67 987 | 75 251 | 75 613 | 77 630 |
| Income tax | 0 | 0 | 0 | 0 | 0 | 0 | 0 | 0 | 0 | 0 |
| Dividends and interest income tax | 0 | 0 | 4 682 | 4 425 | 4 561 | 4 125 | 4 517 | 4 982 | 5 577 | 5 830 |
| Wages and salaries income tax | 0 | 0 | 14 124 | 15 517 | 27 055 | 30 994 | 34 034 | 38 000 | 38 466 | 40 905 |
| Other income tax | 0 | 0 | 2 607 | 2 986 | 4 467 | 5 346 | 5 333 | 5 975 | 6 640 | 6 645 |
| Global income tax | 12 911 | 16 128 | 6 151 | 6 369 | 12 784 | 14 348 | 16 049 | 17 483 | 16 778 | 16 073 |
| Defence tax on income tax | 0 | 0 | 0 | 0 | 0 | 0 | 0 | 0 | 0 | 0 |
| Education tax on income tax | 0 | 0 | 0 | 0 | 0 | 0 | 0 | 0 | 0 | 0 |
| Rural dev. tax on interest, bus. Inc. & cap. gains relief | 149 | 156 | 160 | 179 | 105 | 109 | 104 | 111 | 139 | 225 |
| Inhabitant tax on income tax (local) | 1 526 | 2 285 | 4 260 | 4 459 | 6 772 | 7 106 | 7 950 | 8 700 | 8 013 | 7 952 |
| 1120 On capital gains | 1 957 | 1 381 | 11 292 | 8 163 | 11 856 | 13 683 | 15 134 | 18 023 | 16 101 | 23 656 |
| Capital gains tax | 1 957 | 1 381 | 11 292 | 8 163 | 11 856 | 13 683 | 15 134 | 18 023 | 16 101 | 23 656 |
| 1200 Corporate | 10 158 | 19 271 | 38 963 | 40 807 | 51 551 | 58 792 | 66 299 | 79 702 | 82 326 | 65 278 |
| 1210 On profits | 10 158 | 19 271 | 38 963 | 40 807 | 51 551 | 58 792 | 66 299 | 79 702 | 82 326 | 65 278 |
| Corporation tax - withholding | 5 501 | 8 577 | 8 360 | 9 095 | 12 317 | 11 986 | 11 990 | 13 174 | 14 168 | 13 179 |
| Corporation tax - final returns | 3 924 | 9 302 | 27 057 | 28 173 | 32 713 | 40 130 | 47 187 | 57 763 | 58 006 | 42 335 |
| Defence tax on corporation tax | 0 | 0 | 0 | 0 | 0 | 0 | 0 | 0 | 0 | 0 |
| Inhabitant tax on corporation tax (local) | 733 | 1 142 | 3 152 | 3 094 | 6 217 | 6 270 | 6 785 | 8 307 | 9 729 | 9 293 |
| Rural development tax corporate income | 0 | 251 | 394 | 445 | 304 | 406 | 337 | 458 | 423 | 471 |
| Excess profit tax | 0 | 0 | 0 | 0 | 0 | 0 | 0 | 0 | 0 | 0 |
| 1220 On capital gains | 0 | 0 | 0 | 0 | 0 | 0 | 0 | 0 | 0 | 0 |
| Capital gains tax | .. | .. | .. | .. | .. | .. | .. | .. | .. | .. |
| 1300 Unallocable between 1100 and 1200 | 215 | 33 | 0 | 0 | 0 | 0 | 0 | 0 | 0 | 0 |
| Business income tax | 0 | 0 | .. | .. | .. | .. | .. | .. | .. | .. |
| Real estate income tax | 0 | 0 | .. | .. | .. | .. | .. | .. | .. | .. |
| Defence tax on real estate & business income | 0 | 0 | .. | .. | .. | .. | .. | .. | .. | .. |
| Rural dev. tax on bus. inc. & cap. gains relief | 211 | 30 | .. | .. | .. | .. | .. | .. | .. | .. |
| Inhabitant tax before 1990 (local) | 1 | 0 | .. | .. | .. | .. | .. | .. | .. | .. |
| Farm land tax (local) | 3 | 3 | .. | .. | .. | .. | .. | .. | .. | .. |
| Inhabitant tax on farm land tax (local) | 0 | 0 | .. | .. | .. | .. | .. | .. | .. | .. |
| **2000 Social security contributions** | **14 583** | **22 759** | **53 588** | **69 090** | **104 693** | **112 658** | **119 676** | **128 660** | **140 071** | **150 854** |
| 2100 Employees | 6 376 | 8 578 | 21 773 | 28 213 | 44 281 | 48 077 | 51 125 | 55 257 | 60 682 | 65 384 |
| Veterans' relief fund | 0 | 0 | 0 | 0 | 0 | 0 | 0 | 0 | 0 | 0 |
| Soldiers' annuity fund | 0 | 0 | 0 | 0 | 0 | 0 | 0 | 0 | 0 | 0 |
| Unemployment assurance | 264 | 598 | 1 164 | 1 358 | 3 076 | 3 251 | 3 418 | 3 666 | 4 027 | 4 895 |
| National welfare pension fund | 3 597 | 4 325 | 9 338 | 11 004 | 15 821 | 16 862 | 17 864 | 19 090 | 20 630 | 21 722 |
| Social benefit fund | 0 | 0 | 0 | 0 | 0 | 0 | 0 | 0 | 0 | 0 |
| Health Insurance | 1 149 | 2 066 | 8 180 | 11 783 | 19 868 | 21 470 | 22 814 | 24 920 | 27 911 | 30 184 |
| Teachers' pensions | 219 | 279 | 581 | 868 | 1 125 | 1 410 | 1 507 | 1 595 | 1 678 | 1 780 |
| Government employees pensions | 1 013 | 1 144 | 2 202 | 2 878 | 3 876 | 4 533 | 4 934 | 5 371 | 5 796 | 6 134 |
| Military personal pensions | 134 | 166 | 308 | 322 | 515 | 551 | 588 | 615 | 640 | 669 |
| 2110 On a payroll basis | .. | 8 578 | 21 773 | 28 213 | 44 281 | 48 077 | 51 125 | 55 257 | 60 682 | 65 384 |
| 2120 On an income tax basis | .. | 0 | 0 | 0 | 0 | 0 | 0 | 0 | 0 | 0 |
| 2200 Employers | 5 901 | 9 409 | 23 557 | 30 856 | 47 846 | 51 190 | 54 063 | 58 712 | 63 780 | 67 676 |
| Ind. works' insurance fund | 1 819 | 1 876 | 4 431 | 4 632 | 6 062 | 6 283 | 6 429 | 7 346 | 7 539 | 7 088 |
| Soldiers' annuity fund | 0 | 0 | 0 | 0 | 0 | 0 | 0 | 0 | 0 | 0 |
| Pneumoconiosis fund | 0 | 0 | 0 | 0 | 0 | 0 | 0 | 0 | 0 | 0 |
| Unemployment insurance | 653 | 1 449 | 2 474 | 2 860 | 5 499 | 5 790 | 6 082 | 6 517 | 7 063 | 8 024 |
| Veterans' relief fund | 0 | 0 | 0 | 0 | 0 | 0 | 0 | 0 | 0 | 0 |
| National welfare pension fund | 1 814 | 4 340 | 9 383 | 11 052 | 15 895 | 16 928 | 17 922 | 19 155 | 20 631 | 21 722 |
| Social benefit fund | 0 | 0 | 0 | 0 | 0 | 0 | 0 | 0 | 0 | 0 |
| Health Insurance | 1 459 | 1 547 | 6 844 | 11 718 | 19 493 | 21 074 | 22 397 | 24 346 | 27 110 | 29 288 |
| Teachers' pensions | 156 | 197 | 425 | 594 | 897 | 1 115 | 1 233 | 1 348 | 1 437 | 1 554 |
| Government employees pensions | 0 | 0 | 0 | 0 | 0 | 0 | 0 | 0 | 0 | 0 |
| 2210 On a payroll basis | .. | 9 409 | 23 557 | 30 856 | 47 846 | 51 190 | 54 063 | 58 712 | 63 780 | 67 676 |
| 2220 On an income tax basis | .. | 0 | 0 | 0 | 0 | 0 | 0 | 0 | 0 | .. |
| 2300 Self-employed or non-employed | 2 306 | 4 772 | 8 258 | 10 021 | 12 566 | 13 391 | 14 488 | 14 691 | 15 609 | 17 794 |
| 2310 On a payroll basis | 0 | 0 | 0 | 0 | 0 | 0 | 0 | 0 | 0 | 0 |
| 2320 On an income tax basis | 2 306 | 4 772 | 8 258 | 10 021 | 12 566 | 13 391 | 14 488 | 14 691 | 15 609 | 17 794 |
| 2400 Unallocable between 2100, 2200 and 2300 | 0 | 0 | 0 | 0 | 0 | 0 | 0 | 0 | 0 | 0 |
| 2410 On a payroll basis | .. | .. | .. | .. | .. | .. | .. | .. | .. | .. |
| 2420 On an income tax basis | .. | .. | .. | .. | .. | .. | .. | .. | .. | .. |
| **3000 Taxes on payroll and workforce** | **309** | **258** | **619** | **714** | **1 122** | **1 293** | **1 376** | **1 492** | **1 597** | **1 607** |
| Workshop tax on workforce (local) | 309 | 258 | 619 | 714 | 1 122 | 1 293 | 1 376 | 1 492 | 1 597 | 1 607 |
| Vocational training promotion fund | 0 | 0 | 0 | 0 | 0 | 0 | 0 | 0 | 0 | 0 |
| **4000 Taxes on property** | **13 088** | **16 846** | **33 109** | **33 516** | **48 625** | **49 820** | **54 406** | **58 811** | **59 732** | **76 512** |

| | 1997 | 2000 | 2007 | 2010 | 2015 | 2016 | 2017 | 2018 | 2019 | 2020 |
|---|---|---|---|---|---|---|---|---|---|---|
| 4100 Recurrent taxes on immovable property | 2 986 | 3 385 | 9 196 | 9 270 | 12 486 | 13 095 | 14 319 | 15 589 | 17 750 | 20 044 |
| Property tax (local) | 577 | 728 | 3 755 | 4 817 | 9 294 | 9 930 | 10 662 | 11 532 | 12 677 | 13 773 |
| City planning tax on urban real estate (local) | 731 | 815 | 1 883 | 2 465 | 0 | 0 | 0 | 0 | 0 | 0 |
| Community facilities tax (local) | 268 | 341 | 543 | 650 | 1 351 | 1 450 | 1 513 | 1 626 | 1 681 | 1 777 |
| Tax on excessive land holdings (local) | 0 | 0 | 0 | 0 | 0 | 0 | 0 | 0 | 0 | 0 |
| Tax on aggregate land holdings (local) | 1 279 | 1 282 | 5 | 0 | 0 | 0 | 0 | 0 | 0 | 0 |
| Rural dev. tax on local agg. land holdings tax | 63 | 81 | 1 | 0 | 0 | 0 | 0 | 0 | 0 | 0 |
| Tax on excessively increased land value | -1 | 0 | 0 | 0 | 0 | 0 | 0 | 0 | 0 | 0 |
| Comprehensive real estate tax | 0 | 0 | 2 414 | 1 029 | 1 399 | 1 294 | 1 652 | 1 873 | 2 671 | 3 601 |
| Rural dev. tax on comprehensive real estate tax | 0 | 0 | 483 | 208 | 267 | 240 | 302 | 356 | 505 | 680 |
| 4110 Households | 0 | 0 | 0 | 0 | 0 | 0 | 0 | 0 | 0 | 0 |
| 4120 Others | 68 | 138 | 112 | 101 | 175 | 181 | 190 | 202 | 216 | 213 |
| Workshop tax on property (local) | 68 | 138 | 112 | 101 | 175 | 181 | 190 | 202 | 216 | 213 |
| 4200 Recurrent taxes on net wealth | 0 | 0 | 0 | 0 | 0 | 0 | 0 | 0 | 0 | 0 |
| 4210 Individual | .. | .. | .. | .. | .. | .. | .. | .. | .. | .. |
| 4220 Corporate | .. | .. | .. | .. | .. | .. | .. | .. | .. | .. |
| 4300 Estate, inheritance and gift taxes | 1 161 | 989 | 2 842 | 3 076 | 5 044 | 5 350 | 6 785 | 7 359 | 8 329 | 10 375 |
| 4310 Estate and inheritance taxes | 605 | 449 | 1 059 | 1 203 | 1 944 | 1 995 | 2 342 | 2 832 | 3 154 | 3 904 |
| Inheritance tax | 605 | 449 | 1 059 | 1 203 | 1 944 | 1 995 | 2 342 | 2 832 | 3 154 | 3 904 |
| Defence tax on inheritance tax | 0 | 0 | 0 | 0 | 0 | 0 | 0 | 0 | 0 | 0 |
| 4320 Gift taxes | 556 | 540 | 1 783 | 1 873 | 3 100 | 3 355 | 4 443 | 4 527 | 5 175 | 6 471 |
| Gift tax | 556 | 540 | 1 783 | 1 873 | 3 100 | 3 355 | 4 443 | 4 527 | 5 175 | 6 471 |
| Defence tax on gift tax | 0 | 0 | 0 | 0 | 0 | 0 | 0 | 0 | 0 | 0 |
| 4400 Taxes on financial and capital transactions | 8 774 | 11 935 | 21 071 | 21 170 | 31 095 | 31 375 | 33 302 | 35 863 | 33 653 | 46 093 |
| Registration tax (local) | 4 257 | 4 528 | 7 254 | 7 370 | 1 831 | 1 708 | 1 608 | 1 718 | 1 837 | 2 053 |
| Registration tax | 0 | 0 | 0 | 0 | 0 | 0 | 0 | 0 | 0 | 0 |
| Defence tax on registration tax | 0 | 0 | 0 | 0 | 0 | 0 | 0 | 0 | 0 | 0 |
| Rural dev. tax on local acquisition tax | 164 | 246 | 627 | 632 | 969 | 954 | 1 028 | 993 | 947 | 1 164 |
| Rural dev. tax on local registration tax | 211 | 66 | 143 | 144 | 1 | 0 | 0 | 0 | 0 | 0 |
| Securities transactions tax | 262 | 2 736 | 3 469 | 3 667 | 4 670 | 4 468 | 4 508 | 6 241 | 4 473 | 8 759 |
| Rural dev. tax on securities transaction tax | 170 | 823 | 1 729 | 2 010 | 1 861 | 1 637 | 1 775 | 2 217 | 1 635 | 3 616 |
| Acquisition tax (local) | 3 319 | 3 148 | 7 261 | 6 825 | 20 810 | 21 702 | 23 487 | 23 813 | 23 915 | 29 536 |
| Stamp tax | 390 | 388 | 588 | 522 | 953 | 906 | 896 | 881 | 846 | 965 |
| 4500 Non-recurrent taxes | 167 | 537 | 0 | 0 | 0 | 0 | 0 | 0 | 0 | 0 |
| Asset revaluation tax | 167 | 537 | .. | .. | .. | .. | .. | .. | .. | .. |
| 4510 On net wealth | 0 | 0 | .. | .. | .. | .. | .. | .. | .. | .. |
| 4520 Other non-recurrent taxes | 0 | 0 | .. | .. | .. | .. | .. | .. | .. | .. |
| 4600 Other recurrent taxes on property | 0 | 0 | 0 | 0 | 0 | 0 | 0 | 0 | 0 | 0 |
| **5000 Taxes on goods and services** | **43 978** | **52 271** | **80 861** | **99 769** | **110 326** | **121 197** | **129 065** | **133 095** | **135 276** | **131 353** |
| 5100 Taxes on production, sale, transfer, etc. | 41 699 | 50 023 | 78 414 | 96 573 | 103 254 | 113 644 | 121 293 | 125 207 | 127 551 | 123 219 |
| 5110 General taxes | 19 488 | 23 212 | 40 942 | 51 800 | 60 162 | 68 229 | 74 361 | 77 471 | 82 174 | 81 452 |
| 5111 Value added taxes | 19 488 | 23 212 | 40 942 | 51 800 | 60 162 | 68 229 | 74 361 | 77 471 | 82 174 | 81 452 |
| Value added tax | 19 488 | 23 212 | 40 942 | 51 800 | 60 162 | 68 229 | 74 361 | 77 471 | 82 174 | 81 452 |
| 5112 Sales tax | 0 | 0 | 0 | 0 | 0 | 0 | 0 | 0 | 0 | 0 |
| Business tax | .. | .. | .. | .. | .. | .. | .. | .. | .. | .. |
| 5113 Other | 0 | 0 | 0 | 0 | 0 | 0 | 0 | 0 | 0 | 0 |
| 5120 Taxes on specific goods and services | 22 211 | 26 811 | 37 472 | 44 773 | 43 092 | 45 415 | 46 932 | 47 736 | 45 377 | 41 767 |
| 5121 Excise duties | 14 616 | 18 155 | 27 880 | 31 340 | 31 857 | 34 762 | 35 779 | 36 218 | 34 691 | 33 013 |
| Commodity tax | 0 | 0 | 0 | 0 | 0 | 0 | 0 | 0 | 0 | 0 |
| Defence tax on commodity tax | 0 | 0 | 0 | 0 | 0 | 0 | 0 | 0 | 0 | 0 |
| Liquor tax | 1 790 | 1 963 | 2 268 | 2 878 | 3 228 | 3 209 | 3 035 | 3 261 | 3 504 | 3 008 |
| Defence tax on liquor tax | 0 | 0 | 0 | 0 | 0 | 0 | 0 | 0 | 0 | 0 |
| Education tax on liquor tax | 418 | 516 | 580 | 724 | 808 | 813 | 745 | 788 | 844 | 733 |
| Textile tax | 0 | 0 | 0 | 0 | 0 | 0 | 0 | 0 | 0 | 0 |
| Petroleum tax | 0 | 0 | 0 | 0 | 0 | 0 | 0 | 0 | 0 | 0 |
| Transport tax on petrol products | 5 547 | 8 404 | 11 464 | 13 970 | 14 055 | 15 303 | 15 553 | 15 335 | 14 563 | 13 938 |
| Education tax on transport tax | 758 | 1 247 | 1 715 | 2 133 | 2 154 | 2 289 | 2 320 | 2 304 | 2 190 | 2 041 |
| Electricity and gas tax | 0 | 0 | 0 | 0 | 0 | 0 | 0 | 0 | 0 | 0 |
| Special excise tax | 3 036 | 2 985 | 5 161 | 5 066 | 8 001 | 8 881 | 9 861 | 10 451 | 9 719 | 9 218 |
| Defence tax on special excise tax | 0 | 0 | 0 | 0 | 0 | 0 | 0 | 0 | 0 | 0 |
| Education tax on special excise tax | 804 | 498 | 607 | 501 | 515 | 463 | 602 | 545 | 455 | 440 |
| Rural development on special excise tax | 26 | 37 | 54 | 24 | 61 | 60 | 60 | 56 | 58 | 57 |
| Tobacco sales tax (local) | 0 | 0 | 0 | 0 | 0 | 0 | 0 | 0 | 0 | 0 |
| Tobacco consumption tax (local) | 2 236 | 2 251 | 2 761 | 2 875 | 3 035 | 3 744 | 3 603 | 3 478 | 3 358 | 3 578 |
| Motor fuel tax (local) | 0 | 254 | 3 270 | 3 169 | 0 | 0 | 0 | 0 | 0 | 0 |
| 5122 Profits of fiscal monopolies | 0 | 0 | 0 | 0 | 0 | 0 | 0 | 0 | 0 | 0 |
| Monopoly profit | .. | .. | .. | .. | .. | .. | .. | .. | .. | .. |

| | 1997 | 2000 | 2007 | 2010 | 2015 | 2016 | 2017 | 2018 | 2019 | 2020 |
|---|---|---|---|---|---|---|---|---|---|---|
| 5123 Customs and import duties | 5 941 | 5 936 | 7 690 | 11 046 | 8 907 | 8 434 | 8 938 | 9 213 | 8 250 | 7 413 |
| Customs duties | 5 798 | 5 800 | 7 411 | 10 666 | 8 495 | 8 045 | 8 529 | 8 815 | 7 882 | 7 059 |
| Defence tax on customs duties | 0 | 0 | 0 | 0 | 0 | 0 | 0 | 0 | 0 | 0 |
| Special customs duties | 0 | 0 | 0 | 0 | 0 | 0 | 0 | 0 | 0 | 0 |
| Tonnage tax | 0 | 0 | 0 | 0 | 0 | 0 | 0 | 0 | 0 | 0 |
| Education tax on imports | 116 | 99 | 234 | 336 | 390 | 366 | 382 | 370 | 345 | 341 |
| Rural dev. tax on customs exemptions | 27 | 37 | 45 | 44 | 22 | 23 | 27 | 28 | 23 | 13 |
| Previous year receipts | 0 | 0 | 0 | 0 | 0 | 0 | 0 | 0 | 0 | 0 |
| 5124 Taxes on exports | 0 | 0 | 0 | 0 | 0 | 0 | 0 | 0 | 0 | 0 |
| 5125 Taxes on investment goods | 0 | 0 | 0 | 0 | 0 | 0 | 0 | 0 | 0 | 0 |
| 5126 Taxes on specific services | 1 654 | 2 720 | 1 902 | 2 387 | 2 328 | 2 219 | 2 215 | 2 305 | 2 436 | 1 341 |
| Telephone tax | 789 | 1 457 | 0 | 0 | 0 | 0 | 0 | 0 | 0 | 0 |
| Defence tax on telephone tax | 0 | 0 | 0 | 0 | 0 | 0 | 0 | 0 | 0 | 0 |
| Entertainment tax | 0 | 0 | 0 | 0 | 0 | 0 | 0 | 0 | 0 | 0 |
| Defence tax on entertainment tax | 0 | 0 | 0 | 0 | 0 | 0 | 0 | 0 | 0 | 0 |
| Entertainment tax (local) | 0 | 0 | 0 | 0 | 0 | 0 | 0 | 0 | 0 | 0 |
| Travel tax | 0 | 0 | 0 | 0 | 0 | 0 | 0 | 0 | 0 | 0 |
| Admission tax | 0 | 0 | 0 | 0 | 0 | 0 | 0 | 0 | 0 | 0 |
| Defence tax on admission tax | 0 | 0 | 0 | 0 | 0 | 0 | 0 | 0 | 0 | 0 |
| Education tax on banking & insurance | 369 | 473 | 721 | 951 | 1 004 | 951 | 959 | 1 092 | 1 277 | 1 138 |
| Horse race tax (local) | 361 | 566 | 864 | 1 068 | 1 089 | 1 060 | 1 051 | 1 016 | 970 | 169 |
| Rural dev. tax on horse race tax | 18 | 84 | 165 | 215 | 235 | 208 | 205 | 197 | 189 | 34 |
| Butchery tax (local) | 47 | 51 | 52 | 58 | 0 | 0 | 0 | 0 | 0 | 0 |
| Regional development tax (local) | 71 | 89 | 100 | 95 | 0 | 0 | 0 | 0 | 0 | 0 |
| 5127 Other taxes on internat. trade and transactions | 0 | 0 | 0 | 0 | 0 | 0 | 0 | 0 | 0 | 0 |
| 5128 Other taxes | 0 | 0 | 0 | 0 | 0 | 0 | 0 | 0 | 0 | 0 |
| 5130 Unallocable between 5110 and 5120 | 0 | 0 | 0 | 0 | 0 | 0 | 0 | 0 | 0 | 0 |
| 5200 Taxes on use of goods and perform activities | 2 279 | 2 248 | 2 447 | 3 196 | 7 072 | 7 553 | 7 772 | 7 888 | 7 725 | 8 134 |
| 5210 Recurrent taxes | 2 279 | 2 248 | 2 447 | 3 196 | 7 072 | 7 553 | 7 772 | 7 888 | 7 725 | 8 134 |
| License tax (local) | 225 | 241 | 77 | 76 | 0 | 0 | 0 | 0 | 0 | 0 |
| Automobile tax (local) | 2 054 | 2 007 | 2 370 | 3 120 | 7 072 | 7 553 | 7 772 | 7 888 | 7 725 | 8 134 |
| 5211 Paid by households: motor vehicles | .. | .. | .. | .. | .. | .. | .. | .. | .. | .. |
| 5212 Paid by others: motor vehicles | .. | .. | .. | .. | .. | .. | .. | .. | .. | .. |
| 5213 Paid in respect of other goods | .. | .. | .. | .. | .. | .. | .. | .. | .. | .. |
| 5220 Non-recurrent taxes | 0 | 0 | 0 | 0 | 0 | 0 | 0 | 0 | 0 | 0 |
| 5300 Unallocable between 5100 and 5200 | 0 | 0 | 0 | 0 | 0 | 0 | 0 | 0 | 0 | 0 |
| **6000 Other taxes** | **4 041** | **4 907** | **8 155** | **9 974** | **9 642** | **11 281** | **11 527** | **11 514** | **13 269** | **11 560** |
| 6100 Paid solely by business | 0 | 0 | 0 | 0 | 0 | 0 | 0 | 0 | 0 | 0 |
| 6200 Other | 4 041 | 4 907 | 8 155 | 9 974 | 9 642 | 11 281 | 11 527 | 11 514 | 13 269 | 11 560 |
| Unallocable tax revenue | 0 | 0 | 0 | 0 | 0 | 0 | 0 | 0 | 0 | 0 |
| Previous year tax | 779 | 1 474 | 2 965 | 4 449 | 3 435 | 4 147 | 4 389 | 4 430 | 5 873 | 4 165 |
| Previous year tax (local) | 340 | 474 | 672 | 654 | 392 | 868 | 715 | 540 | 719 | 259 |
| Unallocable defence tax | -8 | -3 | 0 | 0 | 0 | 0 | 0 | 0 | 0 | 0 |
| Education tax on local taxes | 2 931 | 2 962 | 4 518 | 4 871 | 5 815 | 6 266 | 6 423 | 6 544 | 6 677 | 7 136 |

.. Not available

Note: Year ending 31st December.

Data are on cash basis.

Heading 2000: From 1997 the contributions to the three funds (civil servant pension fund, private school teachers pension fund and medical insurance fund) are classified as security social contributions. The reasons for the change are that the contributions either became mandatory or the fund started to be managed by public authorities in that year, thereby meeting the OECD definition of social security contributions.

Heading 2200: From 2007, this includes long-term care insurance.

Source: Ministry of Finance and Economy, Ministry of Home Affairs.

StatLink https://stat.link/c0bjzm

## Table 4.12. Kyrgyzstan: Details of tax revenue

Million KGS

| | 1997 | 2000 | 2007 | 2010 | 2015 | 2016 | 2017 | 2018 | 2019 | 2020 | |
|---|---|---|---|---|---|---|---|---|---|---|---|
| **Total tax revenue** | | **3 792** | **7 639** | **26 087** | **39 157** | **82 234** | **92 929** | **102 184** | **115 483** | **120 064** | **104 906** |
| **1000 Taxes on income, profits and capital gains** | **675** | **1 371** | **4 338** | **8 746** | **15 899** | **16 673** | **17 940** | **19 738** | **22 268** | | **22 732** |
| 1100 Of individuals | 332 | 754 | 2 323 | 4 407 | 9 514 | 10 594 | 11 110 | 11 474 | 12 862 | | 12 151 |
| 1110 On income and profits | 332 | 754 | 2 323 | 4 407 | 9 514 | 10 594 | 11 110 | 11 474 | 12 862 | | 12 151 |
| 1120 On capital gains | .. | .. | .. | .. | .. | .. | .. | .. | .. | | .. |
| 1200 Corporate | 336 | 573 | 1 736 | 1 932 | 4 111 | 3 659 | 4 301 | 5 504 | 6 465 | | 8 356 |
| 1210 On profits | 336 | 573 | 1 736 | 1 932 | 4 111 | 3 659 | 4 301 | 5 504 | 6 465 | | 8 356 |
| 1220 On capital gains of corporates | .. | .. | .. | .. | .. | .. | .. | .. | .. | | .. |
| 1300 Unallocable between 1100 and 1200 | 7 | 44 | 279 | 2 408 | 2 274 | 2 419 | 2 529 | 2 760 | 2 941 | | 2 226 |
| Single tax for small businesses | 0 | 0 | 56 | 131 | 178 | 211 | 202 | 229 | 272 | | 237 |
| Patent based tax | 0 | 0 | 223 | 1 493 | 2 097 | 2 208 | 2 327 | 2 531 | 2 669 | | 1 988 |
| Tax on special funds of budgetary organisations | 0 | 0 | 0 | 784 | 0 | 0 | 0 | 0 | 0 | | 0 |
| Others | 7 | 44 | 0 | 0 | 0 | 0 | 0 | 0 | 0 | | 0 |
| **2000 Social security contributions** | **0** | **0** | **0** | **0** | **0** | **0** | **0** | **0** | **0** | | **0** |
| 2100 Employees | .. | .. | .. | .. | .. | .. | .. | .. | .. | | .. |
| 2110 On a payroll basis | .. | .. | .. | .. | .. | .. | .. | .. | .. | | .. |
| 2120 On an income tax basis | .. | .. | .. | .. | .. | .. | .. | .. | .. | | .. |
| 2200 Employers | .. | .. | .. | .. | .. | .. | .. | .. | .. | | .. |
| 2210 On a payroll basis | .. | .. | .. | .. | .. | .. | .. | .. | .. | | .. |
| 2220 On an income tax basis | .. | .. | .. | .. | .. | .. | .. | .. | .. | | .. |
| 2300 Self-employed or non-employed | .. | .. | .. | .. | .. | .. | .. | .. | .. | | .. |
| 2310 On a payroll basis | .. | .. | .. | .. | .. | .. | .. | .. | .. | | .. |
| 2320 On an income tax basis | .. | .. | .. | .. | .. | .. | .. | .. | .. | | .. |
| 2400 Unallocable between 2100, 2200 and 2300 | .. | .. | .. | .. | .. | .. | .. | .. | .. | | .. |
| 2410 On a payroll basis | .. | .. | .. | .. | .. | .. | .. | .. | .. | | .. |
| 2420 On an income tax basis | .. | .. | .. | .. | .. | .. | .. | .. | .. | | .. |
| **3000 Taxes on payroll and workforce** | **0** | **0** | **0** | **0** | **0** | **0** | **0** | **0** | **0** | | **0** |
| **4000 Taxes on property** | **274** | **179** | **587** | **1 264** | **1 597** | **1 698** | **1 818** | **1 966** | **2 107** | | **2 019** |
| 4100 Recurrent taxes on immovable property | 274 | 179 | 587 | 1 264 | 1 597 | 1 698 | 1 818 | 1 966 | 2 107 | | 2 019 |
| Real estate tax | 0 | 0 | 0 | 465 | 643 | 708 | 766 | 838 | 878 | | 897 |
| Land tax | 274 | 179 | 587 | 799 | 954 | 990 | 1 052 | 1 128 | 1 229 | | 1 123 |
| 4110 Households | .. | .. | .. | .. | .. | .. | .. | .. | .. | | .. |
| 4120 Others | .. | .. | .. | .. | .. | .. | .. | .. | .. | | .. |
| 4200 Recurrent taxes on net wealth | -1 | 0 | 0 | 0 | 0 | 0 | 0 | 0 | 0 | | 0 |
| 4210 Individual | .. | .. | .. | .. | .. | .. | .. | .. | .. | | .. |
| 4220 Corporate | .. | .. | .. | .. | .. | .. | .. | .. | .. | | .. |
| 4300 Estate, inheritance and gift taxes | 0 | 0 | 0 | 0 | 0 | 0 | 0 | 0 | 0 | | 0 |
| 4310 Estate and inheritance taxes | .. | .. | .. | .. | .. | .. | .. | .. | .. | | .. |
| 4320 Gift taxes | .. | .. | .. | .. | .. | .. | .. | .. | .. | | .. |
| 4400 Taxes on financial and capital transactions | 0 | 0 | 0 | 0 | 0 | 0 | 0 | 0 | 0 | | 0 |
| 4500 Other non-reccurrent taxes on property | 0 | 0 | 0 | 0 | 0 | 0 | 0 | 0 | 0 | | 0 |
| 4510 On net wealth | .. | .. | .. | .. | .. | .. | .. | .. | .. | | .. |
| 4520 Other non-recurrent taxes | .. | .. | .. | .. | .. | .. | .. | .. | .. | | .. |
| 4600 Other recurrent taxes on property | 0 | 0 | 0 | 0 | 0 | 0 | 0 | 0 | 0 | | 0 |
| **5000 Taxes on goods and services** | **2 836** | **6 089** | **21 162** | **29 145** | **64 736** | **74 556** | **82 423** | **93 778** | **95 655** | | **80 151** |
| 5100 Taxes on production, sale, transfer, etc | 2 637 | 5 609 | 21 036 | 28 744 | 64 047 | 73 759 | 81 616 | 92 649 | 94 591 | | 79 162 |
| 5110 General taxes on goods and services | 1 940 | 3 797 | 15 736 | 22 707 | 46 606 | 50 891 | 55 617 | 64 033 | 62 678 | | 52 862 |
| 5111 Value added taxes | 1 728 | 2 976 | 12 702 | 14 602 | 33 221 | 39 297 | 45 131 | 52 786 | 50 912 | | 39 461 |
| VAT on domestic products | 1 145 | 1 237 | 2 680 | 4 232 | 9 173 | 11 942 | 12 560 | 11 885 | 12 092 | | 10 654 |
| VAT on imported products | 583 | 1 739 | 10 022 | 10 370 | 24 047 | 27 355 | 32 571 | 40 901 | 38 820 | | 28 807 |
| 5112 Sales tax | 0 | 0 | 1 121 | 3 699 | 7 508 | 6 014 | 4 034 | 4 283 | 4 216 | | 3 782 |
| 5113 Other | 212 | 821 | 1 913 | 4 406 | 5 876 | 5 580 | 6 452 | 6 964 | 7 550 | | 9 619 |
| Road tax | 0 | 0 | 636 | 48 | 2 | 0 | 0 | 0 | 0 | | 0 |
| Deductions for the prevention and liquidation of emergency situations | 212 | 589 | 1 277 | -6 | 1 | 0 | 0 | 0 | 0 | | 0 |
| Tax on gross income from Kumtor | 0 | 0 | 0 | 4 364 | 5 874 | 5 580 | 6 452 | 6 964 | 7 550 | | 9 619 |
| Others | 0 | 232 | 0 | 0 | 0 | 0 | 0 | 0 | 0 | | 0 |
| 5120 Taxes on specific goods and services | 696 | 1 812 | 5 300 | 6 037 | 17 441 | 22 868 | 25 999 | 28 616 | 31 913 | | 26 300 |
| 5121 Excises | 451 | 1 518 | 1 448 | 1 689 | 7 757 | 9 059 | 9 506 | 10 296 | 9 945 | | 8 994 |
| Excises on domestic products | 280 | 1 052 | 481 | 521 | 1 229 | 1 745 | 1 763 | 1 767 | 1 275 | | 977 |
| Excises on imported products | 171 | 466 | 967 | 1 169 | 6 528 | 7 314 | 7 744 | 8 529 | 8 670 | | 8 017 |
| 5122 Profits of fiscal monopolies | 0 | 0 | 0 | 0 | 0 | 0 | 0 | 0 | 0 | | 0 |
| 5123 Customs and import duties | 0 | 275 | 3 789 | 4 342 | 9 682 | 13 803 | 16 474 | 18 300 | 21 965 | | 17 296 |
| 5124 Taxes on exports | 0 | 0 | 0 | 6 | 2 | 7 | 19 | 19 | 3 | | 10 |
| 5125 Taxes on investment goods | 0 | 0 | 0 | 0 | 0 | 0 | 0 | 0 | 0 | | 0 |
| 5126 Taxes on specific services | 0 | 18 | 62 | 0 | 0 | 0 | 0 | 0 | 0 | | 0 |
| 5127 Other taxes on internat. trade and transactions | 245 | 0 | 0 | 0 | 0 | 0 | 0 | 0 | 0 | | 0 |
| 5128 Other taxes | 0 | 0 | 0 | 0 | 0 | 0 | 0 | 0 | 0 | | 0 |
| 5130 Unallocable between 5110 and 5120 | 0 | 0 | 0 | 0 | 0 | 0 | 0 | 0 | 0 | | 0 |

| | 1997 | 2000 | 2007 | 2010 | 2015 | 2016 | 2017 | 2018 | 2019 | 2020 |
|---|---|---|---|---|---|---|---|---|---|---|
| 5200 Taxes on use of goods and to perform activities | 199 | 480 | 127 | 401 | 689 | 797 | 807 | 1 129 | 1 064 | 989 |
| 5210 Recurrent taxes | 199 | 480 | 127 | 401 | 689 | 797 | 807 | 844 | 843 | 784 |
| 5211 Paid by households: motor vehicles | 3 | 35 | 127 | 401 | 577 | 675 | 688 | 727 | 737 | 680 |
| 5212 Paid by others: motor vehicles | 104 | 435 | 0 | 0 | 112 | 122 | 119 | 116 | 106 | 104 |
| 5213 Paid in respect of other goods | 92 | 10 | 0 | 0 | 0 | 0 | 0 | 0 | 0 | 0 |
| 5220 Non-recurrent taxes | 0 | 0 | 0 | 0 | 0 | 0 | 0 | 285 | 221 | 204 |
| 5300 Unallocable between 5100 and 5200 | 0 | 0 | 0 | 0 | 0 | 0 | 0 | 0 | 0 | 0 |
| **6000 Other taxes** | **8** | **0** | **0** | **2** | **2** | **3** | **2** | **1** | **34** | **3** |
| 6100 Paid solely by business | 0 | .. | .. | 0 | 0 | 0 | 0 | 0 | 0 | 0 |
| 6200 Other | 8 | .. | .. | 2 | 2 | 3 | 2 | 1 | 34 | 3 |

.. Not available

Note: Year ending 31st December.

The data are on a cash basis.

The figures refer to state government revenues which included both central and local government revenues.

Data are classified according to the OECD Interpretative Guide, which differs from the national classification. The totals shown for tax and non-tax revenue are therefore different from the totals presented on the website of the National Statistical Committee.

Heading 2000: Data for social security contributions are not available.

Source: National Statistical Committee of Kyrgyzstan.

StatLink https://stat.link/6xbsqm

# Table 4.13. Lao PDR: Details of tax revenue

Billion LAK

| | 1997 | 2000 | 2007 | 2010 | 2015 | 2016 | 2017 | 2018 | 2019 | 2020 |
|---|---|---|---|---|---|---|---|---|---|---|
| **Total tax revenue** | .. | .. | .. | **7 101** | **14 719** | **15 393** | **15 532** | **16 565** | **17 185** | **15 377** |
| **1000 Taxes on income, profits and capital gains** | .. | .. | .. | **1 613** | **3 347** | **3 375** | **3 582** | **3 692** | **3 856** | **3 179** |
| 1100 Of individuals | .. | .. | .. | 482 | 1 140 | 1 624 | 1 603 | 1 619 | 1 646 | 1 451 |
| 1110 On income and profits | .. | .. | .. | 482 | 1 140 | 1 624 | 1 603 | 1 619 | 1 646 | 1 451 |
| 1120 On capital gains | .. | .. | .. | 0 | 0 | 0 | 0 | 0 | 0 | 0 |
| 1200 Corporate | .. | .. | .. | 1 131 | 2 206 | 1 751 | 1 980 | 2 073 | 2 209 | 1 728 |
| 1210 On profits | .. | .. | .. | 1 131 | 2 206 | 1 751 | 1 980 | 2 073 | 2 209 | 1 728 |
| 1220 On capital gains of corporates | .. | .. | .. | 0 | 0 | 0 | 0 | 0 | 0 | 0 |
| 1300 Unallocable between 1100 and 1200 | .. | .. | .. | 0 | 0 | 0 | 0 | 0 | 0 | 0 |
| **2000 Social security contributions** | .. | .. | .. | **0** | **0** | **0** | **0** | **0** | **0** | **0** |
| 2100 Employees | .. | .. | .. | .. | .. | .. | .. | .. | .. | .. |
| 2110 On a payroll basis | .. | .. | .. | .. | .. | .. | .. | .. | .. | .. |
| 2120 On an income tax basis | .. | .. | .. | .. | .. | .. | .. | .. | .. | .. |
| 2200 Employers | .. | .. | .. | .. | .. | .. | .. | .. | .. | .. |
| 2210 On a payroll basis | .. | .. | .. | .. | .. | .. | .. | .. | .. | .. |
| 2220 On an income tax basis | .. | .. | .. | .. | .. | .. | .. | .. | .. | .. |
| 2300 Self-employed or non-employed | .. | .. | .. | .. | .. | .. | .. | .. | .. | .. |
| 2310 On a payroll basis | .. | .. | .. | .. | .. | .. | .. | .. | .. | .. |
| 2320 On an income tax basis | .. | .. | .. | .. | .. | .. | .. | .. | .. | .. |
| 2400 Unallocable between 2100, 2200 and 2300 | .. | .. | .. | .. | .. | .. | .. | .. | .. | .. |
| 2410 On a payroll basis | .. | .. | .. | .. | .. | .. | .. | .. | .. | .. |
| 2420 On an income tax basis | .. | .. | .. | .. | .. | .. | .. | .. | .. | .. |
| **3000 Taxes on payroll and workforce** | .. | .. | .. | **0** | **0** | **0** | **0** | **0** | **0** | **0** |
| **4000 Taxes on property** | .. | .. | .. | **76** | **130** | **105** | **113** | **188** | **201** | **188** |
| 4100 Recurrent taxes on immovable property | .. | .. | .. | 76 | 130 | 105 | 113 | 188 | 201 | 188 |
| 4110 Households | .. | .. | .. | .. | .. | .. | .. | .. | .. | .. |
| 4120 Others | .. | .. | .. | .. | .. | .. | .. | .. | .. | .. |
| 4200 Recurrent taxes on net wealth | .. | .. | .. | 0 | 0 | 0 | 0 | 0 | 0 | 0 |
| 4210 Individual | .. | .. | .. | .. | .. | .. | .. | .. | .. | .. |
| 4220 Corporate | .. | .. | .. | .. | .. | .. | .. | .. | .. | .. |
| 4300 Estate, inheritance and gift taxes | .. | .. | .. | 0 | 0 | 0 | 0 | 0 | 0 | 0 |
| 4310 Estate and inheritance taxes | .. | .. | .. | .. | .. | .. | .. | .. | .. | .. |
| 4320 Gift taxes | .. | .. | .. | .. | .. | .. | .. | .. | .. | .. |
| 4400 Taxes on financial and capital transactions | .. | .. | .. | 0 | 0 | 0 | 0 | 0 | 0 | 0 |
| 4500 Other non-reccurrent taxes on property | .. | .. | .. | 0 | 0 | 0 | 0 | 0 | 0 | 0 |
| 4510 On net wealth | .. | .. | .. | .. | .. | .. | .. | .. | .. | .. |
| 4520 Other non-recurrent taxes | .. | .. | .. | .. | .. | .. | .. | .. | .. | .. |
| 4600 Other recurrent taxes on property | .. | .. | .. | 0 | 0 | 0 | 0 | 0 | 0 | 0 |
| **5000 Taxes on goods and services** | .. | .. | .. | **5 412** | **11 242** | **11 913** | **11 837** | **12 684** | **13 128** | **12 010** |
| 5100 Taxes on production, sale, transfer, etc | .. | .. | .. | 4 720 | 9 834 | 10 524 | 10 172 | 11 718 | 12 059 | 10 000 |
| 5110 General taxes on goods and services | .. | .. | .. | 2 033 | 4 988 | 4 688 | 4 934 | 5 201 | 5 389 | 4 706 |
| 5111 Value added taxes | .. | .. | .. | 400 | 4 744 | 4 688 | 4 934 | 5 201 | 5 389 | 4 706 |
| 5112 Sales tax | .. | .. | .. | 0 | 0 | 0 | 0 | 0 | 0 | 0 |
| 5113 Other | .. | .. | .. | 1 633 | 244 | 0 | 0 | 0 | 0 | 0 |
| 5120 Taxes on specific goods and services | .. | .. | .. | 2 687 | 4 846 | 5 836 | 5 238 | 6 516 | 6 670 | 5 295 |
| 5121 Excises | .. | .. | .. | 1 749 | 3 253 | 4 124 | 4 234 | 4 743 | 4 972 | 3 602 |
| 5122 Profits of fiscal monopolies | .. | .. | .. | 0 | 0 | 0 | 0 | 0 | 0 | 0 |
| 5123 Customs and import duties | .. | .. | .. | 855 | 1 382 | 1 655 | 971 | 1 059 | 967 | 1 070 |
| 5124 Taxes on exports | .. | .. | .. | 70 | 205 | 49 | 29 | 38 | 45 | 15 |
| 5125 Taxes on investment goods | .. | .. | .. | 0 | 0 | 0 | 0 | 0 | 0 | 0 |
| 5126 Taxes on specific services | .. | .. | .. | 12 | 6 | 7 | 4 | 676 | 686 | 608 |
| 5127 Other taxes on internat. trade and transactions | .. | .. | .. | 0 | 0 | 0 | 0 | 0 | 0 | 0 |
| 5128 Other taxes | .. | .. | .. | 0 | 0 | 0 | 0 | 0 | 0 | 0 |
| 5130 Unallocable between 5110 and 5120 | .. | .. | .. | 0 | 0 | 0 | 0 | 0 | 0 | 0 |
| 5200 Taxes on use of goods and to perform activities | .. | .. | .. | 692 | 1 408 | 1 389 | 1 665 | 966 | 1 068 | 2 009 |
| 5210 Recurrent taxes | .. | .. | .. | 692 | 1 408 | 1 389 | 1 665 | 966 | 1 068 | 2 009 |
| 5211 Paid by households: motor vehicles | .. | .. | .. | 0 | 0 | 0 | 0 | 0 | 0 | 0 |
| 5212 Paid by others: motor vehicles | .. | .. | .. | 0 | 0 | 0 | 0 | 0 | 0 | 0 |
| 5213 Paid in respect of other goods | .. | .. | .. | 692 | 1 408 | 1 389 | 1 665 | 966 | 1 068 | 2 009 |
| 5220 Non-recurrent taxes | .. | .. | .. | 0 | 0 | 0 | 0 | 0 | 0 | 0 |
| 5300 Unallocable between 5100 and 5200 | .. | .. | .. | 0 | 0 | 0 | 0 | 0 | 0 | 0 |

| | 1997 | 2000 | 2007 | 2010 | 2015 | 2016 | 2017 | 2018 | 2019 | 2020 |
|---|---|---|---|---|---|---|---|---|---|---|
| **6000 Other taxes** | .. | .. | .. | 0 | 0 | 0 | 0 | 0 | 0 | 0 |
| 6100 Paid solely by business | .. | .. | .. | .. | .. | .. | .. | .. | .. | .. |
| 6200 Other | .. | .. | .. | .. | .. | .. | .. | .. | .. | .. |

.. Not available

Note: Data are reported on a calendar year.

The data are on a cash basis.

Heading 2000: Detailed data on revenues from social security contributions were not available.

Revenues from the natural resource tax are not included in this table. Although considered to be tax revenues by Lao PDR, these revenues are considered to be non-tax revenue under with the OECD classification, as set out in the Interpretative Guides in Annex A and B.

Source: Ministry of Finance, Lao PDR.

StatLink https://stat.link/po0aqm

## Table 4.14. Malaysia: Details of tax revenue

Million MYR

| | 1997 | 2000 | 2007 | 2010 | 2015 | 2016 | 2017 | 2018 | 2019 | 2020 |
|---|---|---|---|---|---|---|---|---|---|---|
| **Total tax revenue** | **55 493** | **50 083** | **98 569** | **113 573** | **170 962** | **175 325** | **183 537** | **181 064** | **188 328** | **161 454** |
| **1000 Taxes on income, profits and capital gains** | **27 648** | **27 339** | **65 671** | **75 058** | **105 751** | **103 967** | **110 260** | **123 953** | **128 307** | **106 572** |
| 1100 Of individuals | 6 429 | 7 015 | 11 661 | 17 805 | 26 321 | 27 566 | 28 945 | 32 605 | 38 680 | 38 953 |
| 1110 On income and profits | 6 429 | 7 015 | 11 661 | 17 805 | 26 321 | 27 566 | 28 945 | 32 605 | 38 680 | 38 953 |
| 1120 On capital gains | .. | .. | .. | .. | .. | .. | .. | .. | .. | .. |
| 1200 Corporate | 20 552 | 19 923 | 52 615 | 55 156 | 75 275 | 72 127 | 76 226 | 86 556 | 84 534 | 62 837 |
| 1210 On profits | 20 552 | 19 923 | 52 615 | 55 156 | 75 275 | 72 127 | 76 226 | 86 556 | 84 534 | 62 837 |
| Company income tax | 16 688 | 13 905 | 32 149 | 36 266 | 63 679 | 63 625 | 64 465 | 66 474 | 63 751 | 50 065 |
| Petroleum income tax | 3 861 | 6 010 | 20 453 | 18 713 | 11 559 | 8 422 | 11 761 | 20 082 | 20 783 | 12 772 |
| Offshore business activity tax | 3 | 8 | 13 | 15 | 37 | 81 | 0 | 0 | 0 | 0 |
| Levy on Electricity | 0 | 0 | 0 | 162 | 0 | 0 | 0 | 0 | 0 | 0 |
| 1220 On capital gains of corporates | .. | .. | .. | .. | .. | .. | .. | .. | .. | .. |
| 1300 Unallocable between 1100 and 1200 | 666 | 402 | 1 395 | 2 097 | 4 155 | 4 274 | 5 089 | 4 792 | 5 093 | 4 782 |
| Cooperatives income tax | 143 | 87 | 189 | 378 | 80 | 90 | 74 | 171 | 189 | 59 |
| Withholding income tax | 0 | 0 | 1 190 | 1 268 | 2 316 | 2 562 | 3 266 | 3 117 | 3 061 | 2 993 |
| Other income tax | 0 | 0 | 17 | 21 | 30 | 43 | 51 | 37 | 43 | 43 |
| Real property gains tax | 523 | 247 | 0 | 303 | 1 729 | 1 492 | 1 697 | 1 467 | 1 800 | 1 687 |
| Exit levy | 0 | 41 | 0 | 0 | 0 | 0 | 0 | 0 | 0 | 0 |
| Windfall levy on crude palm oil | 0 | 0 | 0 | 0 | 0 | 0 | 0 | 0 | 0 | 0 |
| Windfall levy on crude palm kernel oil | 0 | 26 | 0 | 0 | 0 | 0 | 0 | 0 | 0 | 0 |
| Levy on fresh fruit bunch | 0 | 0 | 0 | 127 | 1 | 87 | 0 | 0 | 0 | 0 |
| **2000 Social security contributions** | **..** | **990** | **1 690** | **2 008** | **2 838** | **3 216** | **3 561** | **4 301** | **4 783** | **4 121** |
| 2100 Employees | .. | 218 | 371 | 439 | .. | .. | .. | .. | .. | .. |
| 2110 On a payroll basis | .. | 218 | 371 | 439 | .. | .. | .. | .. | .. | .. |
| 2120 On an income tax basis | .. | 0 | 0 | 0 | .. | .. | .. | .. | .. | .. |
| 2200 Employers | .. | 772 | 1 319 | 1 569 | .. | .. | .. | .. | .. | .. |
| 2210 On a payroll basis | .. | 772 | 1 319 | 1 569 | .. | .. | .. | .. | .. | .. |
| 2220 On an income tax basis | .. | 0 | 0 | 0 | .. | .. | .. | .. | .. | .. |
| 2300 Self-employed or non-employed | .. | 0 | 0 | 0 | .. | .. | .. | .. | .. | .. |
| 2310 On a payroll basis | .. | .. | .. | .. | .. | .. | .. | .. | .. | .. |
| 2320 On an income tax basis | .. | .. | .. | .. | .. | .. | .. | .. | .. | .. |
| 2400 Unallocable between 2100, 2200 and 2300 | .. | 0 | 0 | 0 | 2 838 | 3 216 | 3 561 | 4 301 | 4 783 | 4 121 |
| 2410 On a payroll basis | .. | .. | .. | .. | .. | .. | .. | .. | .. | .. |
| 2420 On an income tax basis | .. | .. | .. | .. | .. | .. | .. | .. | .. | .. |
| **3000 Taxes on payroll and workforce** | **0** | **0** | **0** | **0** | **0** | **0** | **0** | **0** | **0** | **0** |
| **4000 Taxes on property** | **19** | **2** | **..** | **..** | **1** | **3** | **0** | **0** | **0** | **0** |
| 4100 Recurrent taxes on immovable property | 0 | 0 | .. | .. | 0 | 0 | .. | .. | .. | .. |
| 4110 Households | .. | .. | .. | .. | .. | .. | .. | .. | .. | .. |
| 4120 Others | .. | .. | .. | .. | .. | .. | .. | .. | .. | .. |
| 4200 Recurrent taxes on net wealth | 0 | 0 | .. | .. | 0 | 0 | .. | .. | .. | .. |
| 4210 Individual | .. | .. | .. | .. | .. | .. | .. | .. | .. | .. |
| 4220 Corporate | .. | .. | .. | .. | .. | .. | .. | .. | .. | .. |
| 4300 Estate, inheritance and gift taxes | 19 | 2 | .. | .. | 1 | 3 | .. | .. | .. | .. |
| 4310 Estate and inheritance taxes | 19 | 2 | .. | .. | 1 | 3 | .. | .. | .. | .. |
| Estate Duty | 19 | 2 | .. | .. | 1 | 3 | .. | .. | .. | .. |
| 4320 Gift taxes | 0 | 0 | .. | .. | 0 | 0 | .. | .. | .. | .. |
| 4400 Taxes on financial and capital transactions | 0 | 0 | .. | .. | 0 | 0 | .. | .. | .. | .. |
| 4500 Other non-reccurrent taxes on property | 0 | 0 | .. | .. | 0 | 0 | .. | .. | .. | .. |
| 4510 On net wealth | .. | .. | .. | .. | .. | .. | .. | .. | .. | .. |
| 4520 Other non-recurrent taxes | .. | .. | .. | .. | .. | .. | .. | .. | .. | .. |
| 4600 Other recurrent taxes on property | 0 | 0 | .. | .. | 0 | 0 | .. | .. | .. | .. |
| **5000 Taxes on goods and services** | **25 061** | **19 910** | **27 483** | **32 268** | **56 353** | **62 415** | **63 952** | **46 729** | **48 823** | **44 822** |
| 5100 Taxes on production, sale, transfer, etc | 23 195 | 17 990 | 25 772 | 30 218 | 53 669 | 59 649 | 61 148 | 43 810 | 45 843 | 41 887 |
| 5110 General taxes on goods and services | 6 167 | 5 968 | 6 642 | 8 171 | 32 235 | 41 309 | 44 337 | 24 207 | 15 385 | 14 767 |
| 5111 Value added taxes | 0 | 0 | 0 | 0 | 27 012 | 41 206 | 44 290 | 20 236 | 0 | 0 |
| 5112 Sales tax | 6 167 | 5 968 | 6 642 | 8 171 | 5 223 | 103 | 47 | 3 971 | 15 385 | 14 767 |
| Sales tax on local goods | 4 160 | 3 894 | 4 178 | 4 886 | 3 207 | .. | 46 | 1 095 | 6 445 | 6 494 |
| Sales tax on imported goods | 2 008 | 2 074 | 2 464 | 3 285 | 2 016 | .. | 2 | 2 876 | 8 940 | 8 273 |
| 5113 Other | 0 | 0 | 0 | 0 | 0 | 0 | 0 | 0 | 0 | 0 |
| 5120 Taxes on specific goods and services | 15 266 | 10 245 | 16 897 | 19 624 | 18 862 | 15 854 | 14 266 | 16 986 | 27 038 | 25 411 |
| 5121 Excises | 6 053 | 3 803 | 8 990 | 11 770 | 11 890 | 11 705 | 10 112 | 10 779 | 10 511 | 9 856 |
| Excise duties on domestic goods | 6 053 | 3 803 | 7 910 | 9 350 | 7 999 | 7 721 | 5 519 | 4 918 | 5 131 | 4 719 |
| Malt beer (domestic) | .. | .. | .. | .. | .. | .. | .. | 1 696 | 1 861 | 1 619 |
| Cigarettes (domestic) | .. | .. | .. | .. | .. | .. | .. | 234 | 66 | 37 |
| Passenger vehicles (domestic) | .. | .. | .. | .. | .. | .. | .. | 2 483 | 2 443 | 2 373 |
| Other products (domestic) | .. | .. | .. | .. | .. | .. | .. | 505 | 760 | 690 |
| Excise duties on imported goods | 0 | 0 | 1 081 | 2 420 | 3 891 | 3 984 | 4 593 | 5 861 | 5 380 | 5 136 |
| Cigarettes (imported) | .. | .. | .. | .. | .. | .. | .. | 2 681 | 2 522 | 2 748 |
| Motor vehicles (imported) | .. | .. | .. | .. | .. | .. | .. | 2 803 | 2 466 | 2 023 |

| | 1997 | 2000 | 2007 | 2010 | 2015 | 2016 | 2017 | 2018 | 2019 | 2020 |
|---|---|---|---|---|---|---|---|---|---|---|
| Other products (imported) | .. | .. | .. | .. | .. | .. | .. | 378 | 392 | 365 |
| 5122 Profits of fiscal monopolies | 0 | 0 | 0 | 0 | 0 | 0 | 0 | 0 | 0 | 0 |
| 5123 Customs and import duties | 6 524 | 3 599 | 2 424 | 1 966 | 2 732 | 2 905 | 2 784 | 2 897 | 2 733 | 2 346 |
| Import duty on vehicles | .. | .. | .. | .. | .. | .. | .. | 562 | 479 | 426 |
| Import duty on motors, machines and spare parts | .. | .. | .. | .. | .. | .. | .. | 681 | 675 | 517 |
| Import duty on alcoholic beverages | .. | .. | .. | .. | .. | .. | .. | 100 | 99 | 74 |
| Import duty on steel and metal products | .. | .. | .. | .. | .. | .. | .. | 305 | 298 | 241 |
| Import duty on other products | .. | .. | .. | .. | .. | .. | .. | 1 248 | 1 182 | 1 089 |
| 5124 Taxes on exports | 1 053 | 1 032 | 2 322 | 1 810 | 1 039 | 980 | 1 355 | 1 725 | 1 126 | 746 |
| Export duty on petroleom | .. | .. | .. | .. | .. | .. | .. | 1 513 | 1 091 | 634 |
| Export duty on other products | .. | .. | .. | .. | .. | .. | .. | 212 | 35 | 112 |
| 5125 Taxes on investment goods | 0 | 0 | 0 | 0 | 0 | 0 | 0 | 0 | 0 | 0 |
| 5126 Taxes on specific services | 1 475 | 1 701 | 3 013 | 3 926 | 3 038 | 103 | 15 | 1 473 | 12 499 | 12 074 |
| Service tax | 1 475 | 1 701 | 3 013 | 3 926 | 3 038 | 103 | 15 | 1 473 | 12 283 | 12 006 |
| Other taxes on specific services | 0 | 0 | 0 | 0 | 0 | 0 | 0 | 0 | 216 | 68 |
| 5127 Other taxes on internat. trade and transactions | 160 | 110 | 147 | 151 | 163 | 160 | 0 | 113 | 169 | 389 |
| 5128 Other taxes | 0 | 0 | 0 | 0 | 0 | 0 | 0 | 0 | 0 | 0 |
| 5130 Unallocable between 5110 and 5120 | 1 761 | 1 777 | 2 233 | 2 423 | 2 572 | 2 486 | 2 545 | 2 617 | 3 420 | 1 709 |
| 5200 Taxes on use of goods and to perform activities | 1 866 | 1 920 | 1 711 | 2 050 | 2 684 | 2 766 | 2 805 | 2 919 | 2 979 | 2 936 |
| 5210 Recurrent taxes | 1 863 | 1 918 | 1 709 | 2 047 | 2 681 | 2 763 | 2 805 | 2 919 | 2 979 | 2 936 |
| 5211 Paid by households: motor vehicles | 1 852 | 1 909 | 1 688 | 1 992 | 2 630 | 2 714 | 2 805 | 2 919 | 2 979 | 2 936 |
| Motor vehicle licences | 1 852 | 1 909 | 1 688 | 1 992 | 2 630 | 2 714 | 2 805 | 2 919 | 2 979 | 2 936 |
| 5212 Paid by others: motor vehicles | 11 | 9 | 20 | 18 | 3 | 3 | 0 | 0 | 0 | 0 |
| Commercial vehicle licences | 11 | 9 | 19 | 17 | 3 | 3 | .. | .. | .. | .. |
| Tour vehicle licences | 0 | 0 | 1 | 1 | 0 | 0 | .. | .. | .. | .. |
| 5213 Paid in respect of other goods | 0 | 0 | 0 | 38 | 48 | 46 | 0 | 0 | 0 | 0 |
| Petroleum Permits | 0 | 0 | 0 | 1 | 2 | 2 | .. | .. | .. | .. |
| Bank Licences Fees | 0 | 0 | 0 | 37 | 46 | 44 | .. | .. | .. | .. |
| 5220 Non-recurrent taxes | 3 | 2 | 3 | 2 | 3 | 3 | 0 | 0 | 0 | 0 |
| Environment Pollution Licences | 2 | 2 | 3 | 2 | 3 | 3 | .. | .. | .. | .. |
| Film rental tax | 1 | 0 | 0 | 0 | 0 | 0 | .. | .. | .. | .. |
| 5300 Unallocable between 5100 and 5200 | 0 | 0 | 0 | 0 | 0 | 0 | 0 | 0 | 0 | 0 |
| **6000 Other taxes** | **2 764** | **1 841** | **3 725** | **4 240** | **6 018** | **5 724** | **5 764** | **6 081** | **6 416** | **5 939** |
| 6100 Paid solely by business | 0 | 0 | 0 | 0 | 0 | 0 | 0 | 0 | 0 | 0 |
| 6200 Other | 2 764 | 1 841 | 3 725 | 4 240 | 6 018 | 5 724 | 5 764 | 6 081 | 6 416 | 5 939 |
| Share transfer tax | 0 | 0 | 0 | 0 | 0 | 0 | 0 | 0 | 0 | 0 |
| Stamp duties | 2 714 | 1 799 | 3 404 | 4 192 | 5 974 | 5 688 | 5 665 | 5 924 | 6 213 | 5 506 |
| Other direct taxes | 50 | 42 | 321 | 48 | 45 | 37 | 99 | 157 | 203 | 433 |

.. Not available

Note: Year ending 31st December.

The data are on a cash basis.

Heading 2000: Starting from 2015, Social Security Contribution data is given as a lump sum. Data for 2020 is estimated.

Heading 5111: Starting from 2015, VAT (GST, Goods and Services Tax) is sourced from the IMF's Government Finance Statistics dataset. GST was abolished by the government in 2018 and replaced by sales tax and service tax.

Source: Ministry of Finance of Malaysia; Social Security Organisation of Malaysia (PERKESO).

StatLink https://stat.link/kuicam

## Table 4.15. Maldives: Details of tax revenue

Million MVR

| | 1997 | 2000 | 2007 | 2010 | 2015 | 2016 | 2017 | 2018 | 2019 | 2020 |
|---|---|---|---|---|---|---|---|---|---|---|
| **Total tax revenue** | .. | .. | **2 855** | **2 962** | **12 232** | **13 265** | **14 720** | **15 818** | **16 512** | **10 989** |
| **1000 Taxes on income, profits and capital gains** | .. | .. | **169** | **203** | **3 186** | **3 240** | **3 327** | **3 275** | **3 513** | **3 654** |
| 1100 Of individuals | .. | .. | 0 | 0 | 0 | 0 | 0 | 0 | 0 | 83 |
| 1110 On income and profits | .. | .. | 0 | 0 | 0 | 0 | 0 | 0 | 0 | 83 |
| 1120 On capital gains | .. | .. | 0 | 0 | 0 | 0 | 0 | 0 | 0 | 0 |
| 1200 Corporate | .. | .. | 169 | 203 | 3 186 | 3 240 | 3 327 | 3 275 | 3 513 | 3 571 |
| 1210 On profits | .. | .. | 169 | 203 | 3 186 | 3 240 | 3 327 | 3 275 | 3 513 | 3 571 |
| Business profit tax | .. | .. | 0 | 0 | 2 674 | 2 216 | 2 107 | 2 078 | 2 210 | 2 134 |
| Bank profit tax | .. | .. | 169 | 203 | 513 | 492 | 650 | 564 | 614 | 954 |
| Withholding tax | .. | .. | 0 | 0 | 0 | 532 | 570 | 633 | 688 | 484 |
| 1220 On capital gains of corporates | .. | .. | 0 | 0 | 0 | 0 | 0 | 0 | 0 | 0 |
| 1300 Unallocable between 1100 and 1200 | .. | .. | 0 | 0 | 0 | 0 | 0 | 0 | 0 | 0 |
| **2000 Social security contributions** | .. | .. | **0** | **0** | **0** | **0** | **0** | **0** | **0** | **0** |
| 2100 Employees | .. | .. | .. | .. | .. | .. | .. | .. | .. | .. |
| 2110 On a payroll basis | .. | .. | .. | .. | .. | .. | .. | .. | .. | .. |
| 2120 On an income tax basis | .. | .. | .. | .. | .. | .. | .. | .. | .. | .. |
| 2200 Employers | .. | .. | .. | .. | .. | .. | .. | .. | .. | .. |
| 2210 On a payroll basis | .. | .. | .. | .. | .. | .. | .. | .. | .. | .. |
| 2220 On an income tax basis | .. | .. | .. | .. | .. | .. | .. | .. | .. | .. |
| 2300 Self-employed or non-employed | .. | .. | .. | .. | .. | .. | .. | .. | .. | .. |
| 2310 On a payroll basis | .. | .. | .. | .. | .. | .. | .. | .. | .. | .. |
| 2320 On an income tax basis | .. | .. | .. | .. | .. | .. | .. | .. | .. | .. |
| 2400 Unallocable between 2100, 2200 and 2300 | .. | .. | .. | .. | .. | .. | .. | .. | .. | .. |
| 2410 On a payroll basis | .. | .. | .. | .. | .. | .. | .. | .. | .. | .. |
| 2420 On an income tax basis | .. | .. | .. | .. | .. | .. | .. | .. | .. | .. |
| **3000 Taxes on payroll and workforce** | .. | .. | **0** | **0** | **0** | **0** | **0** | **0** | **0** | **0** |
| **4000 Taxes on property** | .. | .. | **12** | **13** | **33** | **24** | **96** | **40** | **31** | **1** |
| 4100 Recurrent taxes on immovable property | .. | .. | 0 | 0 | 0 | 0 | 0 | 0 | 0 | 0 |
| 4110 Households | .. | .. | .. | .. | .. | .. | .. | .. | .. | .. |
| 4120 Others | .. | .. | .. | .. | .. | .. | .. | .. | .. | .. |
| 4200 Recurrent taxes on net wealth | .. | .. | 0 | 0 | 0 | 0 | 0 | 0 | 0 | 0 |
| 4210 Individual | .. | .. | .. | .. | .. | .. | .. | .. | .. | .. |
| 4220 Corporate | .. | .. | .. | .. | .. | .. | .. | .. | .. | .. |
| 4300 Estate, inheritance and gift taxes | .. | .. | 0 | 0 | 0 | 0 | 0 | 0 | 0 | 0 |
| 4310 Estate and inheritance taxes | .. | .. | .. | .. | .. | .. | .. | .. | .. | .. |
| 4320 Gift taxes | .. | .. | .. | .. | .. | .. | .. | .. | .. | .. |
| 4400 Taxes on financial and capital transactions | .. | .. | 12 | 13 | 33 | 24 | 96 | 40 | 31 | 1 |
| 4500 Other non-reccurrent taxes on property | .. | .. | 0 | 0 | 0 | 0 | 0 | 0 | 0 | 0 |
| 4510 On net wealth | .. | .. | .. | .. | .. | .. | .. | .. | .. | .. |
| 4520 Other non-recurrent taxes | .. | .. | .. | .. | .. | .. | .. | .. | .. | .. |
| 4600 Other recurrent taxes on property | .. | .. | 0 | 0 | 0 | 0 | 0 | 0 | 0 | 0 |
| **5000 Taxes on goods and services** | .. | .. | **2 674** | **2 745** | **9 013** | **10 001** | **11 297** | **12 504** | **12 968** | **7 333** |
| 5100 Taxes on production, sale, transfer, etc | .. | .. | 2 634 | 2 689 | 8 935 | 9 911 | 11 198 | 12 395 | 12 845 | 7 214 |
| 5110 General taxes on goods and services | .. | .. | 0 | 0 | 6 054 | 6 249 | 6 882 | 7 689 | 7 748 | 4 307 |
| 5111 Value added taxes | .. | .. | 0 | 0 | 6 054 | 6 249 | 6 882 | 7 689 | 7 748 | 4 307 |
| Tourism Goods and Services Tax | .. | .. | 0 | 0 | 4 150 | 3 921 | 4 199 | 4 783 | 4 903 | 2 220 |
| Goods and Services Tax | .. | .. | 0 | 0 | 1 904 | 2 328 | 2 683 | 2 906 | 2 845 | 2 087 |
| 5112 Sales tax | .. | .. | 0 | 0 | 0 | 0 | 0 | 0 | 0 | 0 |
| 5113 Other | .. | .. | 0 | 0 | 0 | 0 | 0 | 0 | 0 | 0 |
| 5120 Taxes on specific goods and services | .. | .. | 2 634 | 2 689 | 2 880 | 3 663 | 4 316 | 4 706 | 5 097 | 2 908 |
| 5121 Excises | .. | .. | 0 | 0 | 0 | 0 | 0 | 0 | 0 | 0 |
| 5122 Profits of fiscal monopolies | .. | .. | 0 | 0 | 0 | 0 | 0 | 0 | 0 | 0 |
| 5123 Customs and import duties | .. | .. | 2 087 | 2 056 | 2 346 | 2 487 | 2 799 | 3 149 | 3 412 | 2 264 |
| 5124 Taxes on exports | .. | .. | 0 | 0 | 0 | 15 | 114 | 102 | 103 | 9 |
| Remittance tax | .. | .. | 0 | 0 | 0 | 15 | 114 | 102 | 103 | 9 |
| 5125 Taxes on investment goods | .. | .. | 0 | 0 | 0 | 0 | 0 | 0 | 0 | 0 |
| 5126 Taxes on specific services | .. | .. | 547 | 633 | 534 | 1 161 | 1 402 | 1 455 | 1 582 | 635 |
| Green tax | .. | .. | 0 | 0 | 37 | 623 | 696 | 811 | 851 | 352 |
| Airport service charge | .. | .. | 0 | 36 | 497 | 538 | 706 | 645 | 731 | 283 |
| Tourism tax | .. | .. | 547 | 597 | 1 | 0 | 0 | 0 | 0 | 0 |
| 5127 Other taxes on internat. trade and transactions | .. | .. | 0 | 0 | 0 | 0 | 0 | 0 | 0 | 0 |
| 5128 Other taxes | .. | .. | 0 | 0 | 0 | 0 | 0 | 0 | 0 | 0 |
| 5130 Unallocable between 5110 and 5120 | .. | .. | 0 | 0 | 0 | 0 | 0 | 0 | 0 | 0 |
| 5200 Taxes on use of goods and to perform activities | .. | .. | 40 | 57 | 78 | 90 | 99 | 108 | 123 | 119 |
| 5210 Recurrent taxes | .. | .. | 39 | 55 | 75 | 87 | 97 | 106 | 121 | 115 |
| 5211 Paid by households: motor vehicles | .. | .. | 0 | 0 | 0 | 0 | 0 | 0 | 0 | 0 |
| 5212 Paid by others: motor vehicles | .. | .. | 37 | 47 | 62 | 76 | 84 | 92 | 107 | 103 |
| 5213 Paid in respect of other goods | .. | .. | 2 | 8 | 12 | 11 | 13 | 14 | 13 | 12 |
| 5220 Non-recurrent taxes | .. | .. | 1 | 2 | 3 | 3 | 2 | 2 | 2 | 4 |

| | 1997 | 2000 | 2007 | 2010 | 2015 | 2016 | 2017 | 2018 | 2019 | 2020 |
|---|---|---|---|---|---|---|---|---|---|---|
| 5300 Unallocable between 5100 and 5200 | .. | .. | 0 | 0 | 0 | 0 | 0 | 0 | 0 | 0 |
| **6000 Other taxes** | **..** | **..** | **0** | **0** | **0** | **0** | **0** | **0** | **0** | **0** |
| 6100 Paid solely by business | .. | .. | 0 | 0 | 0 | 0 | 0 | 0 | 0 | 0 |
| 6200 Other | .. | .. | 0 | 0 | 0 | 0 | 0 | 0 | 0 | 0 |

.. Not available

Note: Data are reported on a calendar year.
The data are on a cash basis.

Source: Ministry of Finance, Maldives.

StatLink https://stat.link/a23ulp

## Table 4.16. Mongolia: Details of tax revenue

Billion MNT

| | 1997 | 2000 | 2007 | 2010 | 2015 | 2016 | 2017 | 2018 | 2019 | 2020 |
|---|---|---|---|---|---|---|---|---|---|---|
| **Total tax revenue** | .. | .. | **1 406** | **2 470** | **4 421** | **4 567** | **6 005** | **7 788** | **9 033** | **7 951** |
| **1000 Taxes on income, profits and capital gains** | .. | .. | **649** | **975** | **1 171** | **1 043** | **1 613** | **2 091** | **2 556** | **2 227** |
| 1100 Of individuals | .. | .. | 75 | 161 | 482 | 523 | 651 | 814 | 895 | 829 |
| 1110 On income and profits | .. | .. | 75 | 161 | 482 | 523 | 651 | 814 | 895 | 829 |
| 1120 On capital gains | .. | .. | 0 | 0 | 0 | 0 | 0 | 0 | 0 | 0 |
| 1200 Corporate | .. | .. | 574 | 814 | 689 | 520 | 962 | 1 277 | 1 661 | 1 399 |
| 1210 On profits | .. | .. | 574 | 814 | 689 | 520 | 962 | 1 277 | 1 661 | 1 399 |
| Corporate tax income revenue | .. | .. | 220 | 391 | 689 | 520 | 962 | 1 277 | 1 661 | 1 399 |
| Windfall profit tax | .. | .. | 354 | 423 | 0 | 0 | 0 | 0 | 0 | 0 |
| 1220 On capital gains of corporates | .. | .. | 0 | 0 | 0 | 0 | 0 | 0 | 0 | 0 |
| 1300 Unallocable between 1100 and 1200 | .. | .. | 0 | 0 | 0 | 0 | 0 | 0 | 0 | 0 |
| **2000 Social security contributions** | .. | .. | **161** | **323** | **972** | **1 058** | **1 259** | **1 569** | **1 787** | **1 487** |
| 2100 Employees | .. | .. | 8 | 170 | 438 | 465 | 535 | 541 | 701 | 523 |
| 2110 On a payroll basis | .. | .. | .. | .. | .. | .. | .. | .. | .. | .. |
| 2120 On an income tax basis | .. | .. | .. | .. | .. | .. | .. | .. | .. | .. |
| 2200 Employers | .. | .. | 147 | 129 | 447 | 494 | 578 | 640 | 776 | 464 |
| 2210 On a payroll basis | .. | .. | .. | .. | .. | .. | .. | .. | .. | .. |
| 2220 On an income tax basis | .. | .. | .. | .. | .. | .. | .. | .. | .. | .. |
| 2300 Self-employed or non-employed | .. | .. | 0 | 0 | 0 | 0 | 0 | 0 | 0 | 0 |
| 2310 On a payroll basis | .. | .. | .. | .. | .. | .. | .. | .. | .. | .. |
| 2320 On an income tax basis | .. | .. | .. | .. | .. | .. | .. | .. | .. | .. |
| 2400 Unallocable between 2100, 2200 and 2300 | .. | .. | 6 | 24 | 87 | 99 | 146 | 388 | 310 | 500 |
| 2410 On a payroll basis | .. | .. | .. | .. | .. | .. | .. | .. | .. | .. |
| 2420 On an income tax basis | .. | .. | .. | .. | .. | .. | .. | .. | .. | .. |
| **3000 Taxes on payroll and workforce** | .. | .. | **0** | **0** | **0** | **0** | **0** | **0** | **0** | **0** |
| **4000 Taxes on property** | .. | .. | **28** | **47** | **117** | **125** | **157** | **169** | **222** | **228** |
| 4100 Recurrent taxes on immovable property | .. | .. | 20 | 33 | 60 | 54 | 62 | 67 | 110 | 120 |
| 4110 Households | .. | .. | .. | .. | .. | .. | .. | .. | .. | .. |
| 4120 Others | .. | .. | .. | .. | .. | .. | .. | .. | .. | .. |
| 4200 Recurrent taxes on net wealth | .. | .. | 8 | 14 | 58 | 72 | 94 | 102 | 112 | 108 |
| 4210 Individual | .. | .. | 0 | 0 | 0 | 0 | 0 | 0 | 0 | 0 |
| 4220 Corporate | .. | .. | 8 | 14 | 58 | 72 | 94 | 102 | 112 | 108 |
| 4300 Estate, inheritance and gift taxes | .. | .. | 0 | 0 | 0 | 0 | 0 | 0 | 0 | 0 |
| 4310 Estate and inheritance taxes | .. | .. | .. | .. | .. | .. | .. | .. | .. | .. |
| 4320 Gift taxes | .. | .. | .. | .. | .. | .. | .. | .. | .. | .. |
| 4400 Taxes on financial and capital transactions | .. | .. | 0 | 0 | 0 | 0 | 0 | 0 | 0 | 0 |
| 4500 Other non-reccurrent taxes on property | .. | .. | 0 | 0 | 0 | 0 | 0 | 0 | 0 | 0 |
| 4510 On net wealth | .. | .. | .. | .. | .. | .. | .. | .. | .. | .. |
| 4520 Other non-recurrent taxes | .. | .. | .. | .. | .. | .. | .. | .. | .. | .. |
| 4600 Other recurrent taxes on property | .. | .. | 0 | 0 | 0 | 0 | 0 | 0 | 0 | 0 |
| **5000 Taxes on goods and services** | .. | .. | **568** | **1 125** | **2 161** | **2 341** | **2 976** | **3 960** | **4 469** | **4 009** |
| 5100 Taxes on production, sale, transfer, etc | .. | .. | 508 | 1 048 | 1 990 | 2 129 | 2 686 | 3 671 | 4 182 | 3 768 |
| 5110 General taxes on goods and services | .. | .. | 265 | 579 | 1 050 | 1 141 | 1 619 | 2 196 | 2 486 | 2 209 |
| 5111 Value added taxes | .. | .. | 265 | 579 | 1 050 | 1 141 | 1 619 | 2 196 | 2 486 | 2 209 |
| Domestic VAT | .. | .. | 108 | 208 | 485 | 558 | 734 | 898 | 1 088 | 1 053 |
| Import VAT | .. | .. | 199 | 423 | 672 | 684 | 1 032 | 1 412 | 1 633 | 1 504 |
| VAT refunds | .. | .. | -42 | -51 | -107 | -102 | -148 | -114 | -235 | -348 |
| 5112 Sales tax | .. | .. | 0 | 0 | 0 | 0 | 0 | 0 | 0 | 0 |
| 5113 Other | .. | .. | 0 | 0 | 0 | 0 | 0 | 0 | 0 | 0 |
| 5120 Taxes on specific goods and services | .. | .. | 243 | 469 | 941 | 989 | 1 067 | 1 475 | 1 696 | 1 559 |
| 5121 Excises | .. | .. | 140 | 276 | 604 | 641 | 532 | 768 | 880 | 794 |
| Alcoholic drinks (excluding beer) | .. | .. | 48 | 93 | 210 | 222 | 247 | 269 | 310 | 297 |
| Beer | .. | .. | 7 | 17 | 28 | 27 | 27 | 29 | 32 | 28 |
| Tobacco | .. | .. | 10 | 11 | 32 | 33 | 33 | 29 | 29 | 27 |
| Vehicles | .. | .. | 39 | 55 | 44 | 27 | 89 | 214 | 232 | 172 |
| Fuel and gasoline | .. | .. | 36 | 100 | 291 | 332 | 137 | 227 | 277 | 270 |
| 5122 Profits of fiscal monopolies | .. | .. | 0 | 0 | 0 | 0 | 0 | 0 | 0 | 0 |
| 5123 Customs and import duties | .. | .. | 96 | 193 | 321 | 328 | 512 | 682 | 790 | 741 |
| 5124 Taxes on exports | .. | .. | 6 | 0 | 0 | 0 | 0 | 0 | 0 | 0 |
| 5125 Taxes on investment goods | .. | .. | 0 | 0 | 0 | 0 | 0 | 0 | 0 | 0 |
| 5126 Taxes on specific services | .. | .. | 0 | 0 | 16 | 19 | 23 | 25 | 26 | 24 |
| 5127 Other taxes on internat. trade and transactions | .. | .. | 0 | 0 | 0 | 0 | 0 | 0 | 0 | 0 |
| 5128 Other taxes | .. | .. | 0 | 0 | 0 | 0 | 0 | 0 | 0 | 0 |
| 5130 Unallocable between 5110 and 5120 | .. | .. | 0 | 0 | 0 | 0 | 0 | 0 | 0 | 0 |
| 5200 Taxes on use of goods and to perform activities | .. | .. | 60 | 77 | 171 | 212 | 290 | 289 | 286 | 241 |
| 5210 Recurrent taxes | .. | .. | 60 | 74 | 157 | 192 | 253 | 247 | 237 | 209 |
| 5211 Paid by households: motor vehicles | .. | .. | 6 | 10 | 29 | 32 | 36 | 38 | 41 | 46 |
| 5212 Paid by others: motor vehicles | .. | .. | 0 | 0 | 0 | 0 | 0 | 0 | 0 | 0 |
| 5213 Paid in respect of other goods | .. | .. | 54 | 63 | 128 | 160 | 218 | 208 | 196 | 163 |

| | 1997 | 2000 | 2007 | 2010 | 2015 | 2016 | 2017 | 2018 | 2019 | 2020 |
|---|---|---|---|---|---|---|---|---|---|---|
| 5220 Non-recurrent taxes | .. | .. | 0 | 3 | 14 | 20 | 37 | 42 | 49 | 32 |
| 5300 Unallocable between 5100 and 5200 | .. | .. | 0 | 0 | 0 | 0 | 0 | 0 | 0 | 0 |
| **6000 Other taxes** | **..** | **..** | **0** | **0** | **0** | **0** | **0** | **0** | **0** | **0** |
| 6100 Paid solely by business | .. | .. | 0 | 0 | 0 | 0 | 0 | 0 | 0 | 0 |
| 6200 Other | .. | .. | 0 | 0 | 0 | 0 | 0 | 0 | 0 | 0 |

.. Not available
Note: Year ending December 31st.
The data are on a cash basis.
Source: Ministry of Finance of Mongolia.

StatLink https://stat.link/iue1aw

## Table 4.17. Nauru: Details of tax revenue

Thousand AUD

| | 1997 | 2000 | 2007 | 2010 | 2015 | 2016 | 2017 | 2018 | 2019 | 2020 |
|---|---|---|---|---|---|---|---|---|---|---|
| **Total tax revenue** | .. | .. | .. | .. | **24 106** | **21 459** | **42 087** | **56 565** | **80 022** | **81 014** |
| **1000 Taxes on income, profits and capital gains** | .. | .. | .. | .. | **12 593** | **12 590** | **27 320** | **39 731** | **62 927** | **63 468** |
| 1100 Of individuals | .. | .. | .. | .. | 0 | 0 | 0 | 0 | 0 | 0 |
| 1110 On income and profits | .. | .. | .. | .. | 0 | 0 | 0 | 0 | 0 | 0 |
| 1120 On capital gains | .. | .. | .. | .. | 0 | 0 | 0 | 0 | 0 | 0 |
| 1200 Corporate | .. | .. | .. | .. | 0 | 0 | 0 | 0 | 0 | 0 |
| 1210 On profits | .. | .. | .. | .. | 0 | 0 | 0 | 0 | 0 | 0 |
| 1220 On capital gains of corporates | .. | .. | .. | .. | 0 | 0 | 0 | 0 | 0 | 0 |
| 1300 Unallocable between 1100 and 1200 | .. | .. | .. | .. | 12 593 | 12 590 | 27 320 | 39 731 | 62 927 | 63 468 |
| Employment Services Tax | .. | .. | .. | .. | 12 593 | 10 131 | 8 657 | 17 531 | 19 935 | 19 518 |
| Business Tax | .. | .. | .. | .. | 0 | 2 459 | 18 663 | 22 200 | 42 992 | 43 950 |
| **2000 Social security contributions** | .. | .. | .. | .. | **0** | **0** | **0** | **0** | **0** | **0** |
| 2100 Employees | .. | .. | .. | .. | .. | .. | .. | .. | .. | .. |
| 2110 On a payroll basis | .. | .. | .. | .. | .. | .. | .. | .. | .. | .. |
| 2120 On an income tax basis | .. | .. | .. | .. | .. | .. | .. | .. | .. | .. |
| 2200 Employers | .. | .. | .. | .. | .. | .. | .. | .. | .. | .. |
| 2210 On a payroll basis | .. | .. | .. | .. | .. | .. | .. | .. | .. | .. |
| 2220 On an income tax basis | .. | .. | .. | .. | .. | .. | .. | .. | .. | .. |
| 2300 Self-employed or non-employed | .. | .. | .. | .. | .. | .. | .. | .. | .. | .. |
| 2310 On a payroll basis | .. | .. | .. | .. | .. | .. | .. | .. | .. | .. |
| 2320 On an income tax basis | .. | .. | .. | .. | .. | .. | .. | .. | .. | .. |
| 2400 Unallocable between 2100, 2200 and 2300 | .. | .. | .. | .. | .. | .. | .. | .. | .. | .. |
| 2410 On a payroll basis | .. | .. | .. | .. | .. | .. | .. | .. | .. | .. |
| 2420 On an income tax basis | .. | .. | .. | .. | .. | .. | .. | .. | .. | .. |
| **3000 Taxes on payroll and workforce** | .. | .. | .. | .. | **0** | **0** | **0** | **0** | **0** | **0** |
| **4000 Taxes on property** | .. | .. | .. | .. | **0** | **0** | **0** | **0** | **0** | **0** |
| 4100 Recurrent taxes on immovable property | .. | .. | .. | .. | .. | .. | .. | .. | .. | .. |
| 4110 Households | .. | .. | .. | .. | .. | .. | .. | .. | .. | .. |
| 4120 Others | .. | .. | .. | .. | .. | .. | .. | .. | .. | .. |
| 4200 Recurrent taxes on net wealth | .. | .. | .. | .. | .. | .. | .. | .. | .. | .. |
| 4210 Individual | .. | .. | .. | .. | .. | .. | .. | .. | .. | .. |
| 4220 Corporate | .. | .. | .. | .. | .. | .. | .. | .. | .. | .. |
| 4300 Estate, inheritance and gift taxes | .. | .. | .. | .. | .. | .. | .. | .. | .. | .. |
| 4310 Estate and inheritance taxes | .. | .. | .. | .. | .. | .. | .. | .. | .. | .. |
| 4320 Gift taxes | .. | .. | .. | .. | .. | .. | .. | .. | .. | .. |
| 4400 Taxes on financial and capital transactions | .. | .. | .. | .. | .. | .. | .. | .. | .. | .. |
| 4500 Other non-reccurrent taxes on property | .. | .. | .. | .. | .. | .. | .. | .. | .. | .. |
| 4510 On net wealth | .. | .. | .. | .. | .. | .. | .. | .. | .. | .. |
| 4520 Other non-recurrent taxes | .. | .. | .. | .. | .. | .. | .. | .. | .. | .. |
| 4600 Other recurrent taxes on property | .. | .. | .. | .. | .. | .. | .. | .. | .. | .. |
| **5000 Taxes on goods and services** | .. | .. | .. | .. | **11 513** | **8 869** | **14 767** | **16 834** | **17 094** | **17 546** |
| 5100 Taxes on production, sale, transfer, etc | .. | .. | .. | .. | 10 747 | 8 200 | 14 011 | 15 750 | 15 953 | 16 446 |
| 5110 General taxes on goods and services | .. | .. | .. | .. | 0 | 0 | 0 | 0 | 0 | 0 |
| 5111 Value added taxes | .. | .. | .. | .. | 0 | 0 | 0 | 0 | 0 | 0 |
| 5112 Sales tax | .. | .. | .. | .. | 0 | 0 | 0 | 0 | 0 | 0 |
| 5113 Other | .. | .. | .. | .. | 0 | 0 | 0 | 0 | 0 | 0 |
| 5120 Taxes on specific goods and services | .. | .. | .. | .. | 10 747 | 8 200 | 14 011 | 15 750 | 15 953 | 16 446 |
| 5121 Excises | .. | .. | .. | .. | 0 | 0 | 0 | 0 | 0 | 0 |
| 5122 Profits of fiscal monopolies | .. | .. | .. | .. | 0 | 0 | 0 | 0 | 0 | 0 |
| 5123 Customs and import duties | .. | .. | .. | .. | 8 271 | 5 121 | 12 055 | 10 000 | 11 604 | 13 105 |
| 5124 Taxes on exports | .. | .. | .. | .. | 0 | 0 | 0 | 0 | 0 | 0 |
| 5125 Taxes on investment goods | .. | .. | .. | .. | 0 | 0 | 0 | 0 | 0 | 0 |
| 5126 Taxes on specific services | .. | .. | .. | .. | 2 476 | 3 079 | 1 955 | 5 750 | 4 349 | 3 341 |
| DCA Departure tax | .. | .. | .. | .. | 579 | 615 | 259 | 1 747 | 811 | 0 |
| DCA Pax levy | .. | .. | .. | .. | 991 | 689 | 289 | 1 846 | 949 | 0 |
| Telecom tax | .. | .. | .. | .. | 906 | 1 775 | 1 407 | 2 158 | 2 589 | 3 341 |
| 5127 Other taxes on internat. trade and transactions | .. | .. | .. | .. | 0 | 0 | 0 | 0 | 0 | 0 |
| 5128 Other taxes | .. | .. | .. | .. | 0 | 0 | 0 | 0 | 0 | 0 |
| 5130 Unallocable between 5110 and 5120 | .. | .. | .. | .. | 0 | 0 | 0 | 0 | 0 | 0 |
| 5200 Taxes on use of goods and to perform activities | .. | .. | .. | .. | 766 | 670 | 757 | 1 084 | 1 142 | 1 100 |
| 5210 Recurrent taxes | .. | .. | .. | .. | 228 | 286 | 334 | 455 | 700 | 479 |
| 5211 Paid by households: motor vehicles | .. | .. | .. | .. | 0 | 0 | 0 | 0 | 0 | 0 |
| 5212 Paid by others: motor vehicles | .. | .. | .. | .. | 0 | 0 | 0 | 32 | 44 | 93 |
| 5213 Paid in respect of other goods | .. | .. | .. | .. | 228 | 286 | 334 | 423 | 656 | 386 |
| 5220 Non-recurrent taxes | .. | .. | .. | .. | 538 | 384 | 423 | 629 | 442 | 621 |
| 5300 Unallocable between 5100 and 5200 | .. | .. | .. | .. | 0 | 0 | 0 | 0 | 0 | 0 |

| | 1997 | 2000 | 2007 | 2010 | 2015 | 2016 | 2017 | 2018 | 2019 | 2020 |
|---|---|---|---|---|---|---|---|---|---|---|
| **6000 Other taxes** | .. | .. | .. | .. | 0 | 0 | 0 | 0 | 0 | 0 |
| 6100 Paid solely by business | .. | .. | .. | .. | .. | .. | .. | .. | .. | .. |
| 6200 Other | .. | .. | .. | .. | .. | .. | .. | .. | .. | .. |

.. Not available
Note: Data are on a fiscal year basis beginning 1st July. For example, the data for 2020 represent the period from July 2020 to June 2021.
Source: Nauru Revenue Office.

StatLink https://stat.link/6b5xgw

## Table 4.18. New Zealand: Details of tax revenue

Million NZD

| | 1997 | 2000 | 2007 | 2010 | 2015 | 2016 | 2017 | 2018 | 2019 | 2020 |
|---|---|---|---|---|---|---|---|---|---|---|
| **Total tax revenue** | **35 560** | **39 765** | **64 046** | **62 310** | **81 499** | **86 576** | **92 635** | **99 834** | **99 792** | **109 360** |
| **1000 Taxes on income, profits and capital gains** | **21 260** | **23 861** | **40 308** | **33 494** | **44 723** | **48 109** | **51 489** | **56 173** | **55 016** | **60 418** |
| 1100 Of individuals | 15 669 | 17 126 | 26 965 | 23 519 | 30 297 | 31 844 | 35 004 | 37 467 | 39 677 | 42 208 |
| 1110 On income and profits | 15 669 | 17 126 | 26 965 | 23 519 | 30 297 | 31 844 | 35 004 | 37 467 | 39 677 | 42 208 |
| 1120 On capital gains | 0 | 0 | 0 | 0 | 0 | 0 | 0 | 0 | 0 | 0 |
| 1200 Corporate | 3 926 | 4 914 | 9 069 | 7 609 | 11 407 | 13 461 | 13 584 | 15 559 | 12 415 | 15 691 |
| 1210 On profits | 3 926 | 4 914 | 9 069 | 7 609 | 11 407 | 13 461 | 13 584 | 15 559 | 12 415 | 15 691 |
| 1220 On capital gains | 0 | 0 | 0 | 0 | 0 | 0 | 0 | 0 | 0 | 0 |
| 1300 Unallocable between 1100 and 1200 | 1 665 | 1 821 | 4 274 | 2 366 | 3 019 | 2 804 | 2 901 | 3 147 | 2 924 | 2 519 |
| NRWT | 662 | 760 | 1 506 | 467 | 733 | 594 | 619 | 651 | 570 | 455 |
| Property speculation | 0 | 0 | 0 | 0 | 0 | 0 | 0 | 0 | 0 | 0 |
| Absentee income tax | 0 | 0 | 0 | 0 | 0 | 0 | 0 | 0 | 0 | 0 |
| Interest | 961 | 990 | 2 699 | 1 704 | 1 660 | 1 468 | 1 530 | 1 659 | 1 528 | 1 109 |
| Dividends | 42 | 71 | 69 | 195 | 626 | 742 | 752 | 837 | 826 | 955 |
| Other | 0 | 0 | 0 | 0 | 0 | 0 | 0 | 0 | 0 | 0 |
| **2000 Social security contributions** | **0** | **0** | **0** | **0** | **0** | **0** | **0** | **0** | **0** | **0** |
| 2100 Employees | 0 | 0 | 0 | 0 | 0 | 0 | 0 | 0 | 0 | 0 |
| 2110 On a payroll basis | .. | .. | .. | .. | .. | .. | .. | .. | .. | .. |
| 2120 On an income tax basis | .. | .. | .. | .. | .. | .. | .. | .. | .. | .. |
| 2200 Employers | 0 | 0 | 0 | 0 | 0 | 0 | 0 | 0 | 0 | 0 |
| 2210 On a payroll basis | .. | .. | .. | .. | .. | .. | .. | .. | .. | .. |
| 2220 On an income tax basis | .. | .. | .. | .. | .. | .. | .. | .. | .. | .. |
| 2300 Self-employed or non-employed | 0 | 0 | 0 | 0 | 0 | 0 | 0 | 0 | 0 | 0 |
| 2310 On a payroll basis | .. | .. | .. | .. | .. | .. | .. | .. | .. | .. |
| 2320 On an income tax basis | .. | .. | .. | .. | .. | .. | .. | .. | .. | .. |
| 2400 Unallocable between 2100, 2200 and 2300 | 0 | 0 | 0 | 0 | 0 | 0 | 0 | 0 | 0 | 0 |
| 2410 On a payroll basis | .. | .. | .. | .. | .. | .. | .. | .. | .. | .. |
| 2420 On an income tax basis | .. | .. | .. | .. | .. | .. | .. | .. | .. | .. |
| **3000 Taxes on payroll and workforce** | **0** | **0** | **0** | **0** | **0** | **0** | **0** | **0** | **0** | **0** |
| **4000 Taxes on property** | **1 918** | **2 112** | **3 417** | **4 119** | **5 046** | **5 257** | **5 533** | **5 814** | **6 156** | **6 455** |
| 4100 Recurrent taxes on immovable property | 1 732 | 2 049 | 3 322 | 4 031 | 4 962 | 5 178 | 5 426 | 5 709 | 6 055 | 6 341 |
| Local govt rates and services | 1 732 | 2 049 | 3 322 | 4 031 | 4 962 | 5 178 | 5 426 | 5 709 | 6 055 | 6 341 |
| Land tax | 0 | 0 | 0 | 0 | 0 | 0 | 0 | 0 | 0 | 0 |
| 4110 Households | 0 | .. | .. | .. | .. | .. | .. | .. | .. | .. |
| 4120 Others | 0 | .. | .. | .. | .. | .. | .. | .. | .. | .. |
| 4200 Recurrent taxes on net wealth | 0 | 0 | 0 | 0 | 0 | 0 | 0 | 0 | 0 | 0 |
| 4210 Individual | .. | .. | .. | .. | .. | .. | .. | .. | .. | .. |
| 4220 Corporate | .. | .. | .. | .. | .. | .. | .. | .. | .. | .. |
| 4300 Estate, inheritance and gift taxes | 0 | 2 | 3 | 2 | 0 | 0 | 0 | 0 | 0 | 0 |
| 4310 Estate and inheritance taxes | .. | 0 | 0 | 0 | .. | .. | .. | .. | .. | .. |
| 4320 Gift taxes | .. | 2 | 3 | 2 | .. | .. | .. | .. | .. | .. |
| 4400 Taxes on financial and capital transactions | 186 | 61 | 92 | 86 | 84 | 79 | 107 | 105 | 101 | 114 |
| Instrument duty | 173 | 51 | 85 | 82 | 84 | 79 | 107 | 105 | 101 | 114 |
| Cheque duty | 13 | 10 | 7 | 4 | 0 | 0 | 0 | 0 | 0 | 0 |
| 4500 Non-recurrent taxes | 0 | 0 | 0 | 0 | 0 | 0 | 0 | 0 | 0 | 0 |
| 4510 On net wealth | .. | .. | .. | .. | .. | .. | .. | .. | .. | .. |
| 4520 Other non-recurrent taxes | .. | .. | .. | .. | .. | .. | .. | .. | .. | .. |
| 4600 Other recurrent taxes on property | 0 | 0 | 0 | 0 | 0 | 0 | 0 | 0 | 0 | 0 |
| **5000 Taxes on goods and services** | **12 382** | **13 792** | **20 290** | **24 692** | **31 728** | **33 203** | **35 612** | **37 845** | **38 618** | **42 485** |
| 5100 Taxes on production, sale, transfer, etc. | 11 603 | 12 887 | 18 832 | 23 107 | 29 584 | 30 925 | 33 220 | 35 271 | 36 004 | 39 753 |
| 5110 General taxes | 8 696 | 9 885 | 15 046 | 19 143 | 24 587 | 25 847 | 27 951 | 29 521 | 30 259 | 34 263 |
| 5111 Value added taxes | 8 696 | 9 885 | 15 046 | 19 143 | 24 587 | 25 847 | 27 951 | 29 521 | 30 259 | 34 263 |
| 5112 Sales tax | 0 | 0 | 0 | 0 | 0 | 0 | 0 | 0 | 0 | 0 |
| Motor vehicles | .. | .. | .. | .. | .. | .. | .. | .. | .. | .. |
| Other sales tax | .. | .. | .. | .. | .. | .. | .. | .. | .. | .. |
| 5113 Other | 0 | 0 | 0 | 0 | 0 | 0 | 0 | 0 | 0 | 0 |
| 5120 Taxes on specific goods and services | 2 907 | 3 002 | 3 786 | 3 964 | 4 997 | 5 078 | 5 269 | 5 750 | 5 745 | 5 490 |

| | 1997 | 2000 | 2007 | 2010 | 2015 | 2016 | 2017 | 2018 | 2019 | 2020 |
|---|---|---|---|---|---|---|---|---|---|---|
| 5121 Excise duties | 2 018 | 2 148 | 1 627 | 1 782 | 2 280 | 2 231 | 2 214 | 2 622 | 2 468 | 2 152 |
| On alcoholic beverages | 439 | 436 | 573 | 622 | 672 | 684 | 699 | 722 | 710 | 758 |
| Beer | 218 | 201 | 290 | 207 | 262 | 265 | 265 | 274 | 268 | 286 |
| Wine | 106 | 100 | 163 | 181 | 216 | 218 | 227 | 225 | 221 | 236 |
| Spirits | 115 | 135 | 120 | 234 | 194 | 201 | 207 | 223 | 221 | 236 |
| Tobacco | 681 | 764 | 159 | 220 | 362 | 352 | 399 | 483 | 485 | 41 |
| Motor vehicles | 0 | 0 | 0 | 0 | 0 | 0 | 0 | 0 | 0 | 0 |
| Refined sugar | 0 | 0 | 0 | 0 | 0 | 0 | 0 | 0 | 0 | 0 |
| CA petroleum fuels | 786 | 810 | 819 | 872 | 1 185 | 1 137 | 1 057 | 1 201 | 1 075 | 1 163 |
| NRF fuel excise | 0 | 0 | 0 | 0 | 0 | 0 | 0 | 0 | 0 | 0 |
| Local petroleum fuels | 25 | 27 | 30 | 32 | 33 | 34 | 33 | 190 | 175 | 160 |
| CA mileage tax | 0 | 0 | 0 | 0 | 0 | 0 | 0 | 0 | 0 | 0 |
| NRF mileage tax | 0 | 0 | 0 | 0 | 0 | 0 | 0 | 0 | 0 | 0 |
| Road user charges | 0 | 0 | 0 | 0 | 0 | 0 | 0 | 0 | 0 | 0 |
| Energy resources levy | 87 | 111 | 46 | 36 | 28 | 24 | 26 | 26 | 23 | 30 |
| 5122 Profits of fiscal monopolies | 0 | 0 | 0 | 0 | 0 | 0 | 0 | 0 | 0 | 0 |
| 5123 Customs and import duties | 750 | 648 | 1 857 | 1 916 | 2 442 | 2 550 | 2 738 | 2 814 | 3 001 | 3 019 |
| 5124 Taxes on exports | 0 | 0 | 0 | 0 | 0 | 0 | 0 | 0 | 0 | 0 |
| 5125 Taxes on investment goods | 0 | 0 | 0 | 0 | 0 | 0 | 0 | 0 | 0 | 0 |
| 5126 Taxes on specific services | 139 | 206 | 302 | 266 | 275 | 297 | 317 | 314 | 276 | 319 |
| Lottery (national) | 103 | 167 | 290 | 253 | 260 | 281 | 301 | 299 | 266 | 314 |
| Lottery (overseas) | 0 | 0 | 0 | 0 | 0 | 0 | 0 | 0 | 0 | 0 |
| Racing | 36 | 39 | 12 | 13 | 15 | 16 | 16 | 15 | 10 | 5 |
| Film hire tax | 0 | 0 | 0 | 0 | 0 | 0 | 0 | 0 | 0 | 0 |
| Domestic air travel tax | 0 | 0 | 0 | 0 | 0 | 0 | 0 | 0 | 0 | 0 |
| 5127 Other taxes on internat. trade and transactions | 0 | 0 | 0 | 0 | 0 | 0 | 0 | 0 | 0 | 0 |
| Foreign fishing vessels tax | .. | .. | .. | .. | .. | .. | .. | .. | .. | .. |
| Foreign travel tax | .. | .. | .. | .. | .. | .. | .. | .. | .. | .. |
| International departure tax | .. | .. | .. | .. | .. | .. | .. | .. | .. | .. |
| 5128 Other taxes | 0 | 0 | 0 | 0 | 0 | 0 | 0 | 0 | 0 | 0 |
| 5130 Unallocable between 5110 and 5120 | 0 | 0 | 0 | 0 | 0 | 0 | 0 | 0 | 0 | 0 |
| 5200 Taxes on use of goods and perform activities | 779 | 905 | 1 458 | 1 585 | 2 144 | 2 278 | 2 392 | 2 574 | 2 614 | 2 732 |
| 5210 Recurrent taxes | 779 | 905 | 1 458 | 1 585 | 2 144 | 2 278 | 2 392 | 2 574 | 2 614 | 2 732 |
| Motor vehicle registration | 158 | 181 | 226 | 172 | 214 | 223 | 227 | 227 | 226 | 224 |
| Heavy traffic fees | 466 | 532 | 851 | 1 016 | 1 381 | 1 469 | 1 551 | 1 673 | 1 716 | 1 897 |
| Accident compensation levies | 0 | 0 | 0 | 0 | 0 | 0 | 0 | 0 | 0 | 0 |
| 5211 Paid by households: motor vehicles | 0 | 0 | 0 | 0 | 0 | 0 | 0 | 0 | 0 | 0 |
| 5212 Paid by others: motor vehicles | 0 | 0 | 0 | 0 | 0 | 0 | 0 | 0 | 0 | 0 |
| 5213 Paid in respect of other goods | 155 | 192 | 381 | 397 | 549 | 586 | 614 | 674 | 672 | 611 |
| Local authority fees and charges | 155 | 192 | 381 | 397 | 549 | 586 | 614 | 674 | 672 | 611 |
| 5220 Non-recurrent taxes | 0 | 0 | 0 | 0 | 0 | 0 | 0 | 0 | 0 | 0 |
| 5300 Unallocable between 5100 and 5200 | 0 | 0 | 0 | 0 | 0 | 0 | 0 | 0 | 0 | 0 |
| **6000 Other taxes** | **0** | **0** | **31** | **5** | **2** | **7** | **1** | **2** | **2** | **2** |
| 6100 Paid solely by business | .. | .. | 0 | 0 | 0 | 0 | 0 | 0 | 0 | 0 |
| 6200 Other | .. | .. | 31 | 5 | 2 | 7 | 1 | 2 | 2 | 2 |

.. Not available

Note: The figures follow a financial year ending on 30 June of the following year.

From 1993, data are on accrual basis.

Heading 1000: Tax credits to exporters under the export incentives schemes are non-wastable, but that part of the excess of tax liability paid out to taxpayers is not identifiable.

Heading 1100: The figures up to 1969 include revenues collected by a social security income tax. The base of this tax was the same as the ordinary income tax base and the two have now been incorporated into a single income tax.

Heading 5121: From October 1986 incorporates that portion of the selective impost on wine, spirits, tobacco and motor vehicles which was formerly collected and reported as sales tax. The revenue collected on those imported goods which are subject to the equivalent of the domestic excise has been classified as excise duty. In this respect, there is a discontinuity between the excises recorded before and after October 1986.

Heading 5210: The other local authority licence fees include some small items which could be regarded as non-tax revenues.

Heading for non-wastable tax credits 1110 comprises four Family assistance tax credits. The total in item 1100 is net of the tax expenditure component but not net of the transfer component.

Source: Local Authorities Statistics, Department of Statistics, Wellington.

StatLink https://stat.link/o3cm7u

## Table 4.19. Pakistan: Details of tax revenue

Million PKR

| | 1997 | 2000 | 2007 | 2010 | 2015 | 2016 | 2017 | 2018 | 2019 | 2020 |
|---|---|---|---|---|---|---|---|---|---|---|
| **Total tax revenue** | .. | .. | .. | .. | **3 660 418** | **3 969 248** | **4 469 282** | **4 477 136** | **4 751 049** | **5 742 821** |
| **1000 Taxes on income, profits and capital gains** | .. | .. | .. | .. | **1 191 602** | **1 343 197** | **1 536 636** | **1 445 594** | **1 524 252** | **1 731 860** |
| 1100 Of individuals | .. | .. | .. | .. | .. | .. | .. | .. | .. | .. |
| 1110 On income and profits | .. | .. | .. | .. | .. | .. | .. | .. | .. | .. |
| 1120 On capital gains | .. | .. | .. | .. | .. | .. | .. | .. | .. | .. |
| 1200 Corporate | .. | .. | .. | .. | .. | .. | .. | .. | .. | .. |
| 1210 On profits | .. | .. | .. | .. | .. | .. | .. | .. | .. | .. |
| 1220 On capital gains of corporates | .. | .. | .. | .. | .. | .. | .. | .. | .. | .. |
| 1300 Unallocable between 1100 and 1200 | .. | .. | .. | .. | 1 191 602 | 1 343 197 | 1 536 636 | 1 445 594 | 1 524 252 | 1 731 860 |
| **2000 Social security contributions** | .. | .. | .. | .. | **0** | **0** | **0** | **0** | **0** | **0** |
| 2100 Employees | .. | .. | .. | .. | .. | .. | .. | .. | .. | .. |
| 2110 On a payroll basis | .. | .. | .. | .. | .. | .. | .. | .. | .. | .. |
| 2120 On an income tax basis | .. | .. | .. | .. | .. | .. | .. | .. | .. | .. |
| 2200 Employers | .. | .. | .. | .. | .. | .. | .. | .. | .. | .. |
| 2210 On a payroll basis | .. | .. | .. | .. | .. | .. | .. | .. | .. | .. |
| 2220 On an income tax basis | .. | .. | .. | .. | .. | .. | .. | .. | .. | .. |
| 2300 Self-employed or non-employed | .. | .. | .. | .. | .. | .. | .. | .. | .. | .. |
| 2310 On a payroll basis | .. | .. | .. | .. | .. | .. | .. | .. | .. | .. |
| 2320 On an income tax basis | .. | .. | .. | .. | .. | .. | .. | .. | .. | .. |
| 2400 Unallocable between 2100, 2200 and 2300 | .. | .. | .. | .. | .. | .. | .. | .. | .. | .. |
| 2410 On a payroll basis | .. | .. | .. | .. | .. | .. | .. | .. | .. | .. |
| 2420 On an income tax basis | .. | .. | .. | .. | .. | .. | .. | .. | .. | .. |
| **3000 Taxes on payroll and workforce** | .. | .. | .. | .. | **0** | **0** | **0** | **0** | **0** | **0** |
| **4000 Taxes on property** | .. | .. | .. | .. | **39 344** | **45 203** | **68 305** | **77 422** | **68 799** | **55 217** |
| **Other taxes on property** | .. | .. | .. | .. | **3 860** | **7 036** | **5 551** | **7 026** | **9 651** | **0** |
| 4100 Recurrent taxes on immovable property | .. | .. | .. | .. | 0 | 0 | 0 | 0 | 0 | 0 |
| 4110 Households | .. | .. | .. | .. | .. | .. | .. | .. | .. | .. |
| 4120 Others | .. | .. | .. | .. | .. | .. | .. | .. | .. | .. |
| 4200 Recurrent taxes on net wealth | .. | .. | .. | .. | 0 | 0 | 0 | 0 | 0 | 0 |
| 4210 Individual | .. | .. | .. | .. | .. | .. | .. | .. | .. | .. |
| 4220 Corporate | .. | .. | .. | .. | .. | .. | .. | .. | .. | .. |
| 4300 Estate, inheritance and gift taxes | .. | .. | .. | .. | 0 | 0 | 0 | 0 | 0 | 0 |
| 4310 Estate and inheritance taxes | .. | .. | .. | .. | .. | .. | .. | .. | .. | .. |
| 4320 Gift taxes | .. | .. | .. | .. | .. | .. | .. | .. | .. | .. |
| 4400 Taxes on financial and capital transactions | .. | .. | .. | .. | 35 484 | 38 167 | 62 754 | 70 396 | 59 148 | 55 217 |
| Stamp duties | .. | .. | .. | .. | 35 484 | 38 167 | 62 754 | 70 396 | 59 148 | 55 217 |
| 4500 Other non-reccurrent taxes on property | .. | .. | .. | .. | 0 | 0 | 0 | 0 | 0 | 0 |
| 4510 On net wealth | .. | .. | .. | .. | .. | .. | .. | .. | .. | .. |
| 4520 Other non-recurrent taxes | .. | .. | .. | .. | .. | .. | .. | .. | .. | .. |
| 4600 Other recurrent taxes on property | .. | .. | .. | .. | 0 | 0 | 0 | 0 | 0 | 0 |
| **5000 Taxes on goods and services** | .. | .. | .. | .. | **2 337 870** | **2 498 665** | **2 782 433** | **2 857 677** | **3 050 890** | **3 831 206** |
| 5100 Taxes on production, sale, transfer, etc | .. | .. | .. | .. | 2 318 793 | 2 477 383 | 2 758 310 | 2 832 827 | 3 032 911 | 3 804 427 |
| 5110 General taxes on goods and services | .. | .. | .. | .. | 1 453 437 | 1 494 052 | 1 715 170 | 1 667 768 | 1 829 790 | 2 283 831 |
| 5111 Value added taxes | .. | .. | .. | .. | 1 453 437 | 1 494 052 | 1 715 170 | 1 667 768 | 1 829 790 | 2 283 831 |
| Sales tax | .. | .. | .. | .. | 1 323 685 | 1 323 261 | 1 491 310 | 1 464 887 | 1 596 821 | 1 990 186 |
| Sales tax on services | .. | .. | .. | .. | 129 752 | 170 791 | 223 860 | 202 881 | 232 969 | 293 645 |
| 5112 Sales tax | .. | .. | .. | .. | 0 | 0 | 0 | 0 | 0 | 0 |
| 5113 Other | .. | .. | .. | .. | 0 | 0 | 0 | 0 | 0 | 0 |
| 5120 Taxes on specific goods and services | .. | .. | .. | .. | 865 356 | 983 331 | 1 043 140 | 1 165 059 | 1 203 121 | 1 520 596 |
| 5121 Excises | .. | .. | .. | .. | 459 176 | 487 313 | 434 815 | 479 662 | 576 743 | 755 412 |
| Excise duty | .. | .. | .. | .. | 197 461 | 205 205 | 214 431 | 242 865 | 258 113 | 285 290 |
| Petroleum levy | .. | .. | .. | .. | 149 290 | 166 697 | 178 874 | 206 308 | 293 681 | 424 654 |
| Petroleum levy on LPG | .. | .. | .. | .. | 0 | 0 | 2 122 | 3 714 | 3 247 | 3 507 |
| Gas infrastructure development cess | .. | .. | .. | .. | 79 771 | 42 149 | 15 176 | 21 471 | 9 346 | 19 438 |
| Natural gas development surcharge | .. | .. | .. | .. | 32 654 | 73 262 | 24 212 | 5 304 | 12 356 | 22 523 |
| 5122 Profits of fiscal monopolies | .. | .. | .. | .. | 0 | 0 | 0 | 0 | 0 | 0 |
| 5123 Customs and import duties | .. | .. | .. | .. | 406 180 | 496 018 | 608 325 | 685 397 | 626 378 | 765 184 |
| 5124 Taxes on exports | .. | .. | .. | .. | 0 | 0 | 0 | 0 | 0 | 0 |
| 5125 Taxes on investment goods | .. | .. | .. | .. | 0 | 0 | 0 | 0 | 0 | 0 |
| 5126 Taxes on specific services | .. | .. | .. | .. | 0 | 0 | 0 | 0 | 0 | 0 |
| 5127 Other taxes on internat. trade and transactions | .. | .. | .. | .. | 0 | 0 | 0 | 0 | 0 | 0 |
| 5128 Other taxes | .. | .. | .. | .. | 0 | 0 | 0 | 0 | 0 | 0 |
| 5130 Unallocable between 5110 and 5120 | .. | .. | .. | .. | 0 | 0 | 0 | 0 | 0 | 0 |
| 5200 Taxes on use of goods and to perform activities | .. | .. | .. | .. | 19 077 | 21 282 | 24 123 | 24 850 | 17 979 | 26 779 |
| 5210 Recurrent taxes | .. | .. | .. | .. | 19 077 | 21 282 | 24 123 | 24 850 | 17 979 | 26 779 |
| 5211 Paid by households: motor vehicles | .. | .. | .. | .. | 19 077 | 21 282 | 24 123 | 24 850 | 17 979 | 26 779 |
| 5212 Paid by others: motor vehicles | .. | .. | .. | .. | 0 | 0 | 0 | 0 | 0 | 0 |
| 5213 Paid in respect of other goods | .. | .. | .. | .. | 0 | 0 | 0 | 0 | 0 | 0 |
| 5220 Non-recurrent taxes | .. | .. | .. | .. | 0 | 0 | 0 | 0 | 0 | 0 |

| | 1997 | 2000 | 2007 | 2010 | 2015 | 2016 | 2017 | 2018 | 2019 | 2020 |
|---|---|---|---|---|---|---|---|---|---|---|
| 5300 Unallocable between 5100 and 5200 | .. | .. | .. | .. | 0 | 0 | 0 | 0 | 0 | 0 |
| **6000 Other taxes** | **..** | **..** | **..** | **..** | **91 602** | **82 183** | **81 908** | **96 443** | **107 108** | **124 538** |
| 6100 Paid solely by business | .. | .. | .. | .. | 0 | 0 | 0 | 0 | 0 | 0 |
| 6200 Other | .. | .. | .. | .. | 91 602 | 82 183 | 81 908 | 96 443 | 107 108 | 124 538 |

.. Not available

Note: Data are on a fiscal year basis beginning 1st July. For example, the data for 2020 represent the period from July 2020 to June 2021.

The data are on a cash basis.

Heading 1000: The figures refer to total direct taxes, consisting primarily of income tax and Workers Welfare Fund, both of which are classified as taxes on income and profits according to the OECD Revenue Statistics Interpretative Guide.

Heading 4000: Other taxes on property data are not available separately in 2020. They are included in other local tax revenues classified under heading 6200.

Heading 5121: Excise duty is levied by both federal government and provincial governments. The segregation is not available before 2020, therefore excise duty is attributed entirely to the federal government during this period as the federal portion accounts for the majority according to the segregation in 2020.

Source: Pakistan Bureau of Statistics.

StatLink https://stat.link/265knf

## Table 4.20. Papua New Guinea: Details of tax revenue

Million PGK

| | 1997 | 2000 | 2007 | 2010 | 2015 | 2016 | 2017 | 2018 | 2019 | 2020 |
|---|---|---|---|---|---|---|---|---|---|---|
| **Total tax revenue** | .. | **1 305** | **5 875** | **6 573** | **9 142** | **8 606** | **8 986** | **9 983** | **10 518** | **9 490** |
| **1000 Taxes on income, profits and capital gains** | .. | **936** | **4 287** | **4 562** | **5 956** | **5 286** | **5 474** | **6 119** | **6 055** | **5 655** |
| 1100 Of individuals | .. | 552 | 1 001 | 1 553 | 3 037 | 2 844 | 3 094 | 3 102 | 3 212 | 3 517 |
| 1110 On income and profits | .. | 552 | 1 001 | 1 553 | 3 037 | 2 844 | 3 094 | 3 102 | 3 212 | 3 517 |
| 1120 On capital gains | .. | .. | .. | .. | .. | .. | .. | .. | .. | .. |
| 1200 Corporate | .. | 384 | 3 285 | 3 009 | 2 919 | 2 441 | 2 380 | 3 017 | 2 843 | 2 138 |
| 1210 On profits | .. | 384 | 3 285 | 3 009 | 2 919 | 2 441 | 2 380 | 3 017 | 2 843 | 2 138 |
| Corporate Income Tax | .. | 262 | 724 | 1 201 | 2 375 | 2 094 | 1 950 | 1 933 | 1 697 | 1 554 |
| Mining and Petroleum Tax | .. | 0 | 2 334 | 1 476 | 169 | 92 | 114 | 775 | 760 | 183 |
| Royalty Tax and Management fee | .. | 4 | 5 | 10 | 18 | 44 | 43 | 44 | 43 | 50 |
| Dividend witholding tax | .. | 54 | 204 | 279 | 195 | 133 | 182 | 155 | 215 | 216 |
| Interest witholding tax | .. | 64 | 19 | 42 | 162 | 79 | 91 | 111 | 128 | 135 |
| 1220 On capital gains of corporates | .. | .. | .. | .. | .. | .. | .. | .. | .. | .. |
| 1300 Unallocable between 1100 and 1200 | .. | 0 | 0 | 0 | 0 | 0 | 0 | 0 | 0 | 0 |
| **2000 Social security contributions** | .. | **0** | **0** | **0** | **0** | **0** | **0** | **0** | **0** | **0** |
| 2100 Employees | .. | .. | .. | .. | .. | .. | .. | .. | .. | .. |
| 2110 On a payroll basis | .. | .. | .. | .. | .. | .. | .. | .. | .. | .. |
| 2120 On an income tax basis | .. | .. | .. | .. | .. | .. | .. | .. | .. | .. |
| 2200 Employers | .. | .. | .. | .. | .. | .. | .. | .. | .. | .. |
| 2210 On a payroll basis | .. | .. | .. | .. | .. | .. | .. | .. | .. | .. |
| 2220 On an income tax basis | .. | .. | .. | .. | .. | .. | .. | .. | .. | .. |
| 2300 Self-employed or non-employed | .. | .. | .. | .. | .. | .. | .. | .. | .. | .. |
| 2310 On a payroll basis | .. | .. | .. | .. | .. | .. | .. | .. | .. | .. |
| 2320 On an income tax basis | .. | .. | .. | .. | .. | .. | .. | .. | .. | .. |
| 2400 Unallocable between 2100, 2200 and 2300 | .. | .. | .. | .. | .. | .. | .. | .. | .. | .. |
| 2410 On a payroll basis | .. | .. | .. | .. | .. | .. | .. | .. | .. | .. |
| 2420 On an income tax basis | .. | .. | .. | .. | .. | .. | .. | .. | .. | .. |
| **3000 Taxes on payroll and workforce** | .. | **1** | **2** | **2** | **0** | **14** | **11** | **9** | **2** | **1** |
| **4000 Taxes on property** | .. | **44** | **85** | **65** | **51** | **79** | **42** | **100** | **47** | **43** |
| 4100 Recurrent taxes on immovable property | .. | 0 | 0 | 0 | 0 | 0 | 0 | 0 | 0 | 0 |
| 4110 Households | .. | .. | .. | .. | .. | .. | .. | .. | .. | .. |
| 4120 Others | .. | .. | .. | .. | .. | .. | .. | .. | .. | .. |
| 4200 Recurrent taxes on net wealth | .. | 0 | 0 | 0 | 0 | 0 | 0 | 0 | 0 | 0 |
| 4210 Individual | .. | .. | .. | .. | .. | .. | .. | .. | .. | .. |
| 4220 Corporate | .. | .. | .. | .. | .. | .. | .. | .. | .. | .. |
| 4300 Estate, inheritance and gift taxes | .. | 0 | 0 | 0 | 0 | 0 | 0 | 0 | 0 | 0 |
| 4310 Estate and inheritance taxes | .. | .. | .. | .. | .. | .. | .. | .. | .. | .. |
| 4320 Gift taxes | .. | .. | .. | .. | .. | .. | .. | .. | .. | .. |
| 4400 Taxes on financial and capital transactions | .. | 44 | 85 | 65 | 51 | 79 | 42 | 100 | 47 | 43 |
| 4500 Other non-reccurrent taxes on property | .. | 0 | 0 | 0 | 0 | 0 | 0 | 0 | 0 | 0 |
| 4510 On net wealth | .. | .. | .. | .. | .. | .. | .. | .. | .. | .. |
| 4520 Other non-recurrent taxes | .. | .. | .. | .. | .. | .. | .. | .. | .. | .. |
| 4600 Other recurrent taxes on property | .. | 0 | 0 | 0 | 0 | 0 | 0 | 0 | 0 | 0 |
| **5000 Taxes on goods and services** | .. | **325** | **1 501** | **1 944** | **3 134** | **3 227** | **3 459** | **3 755** | **4 414** | **3 791** |
| 5100 Taxes on production, sale, transfer, etc | .. | 325 | 1 501 | 1 944 | 3 134 | 3 227 | 3 459 | 3 755 | 4 414 | 3 791 |
| 5110 General taxes on goods and services | .. | 325 | 654 | 874 | 1 637 | 1 646 | 1 617 | 1 642 | 1 990 | 1 568 |
| 5111 Value added taxes | .. | 321 | 648 | 865 | 1 571 | 1 638 | 1 581 | 1 622 | 1 973 | 1 560 |
| Goods and services tax (inland Collection) | .. | 177 | 468 | 629 | 1 068 | 1 103 | 1 131 | 1 120 | 1 368 | 982 |
| GST transfers to provinces | .. | 144 | 180 | 236 | 503 | 535 | 450 | 502 | 605 | 578 |
| 5112 Sales tax | .. | 0 | 0 | 0 | 0 | 0 | 0 | 0 | 0 | 0 |
| 5113 Other | .. | 4 | 6 | 9 | 66 | 8 | 36 | 20 | 17 | 8 |
| 5120 Taxes on specific goods and services | .. | .. | 846 | 1 070 | 1 497 | 1 581 | 1 842 | 2 113 | 2 424 | 2 223 |
| 5121 Excises | .. | .. | 455 | 611 | 802 | 876 | 1 105 | 1 168 | 1 361 | 1 281 |
| 5122 Profits of fiscal monopolies | .. | 0 | 0 | 0 | 0 | 0 | 0 | 0 | 0 | 0 |
| 5123 Customs and import duties | .. | .. | 136 | 189 | 243 | 243 | 246 | 325 | 409 | 380 |
| 5124 Taxes on exports | .. | .. | 155 | 174 | 316 | 294 | 297 | 392 | 398 | 399 |
| 5125 Taxes on investment goods | .. | 0 | 0 | 0 | 0 | 0 | 0 | 0 | 0 | 0 |
| 5126 Taxes on specific services | .. | 61 | 100 | 97 | 136 | 168 | 193 | 228 | 256 | 163 |
| Gaming taxes | .. | 58 | 97 | 93 | 126 | 164 | 179 | 205 | 227 | 158 |
| Departure tax | .. | 3 | 3 | 4 | 9 | 4 | 14 | 23 | 29 | 5 |
| 5127 Other taxes on internat. trade and transactions | .. | 0 | 0 | 0 | 0 | 0 | 0 | 0 | 0 | 0 |
| 5128 Other taxes | .. | 0 | 0 | 0 | 0 | 0 | 0 | 0 | 0 | 0 |
| 5130 Unallocable between 5110 and 5120 | .. | 0 | 0 | 0 | 0 | 0 | 0 | 0 | 0 | 0 |
| 5200 Taxes on use of goods and to perform activities | .. | 0 | 0 | 0 | 0 | 0 | 0 | 0 | 0 | 0 |
| 5210 Recurrent taxes | .. | .. | .. | .. | .. | .. | .. | .. | .. | .. |
| 5211 Paid by households: motor vehicles | .. | .. | .. | .. | .. | .. | .. | .. | .. | .. |
| 5212 Paid by others: motor vehicles | .. | .. | .. | .. | .. | .. | .. | .. | .. | .. |
| 5213 Paid in respect of other goods | .. | .. | .. | .. | .. | .. | .. | .. | .. | .. |
| 5220 Non-recurrent taxes | .. | .. | .. | .. | .. | .. | .. | .. | .. | .. |

| | 1997 | 2000 | 2007 | 2010 | 2015 | 2016 | 2017 | 2018 | 2019 | 2020 |
|---|---|---|---|---|---|---|---|---|---|---|
| 5300 Unallocable between 5100 and 5200 | .. | 0 | 0 | 0 | 0 | 0 | 0 | 0 | 0 | 0 |
| **6000 Other taxes** | **..** | **0** | **0** | **0** | **0** | **0** | **0** | **0** | **0** | **0** |
| 6100 Paid solely by business | .. | .. | .. | .. | .. | .. | .. | .. | .. | .. |
| 6200 Other | .. | .. | .. | .. | .. | .. | .. | .. | .. | .. |

.. Not available

Note: Year ending 31st December.

The data are on a cash basis.

Figures exclude tax revenues collected by sub-national governments as the data are not available.

Total tax revenues are not available for 2000 and 2001 as the data are incomplete, and do not include customs revenues for these two years.

Source: Department of Finance; PNG Custom Service; Internal Revenue Comission.

StatLink https://stat.link/zfvxp0

## Table 4.21. Philippines: Details of tax revenue

Million PHP

| | 1997 | 2000 | 2007 | 2010 | 2015 | 2016 | 2017 | 2018 | 2019 | 2020 |
|---|---|---|---|---|---|---|---|---|---|---|
| **Total tax revenue** | **472 087** | **564 322** | **1 121 585** | **1 333 225** | **2 262 535** | **2 456 162** | **2 778 684** | **3 176 982** | **3 525 101** | **3 203 823** |
| **1000 Taxes on income, profits and capital gains** | **176 364** | **217 797** | **453 338** | **522 864** | **910 286** | **990 968** | **1 105 874** | **1 126 014** | **1 257 602** | **1 156 254** |
| 1100 Of individuals | 59 749 | 83 005 | 141 673 | 167 605 | 309 439 | 344 081 | 391 049 | 386 748 | 499 450 | 467 997 |
| 1110 On income and profits | 53 370 | 78 228 | 135 504 | 158 325 | 292 548 | 325 446 | 367 166 | 359 901 | 473 098 | 448 714 |
| 1120 On capital gains | 6 379 | 4 777 | 6 170 | 9 280 | 16 891 | 18 635 | 23 883 | 26 847 | 26 352 | 19 283 |
| 1200 Corporate | 107 385 | 116 980 | 282 504 | 328 124 | 567 542 | 615 493 | 683 092 | 702 415 | 716 690 | 646 695 |
| 1210 On profits | 106 363 | 114 871 | 280 090 | 324 273 | 559 522 | 605 727 | 676 031 | 692 067 | 706 474 | 641 242 |
| 1220 On capital gains of corporates | 1 022 | 2 110 | 2 414 | 3 851 | 8 020 | 9 766 | 7 061 | 10 348 | 10 215 | 5 453 |
| 1300 Unallocable between 1100 and 1200 | 9 231 | 17 812 | 29 160 | 27 135 | 33 305 | 31 395 | 31 732 | 36 851 | 41 462 | 41 563 |
| **2000 Social security contributions** | **36 500** | **74 180** | **131 821** | **168 434** | **319 106** | **343 545** | **372 421** | **433 582** | **503 275** | **503 583** |
| 2100 Employees | .. | .. | .. | .. | .. | .. | .. | .. | .. | .. |
| 2110 On a payroll basis | .. | .. | .. | .. | .. | .. | .. | .. | .. | .. |
| 2120 On an income tax basis | .. | .. | .. | .. | .. | .. | .. | .. | .. | .. |
| 2200 Employers | 2 800 | 19 918 | 26 535 | 34 045 | 97 598 | 101 003 | 111 496 | 128 526 | 149 542 | 151 515 |
| 2210 On a payroll basis | .. | .. | .. | .. | .. | .. | .. | .. | .. | .. |
| 2220 On an income tax basis | .. | .. | .. | .. | .. | .. | .. | .. | .. | .. |
| 2300 Self-employed or non-employed | .. | .. | .. | .. | .. | .. | .. | .. | .. | .. |
| 2310 On a payroll basis | .. | .. | .. | .. | .. | .. | .. | .. | .. | .. |
| 2320 On an income tax basis | .. | .. | .. | .. | .. | .. | .. | .. | .. | .. |
| 2400 Unallocable between 2100, 2200 and 2300 | 33 700 | 54 262 | 105 286 | 134 389 | 221 508 | 242 542 | 260 925 | 305 056 | 353 733 | 352 068 |
| 2410 On a payroll basis | .. | .. | .. | .. | .. | .. | .. | .. | .. | .. |
| 2420 On an income tax basis | .. | .. | .. | .. | .. | .. | .. | .. | .. | .. |
| **3000 Taxes on payroll and workforce** | **0** | **0** | **0** | **0** | **0** | **0** | **0** | **0** | **0** | **0** |
| **4000 Taxes on property** | **15 663** | **17 401** | **32 354** | **40 252** | **63 476** | **65 409** | **77 961** | **82 940** | **87 364** | **85 098** |
| 4100 Recurrent taxes on immovable property | 11 485 | 14 947 | 27 387 | 33 057 | 48 484 | 49 973 | 61 583 | 66 041 | 70 049 | 70 863 |
| Real property tax (local government) | 11 485 | 14 947 | 27 387 | 33 057 | 48 484 | 49 973 | 61 583 | 66 041 | 70 049 | 70 863 |
| 4110 Households | .. | .. | .. | .. | .. | .. | .. | .. | .. | .. |
| 4120 Others | .. | .. | .. | .. | .. | .. | .. | .. | .. | .. |
| 4200 Recurrent taxes on net wealth | 0 | 0 | 0 | 0 | 0 | 0 | 0 | 0 | 0 | 0 |
| 4210 Individual | .. | .. | .. | .. | .. | .. | .. | .. | .. | .. |
| 4220 Corporate | .. | .. | .. | .. | .. | .. | .. | .. | .. | .. |
| 4300 Estate, inheritance and gift taxes | 881 | 480 | 962 | 1 981 | 5 636 | 6 638 | 7 467 | 7 155 | 7 219 | 4 854 |
| 4310 Estate and inheritance taxes | 677 | 302 | 650 | 1 451 | 3 341 | 4 723 | 5 001 | 3 654 | 3 299 | 2 100 |
| 4320 Gift taxes | 204 | 178 | 312 | 531 | 2 294 | 1 915 | 2 466 | 3 501 | 3 920 | 2 754 |
| 4400 Taxes on financial and capital transactions | 3 297 | 1 974 | 4 005 | 5 213 | 9 356 | 8 798 | 8 910 | 9 744 | 10 095 | 9 380 |
| Stock transactions (RA 7717) | 3 297 | 1 974 | 4 005 | 5 213 | 9 356 | 8 798 | 8 910 | 9 744 | 10 095 | 9 380 |
| 4500 Other non-reccurrent taxes on property | 0 | 0 | 0 | 0 | 0 | 0 | 0 | 0 | 0 | 0 |
| 4510 On net wealth | .. | .. | .. | .. | .. | .. | .. | .. | .. | .. |
| 4520 Other non-recurrent taxes | .. | .. | .. | .. | .. | .. | .. | .. | .. | .. |
| 4600 Other recurrent taxes on property | 0 | 0 | 0 | 0 | 0 | 0 | 0 | 0 | 0 | 0 |
| **5000 Taxes on goods and services** | **225 283** | **237 243** | **456 497** | **549 889** | **884 133** | **962 763** | **1 118 976** | **1 365 047** | **1 496 801** | **1 306 842** |
| 5100 Taxes on production, sale, transfer, etc | 222 885 | 234 202 | 448 164 | 540 594 | 872 833 | 949 396 | 1 103 612 | 1 349 435 | 1 481 146 | 1 295 206 |
| 5110 General taxes on goods and services | 89 943 | 96 136 | 274 036 | 330 793 | 563 112 | 619 115 | 702 012 | 784 228 | 832 787 | 676 922 |
| 5111 Value added taxes | 89 943 | 96 136 | 274 036 | 330 793 | 563 112 | 619 115 | 702 012 | 784 228 | 832 787 | 676 922 |
| Domestic VAT | 47 459 | 53 879 | 145 013 | 173 284 | 295 502 | 331 414 | 365 235 | 358 169 | 406 084 | 351 849 |
| VAT on imports | 42 484 | 42 257 | 129 023 | 157 509 | 267 610 | 287 701 | 336 776 | 426 059 | 426 703 | 325 073 |
| 5112 Sales tax | 0 | 0 | 0 | 0 | 0 | 0 | 0 | 0 | 0 | 0 |
| 5113 Other | 0 | 0 | 0 | 0 | 0 | 0 | 0 | 0 | 0 | 0 |
| 5120 Taxes on specific goods and services | 132 942 | 138 066 | 174 128 | 209 802 | 309 721 | 330 281 | 401 600 | 565 207 | 648 359 | 618 284 |
| 5121 Excises | 64 974 | 63 954 | 68 383 | 88 247 | 197 278 | 208 791 | 270 346 | 383 438 | 447 062 | 426 853 |
| Domestic excises | 63 078 | 61 677 | 54 998 | 67 203 | 158 319 | 163 505 | 209 493 | 290 612 | 317 267 | 296 169 |
| Alcohol products | 13 412 | 12 997 | 18 786 | 21 781 | 42 214 | 50 272 | 61 050 | 68 809 | 76 999 | 77 917 |
| Tobacco products | 16 027 | 17 427 | 23 206 | 31 730 | 99 505 | 95 055 | 125 910 | 136 005 | 147 633 | 149 651 |
| Petroleum products | 29 272 | 28 297 | 10 036 | 9 832 | 11 888 | 13 111 | 15 512 | 39 002 | 42 709 | 27 602 |
| Automobiles | 0 | 0 | 0 | 0 | 2 452 | 3 128 | 4 308 | 5 814 | 5 523 | 2 310 |
| Mineral products | 77 | 243 | 942 | 1 306 | 2 079 | 1 758 | 2 251 | 4 918 | 5 453 | 5 900 |
| Others | 4 289 | 2 712 | 2 028 | 2 555 | 182 | 181 | 462 | 36 064 | 38 952 | 32 789 |
| Excises on imports | 1 896 | 2 277 | 13 385 | 21 044 | 38 959 | 45 286 | 60 853 | 92 825 | 129 795 | 130 684 |
| Alcohol products | .. | .. | 953 | 2 807 | 1 324 | 1 521 | 1 888 | 2 293 | 2 746 | 2 011 |
| Tobacco products | .. | .. | 169 | 167 | 3 | 1 | 949 | 498 | 147 | 419 |
| Petroleum products | .. | .. | 6 892 | 9 260 | 13 159 | 10 866 | 15 696 | 43 964 | 85 709 | 100 281 |
| Automobiles | .. | .. | 4 617 | 8 114 | 24 027 | 32 391 | 41 485 | 41 446 | 34 006 | 19 273 |
| Mineral products | .. | .. | 329 | 101 | 254 | 203 | 282 | 1 338 | 3 006 | 4 316 |
| Others | .. | .. | 426 | 596 | 193 | 304 | 554 | 3 286 | 4 181 | 4 385 |
| 5122 Profits of fiscal monopolies | 0 | 0 | 0 | 0 | 0 | 0 | 0 | 0 | 0 | 0 |
| 5123 Customs and import duties | 50 420 | 50 472 | 67 031 | 80 687 | 60 966 | 63 379 | 60 555 | 74 227 | 73 812 | 81 930 |
| 5124 Taxes on exports | 0 | 0 | 0 | 0 | 0 | 0 | 0 | 0 | 0 | 0 |
| 5125 Taxes on investment goods | 0 | 0 | 0 | 0 | 0 | 0 | 0 | 0 | 0 | 0 |

| | 1997 | 2000 | 2007 | 2010 | 2015 | 2016 | 2017 | 2018 | 2019 | 2020 |
|---|---|---|---|---|---|---|---|---|---|---|
| 5126 Taxes on specific services | 17 548 | 23 639 | 38 714 | 40 868 | 51 477 | 58 111 | 70 700 | 107 543 | 127 484 | 109 501 |
| Banks and financial institutions | 9 696 | 9 538 | 19 434 | 22 857 | 26 915 | 29 602 | 33 471 | 33 087 | 50 876 | 45 350 |
| Travel tax (CHED/NCAA) | 386 | 1 043 | 1 581 | 1 512 | 1 770 | 1 694 | 2 894 | 3 084 | 3 487 | 1 203 |
| Immigration tax (BID) | 18 | 47 | 42 | 59 | 72 | 87 | 115 | 165 | 241 | 69 |
| Other | 7 448 | 13 011 | 17 657 | 16 440 | 22 720 | 26 728 | 34 220 | 71 207 | 72 880 | 62 879 |
| 5127 Other taxes on internat. trade and transactions | 0 | 0 | 0 | 0 | 0 | 0 | 0 | 0 | 0 | 0 |
| 5128 Other taxes | 0 | 0 | 0 | 0 | 0 | 0 | 0 | 0 | 0 | 0 |
| 5130 Unallocable between 5110 and 5120 | 0 | 0 | 0 | 0 | 0 | 0 | 0 | 0 | 0 | 0 |
| 5200 Taxes on use of goods and to perform activities | 2 398 | 3 041 | 8 333 | 9 295 | 11 300 | 13 367 | 15 364 | 15 612 | 15 655 | 11 636 |
| 5210 Recurrent taxes | 2 398 | 3 041 | 8 333 | 9 295 | 11 300 | 13 367 | 15 364 | 15 612 | 15 655 | 11 636 |
| LTO-Motor Vehicle Users' Tax | 2 398 | 3 041 | 8 333 | 9 295 | 11 300 | 13 367 | 15 364 | 15 612 | 15 655 | 11 636 |
| 5211 Paid by households: motor vehicles | .. | .. | .. | .. | .. | .. | .. | .. | .. | .. |
| 5212 Paid by others: motor vehicles | .. | .. | .. | .. | .. | .. | .. | .. | .. | .. |
| 5213 Paid in respect of other goods | .. | .. | .. | .. | .. | .. | .. | .. | .. | .. |
| 5220 Non-recurrent taxes | 0 | 0 | 0 | 0 | 0 | 0 | 0 | 0 | 0 | 0 |
| 5300 Unallocable between 5100 and 5200 | 0 | 0 | 0 | 0 | 0 | 0 | 0 | 0 | 0 | 0 |
| **6000 Other taxes** | **18 277** | **17 702** | **47 575** | **51 786** | **85 534** | **93 475** | **103 452** | **169 400** | **180 059** | **152 046** |
| 6100 Paid solely by business | 0 | 0 | 0 | 0 | 0 | 0 | 0 | 0 | 0 | 0 |
| 6200 Other | 18 277 | 17 702 | 47 575 | 51 786 | 85 534 | 93 475 | 103 452 | 169 400 | 180 059 | 152 046 |
| Documentary Stamp Tax | 16 477 | 16 170 | 35 147 | 42 629 | 72 073 | 80 151 | 85 916 | 139 168 | 145 970 | 124 521 |
| DENR-Forest charges | 116 | 175 | 164 | 239 | 128 | 136 | 164 | 192 | 250 | 322 |
| Miscellaneous taxes | 1 683 | 1 356 | 8 944 | 4 391 | 6 219 | 5 888 | 9 086 | 19 708 | 22 684 | 18 244 |
| Other taxes (local government) | 0 | 0 | 3 319 | 4 526 | 7 114 | 7 300 | 8 286 | 10 331 | 11 155 | 8 960 |

.. Not available

Note: Year ending 31st December.

The data are on a cash basis.

Local tax revenues have been expanded with longer time series in this edition based on information from the government.

Heading 5111: The figures include VAT on imports in this edition. It was previously under heading 5123.

Heading 5121: The figures include excises on imports in this edition. They were previously under heading 5123. The category 'Others' cover excise taxes from sweetened beverages, cosmetic procedures, and non-essentials or miscellaneous goods.

Heading 5123: This category includes only import duties and related revenues in this edition.

Source: Department of Finance of the Philippines.

StatLink https://stat.link/zhm6cf

## Table 4.22. Samoa: Details of tax revenue

Million WST

| | 1997 | 2000 | 2007 | 2010 | 2015 | 2016 | 2017 | 2018 | 2019 | 2020 |
|---|---|---|---|---|---|---|---|---|---|---|
| **Total tax revenue** | .. | .. | **330** | **341** | **495** | **514** | **523** | **572** | **563** | **542** |
| **1000 Taxes on income, profits and capital gains** | .. | .. | **78** | **84** | **114** | **117** | **116** | **132** | **130** | **128** |
| 1100 Of individuals | .. | .. | 42 | 46 | 64 | 69 | 68 | 68 | 69 | 69 |
| 1110 On income and profits | .. | .. | 42 | 46 | 64 | 69 | 68 | 68 | 69 | 69 |
| 1120 On capital gains | .. | .. | 0 | 0 | 0 | 0 | 0 | 0 | 0 | 0 |
| 1200 Corporate | .. | .. | 36 | 38 | 51 | 48 | 48 | 64 | 60 | 59 |
| 1210 On profits | .. | .. | 36 | 38 | 51 | 48 | 48 | 64 | 60 | 59 |
| 1220 On capital gains of corporates | .. | .. | 0 | 0 | 0 | 0 | 0 | 0 | 0 | 0 |
| 1300 Unallocable between 1100 and 1200 | .. | .. | 0 | 0 | 0 | 0 | 0 | 0 | 0 | 0 |
| **2000 Social security contributions** | .. | .. | **0** | **0** | **0** | **0** | **0** | **0** | **0** | **0** |
| 2100 Employees | .. | .. | .. | .. | .. | .. | .. | .. | .. | .. |
| 2110 On a payroll basis | .. | .. | .. | .. | .. | .. | .. | .. | .. | .. |
| 2120 On an income tax basis | .. | .. | .. | .. | .. | .. | .. | .. | .. | .. |
| 2200 Employers | .. | .. | .. | .. | .. | .. | .. | .. | .. | .. |
| 2210 On a payroll basis | .. | .. | .. | .. | .. | .. | .. | .. | .. | .. |
| 2220 On an income tax basis | .. | .. | .. | .. | .. | .. | .. | .. | .. | .. |
| 2300 Self-employed or non-employed | .. | .. | .. | .. | .. | .. | .. | .. | .. | .. |
| 2310 On a payroll basis | .. | .. | .. | .. | .. | .. | .. | .. | .. | .. |
| 2320 On an income tax basis | .. | .. | .. | .. | .. | .. | .. | .. | .. | .. |
| 2400 Unallocable between 2100, 2200 and 2300 | .. | .. | .. | .. | .. | .. | .. | .. | .. | .. |
| 2410 On a payroll basis | .. | .. | .. | .. | .. | .. | .. | .. | .. | .. |
| 2420 On an income tax basis | .. | .. | .. | .. | .. | .. | .. | .. | .. | .. |
| **3000 Taxes on payroll and workforce** | .. | .. | **0** | **0** | **0** | **0** | **0** | **0** | **0** | **0** |
| **4000 Taxes on property** | .. | .. | **2** | **0** | **0** | **0** | **0** | **0** | **0** | **0** |
| 4100 Recurrent taxes on immovable property | .. | .. | 0 | .. | .. | .. | .. | .. | .. | .. |
| 4110 Households | .. | .. | .. | .. | .. | .. | .. | .. | .. | .. |
| 4120 Others | .. | .. | .. | .. | .. | .. | .. | .. | .. | .. |
| 4200 Recurrent taxes on net wealth | .. | .. | 0 | .. | .. | .. | .. | .. | .. | .. |
| 4210 Individual | .. | .. | .. | .. | .. | .. | .. | .. | .. | .. |
| 4220 Corporate | .. | .. | .. | .. | .. | .. | .. | .. | .. | .. |
| 4300 Estate, inheritance and gift taxes | .. | .. | 0 | .. | .. | .. | .. | .. | .. | .. |
| 4310 Estate and inheritance taxes | .. | .. | .. | .. | .. | .. | .. | .. | .. | .. |
| 4320 Gift taxes | .. | .. | .. | .. | .. | .. | .. | .. | .. | .. |
| 4400 Taxes on financial and capital transactions | .. | .. | 2 | .. | .. | .. | .. | .. | .. | .. |
| 4500 Other non-reccurrent taxes on property | .. | .. | 0 | .. | .. | .. | .. | .. | .. | .. |
| 4510 On net wealth | .. | .. | .. | .. | .. | .. | .. | .. | .. | .. |
| 4520 Other non-recurrent taxes | .. | .. | .. | .. | .. | .. | .. | .. | .. | .. |
| 4600 Other recurrent taxes on property | .. | .. | 0 | .. | .. | .. | .. | .. | .. | .. |
| **5000 Taxes on goods and services** | .. | .. | **251** | **257** | **380** | **397** | **408** | **440** | **434** | **413** |
| 5100 Taxes on production, sale, transfer, etc | .. | .. | 251 | 257 | 380 | 397 | 408 | 440 | 434 | 413 |
| 5110 General taxes on goods and services | .. | .. | 126 | 119 | 200 | 198 | 209 | 229 | 232 | 218 |
| 5111 Value added taxes | .. | .. | .. | .. | .. | .. | .. | .. | .. | .. |
| VAGST on Imports | .. | .. | 100 | .. | .. | .. | .. | .. | .. | .. |
| VAGST on sales of goods and services | .. | .. | 26 | .. | .. | .. | .. | .. | .. | .. |
| 5112 Sales tax | .. | .. | 0 | 0 | 0 | 0 | 0 | 0 | 0 | 0 |
| 5113 Other | .. | .. | 0 | 0 | 0 | 0 | 0 | 0 | 0 | 0 |
| 5120 Taxes on specific goods and services | .. | .. | 125 | 137 | 181 | 199 | 199 | 211 | 202 | 196 |
| 5121 Excises | .. | .. | 78 | 95 | 120 | 134 | 127 | 133 | 132 | 127 |
| Petroleum Levy | .. | .. | 3 | .. | .. | .. | .. | .. | .. | .. |
| Import Excise | .. | .. | 29 | .. | .. | .. | .. | .. | .. | .. |
| Domestic Excise | .. | .. | 47 | .. | .. | .. | .. | .. | .. | .. |
| 5122 Profits of fiscal monopolies | .. | .. | 0 | 0 | 0 | 0 | 0 | 0 | 0 | 0 |
| 5123 Customs and import duties | .. | .. | 43 | 38 | 54 | 55 | 59 | 63 | 55 | 60 |
| 5124 Taxes on exports | .. | .. | 0 | 0 | 0 | 0 | 0 | 0 | 0 | 0 |
| 5125 Taxes on investment goods | .. | .. | 0 | 0 | 0 | 0 | 0 | 0 | 0 | 0 |
| 5126 Taxes on specific services | .. | .. | 4 | 4 | 6 | 10 | 13 | 15 | 14 | 9 |
| 5127 Other taxes on internat. trade and transactions | .. | .. | 0 | 0 | 0 | 0 | 0 | 0 | 0 | 0 |
| 5128 Other taxes | .. | .. | 0 | 0 | 0 | 0 | 0 | 0 | 0 | 0 |
| 5130 Unallocable between 5110 and 5120 | .. | .. | 0 | 0 | 0 | 0 | 0 | 0 | 0 | 0 |
| 5200 Taxes on use of goods and to perform activities | .. | .. | 0 | 0 | 0 | 0 | 0 | 0 | 0 | 0 |
| 5210 Recurrent taxes | .. | .. | .. | .. | .. | .. | .. | .. | .. | .. |
| 5211 Paid by households: motor vehicles | .. | .. | .. | .. | .. | .. | .. | .. | .. | .. |
| 5212 Paid by others: motor vehicles | .. | .. | .. | .. | .. | .. | .. | .. | .. | .. |
| 5213 Paid in respect of other goods | .. | .. | .. | .. | .. | .. | .. | .. | .. | .. |
| 5220 Non-recurrent taxes | .. | .. | .. | .. | .. | .. | .. | .. | .. | .. |
| 5300 Unallocable between 5100 and 5200 | .. | .. | 0 | 0 | 0 | 0 | 0 | 0 | 0 | 0 |
| **6000 Other taxes** | .. | .. | **0** | **0** | **0** | **0** | **0** | **0** | **0** | **0** |
| 6100 Paid solely by business | .. | .. | .. | .. | .. | .. | .. | .. | .. | .. |
| 6200 Other | .. | .. | .. | .. | .. | .. | .. | .. | .. | .. |

.. Not available

Note: Data are reported on a fiscal year basis beginning 1st July. For example, the data for 2020 represent the period from July 2020 to June 2021.

The data are on a cash basis.

Figures exclude tax revenues collected by sub-national governments as the data are not available.

The data from 2009 were provided on the basis of the IMF's GFSM 2014 classification. Prior to this year, data were provided on a different basis. The differences between the two sets of data are indicated below for the relevant tax revenue categories.

Heading 1000: Income tax revenues from 2009 onwards are net of income tax refunds. Prior to 2009, the income tax revenue figures are gross of refunds

Heading 5111: VAGST revenues from 2009 onwards are net of aid, loan payments by Treasury and VAGST paid by Government departments.

Heading 5123: Import duty from 2009 onwards is net of aid and loan payments by Treasury.

Heading 5126: Data from 2009 include revenues from fisheries' licences. Fisheries' licences revenues are usually classified as non-tax revenues according to the OECD classification set out in Annex A of the Interpretative Guide, but could not be distinguished from other revenues from taxes on specific services.

Source: Bureau of Statistics of Samoa.

StatLink https://stat.link/7t84s6

## Table 4.23. Singapore: Details of tax revenue

Million SGD

| | 1997 | 2000 | 2007 | 2010 | 2015 | 2016 | 2017 | 2018 | 2019 | 2020 |
|---|---|---|---|---|---|---|---|---|---|---|
| **Total tax revenue** | .. | **25 627** | **36 630** | **41 848** | **55 647** | **58 699** | **66 363** | **66 203** | **67 645** | **61 409** |
| **1000 Taxes on income, profits and capital gains** | .. | **13 538** | **16 621** | **18 687** | **24 890** | **26 378** | **32 065** | **30 818** | **32 535** | **32 997** |
| 1100 Of individuals | .. | 3 543 | 4 537 | 6 470 | 9 235 | 10 526 | 10 724 | 11 706 | 12 368 | 12 748 |
| 1110 On income and profits | .. | 3 543 | 4 537 | 6 470 | 9 235 | 10 526 | 10 724 | 11 706 | 12 368 | 12 748 |
| 1120 On capital gains | .. | 0 | 0 | 0 | 0 | 0 | 0 | 0 | 0 | 0 |
| 1200 Corporate | .. | 9 509 | 10 934 | 11 260 | 14 253 | 14 378 | 19 810 | 17 523 | 18 530 | 18 631 |
| 1210 On profits | .. | 9 509 | 10 934 | 11 260 | 14 253 | 14 378 | 19 810 | 17 523 | 18 530 | 18 631 |
| From corporate profits | .. | 8 316 | 9 250 | 10 687 | 13 815 | 13 602 | 14 944 | 16 032 | 16 732 | 16 112 |
| Statutory board contributions | .. | 1 192 | 1 683 | 573 | 438 | 776 | 4 866 | 1 491 | 1 798 | 2 519 |
| 1220 On capital gains | .. | 0 | 0 | 0 | 0 | 0 | 0 | 0 | 0 | 0 |
| 1300 Unallocable between 1100 and 1200 | .. | 486 | 1 150 | 957 | 1 402 | 1 474 | 1 532 | 1 590 | 1 637 | 1 618 |
| Withholding taxes | .. | 486 | 1 150 | 957 | 1 402 | 1 474 | 1 532 | 1 590 | 1 637 | 1 618 |
| **2000 Social security contributions** | .. | **0** | **0** | **0** | **0** | **0** | **0** | **0** | **0** | **0** |
| 2100 Employees | .. | .. | .. | .. | .. | .. | .. | .. | .. | .. |
| 2110 On a payroll basis | .. | .. | .. | .. | .. | .. | .. | .. | .. | .. |
| 2120 On an income tax basis | .. | .. | .. | .. | .. | .. | .. | .. | .. | .. |
| 2200 Employers | .. | .. | .. | .. | .. | .. | .. | .. | .. | .. |
| 2210 On a payroll basis | .. | .. | .. | .. | .. | .. | .. | .. | .. | .. |
| 2220 On an income tax basis | .. | .. | .. | .. | .. | .. | .. | .. | .. | .. |
| 2300 Self-employed or non-employed | .. | .. | .. | .. | .. | .. | .. | .. | .. | .. |
| 2310 On a payroll basis | .. | .. | .. | .. | .. | .. | .. | .. | .. | .. |
| 2320 On an income tax basis | .. | .. | .. | .. | .. | .. | .. | .. | .. | .. |
| 2400 Unallocable between 2100, 2200 and 2300 | .. | .. | .. | .. | .. | .. | .. | .. | .. | .. |
| 2410 On a payroll basis | .. | .. | .. | .. | .. | .. | .. | .. | .. | .. |
| 2420 On an income tax basis | .. | .. | .. | .. | .. | .. | .. | .. | .. | .. |
| **3000 Taxes on payroll and workforce** | .. | **0** | **0** | **0** | **0** | **0** | **0** | **0** | **0** | **0** |
| **4000 Taxes on property** | .. | **2 863** | **6 259** | **6 080** | **7 224** | **7 638** | **9 345** | **9 256** | **8 961** | **7 024** |
| 4100 Recurrent taxes on immovable property | .. | 1 535 | 2 428 | 2 798 | 4 456 | 4 359 | 4 440 | 4 649 | 4 761 | 3 128 |
| 4110 Households | .. | .. | .. | .. | .. | .. | .. | .. | .. | .. |
| 4120 Others | .. | .. | .. | .. | .. | .. | .. | .. | .. | .. |
| 4200 Recurrent taxes on net wealth | .. | 0 | 0 | 0 | 0 | 0 | 0 | 0 | 0 | 0 |
| 4210 Individual | .. | .. | .. | .. | .. | .. | .. | .. | .. | .. |
| 4220 Corporate | .. | .. | .. | .. | .. | .. | .. | .. | .. | .. |
| 4300 Estate, inheritance and gift taxes | .. | 71 | 154 | 5 | -1 | 0 | 0 | 0 | 0 | 0 |
| 4310 Estate and inheritance taxes | .. | 71 | 154 | 5 | -1 | 0 | 0 | 0 | 0 | 0 |
| 4320 Gift taxes | .. | 0 | 0 | 0 | 0 | 0 | 0 | 0 | 0 | 0 |
| 4400 Taxes on financial and capital transactions | .. | 1 257 | 3 677 | 3 277 | 2 769 | 3 278 | 4 905 | 4 607 | 4 199 | 3 896 |
| 4500 Non-recurrent taxes | .. | 0 | 0 | 0 | 0 | 0 | 0 | 0 | 0 | 0 |
| 4510 On net wealth | .. | .. | .. | .. | .. | .. | .. | .. | .. | .. |
| 4520 Other non-recurrent taxes | .. | .. | .. | .. | .. | .. | .. | .. | .. | .. |
| 4600 Other recurrent taxes on property | .. | 0 | 0 | 0 | 0 | 0 | 0 | 0 | 0 | 0 |
| **5000 Taxes on goods and services** | .. | **7 967** | **12 053** | **14 376** | **17 657** | **18 638** | **18 933** | **19 499** | **19 466** | **17 782** |
| 5100 Taxes on production, sale, transfer, etc | .. | 5 462 | 9 864 | 12 525 | 15 897 | 16 490 | 16 781 | 16 876 | 17 047 | 15 442 |
| 5110 General taxes | .. | 2 121 | 6 165 | 8 198 | 10 345 | 11 078 | 10 960 | 11 137 | 11 164 | 10 346 |
| 5111 Value added taxes | .. | 2 121 | 6 165 | 8 198 | 10 345 | 11 078 | 10 960 | 11 137 | 11 164 | 10 346 |
| 5112 Sales tax | .. | 0 | 0 | 0 | 0 | 0 | 0 | 0 | 0 | 0 |
| 5113 Other | .. | 0 | 0 | 0 | 0 | 0 | 0 | 0 | 0 | 0 |
| 5120 Taxes on specific goods and services | .. | 3 341 | 3 699 | 4 327 | 5 552 | 5 412 | 5 821 | 5 739 | 5 883 | 5 096 |
| 5121 Excises | .. | 1 847 | 1 985 | 2 048 | 2 833 | 2 730 | 3 133 | 3 075 | 3 264 | 3 374 |
| Liquors | .. | .. | 414 | 470 | 638 | 640 | 663 | 678 | 678 | 742 |
| Tobacco | .. | .. | 700 | 889 | 1 205 | 986 | 1 174 | 1 122 | 1 160 | 1 476 |
| Petroleum Products | .. | .. | 386 | 419 | 584 | 596 | 827 | 784 | 986 | 874 |
| Motor Vehicles | .. | .. | 483 | 267 | 399 | 502 | 463 | 486 | 435 | 282 |
| Compressed Natural Gas Unit Duty | .. | .. | 0 | 0 | 2 | 1 | 1 | 0 | 0 | 0 |
| Others | .. | .. | 3 | 5 | 5 | 5 | 5 | 6 | 5 | 1 |
| 5122 Profits of fiscal monopolies | .. | 0 | 0 | 0 | 0 | 0 | 0 | 0 | 0 | 0 |
| 5123 Customs and import duties | .. | 0 | 0 | 0 | 0 | 0 | 0 | 0 | 0 | 0 |
| 5124 Taxes on exports | .. | 0 | 0 | 0 | 0 | 0 | 0 | 0 | 0 | 0 |
| 5125 Taxes on investment goods | .. | 0 | 0 | 0 | 0 | 0 | 0 | 0 | 0 | 0 |
| 5126 Taxes on specific services | .. | 1 494 | 1 714 | 2 279 | 2 719 | 2 682 | 2 688 | 2 664 | 2 620 | 1 722 |
| Betting duty | .. | 1 494 | 1 714 | 2 279 | 2 719 | 2 682 | 2 688 | 2 664 | 2 620 | 1 722 |
| 5127 Other taxes on internat. trade and transactions | .. | 0 | 0 | 0 | 0 | 0 | 0 | 0 | 0 | 0 |
| 5128 Other taxes | .. | 0 | 0 | 0 | 0 | 0 | 0 | 0 | 0 | 0 |
| 5130 Unallocable between 5110 and 5120 | .. | 0 | 0 | 0 | 0 | 0 | 0 | 0 | 0 | 0 |
| 5200 Taxes on use of goods and perform activities | .. | 2 506 | 2 189 | 1 851 | 1 760 | 2 148 | 2 153 | 2 623 | 2 419 | 2 341 |
| 5210 Recurrent taxes | .. | .. | .. | .. | .. | .. | .. | .. | .. | .. |
| 5211 Paid by households: motor vehicles | .. | .. | .. | .. | .. | .. | .. | .. | .. | .. |
| 5212 Paid by others: motor vehicles | .. | .. | .. | .. | .. | .. | .. | .. | .. | .. |
| 5213 Paid in respect of other goods | .. | .. | .. | .. | .. | .. | .. | .. | .. | .. |

| | 1997 | 2000 | 2007 | 2010 | 2015 | 2016 | 2017 | 2018 | 2019 | 2020 |
|---|---|---|---|---|---|---|---|---|---|---|
| 5220 Non-recurrent taxes | .. | .. | .. | .. | .. | .. | .. | .. | .. | .. |
| 5300 Unallocable between 5100 and 5200 | .. | 0 | 0 | 0 | 0 | 0 | 0 | 0 | 0 | 0 |
| **6000 Other taxes** | .. | **1 259** | **1 698** | **2 706** | **5 876** | **6 045** | **6 019** | **6 629** | **6 683** | **3 606** |
| 6100 Paid solely by business | .. | 0 | 0 | 0 | 0 | 0 | 0 | 0 | 0 | 0 |
| 6200 Other | .. | 1 259 | 1 698 | 2 706 | 5 876 | 6 045 | 6 019 | 6 629 | 6 683 | 3 606 |

.. Not available

Note: Data are on a fiscal year basis ending 31st March. For example, the data for 2020 represent 1 April 2020 to 31 March 2021.

The data are on a cash basis.

For some headings, components may not sum up to the total due to rounding issues.

Heading 2000: There are no social security contributions in Singapore.

Heading 4100: Recurrent taxes on immovable property includes tax levied on all private properties, as well as properties owned by statutory boards.

Heading 5123: Customs and import duties are included in heading 5121 as disaggregation is not available.

Heading 5220: The figures include carbon tax. Singapore started the collection of carbon tax in fiscal year 2020.

Source: Ministry of Finance of Singapore.

StatLink https://stat.link/7kboy2

## Table 4.24. Solomon Islands: Details of tax revenue

Million SBD

| | 1997 | 2000 | 2007 | 2010 | 2015 | 2016 | 2017 | 2018 | 2019 | 2020 |
|---|---|---|---|---|---|---|---|---|---|---|
| **Total tax revenue** | .. | .. | **819** | **1 376** | **2 392** | **2 367** | **2 632** | **3 013** | **2 623** | **2 382** |
| **1000 Taxes on income, profits and capital gains** | .. | .. | **189** | **418** | **719** | **690** | **780** | **794** | **757** | **690** |
| 1100 Of individuals | .. | .. | 141 | 280 | 437 | 411 | 491 | 505 | 509 | 406 |
| 1110 On income and profits | .. | .. | 141 | 280 | 437 | 411 | 491 | 505 | 509 | 406 |
| 1120 On capital gains | .. | .. | .. | .. | .. | .. | .. | .. | .. | .. |
| 1200 Corporate | .. | .. | 48 | 137 | 283 | 278 | 289 | 288 | 248 | 284 |
| 1210 On profits | .. | .. | 48 | 137 | 283 | 278 | 289 | 288 | 248 | 284 |
| Dividend Withholding Tax (WHT) | .. | .. | 14 | 41 | 118 | 106 | 114 | 86 | 43 | 71 |
| Non-resident WHT | .. | .. | 16 | 43 | 71 | 68 | 66 | 59 | 71 | 74 |
| Resident WHT | .. | .. | 19 | 53 | 94 | 105 | 110 | 143 | 134 | 138 |
| 1220 On capital gains of corporates | .. | .. | .. | .. | .. | .. | .. | .. | .. | .. |
| 1300 Unallocable between 1100 and 1200 | .. | .. | 0 | 0 | 0 | 0 | 0 | 0 | 0 | 0 |
| **2000 Social security contributions** | .. | .. | **0** | **0** | **0** | **0** | **0** | **0** | **0** | **0** |
| 2100 Employees | .. | .. | .. | .. | .. | .. | .. | .. | .. | .. |
| 2110 On a payroll basis | .. | .. | .. | .. | .. | .. | .. | .. | .. | .. |
| 2120 On an income tax basis | .. | .. | .. | .. | .. | .. | .. | .. | .. | .. |
| 2200 Employers | .. | .. | .. | .. | .. | .. | .. | .. | .. | .. |
| 2210 On a payroll basis | .. | .. | .. | .. | .. | .. | .. | .. | .. | .. |
| 2220 On an income tax basis | .. | .. | .. | .. | .. | .. | .. | .. | .. | .. |
| 2300 Self-employed or non-employed | .. | .. | .. | .. | .. | .. | .. | .. | .. | .. |
| 2310 On a payroll basis | .. | .. | .. | .. | .. | .. | .. | .. | .. | .. |
| 2320 On an income tax basis | .. | .. | .. | .. | .. | .. | .. | .. | .. | .. |
| 2400 Unallocable between 2100, 2200 and 2300 | .. | .. | .. | .. | .. | .. | .. | .. | .. | .. |
| 2410 On a payroll basis | .. | .. | .. | .. | .. | .. | .. | .. | .. | .. |
| 2420 On an income tax basis | .. | .. | .. | .. | .. | .. | .. | .. | .. | .. |
| **3000 Taxes on payroll and workforce** | .. | .. | **0** | **0** | **0** | **0** | **0** | **0** | **0** | **0** |
| **4000 Taxes on property** | .. | .. | **9** | **8** | **19** | **17** | **14** | **16** | **15** | **12** |
| 4100 Recurrent taxes on immovable property | .. | .. | 0 | 0 | 0 | 0 | 0 | 0 | 0 | 0 |
| 4110 Households | .. | .. | .. | .. | .. | .. | .. | .. | .. | .. |
| 4120 Others | .. | .. | .. | .. | .. | .. | .. | .. | .. | .. |
| 4200 Recurrent taxes on net wealth | .. | .. | 0 | 0 | 0 | 0 | 0 | 0 | 0 | 0 |
| 4210 Individual | .. | .. | .. | .. | .. | .. | .. | .. | .. | .. |
| 4220 Corporate | .. | .. | .. | .. | .. | .. | .. | .. | .. | .. |
| 4300 Estate, inheritance and gift taxes | .. | .. | 0 | 0 | 0 | 0 | 0 | 0 | 0 | 0 |
| 4310 Estate and inheritance taxes | .. | .. | .. | .. | .. | .. | .. | .. | .. | .. |
| 4320 Gift taxes | .. | .. | .. | .. | .. | .. | .. | .. | .. | .. |
| 4400 Taxes on financial and capital transactions | .. | .. | 9 | 8 | 19 | 17 | 14 | 16 | 15 | 12 |
| 4500 Other non-reccurrent taxes on property | .. | .. | 0 | 0 | 0 | 0 | 0 | 0 | 0 | 0 |
| 4510 On net wealth | .. | .. | .. | .. | .. | .. | .. | .. | .. | .. |
| 4520 Other non-recurrent taxes | .. | .. | .. | .. | .. | .. | .. | .. | .. | .. |
| 4600 Other recurrent taxes on property | .. | .. | 0 | 0 | 0 | 0 | 0 | 0 | 0 | 0 |
| **5000 Taxes on goods and services** | .. | .. | **621** | **951** | **1 654** | **1 660** | **1 838** | **2 204** | **1 852** | **1 680** |
| 5100 Taxes on production, sale, transfer, etc | .. | .. | 616 | 944 | 1 638 | 1 643 | 1 821 | 2 188 | 1 834 | 1 660 |
| 5110 General taxes on goods and services | .. | .. | 621 | 458 | 721 | 682 | 773 | 867 | 750 | 703 |
| 5111 Value added taxes | .. | .. | 0 | 0 | 0 | 0 | 0 | 0 | 0 | 0 |
| 5112 Sales tax | .. | .. | 283 | 458 | 721 | 682 | 773 | 867 | 750 | 703 |
| 5113 Other | .. | .. | 0 | 0 | 0 | 0 | 0 | 0 | 0 | 0 |
| 5120 Taxes on specific goods and services | .. | .. | 333 | 486 | 917 | 961 | 1 047 | 1 321 | 1 084 | 957 |
| 5121 Excises | .. | .. | 53 | 106 | 144 | 163 | 173 | 233 | 198 | 221 |
| Tobacco | .. | .. | 29 | 59 | 89 | 95 | 109 | 139 | 122 | 139 |
| Beer | .. | .. | 23 | 34 | 49 | 61 | 63 | 93 | 55 | 52 |
| Spirits | .. | .. | 0 | 12 | 6 | 7 | 2 | 0 | 18 | 23 |
| Other | .. | .. | 0 | 0 | 0 | 0 | 0 | 0 | 4 | 6 |
| 5122 Profits of fiscal monopolies | .. | .. | 0 | 0 | 0 | 0 | 0 | 0 | 0 | 0 |
| 5123 Customs and import duties | .. | .. | 99 | 136 | 214 | 215 | 243 | 295 | 261 | 256 |
| 5124 Taxes on exports | .. | .. | 182 | 245 | 560 | 582 | 631 | 794 | 624 | 481 |
| Export duty on minerals | .. | .. | 0 | 2 | 1 | 2 | 1 | 1 | 2 | 0 |
| Export duty on shells | .. | .. | 0 | 1 | 1 | 0 | 0 | 1 | 0 | 1 |
| Export duty on fish | .. | .. | 7 | 2 | 1 | 1 | 2 | 1 | 2 | 1 |
| Export duty on timber/log | .. | .. | 174 | 240 | 469 | 579 | 627 | 790 | 618 | 477 |
| Export duty on other products | .. | .. | 0 | 0 | 88 | 1 | 1 | 1 | 2 | 2 |
| 5125 Taxes on investment goods | .. | .. | 0 | 0 | 0 | 0 | 0 | 0 | 0 | 0 |
| 5126 Taxes on specific services | .. | .. | 0 | 0 | 0 | 0 | 0 | 0 | 0 | 0 |
| 5127 Other taxes on internat. trade and transactions | .. | .. | 0 | 0 | 0 | 0 | 0 | 0 | 0 | 0 |
| 5128 Other taxes | .. | .. | 0 | 0 | 0 | 0 | 0 | 0 | 0 | 0 |
| 5130 Unallocable between 5110 and 5120 | .. | .. | 0 | 0 | 0 | 0 | 0 | 0 | 0 | 0 |
| 5200 Taxes on use of goods and to perform activities | .. | .. | 5 | 7 | 16 | 17 | 17 | 16 | 18 | 19 |
| 5210 Recurrent taxes | .. | .. | 5 | 7 | 16 | 17 | 17 | 16 | 18 | 19 |
| 5211 Paid by households: motor vehicles | .. | .. | 0 | 0 | 0 | 0 | 0 | 0 | 0 | 0 |

| | 1997 | 2000 | 2007 | 2010 | 2015 | 2016 | 2017 | 2018 | 2019 | 2020 |
|---|---|---|---|---|---|---|---|---|---|---|
| 5212 Paid by others: motor vehicles | .. | .. | 0 | 0 | 0 | 0 | 0 | 0 | 0 | 0 |
| 5213 Paid in respect of other goods | .. | .. | 5 | 7 | 16 | 17 | 17 | 16 | 18 | 19 |
| 5220 Non-recurrent taxes | .. | .. | 0 | 0 | 0 | 0 | 0 | 0 | 0 | 0 |
| 5300 Unallocable between 5100 and 5200 | .. | .. | 0 | 0 | 0 | 0 | 0 | 0 | 0 | 0 |
| **6000 Other taxes** | **..** | **..** | **0** | **0** | **0** | **0** | **0** | **0** | **0** | **0** |
| 6100 Paid solely by business | .. | .. | .. | .. | .. | .. | .. | .. | .. | .. |
| 6200 Other | .. | .. | .. | .. | .. | .. | .. | .. | .. | .. |

.. Not available

Note: Year ending 31st December.

The data are on a cash basis.

Figures exclude tax revenues collected by sub-national governments as the data are not available.

Some revenues (e.g. customs fees, penalties) amounting to about 1.14 million in 2020 are considered as non-tax revenues according to the OECD classification, described in the interpretative guide in Annex A. The national classification of Solomon Islands classifies these revenues as tax revenues.

Source: Solomon Islands Ministry of Finance and Treasury.

StatLink https://stat.link/5c1l6k

## Table 4.25. Thailand: Details of tax revenue

Million THB

| | 1997 | 2000 | 2007 | 2010 | 2015 | 2016 | 2017 | 2018 | 2019 | 2020 |
|---|---|---|---|---|---|---|---|---|---|---|
| **Total tax revenue** | .. | **740 147** | **1 553 133** | **1 870 452** | **2 568 168** | **2 595 696** | **2 673 414** | **2 856 898** | **2 897 782** | **2 614 153** |
| **1000 Taxes on income, profits and capital gains** | .. | **235 421** | **614 883** | **682 860** | **895 205** | **894 058** | **893 754** | **975 030** | **1 031 929** | **912 618** |
| 1100 Of individuals | .. | 87 420 | 177 205 | 187 687 | 268 290 | 283 003 | 275 928 | 281 123 | 298 444 | 297 266 |
| 1110 On income and profits | .. | .. | .. | .. | .. | .. | .. | .. | .. | .. |
| 1120 On capital gains | .. | .. | .. | .. | .. | .. | .. | .. | .. | .. |
| 1200 Corporate | .. | 148 001 | 437 678 | 495 173 | 626 915 | 611 055 | 617 826 | 693 907 | 733 486 | 615 352 |
| 1210 On profits | .. | .. | .. | .. | .. | .. | .. | .. | .. | .. |
| 1220 On capital gains of corporates | .. | .. | .. | .. | .. | .. | .. | .. | .. | .. |
| 1300 Unallocable between 1100 and 1200 | .. | 0 | 0 | 0 | 0 | 0 | 0 | 0 | 0 | 0 |
| **2000 Social security contributions** | .. | **27 073** | **79 809** | **132 394** | **144 803** | **145 693** | **153 488** | **162 127** | **172 134** | **151 347** |
| 2100 Employees | .. | 12 704 | 37 717 | 0 | 66 027 | 68 574 | 70 993 | 75 249 | 79 418 | 69 116 |
| 2110 On a payroll basis | .. | .. | .. | .. | .. | .. | .. | .. | .. | .. |
| 2120 On an income tax basis | .. | .. | .. | .. | .. | .. | .. | .. | .. | .. |
| 2200 Employers | .. | 14 369 | 40 567 | 127 844 | 70 103 | 72 714 | 74 681 | 78 656 | 83 320 | 73 280 |
| 2210 On a payroll basis | .. | .. | .. | .. | .. | .. | .. | .. | .. | .. |
| 2220 On an income tax basis | .. | .. | .. | .. | .. | .. | .. | .. | .. | .. |
| 2300 Self-employed or non-employed | .. | 0 | 1 525 | 4 549 | 8 674 | 4 405 | 7 814 | 8 222 | 9 396 | 8 951 |
| 2310 On a payroll basis | .. | .. | .. | .. | .. | .. | .. | .. | .. | .. |
| 2320 On an income tax basis | .. | .. | .. | .. | .. | .. | .. | .. | .. | .. |
| 2400 Unallocable between 2100, 2200 and 2300 | .. | 0 | 0 | 0 | 0 | 0 | 0 | 0 | 0 | 0 |
| 2410 On a payroll basis | .. | .. | .. | .. | .. | .. | .. | .. | .. | .. |
| 2420 On an income tax basis | .. | .. | .. | .. | .. | .. | .. | .. | .. | .. |
| **3000 Taxes on payroll and workforce** | .. | **0** | **0** | **0** | **0** | **0** | **0** | **0** | **0** | **0** |
| **4000 Taxes on property** | .. | **16 283** | **18 317** | **24 666** | **68 157** | **60 364** | **73 946** | **78 533** | **78 277** | **37 135** |
| 4100 Recurrent taxes on immovable property | .. | 9 094 | 18 317 | 24 592 | 33 530 | 33 751 | 37 955 | 38 166 | 37 098 | 6 047 |
| 4110 Households | .. | .. | .. | .. | .. | .. | .. | .. | .. | .. |
| 4120 Others | .. | .. | .. | .. | .. | .. | .. | .. | .. | .. |
| 4200 Recurrent taxes on net wealth | .. | 0 | 0 | 74 | 0 | 0 | 0 | 0 | 0 | 0 |
| 4210 Individual | .. | .. | .. | .. | .. | .. | .. | .. | .. | .. |
| 4220 Corporate | .. | .. | .. | .. | .. | .. | .. | .. | .. | .. |
| 4300 Estate, inheritance and gift taxes | .. | 0 | 0 | 0 | 0 | 0 | 65 | 218 | 449 | 158 |
| 4310 Estate and inheritance taxes | .. | .. | .. | .. | .. | .. | .. | .. | .. | .. |
| 4320 Gift taxes | .. | .. | .. | .. | .. | .. | .. | .. | .. | .. |
| 4400 Taxes on financial and capital transactions | .. | 7 189 | 0 | 0 | 34 627 | 26 613 | 35 927 | 40 149 | 40 731 | 30 930 |
| 4500 Other non-reccurrent taxes on property | .. | 0 | 0 | 0 | 0 | 0 | 0 | 0 | 0 | 0 |
| 4510 On net wealth | .. | .. | .. | .. | .. | .. | .. | .. | .. | .. |
| 4520 Other non-recurrent taxes | .. | .. | .. | .. | .. | .. | .. | .. | .. | .. |
| 4600 Other recurrent taxes on property | .. | 0 | 0 | 0 | 0 | 0 | 0 | 0 | 0 | 0 |
| **5000 Taxes on goods and services** | .. | **457 826** | **829 490** | **1 016 829** | **1 442 327** | **1 477 187** | **1 533 483** | **1 620 247** | **1 596 431** | **1 495 090** |
| 5100 Taxes on production, sale, transfer, etc | .. | 444 986 | 808 624 | 990 052 | 1 262 437 | 1 312 202 | 1 386 480 | 1 456 652 | 1 447 646 | 1 335 974 |
| 5110 General taxes on goods and services | .. | 171 113 | 319 655 | 388 856 | 535 121 | 558 192 | 584 342 | 633 623 | 596 676 | 552 496 |
| 5111 Value added taxes | .. | 169 425 | 319 655 | 388 856 | 535 121 | 558 192 | 584 342 | 633 623 | 596 676 | 552 496 |
| 5112 Sales tax | .. | 1 688 | 0 | 0 | 0 | 0 | 0 | 0 | 0 | 0 |
| 5113 Other | .. | 0 | 0 | 0 | 0 | 0 | 0 | 0 | 0 | 0 |
| 5120 Taxes on specific goods and services | .. | 273 873 | 488 969 | 601 197 | 727 316 | 754 010 | 802 138 | 823 029 | 850 969 | 783 479 |
| 5121 Excises | .. | 180 884 | 351 498 | 478 257 | 559 388 | 589 363 | 642 966 | 662 141 | 683 725 | 635 347 |
| 5122 Profits of fiscal monopolies | .. | 5 310 | 8 210 | 4 879 | 8 106 | 5 148 | 7 116 | 174 | 928 | 643 |
| 5123 Customs and import duties | .. | 84 902 | 87 440 | 92 675 | 100 156 | 97 400 | 90 485 | 93 665 | 97 837 | 84 072 |
| 5124 Taxes on exports | .. | 2 329 | 4 164 | 168 | 202 | 103 | 81 | 143 | 209 | 133 |
| 5125 Taxes on investment goods | .. | 0 | 0 | 0 | 0 | 0 | 0 | 0 | 0 | 0 |
| 5126 Taxes on specific services | .. | 448 | 37 657 | 25 218 | 59 463 | 61 996 | 61 490 | 66 905 | 68 270 | 63 283 |
| 5127 Other taxes on internat. trade and transactions | .. | 0 | 0 | 0 | 0 | 0 | 0 | 0 | 0 | 0 |
| 5128 Other taxes | .. | 0 | 0 | 0 | 0 | 0 | 0 | 0 | 0 | 0 |
| 5130 Unallocable between 5110 and 5120 | .. | 0 | 0 | 0 | 0 | 0 | 0 | 0 | 0 | 0 |
| 5200 Taxes on use of goods and to perform activities | .. | 12 840 | 20 866 | 26 777 | 179 890 | 164 985 | 147 003 | 163 595 | 148 785 | 159 116 |
| 5210 Recurrent taxes | .. | .. | .. | .. | .. | .. | .. | .. | .. | .. |
| 5211 Paid by households: motor vehicles | .. | .. | .. | .. | .. | .. | .. | .. | .. | .. |
| 5212 Paid by others: motor vehicles | .. | .. | .. | .. | .. | .. | .. | .. | .. | .. |
| 5213 Paid in respect of other goods | .. | .. | .. | .. | .. | .. | .. | .. | .. | .. |
| 5220 Non-recurrent taxes | .. | .. | .. | .. | .. | .. | .. | .. | .. | .. |
| 5300 Unallocable between 5100 and 5200 | .. | 0 | 0 | 0 | 0 | 0 | 0 | 0 | 0 | 0 |

| | 1997 | 2000 | 2007 | 2010 | 2015 | 2016 | 2017 | 2018 | 2019 | 2020 |
|---|---|---|---|---|---|---|---|---|---|---|
| **6000 Other taxes** | .. | **3 544** | **10 634** | **13 703** | **17 677** | **18 394** | **18 743** | **20 962** | **19 010** | **17 963** |
| 6100 Paid solely by business | .. | .. | .. | .. | .. | .. | .. | .. | .. | .. |
| 6200 Other | .. | .. | .. | .. | .. | .. | .. | .. | .. | .. |

.. Not available

Note: Data are on a fiscal year basis ending 30th September. For example, the data for 2020 represents 1 October 2019 to 30 September 2020.

The data are on a cash basis.

Tax revenues submitted by the Ministry of Finance for 2000 - 2012 are based on data gathered by the IMF.

Source: Ministry of Finance in Thailand.

StatLink https://stat.link/p5oym3

## Table 4.26. Tokelau: Details of tax revenue

Thousand NZD

| | 1997 | 2000 | 2007 | 2010 | 2015 | 2016 | 2017 | 2018 | 2019 | 2020 |
|---|---|---|---|---|---|---|---|---|---|---|
| **Total tax revenue** | .. | .. | **1 198** | **1 694** | **2 151** | **2 176** | **2 518** | **2 843** | **3 040** | **3 279** |
| **1000 Taxes on income, profits and capital gains** | .. | .. | **573** | **866** | **1 100** | **1 188** | **1 404** | **1 346** | **1 631** | **1 667** |
| 1100 Of individuals | .. | .. | 573 | 866 | 1 100 | 1 188 | 1 404 | 1 346 | 1 631 | 1 667 |
| 1110 On income and profits | .. | .. | .. | .. | .. | .. | .. | .. | .. | .. |
| 1120 On capital gains | .. | .. | .. | .. | .. | .. | .. | .. | .. | .. |
| 1200 Corporate | .. | .. | 0 | 0 | 0 | 0 | 0 | 0 | 0 | 0 |
| 1210 On profits | .. | .. | .. | .. | .. | .. | .. | .. | .. | .. |
| 1220 On capital gains of corporates | .. | .. | .. | .. | .. | .. | .. | .. | .. | .. |
| 1300 Unallocable between 1100 and 1200 | .. | .. | 0 | 0 | 0 | 0 | 0 | 0 | 0 | 0 |
| **2000 Social security contributions** | .. | .. | **0** | **0** | **0** | **0** | **0** | **0** | **0** | **0** |
| 2100 Employees | .. | .. | .. | .. | .. | .. | .. | .. | .. | .. |
| 2110 On a payroll basis | .. | .. | .. | .. | .. | .. | .. | .. | .. | .. |
| 2120 On an income tax basis | .. | .. | .. | .. | .. | .. | .. | .. | .. | .. |
| 2200 Employers | .. | .. | .. | .. | .. | .. | .. | .. | .. | .. |
| 2210 On a payroll basis | .. | .. | .. | .. | .. | .. | .. | .. | .. | .. |
| 2220 On an income tax basis | .. | .. | .. | .. | .. | .. | .. | .. | .. | .. |
| 2300 Self-employed or non-employed | .. | .. | .. | .. | .. | .. | .. | .. | .. | .. |
| 2310 On a payroll basis | .. | .. | .. | .. | .. | .. | .. | .. | .. | .. |
| 2320 On an income tax basis | .. | .. | .. | .. | .. | .. | .. | .. | .. | .. |
| 2400 Unallocable between 2100, 2200 and 2300 | .. | .. | .. | .. | .. | .. | .. | .. | .. | .. |
| 2410 On a payroll basis | .. | .. | .. | .. | .. | .. | .. | .. | .. | .. |
| 2420 On an income tax basis | .. | .. | .. | .. | .. | .. | .. | .. | .. | .. |
| **3000 Taxes on payroll and workforce** | .. | .. | **0** | **0** | **0** | **0** | **0** | **0** | **0** | **0** |
| **4000 Taxes on property** | .. | .. | **0** | **0** | **0** | **0** | **0** | **0** | **0** | **0** |
| 4100 Recurrent taxes on immovable property | .. | .. | .. | .. | .. | .. | .. | .. | .. | .. |
| 4110 Households | .. | .. | .. | .. | .. | .. | .. | .. | .. | .. |
| 4120 Others | .. | .. | .. | .. | .. | .. | .. | .. | .. | .. |
| 4200 Recurrent taxes on net wealth | .. | .. | .. | .. | .. | .. | .. | .. | .. | .. |
| 4210 Individual | .. | .. | .. | .. | .. | .. | .. | .. | .. | .. |
| 4220 Corporate | .. | .. | .. | .. | .. | .. | .. | .. | .. | .. |
| 4300 Estate, inheritance and gift taxes | .. | .. | .. | .. | .. | .. | .. | .. | .. | .. |
| 4310 Estate and inheritance taxes | .. | .. | .. | .. | .. | .. | .. | .. | .. | .. |
| 4320 Gift taxes | .. | .. | .. | .. | .. | .. | .. | .. | .. | .. |
| 4400 Taxes on financial and capital transactions | .. | .. | .. | .. | .. | .. | .. | .. | .. | .. |
| 4500 Other non-reccurrent taxes on property | .. | .. | .. | .. | .. | .. | .. | .. | .. | .. |
| 4510 On net wealth | .. | .. | .. | .. | .. | .. | .. | .. | .. | .. |
| 4520 Other non-recurrent taxes | .. | .. | .. | .. | .. | .. | .. | .. | .. | .. |
| 4600 Other recurrent taxes on property | .. | .. | .. | .. | .. | .. | .. | .. | .. | .. |
| **5000 Taxes on goods and services** | .. | .. | **625** | **828** | **1 051** | **988** | **1 114** | **1 497** | **1 409** | **1 612** |
| 5100 Taxes on production, sale, transfer, etc | .. | .. | 625 | 828 | 1 051 | 988 | 1 114 | 1 497 | 1 409 | 1 612 |
| 5110 General taxes on goods and services | .. | .. | 0 | 0 | 0 | 0 | 0 | 0 | 0 | 0 |
| 5111 Value added taxes | .. | .. | 0 | 0 | 0 | 0 | 0 | 0 | 0 | 0 |
| 5112 Sales tax | .. | .. | 0 | 0 | 0 | 0 | 0 | 0 | 0 | 0 |
| 5113 Other | .. | .. | 0 | 0 | 0 | 0 | 0 | 0 | 0 | 0 |
| 5120 Taxes on specific goods and services | .. | .. | 625 | 828 | 1 051 | 988 | 1 114 | 1 497 | 1 409 | 1 612 |
| 5121 Excises | .. | .. | 624 | 827 | 1 050 | 984 | 1 104 | 1 489 | 1 406 | 1 612 |
| Duty On Tobacco | .. | .. | 258 | 379 | 558 | 539 | 702 | 966 | 948 | 1 101 |
| Duty On Liqour | .. | .. | 178 | 222 | 288 | 251 | 200 | 266 | 240 | 288 |
| Duty On General Goods : resale | .. | .. | 188 | 226 | 204 | 194 | 202 | 257 | 218 | 223 |
| 5122 Profits of fiscal monopolies | .. | .. | 0 | 0 | 0 | 0 | 0 | 0 | 0 | 0 |
| 5123 Customs and import duties | .. | .. | 0 | 0 | 0 | 0 | 0 | 0 | 0 | 0 |
| 5124 Taxes on exports | .. | .. | 0 | 0 | 0 | 0 | 0 | 0 | 0 | 0 |
| 5125 Taxes on investment goods | .. | .. | 0 | 0 | 0 | 0 | 0 | 0 | 0 | 0 |
| 5126 Taxes on specific services | .. | .. | 1 | 1 | 1 | 4 | 10 | 8 | 3 | 0 |
| 5127 Other taxes on internat. trade and transactions | .. | .. | 0 | 0 | 0 | 0 | 0 | 0 | 0 | 0 |
| 5128 Other taxes | .. | .. | 0 | 0 | 0 | 0 | 0 | 0 | 0 | 0 |
| 5130 Unallocable between 5110 and 5120 | .. | .. | 0 | 0 | 0 | 0 | 0 | 0 | 0 | 0 |
| 5200 Taxes on use of goods and to perform activities | .. | .. | 0 | 0 | 0 | 0 | 0 | 0 | 0 | 0 |
| 5210 Recurrent taxes | .. | .. | .. | .. | .. | .. | .. | .. | .. | .. |
| 5211 Paid by households: motor vehicles | .. | .. | .. | .. | .. | .. | .. | .. | .. | .. |
| 5212 Paid by others: motor vehicles | .. | .. | .. | .. | .. | .. | .. | .. | .. | .. |
| 5213 Paid in respect of other goods | .. | .. | .. | .. | .. | .. | .. | .. | .. | .. |
| 5220 Non-recurrent taxes | .. | .. | .. | .. | .. | .. | .. | .. | .. | .. |
| 5300 Unallocable between 5100 and 5200 | .. | .. | 0 | 0 | 0 | 0 | 0 | 0 | 0 | 0 |

| | 1997 | 2000 | 2007 | 2010 | 2015 | 2016 | 2017 | 2018 | 2019 | 2020 |
|---|---|---|---|---|---|---|---|---|---|---|
| **6000 Other taxes** | .. | .. | **0** | **0** | **0** | **0** | **0** | **0** | **0** | **0** |
| 6100 Paid solely by business | .. | .. | .. | .. | .. | .. | .. | .. | .. | .. |
| 6200 Other | .. | .. | .. | .. | .. | .. | .. | .. | .. | .. |

.. Not available

Note: Data are reported on a fiscal year basis beginning 1st July. For example, the data for 2020 represent the period from July 2020 to June 2021.
The data are on a cash basis.

Source: National Statistics Office of Tokelau.

StatLink https://stat.link/ibc59o

## Table 4.27. Vanuatu: Details of tax revenue

Million VUV

| | 1997 | 2000 | 2007 | 2010 | 2015 | 2016 | 2017 | 2018 | 2019 | 2020 |
|---|---|---|---|---|---|---|---|---|---|---|
| **Total tax revenue** | .. | **6 098** | **10 267** | **11 089** | **13 477** | **13 324** | **16 249** | **17 976** | **18 254** | **14 732** |
| **1000 Taxes on income, profits and capital gains** | .. | **0** | **0** | **0** | **0** | **0** | **0** | **0** | **0** | **0** |
| 1100 Of individuals | .. | 0 | 0 | 0 | 0 | 0 | 0 | 0 | 0 | 0 |
| 1110 On income and profits | .. | 0 | 0 | 0 | 0 | 0 | 0 | 0 | 0 | 0 |
| 1120 On capital gains | .. | 0 | 0 | 0 | 0 | 0 | 0 | 0 | 0 | 0 |
| 1200 Corporate | .. | 0 | 0 | 0 | 0 | 0 | 0 | 0 | 0 | 0 |
| 1210 On profits | .. | 0 | 0 | 0 | 0 | 0 | 0 | 0 | 0 | 0 |
| 1220 On capital gains of corporates | .. | 0 | 0 | 0 | 0 | 0 | 0 | 0 | 0 | 0 |
| 1300 Unallocable between 1100 and 1200 | .. | 0 | 0 | 0 | 0 | 0 | 0 | 0 | 0 | 0 |
| **2000 Social security contributions** | .. | **0** | **0** | **0** | **0** | **0** | **0** | **0** | **0** | **0** |
| 2100 Employees | .. | .. | .. | .. | .. | .. | .. | .. | .. | .. |
| 2110 On a payroll basis | .. | .. | .. | .. | .. | .. | .. | .. | .. | .. |
| 2120 On an income tax basis | .. | .. | .. | .. | .. | .. | .. | .. | .. | .. |
| 2200 Employers | .. | .. | .. | .. | .. | .. | .. | .. | .. | .. |
| 2210 On a payroll basis | .. | .. | .. | .. | .. | .. | .. | .. | .. | .. |
| 2220 On an income tax basis | .. | .. | .. | .. | .. | .. | .. | .. | .. | .. |
| 2300 Self-employed or non-employed | .. | .. | .. | .. | .. | .. | .. | .. | .. | .. |
| 2310 On a payroll basis | .. | .. | .. | .. | .. | .. | .. | .. | .. | .. |
| 2320 On an income tax basis | .. | .. | .. | .. | .. | .. | .. | .. | .. | .. |
| 2400 Unallocable between 2100, 2200 and 2300 | .. | .. | .. | .. | .. | .. | .. | .. | .. | .. |
| 2410 On a payroll basis | .. | .. | .. | .. | .. | .. | .. | .. | .. | .. |
| 2420 On an income tax basis | .. | .. | .. | .. | .. | .. | .. | .. | .. | .. |
| **3000 Taxes on payroll and workforce** | .. | **0** | **0** | **0** | **0** | **0** | **0** | **0** | **0** | **0** |
| **4000 Taxes on property** | .. | **196** | **449** | **485** | **402** | **383** | **488** | **566** | **648** | **495** |
| 4100 Recurrent taxes on immovable property | .. | .. | .. | .. | .. | .. | .. | .. | .. | .. |
| 4110 Households | .. | .. | .. | .. | .. | .. | .. | .. | .. | .. |
| 4120 Others | .. | .. | .. | .. | .. | .. | .. | .. | .. | .. |
| 4200 Recurrent taxes on net wealth | .. | .. | .. | .. | .. | .. | .. | .. | .. | .. |
| 4210 Individual | .. | .. | .. | .. | .. | .. | .. | .. | .. | .. |
| 4220 Corporate | .. | .. | .. | .. | .. | .. | .. | .. | .. | .. |
| 4300 Estate, inheritance and gift taxes | .. | .. | .. | .. | .. | .. | .. | .. | .. | .. |
| 4310 Estate and inheritance taxes | .. | .. | .. | .. | .. | .. | .. | .. | .. | .. |
| 4320 Gift taxes | .. | .. | .. | .. | .. | .. | .. | .. | .. | .. |
| 4400 Taxes on financial and capital transactions | .. | .. | .. | .. | .. | .. | .. | .. | .. | .. |
| 4500 Other non-reccurrent taxes on property | .. | .. | .. | .. | .. | .. | .. | .. | .. | .. |
| 4510 On net wealth | .. | .. | .. | .. | .. | .. | .. | .. | .. | .. |
| 4520 Other non-recurrent taxes | .. | .. | .. | .. | .. | .. | .. | .. | .. | .. |
| 4600 Other recurrent taxes on property | .. | .. | .. | .. | .. | .. | .. | .. | .. | .. |
| **5000 Taxes on goods and services** | .. | **5 902** | **9 818** | **10 603** | **13 075** | **12 941** | **15 761** | **17 410** | **17 606** | **14 237** |
| 5100 Taxes on production, sale, transfer, etc | .. | 5 902 | 9 818 | 8 829 | 10 898 | 10 708 | 13 024 | 14 713 | 14 598 | 12 269 |
| 5110 General taxes on goods and services | .. | 3 441 | 5 858 | 4 301 | 5 769 | 5 549 | 6 912 | 8 235 | 8 134 | 6 495 |
| 5111 Value added taxes | .. | 3 441 | 5 858 | 4 301 | 5 769 | 5 549 | 6 912 | 8 235 | 8 134 | 6 495 |
| 5112 Sales tax | .. | 0 | 0 | 0 | 0 | 0 | 0 | 0 | 0 | 0 |
| 5113 Other | .. | 0 | 0 | 0 | 0 | 0 | 0 | 0 | 0 | 0 |
| 5120 Taxes on specific goods and services | .. | 2 461 | 3 960 | 4 528 | 5 130 | 5 159 | 6 112 | 6 478 | 6 464 | 5 773 |
| 5121 Excises | .. | 76 | 554 | 1 882 | 2 180 | 2 219 | 2 578 | 2 784 | 2 830 | 2 633 |
| 5122 Profits of fiscal monopolies | .. | 0 | 0 | 0 | 0 | 0 | 0 | 0 | 0 | 0 |
| 5123 Customs and import duties | .. | 2 385 | 3 406 | 2 646 | 2 950 | 2 940 | 3 534 | 3 694 | 3 635 | 3 140 |
| 5124 Taxes on exports | .. | 0 | 0 | 0 | 0 | 0 | 0 | 0 | 0 | 0 |
| 5125 Taxes on investment goods | .. | 0 | 0 | 0 | 0 | 0 | 0 | 0 | 0 | 0 |
| 5126 Taxes on specific services | .. | 0 | 0 | 0 | 0 | 0 | 0 | 0 | 0 | 0 |
| 5127 Other taxes on internat. trade and transactions | .. | 0 | 0 | 0 | 0 | 0 | 0 | 0 | 0 | 0 |
| 5128 Other taxes | .. | 0 | 0 | 0 | 0 | 0 | 0 | 0 | 0 | 0 |
| 5130 Unallocable between 5110 and 5120 | .. | 0 | 0 | 0 | 0 | 0 | 0 | 0 | 0 | 0 |
| 5200 Taxes on use of goods and to perform activities | .. | 0 | 0 | 0 | 0 | 0 | 0 | 0 | 0 | 0 |
| 5210 Recurrent taxes | .. | .. | .. | .. | .. | .. | .. | .. | .. | .. |
| 5211 Paid by households: motor vehicles | .. | .. | .. | .. | .. | .. | .. | .. | .. | .. |
| 5212 Paid by others: motor vehicles | .. | .. | .. | .. | .. | .. | .. | .. | .. | .. |
| 5213 Paid in respect of other goods | .. | .. | .. | .. | .. | .. | .. | .. | .. | .. |
| 5220 Non-recurrent taxes | .. | .. | .. | .. | .. | .. | .. | .. | .. | .. |
| 5300 Unallocable between 5100 and 5200 | .. | 0 | 0 | 1 774 | 2 177 | 2 233 | 2 737 | 2 697 | 3 008 | 1 968 |
| **6000 Other taxes** | .. | **0** | **0** | **0** | **0** | **0** | **0** | **0** | **0** | **0** |
| 6100 Paid solely by business | .. | .. | .. | .. | .. | .. | .. | .. | .. | .. |
| 6200 Other | .. | .. | .. | .. | .. | .. | .. | .. | .. | .. |

.. Not available

Note: Year ending December 31st.

Source: Department of Finance and Treasury of Vanuatu.

StatLink https://stat.link/c7faoj

## Table 4.28. Viet Nam: Details of tax revenue

Billion VND

| | 1997 | 2000 | 2007 | 2010 | 2015 | 2016 | 2017 | 2018 | 2019 | 2020 |
|---|---|---|---|---|---|---|---|---|---|---|
| **Total tax revenue** | .. | .. | **248 381** | **546 771** | **943 196** | **1 035 456** | **1 158 960** | **1 285 632** | **1 458 674** | **1 427 088** |
| **1000 Taxes on income, profits and capital gains** | .. | .. | **111 967** | **174 931** | **256 753** | **254 916** | **295 983** | **345 256** | **380 016** | **374 542** |
| 1100 Of individuals | .. | .. | 7 415 | 26 276 | 56 723 | 65 239 | 78 783 | 94 364 | 109 406 | 115 213 |
| 1110 On income and profits | .. | .. | 7 415 | 26 276 | 56 723 | 65 239 | 78 783 | 94 364 | 109 406 | 115 213 |
| 1120 On capital gains | .. | .. | 0 | 0 | 0 | 0 | 0 | 0 | 0 | 0 |
| 1200 Corporate | .. | .. | 104 552 | 148 655 | 200 030 | 189 677 | 217 200 | 250 892 | 270 610 | 259 329 |
| 1210 On profits | .. | .. | 104 552 | 148 655 | 200 030 | 189 677 | 217 200 | 250 892 | 270 610 | 259 329 |
| 1220 On capital gains of corporates | .. | .. | 0 | 0 | 0 | 0 | 0 | 0 | 0 | 0 |
| 1300 Unallocable between 1100 and 1200 | .. | .. | 0 | 0 | 0 | 0 | 0 | 0 | 0 | 0 |
| **2000 Social security contributions** | .. | .. | .. | **80 855** | **217 755** | **256 391** | **290 861** | **331 611** | **406 947** | **433 147** |
| 2100 Employees | .. | .. | .. | .. | .. | .. | .. | .. | .. | .. |
| 2110 On a payroll basis | .. | .. | .. | .. | .. | .. | .. | .. | .. | .. |
| 2120 On an income tax basis | .. | .. | .. | .. | .. | .. | .. | .. | .. | .. |
| 2200 Employers | .. | .. | .. | .. | .. | .. | .. | .. | .. | .. |
| 2210 On a payroll basis | .. | .. | .. | .. | .. | .. | .. | .. | .. | .. |
| 2220 On an income tax basis | .. | .. | .. | .. | .. | .. | .. | .. | .. | .. |
| 2300 Self-employed or non-employed | .. | .. | .. | .. | .. | .. | .. | .. | .. | .. |
| 2310 On a payroll basis | .. | .. | .. | .. | .. | .. | .. | .. | .. | .. |
| 2320 On an income tax basis | .. | .. | .. | .. | .. | .. | .. | .. | .. | .. |
| 2400 Unallocable between 2100, 2200 and 2300 | .. | .. | .. | 80 855 | 217 755 | 256 391 | 290 861 | 331 611 | 406 947 | 433 147 |
| 2410 On a payroll basis | .. | .. | .. | .. | .. | .. | .. | .. | .. | .. |
| 2420 On an income tax basis | .. | .. | .. | .. | .. | .. | .. | .. | .. | .. |
| **3000 Taxes on payroll and workforce** | .. | .. | **0** | **0** | **0** | **0** | **0** | **0** | **0** | **0** |
| **4000 Taxes on property** | .. | .. | **824** | **1 452** | **1 537** | **1 479** | **1 726** | **1 901** | **2 060** | **2 074** |
| 4100 Recurrent taxes on immovable property | .. | .. | 824 | 1 452 | 1 537 | 1 479 | 1 726 | 1 901 | 2 060 | 2 074 |
| 4110 Households | .. | .. | 711 | 1 396 | 1 479 | 1 419 | 1 687 | 1 874 | 2 040 | 2 068 |
| 4120 Others | .. | .. | 113 | 56 | 58 | 60 | 39 | 27 | 20 | 6 |
| 4200 Recurrent taxes on net wealth | .. | .. | 0 | 0 | 0 | 0 | 0 | 0 | 0 | 0 |
| 4210 Individual | .. | .. | .. | .. | .. | .. | .. | .. | .. | .. |
| 4220 Corporate | .. | .. | .. | .. | .. | .. | .. | .. | .. | .. |
| 4300 Estate, inheritance and gift taxes | .. | .. | 0 | 0 | 0 | 0 | 0 | 0 | 0 | 0 |
| 4310 Estate and inheritance taxes | .. | .. | .. | .. | .. | .. | .. | .. | .. | .. |
| 4320 Gift taxes | .. | .. | .. | .. | .. | .. | .. | .. | .. | .. |
| 4400 Taxes on financial and capital transactions | .. | .. | 0 | 0 | 0 | 0 | 0 | 0 | 0 | 0 |
| 4500 Other non-reccurrent taxes on property | .. | .. | 0 | 0 | 0 | 0 | 0 | 0 | 0 | 0 |
| 4510 On net wealth | .. | .. | .. | .. | .. | .. | .. | .. | .. | .. |
| 4520 Other non-recurrent taxes | .. | .. | .. | .. | .. | .. | .. | .. | .. | .. |
| 4600 Other recurrent taxes on property | .. | .. | 0 | 0 | 0 | 0 | 0 | 0 | 0 | 0 |
| **5000 Taxes on goods and services** | .. | .. | **135 590** | **289 533** | **467 151** | **522 670** | **570 390** | **606 864** | **669 652** | **617 325** |
| 5100 Taxes on production, sale, transfer, etc | .. | .. | 129 954 | 276 922 | 444 746 | 495 359 | 542 777 | 574 455 | 629 462 | 582 503 |
| 5110 General taxes on goods and services | .. | .. | 69 822 | 155 022 | 251 758 | 269 627 | 314 508 | 344 063 | 362 691 | 342 029 |
| 5111 Value added taxes | .. | .. | 69 822 | 155 022 | 251 758 | 269 627 | 314 508 | 344 063 | 362 691 | 342 029 |
| Domestic VAT | .. | .. | 47 860 | 98 739 | 181 770 | 192 562 | 212 518 | 228 840 | 247 100 | 243 253 |
| VAT on imports | .. | .. | 21 962 | 56 283 | 69 988 | 77 065 | 101 990 | 115 223 | 115 591 | 98 776 |
| 5112 Sales tax | .. | .. | 0 | 0 | 0 | 0 | 0 | 0 | 0 | 0 |
| 5113 Other | .. | .. | 0 | 0 | 0 | 0 | 0 | 0 | 0 | 0 |
| 5120 Taxes on specific goods and services | .. | .. | 60 132 | 121 900 | 192 988 | 225 732 | 228 269 | 230 392 | 266 771 | 240 474 |
| 5121 Excises | .. | .. | 60 132 | 121 900 | 192 988 | 225 732 | 228 269 | 230 392 | 266 771 | 240 474 |
| Domestic excises | .. | .. | 17 365 | 37 311 | 66 653 | 85 853 | 86 585 | 96 025 | 106 753 | 101 090 |
| Environmental protection tax | .. | .. | 4 458 | 10 521 | 27 020 | 43 632 | 44 666 | 47 050 | 63 075 | 60 631 |
| Excise tax on imports | .. | .. | 38 309 | 74 068 | 99 315 | 96 247 | 97 018 | 87 317 | 96 943 | 78 753 |
| 5122 Profits of fiscal monopolies | .. | .. | 0 | 0 | 0 | 0 | 0 | 0 | 0 | 0 |
| 5123 Customs and import duties | .. | .. | 0 | 0 | 0 | 0 | 0 | 0 | 0 | 0 |
| 5124 Taxes on exports | .. | .. | 0 | 0 | 0 | 0 | 0 | 0 | 0 | 0 |
| 5125 Taxes on investment goods | .. | .. | 0 | 0 | 0 | 0 | 0 | 0 | 0 | 0 |
| 5126 Taxes on specific services | .. | .. | 0 | 0 | 0 | 0 | 0 | 0 | 0 | 0 |
| 5127 Other taxes on internat. trade and transactions | .. | .. | 0 | 0 | 0 | 0 | 0 | 0 | 0 | 0 |
| 5128 Other taxes | .. | .. | 0 | 0 | 0 | 0 | 0 | 0 | 0 | 0 |
| 5130 Unallocable between 5110 and 5120 | .. | .. | 0 | 0 | 0 | 0 | 0 | 0 | 0 | 0 |
| 5200 Taxes on use of goods and to perform activities | .. | .. | 5 636 | 12 611 | 22 405 | 27 311 | 27 613 | 32 409 | 40 190 | 34 822 |
| 5210 Recurrent taxes | .. | .. | 0 | 0 | 0 | 0 | 0 | 0 | 0 | 0 |
| 5211 Paid by households: motor vehicles | .. | .. | .. | .. | .. | .. | .. | .. | .. | .. |
| 5212 Paid by others: motor vehicles | .. | .. | .. | .. | .. | .. | .. | .. | .. | .. |
| 5213 Paid in respect of other goods | .. | .. | .. | .. | .. | .. | .. | .. | .. | .. |
| 5220 Non-recurrent taxes | .. | .. | 5 636 | 12 611 | 22 405 | 27 311 | 27 613 | 32 409 | 40 190 | 34 822 |
| 5300 Unallocable between 5100 and 5200 | .. | .. | 0 | 0 | 0 | 0 | 0 | 0 | 0 | 0 |
| **6000 Other taxes** | .. | .. | **0** | **0** | **0** | **0** | **0** | **0** | **0** | **0** |
| 6100 Paid solely by business | .. | .. | .. | .. | .. | .. | .. | .. | .. | .. |
| 6200 Other | .. | .. | .. | .. | .. | .. | .. | .. | .. | .. |

.. Not available

Note: Year ending 31st December.

The data are on a cash basis.

The figures include both central government and sub-national government revenues but segregation is not available.

Heading 2000: Social security contribution data for Viet Nam have been included in this edition. The data consist of revenues from social insurance, health insurance and unemployment insurance. Compulsory contributions from employers and employees account for the majority of these revenues which also include a smaller amount of voluntary contributions and other revenues that are not considered as tax revenues according to the OECD classification described in the Interpretative Guide, as they cannot be distinguished from the total. Data are not available before 2010.

Heading 4110: This heading shows the revenues from the land and housing tax. A distinction between the amounts paid by households and the amounts paid by other taxpayers could not be made.

Source: General Statistics Office Viet Nam.

*StatLink* https://stat.link/ka5qeg

# 5 Comparative and country tables, non-tax revenues, 2007-2020

## Non-tax revenue tables, 2007-2020

In all of the following tables a ("..") indicates not available. The main series in this volume cover the years 2007 to 2020.

Complete series for the comparative tables are available on line at OECD (2022), "Revenue Statistics - Asian and Pacific Economies: Comparative tables", OECD Tax statistics (database). Full time series for the country tables can be accessed at https://stats.oecd.org/ within the theme Public Sector, Taxation and Market Regulation/Taxation/Revenue Statistics Asian and Pacific Economies.

## Table 5.1. Total non-tax revenue as percentage of GDP in selected economies, 2007-20

| | 2007 | 2010 | 2012 | 2014 | 2015 | 2016 | 2017 | 2018 | 2019 | 2020 |
|---|---|---|---|---|---|---|---|---|---|---|
| Bhutan | 26.6 | 22.1 | 16.6 | 14.8 | 17.7 | 15.0 | 16.4 | 13.1 | 19.5 | 19.8 |
| Cambodia[1] | 3.6 | 6.4 | 4.4 | 4.4 | 4.0 | 5.1 | 4.7 | 5.1 | 5.1 | 4.3 |
| Cook Islands | 5.6 | 13.5 | 8.4 | 16.2 | 13.9 | 16.4 | 14.3 | 12.9 | 16.0 | 27.4 |
| Fiji | .. | 2.9 | 3.0 | 2.9 | 2.9 | 3.2 | 3.5 | 3.6 | 3.4 | 4.1 |
| Kazakhstan | 1.5 | 1.0 | 1.8 | 1.5 | 1.3 | 1.2 | 1.1 | 1.7 | 1.5 | 1.2 |
| Kyrgyzstan | 6.7 | 8.3 | 7.6 | 9.4 | 10.7 | 7.9 | 8.5 | 6.3 | 7.6 | 7.8 |
| Lao PDR | .. | 9.5 | 10.2 | 9.6 | 7.7 | 4.5 | 5.3 | 5.4 | 5.1 | 3.7 |
| Maldives | 14.9 | 10.2 | 6.3 | 7.0 | 6.7 | 7.2 | 6.8 | 6.8 | 6.4 | 5.7 |
| Mongolia | 9.5 | 6.5 | 6.9 | 7.8 | 6.4 | 5.1 | 4.3 | 4.6 | 4.3 | 3.6 |
| Nauru | .. | .. | .. | 28.6 | 65.2 | 63.7 | 70.8 | 92.7 | 85.3 | 67.5 |
| Pakistan | .. | .. | 3.0 | 3.5 | 2.5 | 2.8 | 2.0 | 1.1 | 3.3 | 2.2 |
| Papua New Guinea | 4.0 | 4.7 | 3.1 | 3.1 | 3.2 | 3.2 | 3.3 | 3.7 | 2.8 | 2.7 |
| Philippines | .. | .. | .. | 1.8 | 2.0 | 1.8 | 1.7 | 1.8 | 2.0 | 2.3 |
| Samoa[2] | 8.3 | 8.9 | 4.8 | 4.8 | 4.7 | 4.5 | 5.3 | 5.6 | 10.9 | 11.6 |
| Singapore | 5.8 | 3.5 | 3.4 | 3.9 | 4.4 | 4.4 | 5.3 | 4.3 | 7.2 | 4.7 |
| Thailand | 2.7 | 3.3 | 2.9 | 3.1 | 3.6 | 3.7 | 3.6 | 3.8 | 3.7 | 4.0 |
| Tokelau[3] | 149.3 | 154.6 | 192.6 | 173.4 | 230.4 | 236.5 | 210.0 | 236.4 | 220.1 | 218.7 |
| Vanuatu | 1.4 | 8.3 | 5.2 | 5.8 | 14.8 | 9.6 | 14.2 | 19.8 | 24.3 | 24.0 |
| Viet Nam | 7.1 | 5.7 | 4.9 | 5.1 | 6.5 | 7.2 | 8.4 | 8.6 | 8.3 | 8.2 |

.. Not available

Note: Figures include non-tax revenue data collected by sub-national governments for Cambodia, Kyrgyzstan, Kazakhstan, Mongolia, Pakistan, the Philippines and Thailand. They exclude non-tax revenue collected by sub-national governments as the data are not available for the remaining economies.

1. Local government revenue data are not available before 2012.
2. The data prior to 2009 are reported on a different basis (for more information see Table 5.11).
3. Tokelau receives significant revenues from foreign vessels for access to Tokelau fishing waters. In the 2008 SNA, these revenues are recorded as part of GNI, but they do not add to GDP.

StatLink https://stat.link/nb0lk7

## Table 5.2. Non-tax revenue of main headings as percentage of GDP in selected economies, 2020

| | Grants | Property income | Sales of goods and services | Fines, penalties and forfeits | Miscellaneous and unidentified revenue |
|---|---|---|---|---|---|
| Bhutan | 8.4 | 6.5 | 4.8 | 0.1 | 0.0 |
| Cambodia | 2.0 | 0.5 | 1.5 | 0.3 | 0.0 |
| Cook Islands | 13.7 | 2.5 | 2.5 | 0.2 | 8.5 |
| Fiji | 1.2 | 1.2 | 1.6 | 0.0 | 0.0 |
| Kazakhstan | 0.0 | 0.9 | 0.2 | 0.1 | 0.0 |
| Kyrgyzstan[1] | 2.0 | 2.0 | 2.2 | 0.3 | 1.4 |
| Lao PDR | 1.5 | 1.2 | 0.9 | 0.0 | 0.2 |
| Maldives | 0.0 | 1.5 | 3.6 | 0.3 | 0.3 |
| Mongolia | 0.4 | 1.6 | 0.2 | 0.4 | 1.0 |
| Nauru | 0.0 | 37.0 | 18.2 | 0.0 | 12.4 |
| Pakistan | 0.1 | 1.6 | 0.1 | 0.0 | 0.4 |
| Papua New Guinea | 1.7 | 0.9 | 0.0 | 0.0 | 0.0 |
| Philippines | 0.0 | 1.3 | 0.3 | 0.0 | 0.6 |
| Samoa[2] | 6.8 | 1.5 | 3.2 | 0.0 | 0.0 |
| Singapore | 0.0 | 3.7 | 0.8 | 0.1 | 0.1 |
| Thailand | 0.0 | 2.1 | 1.3 | 0.1 | 0.4 |
| Tokelau[3] | 79.1 | 130.5 | 9.2 | 0.0 | 0.0 |
| Vanuatu | 7.9 | .. | .. | .. | 16.1 |
| Viet Nam | 0.1 | 0.5 | 4.5 | 0.0 | 3.1 |

.. Not available

Note: Figures include non-tax revenue data collected by sub-national governments for Cambodia, Kyrgyzstan, Kazakhstan, Mongolia, Pakistan, the Philippines and Thailand. They exclude non-tax revenue collected by sub-national governments as the data are not available for the remaining economies.

1. Grants: "Other transfers received" are not classified as non-tax revenue in Kyrgyzstan but are considered as non-tax revenues under the OECD Interpretative Guide.
2. The data prior to 2009 are reported on a different basis (for more information see Table 5.11).
3. Tokelau receives significant revenues from foreign vessels for access to Tokelau fishing waters. In the 2008 SNA, these revenues are recorded as part of GNI, but they do not add to GDP.

StatLink https://stat.link/h5xc43

## Table 5.3. Non-tax revenue of main headings as percentage of total non-tax revenues in selected economies, 2020

| | Grants | Property income | Sales of goods and services | Fines, penalties and forfeits | Miscellaneous and unidentified revenue |
|---|---|---|---|---|---|
| Bhutan | 42.6 | 32.9 | 24.2 | 0.3 | 0.0 |
| Cambodia | 45.8 | 12.7 | 34.1 | 7.3 | 0.1 |
| Cook Islands | 49.9 | 9.2 | 9.1 | 0.8 | 31.0 |
| Fiji | 29.6 | 28.8 | 40.1 | 0.5 | 0.9 |
| Kazakhstan | 0.0 | 75.2 | 16.2 | 8.6 | 0.0 |
| Kyrgyzstan[1] | 25.1 | 26.0 | 27.7 | 3.5 | 17.7 |
| Lao PDR | 39.7 | 30.7 | 23.6 | 0.6 | 5.3 |
| Maldives | 0.0 | 26.0 | 64.4 | 4.6 | 5.0 |
| Mongolia | 12.4 | 43.6 | 6.0 | 11.6 | 26.5 |
| Nauru | 0.0 | 54.7 | 26.9 | 0.0 | 18.3 |
| Pakistan | 2.8 | 74.9 | 2.3 | 0.0 | 20.0 |
| Papua New Guinea | 65.4 | 34.0 | 0.4 | 0.1 | 0.0 |
| Philippines | 0.1 | 58.0 | 14.1 | 0.0 | 27.8 |
| Samoa | 59.0 | 13.3 | 27.4 | 0.3 | 0.0 |
| Singapore | 0.0 | 78.8 | 16.6 | 2.4 | 2.2 |
| Thailand | 0.2 | 53.2 | 33.0 | 2.4 | 11.1 |
| Tokelau | 36.2 | 59.6 | 4.2 | 0.0 | 0.0 |
| Vanuatu | 32.8 | .. | .. | .. | 67.2 |
| Viet Nam | 0.9 | 5.9 | 55.5 | 0.0 | 37.7 |

.. Not available

Note: Figures include non-tax revenue data collected by sub-national governments for Cambodia, Kyrgyzstan, Kazakhstan, Mongolia, Pakistan, the Philippines and Thailand. They exclude non-tax revenue collected by sub-national governments as the data are not available for the remaining economies.

1. Grants: "Other transfers received" are not classified as non-tax revenue in Kyrgyzstan but are considered as non-tax revenues under the OECD Interpretative Guide.

StatLink https://stat.link/zonxla

## Table 5.4. Total non-tax revenue in selected economies in millions of US dollars at market exchange rates

| | 2007 | 2010 | 2012 | 2014 | 2015 | 2016 | 2017 | 2018 | 2019 | 2020 |
|---|---|---|---|---|---|---|---|---|---|---|
| Bhutan | 306.2 | 364.0 | 326.3 | 295.5 | 391.2 | 344.2 | 404.4 | 349.0 | 484.4 | 481.7 |
| Cambodia | 0.3 | 0.7 | 0.6 | 0.7 | 0.7 | 1.0 | 1.0 | 1.2 | 1.4 | 1.1 |
| Cook Islands | 12.6 | 34.6 | 24.7 | 50.2 | 42.5 | 53.7 | 50.6 | 47.8 | 52.8 | 76.8 |
| Fiji | .. | 89.8 | 118.6 | 142.9 | 134.7 | 158.0 | 187.6 | 199.0 | 188.3 | 182.3 |
| Kazakhstan | 1 619.2 | 1 451.3 | 3 843.4 | 3 211.3 | 2 460.0 | 1 651.2 | 1 760.1 | 3 108.5 | 2 705.3 | 1 983.1 |
| Kyrgyzstan | 0.3 | 0.4 | 0.5 | 0.7 | 0.7 | 0.5 | 0.7 | 0.5 | 0.7 | 0.6 |
| Lao PDR | .. | 711.5 | 1 035.2 | 1 269.5 | 1 104.3 | 709.8 | 896.1 | 974.7 | 957.3 | 712.5 |
| Maldives | 277.6 | 264.2 | 183.0 | 258.0 | 274.8 | 316.4 | 322.0 | 359.6 | 359.8 | 211.8 |
| Mongolia | 403.6 | 470.4 | 851.1 | 948.6 | 740.4 | 566.0 | 494.6 | 602.5 | 610.3 | 477.2 |
| Nauru | .. | .. | .. | 26.8 | 50.8 | 66.1 | 77.8 | 106.8 | 97.8 | 79.2 |
| Pakistan | .. | .. | 8.4 | 10.5 | 8.0 | 9.5 | 7.5 | 4.2 | 11.3 | 7.5 |
| Papua New Guinea | 381.7 | 671.6 | 657.6 | 718.5 | 703.0 | 658.8 | 753.3 | 890.9 | 691.9 | 629.5 |
| Philippines | .. | .. | .. | 5 259.0 | 6 201.4 | 5 660.9 | 5 574.2 | 6 342.4 | 7 349.7 | 8 360.3 |
| Samoa | 46.0 | 61.8 | 36.8 | 39.8 | 40.4 | 38.2 | 47.1 | 53.5 | 97.2 | 92.9 |
| Singapore | 10 656.9 | 8 539.4 | 10 253.3 | 12 519.6 | 13 526.3 | 14 340.4 | 18 536.4 | 16 463.0 | 26 838.4 | 16 476.6 |
| Thailand | 6 825.1 | 11 147.6 | 11 078.6 | 12 659.8 | 14 140.3 | 14 942.5 | 16 003.4 | 19 019.7 | 20 246.0 | 20 143.9 |
| Tokelau | 9.0 | 11.2 | 16.6 | 16.2 | 22.8 | 24.7 | 22.1 | 25.1 | 22.7 | 22.4 |
| Vanuatu | 7.6 | 56.4 | 40.3 | 47.6 | 114.4 | 76.3 | 125.0 | 184.1 | 225.5 | 238.3 |
| Viet Nam | 5 464.7 | 6 403.8 | 7 664.3 | 9 440.8 | 12 442.3 | 14 411.1 | 18 514.2 | 20 748.4 | 21 607.6 | 22 123.5 |

.. Not available

Note: This table is derived by dividing the total non-tax revenue figures for each country (in millions of national currency) by the exchange rate figures shown in Table 3.20.

StatLink https://stat.link/0tovpu

## Table 5.5. Bhutan: Details of non-tax revenue

Million NU

| | 1997 | 2000 | 2007 | 2010 | 2015 | 2016 | 2017 | 2018 | 2019 | 2020 |
|---|---|---|---|---|---|---|---|---|---|---|
| **Total non-tax revenue** | **3 558** | **6 437** | **13 532** | **16 981** | **24 270** | **22 838** | **26 864** | **22 737** | **34 168** | **34 909** |
| Grants | 1 816 | 3 711 | 5 935 | 10 498 | 14 890 | 12 987 | 14 847 | 10 516 | 16 426 | 14 882 |
| Property income | 1 187 | 2 193 | 5 054 | 5 627 | 8 295 | 8 748 | 10 763 | 10 838 | 12 850 | 11 477 |
| Rents and royalties | 170 | 286 | 573 | 711 | 1 565 | 1 938 | 3 855 | 4 640 | 4 346 | 4 866 |
| Interest and dividends | 1 017 | 1 907 | 4 481 | 4 915 | 6 729 | 6 810 | 6 907 | 6 198 | 8 505 | 6 611 |
| Druk Holding and Investments (DHI) dividends | 0 | 0 | 368 | 1 470 | 3 781 | 4 037 | 4 020 | 3 349 | 4 551 | 3 020 |
| DGPC dividends | 856 | 1 201 | 1 749 | 1 519 | 0 | 0 | 0 | 0 | 0 | 0 |
| Other dividends | 65 | 95 | 363 | 8 | 5 | 5 | 41 | 57 | 55 | 19 |
| Net surplus transfers from the Royal Monetary Authority (RMA) | 50 | 562 | 341 | 187 | 789 | 874 | 1 001 | 1 550 | 3 011 | 2 001 |
| Interest receipt from corporations | .. | .. | .. | 1 731 | 2 155 | 1 895 | 1 846 | 1 242 | 887 | 1 571 |
| Other property income | 0 | 0 | 0 | 0 | 0 | 0 | 0 | 0 | 0 | 0 |
| Sales of goods and services | 552 | 531 | 2 520 | 838 | 993 | 1 026 | 1 148 | 1 186 | 4 823 | 8 444 |
| Fines, penalties and forfeits | 0 | 0 | 0 | 0 | 92 | 77 | 107 | 197 | 69 | 106 |
| Miscellaneous and unidentified revenue | 3 | 2 | 23 | 19 | 0 | 0 | 0 | 0 | 0 | 0 |
| *Total tax and non-tax revenue* | 4 767 | 8 288 | 18 145 | 27 797 | 42 788 | 42 487 | 49 268 | 44 483 | 52 565 | 50 653 |

.. Not available

Note: Data are reported on a fiscal year basis beginning 1st July. For example, the data for 2020 represent the period from July 2020 to June 2021.

The data are on a cash basis.

Grants: 2020 data are sourced from IMF World Economic Outlook April 2022.

Source: Ministry of Finance, Bhutan.

StatLink https://stat.link/oyqfia

## Table 5.6. Cambodia: Details of non-tax revenue

Million KHR

| | 1997 | 2000 | 2007 | 2010 | 2015 | 2016 | 2017 | 2018 | 2019 | 2020 |
|---|---|---|---|---|---|---|---|---|---|---|
| Total non-tax revenue | .. | .. | 1 276 218 | 3 011 113 | 2 941 166 | 4 113 236 | 4 194 068 | 5 038 225 | 5 639 402 | 4 445 400 |
| Grants | .. | .. | 753 802 | 2 318 638 | 1 427 542 | 2 010 468 | 1 706 636 | 2 132 905 | 2 200 916 | 2 036 914 |
| Property income | .. | .. | 84 189 | 178 391 | 153 388 | 194 870 | 222 774 | 363 058 | 424 095 | 566 121 |
| Rents and royalties | .. | .. | 36 313 | 148 220 | 61 654 | 91 227 | 109 733 | 119 046 | 126 135 | 141 450 |
| Interest and dividends | .. | .. | 47 876 | 30 151 | 91 699 | 103 606 | 113 000 | 243 958 | 297 894 | 424 585 |
| Other property income | .. | .. | 0 | 21 | 35 | 37 | 41 | 53 | 66 | 86 |
| Sales of goods and services | .. | .. | 405 711 | 480 520 | 1 239 273 | 1 779 585 | 2 080 861 | 2 326 094 | 2 747 769 | 1 514 256 |
| Fines, penalties and forfeits | .. | .. | 3 954 | 33 480 | 118 553 | 125 687 | 180 720 | 212 066 | 250 971 | 323 612 |
| Miscellaneous and unidentified revenue | .. | .. | 28 562 | 83 | 2 410 | 2 627 | 3 076 | 4 103 | 15 651 | 4 497 |
| Total tax and non-tax revenue | .. | .. | 4 674 253 | 6 452 084 | 14 409 681 | 16 913 325 | 19 386 752 | 23 599 112 | 29 461 178 | 25 327 113 |

.. Not available

Note: Year ending 31st December.

The data are on an accrual basis.

Local government revenue data are not available before 2012.

Source: Ministry of Economy and Finance of Cambodia.

StatLink https://stat.link/rox58l

## Table 5.7. Cook Islands: Details of non-tax revenue

Thousand NZD

| | 1997 | 2000 | 2007 | 2010 | 2015 | 2016 | 2017 | 2018 | 2019 | 2020 |
|---|---|---|---|---|---|---|---|---|---|---|
| **Total non-tax revenue** | .. | .. | **17 586** | **45 942** | **60 999** | **76 336** | **72 214** | **70 821** | **80 832** | **118 298** |
| Grants | .. | .. | 5 034 | 22 411 | 35 902 | 47 172 | 47 449 | 33 060 | 52 827 | 59 038 |
| Green Climate Fund (GCF) | .. | .. | 0 | 0 | 0 | 0 | 0 | 1 823 | 7 704 | 500 |
| OIDGF Aid Fund | .. | .. | 177 | 306 | 0 | 7 730 | 0 | 0 | 0 | 0 |
| NZODA Revenue | .. | .. | 4 097 | 20 123 | 20 889 | 26 081 | 25 021 | 21 876 | 32 496 | 53 162 |
| AusAid Revenue | .. | .. | 0 | 0 | 498 | 84 | 2 250 | 66 | 0 | 0 |
| UNESCO Revenue | .. | .. | 65 | 0 | 84 | 110 | 1 371 | 0 | 0 | 25 |
| UNDP Revenue | .. | .. | 223 | 619 | 1 559 | 206 | 2 302 | 2 183 | 6 887 | 0 |
| EU Revenue | .. | .. | 22 | 179 | 603 | 6 826 | 6 587 | 945 | 0 | 1 138 |
| Global Environment Facility (GEF) | .. | .. | 0 | 0 | 0 | 0 | 0 | 3 140 | 3 614 | 1 139 |
| Other | .. | .. | 451 | 1 183 | 12 269 | 6 135 | 9 918 | 3 027 | 2 126 | 3 074 |
| Property income | .. | .. | 9 768 | 9 327 | 11 307 | 21 366 | 18 680 | 28 321 | 17 550 | 10 830 |
| Rents and royalties | .. | .. | 595 | 3 528 | 7 714 | 18 057 | 12 797 | 20 522 | 13 262 | 9 903 |
| Fishing Licences | .. | .. | 595 | 3 528 | 7 714 | 14 197 | 7 651 | 15 164 | 5 219 | 4 015 |
| Fisheries Catch Revenue | .. | .. | 0 | 0 | 0 | 2 312 | 255 | 0 | 0 | 0 |
| Fisheries - US Treaties | .. | .. | 0 | 0 | 0 | 1 548 | 4 890 | 5 358 | 8 043 | 5 888 |
| Interest and dividends | .. | .. | 9 173 | 5 800 | 3 593 | 3 309 | 5 883 | 7 799 | 4 288 | 926 |
| Dividend Income | .. | .. | 2 350 | 2 672 | 0 | 0 | 0 | 0 | 0 | 0 |
| Interest Income (Crown Accounts) | .. | .. | 3 795 | 3 100 | 1 673 | 2 140 | 2 372 | 2 483 | 2 968 | 926 |
| Interest Inc from SOE Advances | .. | .. | 69 | 28 | 1 102 | 787 | 791 | 760 | 360 | 0 |
| Other dividends | .. | .. | 2 958 | 0 | 818 | 382 | 2 720 | 4 556 | 960 | 0 |
| Other property income | .. | .. | 0 | 0 | 0 | 0 | 0 | 0 | 0 | 0 |
| Sales of goods and services | .. | .. | 2 157 | 2 843 | 3 497 | 2 401 | 3 682 | 3 176 | 2 794 | 10 821 |
| Immigration Fees | .. | .. | 495 | 496 | 715 | 886 | 935 | 1 064 | 965 | 856 |
| Financial Supervisory Comm | .. | .. | 325 | 605 | 917 | 324 | 262 | 279 | 319 | 8 664 |
| Numismatic Revenue | .. | .. | 386 | 457 | 600 | 354 | 511 | 537 | 172 | 662 |
| Drivers Licence Fees | .. | .. | 403 | 718 | 292 | 87 | 214 | 289 | 256 | 119 |
| Censorship Fees | .. | .. | 0 | 12 | 2 | 2 | 3 | 2 | 1 | 1 |
| Upper Air Space Fees | .. | .. | 354 | 442 | 545 | 545 | 545 | 577 | 922 | 186 |
| Other fees | .. | .. | 193 | 112 | 426 | 203 | 1 212 | 428 | 159 | 133 |
| Seabed Exploration Licenses | .. | .. | 0 | 0 | 0 | 0 | 0 | 0 | 0 | 200 |
| Fines, penalties and forfeits | .. | .. | 81 | 72 | 23 | 553 | 248 | 2 302 | 246 | 924 |
| Miscellaneous and unidentified revenue | .. | .. | 545 | 11 289 | 10 271 | 4 844 | 2 155 | 3 962 | 7 415 | 36 686 |
| *Total tax and non-tax revenue* | .. | .. | 95 916 | 137 104 | 178 444 | 202 346 | 214 752 | 234 243 | 222 238 | 203 201 |

.. Not available

Note: Data are reported on a fiscal year basis beginning 1st July. For example, the data for 2020 represent the period from July 2020 to June 2021.
The data are on a cash basis.
Figures exclude non-tax revenues collected by sub-national governments as the data are not available.
Other grants include revenue from Japan, China, India as well as other sources.

Source: Ministry of Finance and Economic Management of the Cook Islands.

StatLink https://stat.link/uzb8ds

## Table 5.8. Fiji: Details of non-tax revenue

Million FJD

| | 1997 | 2000 | 2007 | 2010 | 2015 | 2016 | 2017 | 2018 | 2019 | 2020 |
|---|---|---|---|---|---|---|---|---|---|---|
| **Total non-tax revenue** | .. | .. | .. | **172** | **282** | **331** | **388** | **415** | **407** | **395** |
| Grants | .. | .. | .. | 9 | 18 | 26 | 20 | 57 | 46 | 117 |
| Property income | .. | .. | .. | 54 | 109 | 143 | 174 | 178 | 186 | 114 |
| Rents and royalties | .. | .. | .. | 1 | 40 | 49 | 63 | 81 | 74 | 54 |
| Interest and dividends | .. | .. | .. | 52 | 70 | 94 | 111 | 97 | 112 | 60 |
| Other property income | .. | .. | .. | 0 | 0 | 0 | 0 | 0 | 0 | 0 |
| Sales of goods and services | .. | .. | .. | 99 | 136 | 136 | 178 | 169 | 169 | 159 |
| Fines, penalties and forfeits | .. | .. | .. | 3 | 3 | 3 | 3 | 2 | 2 | 2 |
| Miscellaneous and unidentified revenue | .. | .. | .. | 8 | 16 | 22 | 13 | 9 | 5 | 4 |
| *Total tax and non-tax revenue* | .. | .. | .. | 1 476 | 2 601 | 2 719 | 3 067 | 3 155 | 3 044 | 2 003 |

.. Not available

Note: Year ending 31st December.
The data are on a cash basis.
Figures exclude non-tax revenues collected by sub-national governments as the data are not available.

Source: Ministry of Economy, Fiji.

StatLink https://stat.link/h1akm2

## Table 5.9. Kazakhstan: Details of non-tax revenue

Million KZT

| | 1997 | 2000 | 2007 | 2010 | 2015 | 2016 | 2017 | 2018 | 2019 | 2020 |
|---|---|---|---|---|---|---|---|---|---|---|
| **Total non-tax revenue** | .. | **8 577** | **198 439** | **213 863** | **545 447** | **564 930** | **573 780** | **1 071 522** | **1 035 462** | **818 944** |
| Grants | .. | 0 | 0 | 0 | 0 | 0 | 0 | 0 | 0 | 0 |
| Property income | .. | 52 | 91 107 | 121 760 | 351 753 | 305 424 | 342 509 | 872 985 | 809 180 | 615 501 |
| Rents and royalties | .. | 0 | 55 466 | 103 118 | 303 211 | 278 626 | 309 080 | 837 280 | 727 203 | 461 585 |
| Interest and dividends | .. | 52 | 31 871 | 16 289 | 46 163 | 24 014 | 30 784 | 33 709 | 79 558 | 150 530 |
| Other property income | .. | 0 | 3 770 | 2 352 | 2 379 | 2 785 | 2 645 | 1 996 | 2 419 | 3 386 |
| Sales of goods and services | .. | 8 525 | 42 383 | 59 965 | 122 511 | 183 868 | 129 057 | 123 938 | 138 926 | 132 753 |
| Fines, penalties and forfeits | .. | 0 | 7 083 | 32 138 | 68 087 | 69 673 | 102 234 | 74 572 | 87 333 | 70 661 |
| Miscellaneous and unidentified revenue | .. | 0 | 57 866 | 0 | 3 096 | 5 965 | -21 | 26 | 21 | 30 |
| *Total tax and non-tax revenue* | .. | 526 354 | 3 547 757 | 5 396 242 | 6 898 410 | 7 570 983 | 9 281 536 | 11 555 937 | 12 630 402 | 10 753 250 |

.. Not available

Note: Year ending 31st December.

Data are on a cash basis.

The share of the Republic of Kazakhstan under production sharing contracts of oil companies, the bonuses of oil and non-oil sector companies, the levy for the use of the radio-frequency spectrum, the payment to compensate for historic costs as well as certain other items are classified as non-tax revenues according to the OECD Interpretative Guide, but are considered as tax revenues in Kazakhstan.

Source: Ministry of Finance of the Republic of Kazakhstan.

StatLink https://stat.link/4j0132

## Table 5.10. Kyrgyzstan: Details of non-tax revenue

Million KGS

| | 1997 | 2000 | 2007 | 2010 | 2015 | 2016 | 2017 | 2018 | 2019 | 2020 |
|---|---|---|---|---|---|---|---|---|---|---|
| Total non-tax revenue | 1 112 | 2 215 | 9 436 | 18 228 | 46 058 | 37 574 | 44 905 | 36 058 | 47 264 | 47 145 |
| Grants | 195 | 608 | 1 790 | 7 022 | 9 309 | 9 877 | 13 467 | 9 216 | 13 489 | 11 818 |
| Property income | 61 | 334 | 3 023 | 5 005 | 16 326 | 10 226 | 8 641 | 9 813 | 9 302 | 12 270 |
| Rents and royalties | 43 | 33 | 2 031 | 3 331 | 8 769 | 1 929 | 2 673 | 3 177 | 3 662 | 3 778 |
| Interest and dividends | 10 | 129 | 991 | 1 674 | 7 557 | 8 296 | 5 968 | 6 636 | 5 640 | 8 493 |
| Other property income | 8 | 172 | 0 | 0 | 0 | 0 | 0 | 0 | 0 | 0 |
| Sales of goods and services | 748 | 1 150 | 4 234 | 5 389 | 13 461 | 13 952 | 13 294 | 13 388 | 15 363 | 13 038 |
| Fines, penalties and forfeits | 24 | 32 | 143 | 244 | 849 | 659 | 767 | 1 043 | 1 332 | 1 666 |
| Miscellaneous and unidentified revenue | 83 | 91 | 247 | 568 | 6 113 | 2 861 | 8 737 | 2 597 | 7 778 | 8 353 |
| Total tax and non-tax revenue | 4 904 | 9 854 | 35 523 | 57 385 | 128 292 | 130 503 | 147 090 | 151 540 | 167 329 | 152 051 |

Note: Year ending 31st December.

The data are on a cash basis.

The figures refer to state government revenues which included both central and local government revenues.

Data are classified according to the OECD Interpretative Guide, which differs from the national classification. The totals shown for tax and non-tax revenue are therefore different from the totals presented on the website of the National Statistical Committee.

Grants: "Other transfers received" are not classified as non-tax revenue in Kyrgyzstan but are considered as non-tax revenues under the OECD Interpretative Guide.

Source: National Statistical Committee of Kyrgyzstan.

StatLink https://stat.link/l8xm3s

## Table 5.11. Lao PDR: Details of non-tax revenue

Million LAK

| | 1997 | 2000 | 2007 | 2010 | 2015 | 2016 | 2017 | 2018 | 2019 | 2020 |
|---|---|---|---|---|---|---|---|---|---|---|
| **Total non-tax revenue** | .. | .. | .. | **5 877** | **8 980** | **5 770** | **7 393** | **8 194** | **8 317** | **6 454** |
| Grants | .. | .. | .. | 3 931 | 4 618 | 1 749 | 2 346 | 2 929 | 2 829 | 2 565 |
| Property income | .. | .. | .. | 1 417 | 2 696 | 2 019 | 3 089 | 3 156 | 2 858 | 1 984 |
| Rents and royalties | .. | .. | .. | 701 | 1 545 | 971 | 1 316 | 1 097 | 1 180 | 926 |
| Timber royalties | .. | .. | .. | 48 | 546 | 127 | 335 | 38 | 22 | 44 |
| Hydro-power royalties | .. | .. | .. | 140 | 378 | 369 | 371 | 418 | 538 | 319 |
| Natural resource taxes | .. | .. | .. | 513 | 620 | 474 | 610 | 641 | 620 | 563 |
| Interest and dividends | .. | .. | .. | 716 | 1 152 | 1 048 | 1 773 | 2 058 | 1 678 | 1 058 |
| Other property income | .. | .. | .. | 0 | 0 | 0 | 0 | 0 | 0 | 0 |
| Sales of goods and services | .. | .. | .. | 486 | 1 533 | 1 800 | 1 744 | 1 869 | 1 971 | 1 525 |
| Fines, penalties and forfeits | .. | .. | .. | 37 | 124 | 180 | 83 | 49 | 35 | 36 |
| Miscellaneous and unidentified revenue | .. | .. | .. | 5 | 9 | 23 | 131 | 191 | 624 | 343 |
| *Total tax and non-tax revenue* | .. | .. | .. | 12 978 | 23 699 | 21 163 | 22 925 | 24 758 | 25 502 | 21 831 |

.. Not available

Note: Data are reported on a calendar year.

The data are on a cash basis.

Miscellaneous and unidentified revenue: Social contribution has been included under the heading in this edition.

Source: Ministry of Finance, Lao PDR.

StatLink https://stat.link/ory834

## Table 5.12. Maldives: Details of non-tax revenue

Million MVR

| | 1997 | 2000 | 2007 | 2010 | 2015 | 2016 | 2017 | 2018 | 2019 | 2020 |
|---|---|---|---|---|---|---|---|---|---|---|
| **Total non-tax revenue** | .. | .. | **3 553** | **3 381** | **4 234** | **4 875** | **4 962** | **5 541** | **5 544** | **3 264** |
| Grants | .. | .. | 0 | 0 | 0 | 0 | 0 | 0 | 0 | 0 |
| Property income | .. | .. | 1 102 | 1 244 | 627 | 758 | 1 008 | 1 152 | 1 048 | 848 |
| Rents and royalties | .. | .. | 141 | 93 | 104 | 94 | 102 | 104 | 115 | 41 |
| Interest and dividends | .. | .. | 961 | 1 151 | 523 | 664 | 907 | 1 048 | 933 | 808 |
| Other property income | .. | .. | 0 | 0 | 0 | 0 | 0 | 0 | 0 | 0 |
| Sales of goods and services | .. | .. | 2 306 | 1 737 | 3 260 | 3 718 | 3 610 | 3 904 | 3 987 | 2 101 |
| Fines, penalties and forfeits | .. | .. | 58 | 114 | 269 | 327 | 244 | 278 | 235 | 152 |
| Miscellaneous and unidentified revenue | .. | .. | 87 | 287 | 78 | 72 | 100 | 208 | 274 | 163 |
| *Total tax and non-tax revenue* | .. | .. | 6 408 | 6 343 | 16 467 | 18 141 | 19 682 | 21 359 | 22 056 | 14 252 |

.. Not available

Note: Data are reported on a calendar year.

The data are on a cash basis.

Source: Ministry of Finance, Maldives.

StatLink https://stat.link/gb9r7j

## Table 5.13. Mongolia: Details of non-tax revenue

Billion MNT

| | 1997 | 2000 | 2007 | 2010 | 2015 | 2016 | 2017 | 2018 | 2019 | 2020 |
|---|---|---|---|---|---|---|---|---|---|---|
| **Total non-tax revenue** | .. | .. | **472** | **639** | **1 459** | **1 214** | **1 207** | **1 486** | **1 626** | **1 343** |
| Grants | .. | .. | 22 | 39 | 53 | 77 | 62 | 89 | 88 | 166 |
| Property income | .. | .. | 249 | 320 | 824 | 470 | 482 | 670 | 793 | 585 |
| Rents and royalties | .. | .. | 107 | 265 | 813 | 466 | 446 | 593 | 766 | 564 |
| Interest and dividends | .. | .. | 142 | 55 | 12 | 4 | 36 | 77 | 27 | 21 |
| Other property income | .. | .. | 0 | 0 | 0 | 0 | 0 | 0 | 0 | 0 |
| Sales of goods and services | .. | .. | 25 | 33 | 98 | 118 | 150 | 170 | 158 | 80 |
| Fines, penalties and forfeits | .. | .. | 34 | 36 | 178 | 193 | 75 | 113 | 159 | 155 |
| Miscellaneous and unidentified revenue | .. | .. | 142 | 211 | 305 | 355 | 438 | 445 | 427 | 356 |
| *Total tax and non-tax revenue* | .. | .. | 1 878 | 3 109 | 5 879 | 5 781 | 7 211 | 9 275 | 10 659 | 9 293 |

.. Not available

Note: Year ending December 31st.

Data are on a cash basis.

Source: Ministry of Finance, Mongolia.

StatLink https://stat.link/n4ivx7

## Table 5.14. Nauru: Details of non-tax revenue

Thousand AUD

| | 1997 | 2000 | 2007 | 2010 | 2015 | 2016 | 2017 | 2018 | 2019 | 2020 |
|---|---|---|---|---|---|---|---|---|---|---|
| **Total non-tax revenue** | .. | .. | .. | .. | **67 971** | **87 636** | **102 887** | **148 266** | **141 381** | **115 104** |
| Grants | .. | .. | .. | .. | 20 | 32 | 31 | 33 | 21 | 32 |
| Property income | .. | .. | .. | .. | 38 618 | 48 042 | 48 170 | 73 684 | 76 021 | 63 006 |
| Rents and royalties | .. | .. | .. | .. | 38 160 | 46 910 | 47 111 | 72 492 | 73 771 | 60 284 |
| Fishing days, licences and support vessels | .. | .. | .. | .. | 37 477 | 46 897 | 46 363 | 71 374 | 73 279 | 59 798 |
| DCA Air navigation and rental fees | .. | .. | .. | .. | 683 | 13 | 748 | 1 118 | 492 | 486 |
| Interest and dividends | .. | .. | .. | .. | 458 | 1 132 | 1 059 | 1 192 | 2 250 | 2 722 |
| Other property income | .. | .. | .. | .. | 0 | 0 | 0 | 0 | 0 | 0 |
| Sales of goods and services | .. | .. | .. | .. | 28 038 | 33 587 | 49 800 | 57 660 | 46 396 | 31 001 |
| Visa Fees RPB | .. | .. | .. | .. | 24 978 | 27 844 | 28 357 | 20 282 | 21 113 | 5 772 |
| DJBC Operations | .. | .. | .. | .. | 729 | 3 740 | 2 657 | 5 450 | 3 370 | 4 212 |
| Other sales of goods and services | .. | .. | .. | .. | 2 331 | 2 003 | 18 785 | 31 929 | 21 913 | 21 017 |
| Fines, penalties and forfeits | .. | .. | .. | .. | 0 | 0 | 0 | 0 | 0 | 0 |
| Miscellaneous and unidentified revenue | .. | .. | .. | .. | 1 295 | 5 975 | 4 887 | 16 889 | 18 943 | 21 066 |
| *Total tax and non-tax revenue* | .. | .. | .. | .. | 92 076 | 109 095 | 144 975 | 204 831 | 221 403 | 196 119 |

.. Not available

Note: Data are on a fiscal year basis beginning 1st July. For example, the data for 2020 represent the period from July 2020 to June 2021.

Source: Nauru Revenue Office; Grant data are taken from the IMF World Economic Outlook April 2022.

StatLink https://stat.link/gd7vel

## Table 5.15. Pakistan: Details of non-tax revenue

Million PKR

| | 1997 | 2000 | 2007 | 2010 | 2015 | 2016 | 2017 | 2018 | 2019 | 2020 |
|---|---|---|---|---|---|---|---|---|---|---|
| Total non-tax revenue | .. | .. | .. | .. | 808 931 | 996 249 | 784 011 | 460 542 | 1 554 142 | 1 194 032 |
| Grants | .. | .. | .. | .. | 22 370 | 28 774 | 25 278 | 36 954 | 33 023 | 33 483 |
| Property income | .. | .. | .. | .. | 477 015 | 494 498 | 465 532 | 236 268 | 1 305 300 | 893 944 |
| Rents and royalties | .. | .. | .. | .. | 68 490 | 63 724 | 71 230 | 109 611 | 97 528 | 84 250 |
| Interest and dividends | .. | .. | .. | .. | 408 525 | 430 774 | 394 302 | 126 657 | 1 207 772 | 809 694 |
| Other property income | .. | .. | .. | .. | 0 | 0 | 0 | 0 | 0 | 0 |
| Sales of goods and services | .. | .. | .. | .. | 127 830 | 87 828 | 28 710 | 38 645 | 32 165 | 27 900 |
| Fines, penalties and forfeits | .. | .. | .. | .. | 0 | 0 | 0 | 0 | 0 | 0 |
| Miscellaneous and unidentified revenue | .. | .. | .. | .. | 181 716 | 385 149 | 264 491 | 148 675 | 183 654 | 238 705 |
| Total tax and non-tax revenue | .. | .. | .. | .. | 4 469 349 | 4 965 497 | 5 253 293 | 4 937 678 | 6 305 191 | 6 936 853 |

.. Not available

Note: Data are on a fiscal year basis beginning 1st July. For example, the data for 2020 represent the period from July 2020 to June 2021.

The data are on a cash basis.

Local non-tax revenue data are only available in 2020 and they cannot be distinguished from federal non-tax revenues in previous years.

Source: Pakistan Bureau of Statistics.

StatLink https://stat.link/wpy36k

## Table 5.16. Papua New Guinea: Details of non-tax revenue

Million PGK

| | 1997 | 2000 | 2007 | 2010 | 2015 | 2016 | 2017 | 2018 | 2019 | 2020 |
|---|---|---|---|---|---|---|---|---|---|---|
| **Total non-tax revenue** | **..** | **..** | **1 132** | **1 826** | **1 946** | **2 064** | **2 402** | **2 934** | **2 344** | **2 178** |
| Grants | .. | .. | 721 | 1 391 | 820 | 1 430 | 1 440 | 1 836 | 1 776 | 1 425 |
| Property income | .. | .. | 291 | 341 | 911 | 529 | 842 | 1 064 | 529 | 741 |
| Rents and royalties | .. | .. | 0 | 0 | 0 | 0 | 0 | 30 | 28 | 23 |
| Interest and dividends | .. | .. | 291 | 341 | 911 | 529 | 842 | 1 034 | 501 | 719 |
| Dividends | .. | .. | 65 | 40 | 455 | 228 | 279 | 380 | 120 | 150 |
| Mining and Petroleum Dividends | .. | .. | 226 | 299 | 456 | 301 | 562 | 654 | 381 | 569 |
| SWF Receipts | .. | .. | 0 | 0 | 0 | 0 | 0 | 0 | 0 | 0 |
| Interests and fees from lending | .. | .. | 1 | 1 | 0 | 0 | 0 | 0 | 0 | 0 |
| Other property income | .. | .. | 0 | 0 | 0 | 0 | 0 | 0 | 0 | 0 |
| Sales of goods and services | .. | .. | 0 | 0 | 0 | 0 | 0 | 32 | 37 | 9 |
| Fines, penalties and forfeits | .. | .. | 0 | 0 | 0 | 0 | 0 | 3 | 2 | 3 |
| Miscellaneous and unidentified revenue | .. | .. | 120 | 95 | 215 | 105 | 121 | 0 | 0 | 0 |
| *Total tax and non-tax revenue* | .. | .. | 7 007 | 8 399 | 11 088 | 10 670 | 11 388 | 12 917 | 12 862 | 11 668 |

.. Not available

Note: Year ending 31st December.

The data are on a cash basis.

Figures exclude non-tax revenues collected by sub-national governments as the data are not available.

Source: Department of Finance; PNG Custom Service; Internal Revenue Comission.

StatLink https://stat.link/i16zxe

## Table 5.17. Philippines: Details of non-tax revenue

Million PHP

| | 1997 | 2000 | 2007 | 2010 | 2015 | 2016 | 2017 | 2018 | 2019 | 2020 |
|---|---|---|---|---|---|---|---|---|---|---|
| **Total non-tax revenue** | **..** | **..** | **..** | **..** | **282 183** | **268 852** | **280 960** | **334 001** | **380 683** | **414 872** |
| Grants | .. | .. | .. | .. | 164 | 78 | 39 | 51 | 259 | 241 |
| Property income | .. | .. | .. | .. | 123 845 | 117 166 | 118 089 | 135 414 | 170 546 | 240 737 |
| Rents and royalties | .. | .. | .. | .. | 1 307 | 1 086 | 1 126 | 1 187 | 1 405 | 1 799 |
| Interest and dividends | .. | .. | .. | .. | 0 | 0 | 0 | 0 | 0 | 0 |
| Other property income | .. | .. | .. | .. | 122 537 | 116 080 | 116 963 | 134 227 | 169 140 | 238 938 |
| Sales of goods and services | .. | .. | .. | .. | 66 893 | 72 456 | 76 590 | 91 329 | 96 055 | 58 397 |
| Fines, penalties and forfeits | .. | .. | .. | .. | 0 | 0 | 0 | 0 | 0 | 0 |
| Miscellaneous and unidentified revenue | .. | .. | .. | .. | 91 281 | 79 152 | 86 242 | 107 206 | 113 823 | 115 497 |
| *Total tax and non-tax revenue* | .. | .. | .. | .. | 2 544 718 | 2 725 013 | 3 059 644 | 3 510 983 | 3 905 784 | 3 618 696 |

.. Not available

Note: Year ending 31st December.

The data are on a cash basis.

Source: Department of Finance of the Philippines.

StatLink https://stat.link/jwfuak

## Table 5.18. Samoa: Details of non-tax revenue

Million WST

| | 1997 | 2000 | 2007 | 2010 | 2015 | 2016 | 2017 | 2018 | 2019 | 2020 |
|---|---|---|---|---|---|---|---|---|---|---|
| **Total non-tax revenue** | .. | .. | **125** | **157** | **98** | **100** | **120** | **135** | **255** | **251** |
| Grants | .. | .. | 77 | 105 | 45 | 41 | 61 | 46 | 179 | 148 |
| Property income | .. | .. | 24 | 8 | 7 | 6 | 7 | 22 | 12 | 33 |
| Rents and royalties | .. | .. | 24 | 1 | 1 | 1 | 2 | 3 | 2 | 1 |
| Interest and dividends | .. | .. | 0 | 7 | 6 | 6 | 6 | 18 | 10 | 33 |
| Other property income | .. | .. | 0 | 0 | 0 | 0 | 0 | 0 | 0 | 0 |
| Sales of goods and services | .. | .. | 23 | 31 | 37 | 41 | 40 | 67 | 63 | 69 |
| Administrative fees | .. | .. | .. | 28 | 26 | 28 | 24 | 38 | 30 | 28 |
| Incidental sales by nonmarket establishments | .. | .. | .. | 2 | 11 | 13 | 17 | 30 | 32 | 41 |
| Fines, penalties and forfeits | .. | .. | 0 | 1 | 8 | 11 | 11 | 0 | 1 | 1 |
| Miscellaneous and unidentified revenue | .. | .. | 0 | 11 | 0 | 0 | 0 | 0 | 0 | 0 |
| *Total tax and non-tax revenue* | .. | .. | 455 | 498 | 593 | 614 | 643 | 706 | 818 | 792 |

.. Not available

Note: Data are reported on a fiscal year basis beginning 1st July. For example, the data for 2020 represent the period from July 2020 to June 2021.

The data are on a cash basis.

Figures exclude non-tax revenues collected by sub-national governments as the data are not available.

The data from 2009 were provided on the basis of the IMF's GFSM 2014 classification. Prior to this year, data were provided on a different basis. The differences between the two sets of data are indicated below for the relevant non-tax revenue categories.

Heading Grants: Data from 2009 includes only cash grants whereas data prior to that year also includes aid-funded projects.

Heading Sales of Goods and services: Data from 2009 exclude fisheries' licences currently included in tax revenue under heading "5126 taxes on specific services" (more information can be found in Table 4.12). Fisheries' licences revenues are usually classified as non-tax revenues according to the the OECD classification set out in Annex B of the Interpretative Guide.

Source: Bureau of Statistics of Samoa.

StatLink https://stat.link/2yjwaf

## Table 5.19. Singapore: Details of non-tax revenue

Million SGD

| | 1997 | 2000 | 2007 | 2010 | 2015 | 2016 | 2017 | 2018 | 2019 | 2020 |
|---|---|---|---|---|---|---|---|---|---|---|
| **Total non-tax revenue** | .. | **17 088** | **16 061** | **11 644** | **18 596** | **19 812** | **25 597** | **22 206** | **36 612** | **22 733** |
| Grants | .. | 0 | 0 | 0 | 0 | 0 | 0 | 0 | 0 | 0 |
| Property income | .. | 11 154 | 13 040 | 8 348 | 10 821 | 10 865 | 17 428 | 16 106 | 31 391 | 17 915 |
| Rents and royalties | .. | .. | .. | .. | 1 400 | 1 319 | 1 284 | 1 436 | 1 408 | 1 150 |
| Interest and dividends | .. | .. | .. | .. | 9 420 | 9 547 | 16 144 | 14 670 | 29 983 | 16 765 |
| Other property income | .. | .. | .. | .. | .. | .. | .. | .. | .. | .. |
| Sales of goods and services | .. | 4 921 | 2 738 | 2 844 | 6 943 | 8 152 | 7 425 | 5 284 | 4 530 | 3 785 |
| Fines, penalties and forfeits | .. | 187 | 168 | 226 | 331 | 289 | 367 | 386 | 336 | 544 |
| Miscellaneous and unidentified revenue | .. | 826 | 115 | 226 | 502 | 506 | 378 | 430 | 354 | 489 |
| *Total tax and non-tax revenue* | .. | 42 715 | 52 691 | 53 492 | 74 243 | 78 511 | 91 960 | 88 409 | 104 257 | 84 142 |

.. Not available

Note: Data are on a fiscal year basis ending 31st March. For example, the data for 2020 represent 1 April 2020 to 31 March 2021.

The data are on a cash basis.

Scope of data provided is limited to the Budgetary Central Government.

Source: Ministry of Finance of Singapore.

StatLink https://stat.link/jmbdyo

## Table 5.20. Thailand: Details of non-tax revenue

Million THB

| | 1997 | 2000 | 2007 | 2010 | 2015 | 2016 | 2017 | 2018 | 2019 | 2020 |
|---|---|---|---|---|---|---|---|---|---|---|
| **Total non-tax revenue** | .. | .. | **235 534** | **353 402** | **484 461** | **527 248** | **542 953** | **614 782** | **628 652** | **630 292** |
| Grants | .. | .. | 1 687 | 2 081 | 1 450 | 2 984 | 2 415 | 2 401 | 1 584 | 1 449 |
| Property income | .. | .. | 155 317 | 191 289 | 306 528 | 281 647 | 300 896 | 311 258 | 331 914 | 335 508 |
| Rents and royalties | .. | .. | 41 537 | 46 429 | 88 895 | 80 580 | 75 554 | 78 839 | 83 980 | 73 199 |
| Interest and dividends | .. | .. | 113 780 | 144 442 | 217 633 | 201 067 | 225 343 | 232 420 | 247 934 | 262 310 |
| Other property income | .. | .. | 0 | 418 | 0 | 0 | 0 | 0 | 0 | 0 |
| Sales of goods and services | .. | .. | 65 093 | 103 797 | 127 522 | 185 322 | 171 104 | 220 257 | 202 721 | 208 127 |
| Fines, penalties and forfeits | .. | .. | 7 640 | 9 197 | 13 287 | 23 063 | 14 095 | 17 733 | 19 330 | 15 416 |
| Miscellaneous and unidentified revenue | .. | .. | 5 797 | 47 037 | 35 672 | 34 231 | 54 443 | 63 133 | 73 102 | 69 791 |
| *Total tax and non-tax revenue* | .. | .. | 1 788 667 | 2 223 854 | 3 052 629 | 3 122 944 | 3 216 367 | 3 471 680 | 3 526 434 | 3 244 445 |

.. Not available

Note: Data are on a fiscal year basis ending 30th September. For example, the data for 2020 represents 1 October 2019 to 30 September 2020.

The data are on a cash basis.

Source: Ministry of Finance in Thailand.

StatLink https://stat.link/ovrq39

## Table 5.21. Tokelau: Details of non-tax revenue

Thousand NZD

| | 1997 | 2000 | 2007 | 2010 | 2015 | 2016 | 2017 | 2018 | 2019 | 2020 |
|---|---|---|---|---|---|---|---|---|---|---|
| **Total non-tax revenue** | .. | .. | **12 537** | **14 836** | **32 773** | **35 088** | **31 507** | **37 212** | **34 780** | **34 562** |
| Grants | .. | .. | 10 508 | 13 115 | 12 000 | 12 000 | 11 010 | 13 500 | 15 538 | 12 500 |
| New Zealand Budgetary Grants | .. | .. | 10 508 | 13 115 | 12 000 | 12 000 | 11 010 | 13 500 | 15 538 | 12 500 |
| External donor funding | .. | .. | 0 | 0 | 0 | 0 | 0 | 0 | 0 | 0 |
| Property income | .. | .. | 1 478 | 1 051 | 20 001 | 22 340 | 19 726 | 22 335 | 17 810 | 20 614 |
| Rents and royalties | .. | .. | 1 257 | 955 | 19 901 | 21 866 | 18 909 | 21 684 | 17 259 | 20 573 |
| Tokelau EEZ Revenues | .. | .. | 1 257 | 955 | 19 901 | 21 866 | 18 909 | 21 684 | 17 259 | 20 573 |
| Interest and dividends | .. | .. | 221 | 96 | 100 | 474 | 817 | 651 | 551 | 41 |
| Other property income | .. | .. | 0 | 0 | 0 | 0 | 0 | 0 | 0 | 0 |
| Sales of goods and services | .. | .. | 551 | 670 | 772 | 748 | 771 | 1 377 | 1 432 | 1 448 |
| Handicrafts & Tourism (ENDRE) | .. | .. | 0 | 0 | 154 | 4 | 7 | 7 | 10 | 6 |
| Commemorative coins | .. | .. | 0 | 0 | 0 | 0 | 0 | 115 | 32 | 292 |
| Stamp sales | .. | .. | 0 | 0 | 0 | 0 | 0 | 0 | 5 | 2 |
| Transport - Boatfares | .. | .. | 159 | 117 | 123 | 174 | 243 | 295 | 215 | 29 |
| Transport - Freights Payments | .. | .. | 291 | 409 | 386 | 430 | 398 | 618 | 649 | 584 |
| Transport - Sale of Assets | .. | .. | 0 | 1 | 6 | 10 | 0 | 4 | 0 | 19 |
| Charter fees | .. | .. | 25 | 10 | 0 | 0 | 0 | 171 | 323 | 381 |
| Postage | .. | .. | 2 | 3 | 1 | 0 | 0 | 0 | 0 | 0 |
| Registry Certificates: Birth & Death | .. | .. | 1 | 1 | 2 | 4 | 5 | 10 | 4 | 2 |
| Service Fees | .. | .. | 19 | 45 | 20 | 37 | 31 | 73 | 82 | 68 |
| Miscellaneous Revenues | .. | .. | 1 | 1 | 0 | 0 | 0 | 3 | 51 | 5 |
| Revenue - Debt Recovery (MISC) | .. | .. | 0 | 0 | 0 | 2 | 0 | 0 | 0 | 0 |
| Gains - Sale of Assets (Vehicles) | .. | .. | 0 | 0 | 66 | 19 | 0 | 0 | 0 | 0 |
| House Rental Subsidies | .. | .. | 22 | 46 | 1 | 55 | 74 | 62 | 51 | 56 |
| Tokelau Savings Bank Passbook Fees | .. | .. | 0 | 0 | 2 | 1 | 0 | 1 | 1 | 1 |
| Tokelau Higano: accommodation | .. | .. | 31 | 37 | 11 | 12 | 13 | 18 | 9 | 3 |
| Fines, penalties and forfeits | .. | .. | 0 | 0 | 0 | 0 | 0 | 0 | 0 | 0 |
| Miscellaneous and unidentified revenue | .. | .. | 0 | 0 | 0 | 0 | 0 | 0 | 0 | 0 |
| *Total tax and non-tax revenue* | .. | .. | 13 735 | 16 530 | 34 924 | 37 264 | 34 025 | 40 055 | 37 820 | 37 841 |

.. Not available

Note: Data are reported on a fiscal year basis beginning 1st July. For example, the data for 2020 represent the period from July 2020 to June 2021. The data are on a cash basis.

Source: Tokelau National Statistics Office.

StatLink https://stat.link/ruqemd

## Table 5.22. Vanuatu: Details of non-tax revenue

Million VUV

| | 1997 | 2000 | 2007 | 2010 | 2015 | 2016 | 2017 | 2018 | 2019 | 2020 |
|---|---|---|---|---|---|---|---|---|---|---|
| **Total non-tax revenue** | .. | **388** | **774** | **5 619** | **12 244** | **8 340** | **13 470** | **19 984** | **26 064** | **24 810** |
| Grants | .. | 373 | 745 | 4 431 | 8 943 | 4 551 | 7 032 | 7 807 | 11 113 | 8 143 |
| Property income | .. | .. | .. | .. | .. | .. | .. | .. | .. | .. |
| Rents and royalties | .. | .. | .. | .. | .. | .. | .. | .. | .. | .. |
| Interest and dividends | .. | .. | .. | .. | .. | .. | .. | .. | .. | .. |
| Other property income | .. | .. | .. | .. | .. | .. | .. | .. | .. | .. |
| Sales of goods and services | .. | .. | .. | .. | .. | .. | .. | .. | .. | .. |
| Fines, penalties and forfeits | .. | .. | .. | .. | .. | .. | .. | .. | .. | .. |
| Miscellaneous and unidentified revenue | .. | 15 | 29 | 1 187 | 3 302 | 3 789 | 6 438 | 12 177 | 14 950 | 16 667 |
| *Total tax and non-tax revenue* | .. | 6 486 | 11 041 | 16 708 | 25 721 | 21 664 | 29 719 | 37 960 | 44 318 | 39 542 |

.. Not available

Note: Year ending December 31st.

Source: Department of Finance and Treasury of Vanuatu.

StatLink https://stat.link/b7l2yx

# Table 5.23. Viet Nam: Details of non-tax revenue

Billion VND

| | 1997 | 2000 | 2007 | 2010 | 2015 | 2016 | 2017 | 2018 | 2019 | 2020 |
|---|---|---|---|---|---|---|---|---|---|---|
| **Total non-tax revenue** | .. | .. | **87 893** | **122 514** | **272 776** | **322 312** | **420 566** | **477 639** | **501 884** | **513 904** |
| Grants | .. | .. | 6 012 | 11 868 | 11 844 | 8 519 | 7 910 | 7 780 | 5 133 | 4 825 |
| Property income | .. | .. | 21 461 | 26 316 | 29 110 | 27 080 | 32 822 | 38 195 | 36 768 | 30 148 |
| Rents and royalties | .. | .. | 21 461 | 26 316 | 29 110 | 27 080 | 32 822 | 38 195 | 36 768 | 30 148 |
| Interest and dividends | .. | .. | 0 | 0 | 0 | 0 | 0 | 0 | 0 | 0 |
| Other property income | .. | .. | 0 | 0 | 0 | 0 | 0 | 0 | 0 | 0 |
| Sales of goods and services | .. | .. | 43 039 | 66 702 | 113 628 | 143 685 | 216 679 | 245 849 | 266 196 | 285 339 |
| Fees and charges | .. | .. | 7 366 | 11 347 | 27 200 | 19 177 | 36 062 | 37 530 | 41 011 | 35 099 |
| Land rents | .. | .. | 4 668 | 5 987 | 17 434 | 25 755 | 27 432 | 31 064 | 33 829 | 39 370 |
| Revenue from land user right assignment | .. | .. | 31 005 | 49 368 | 68 994 | 98 753 | 125 287 | 147 815 | 157 448 | 174 161 |
| Lottery revenue | .. | .. | 0 | 0 | 0 | 0 | 27 898 | 29 440 | 33 908 | 36 709 |
| Fines, penalties and forfeits | .. | .. | 0 | 0 | 0 | 0 | 0 | 0 | 0 | 0 |
| Miscellaneous and unidentified revenue | .. | .. | 17 381 | 17 628 | 118 194 | 143 028 | 163 155 | 185 815 | 193 787 | 193 592 |
| *Total tax and non-tax revenue* | .. | .. | 336 274 | 588 430 | 998 217 | 1 101 377 | 1 288 665 | 1 431 660 | 1 553 611 | 1 507 845 |

.. Not available

Note: Year ending 31st December.

The data are on a cash basis.

Source: General Statistics Office Viet Nam.

StatLink https://stat.link/uhxypv

# Annex A. The OECD Classification of Taxes and Interpretative Guide

## Table of contents

## A.1 The OECD Classification of Taxes

1. **1000. Taxes on income, profits and capital gains**
    - 1100. Taxes on income, profits and capital gains of individuals
        - 1110. On income and profits
        - 1120. On capital gains
    - 1200. Corporate taxes on income, profits and capital gains
        - 1210. On income and profits
        - 1220. On capital gains
    - 1300. Unallocable as between 1100 and 1200
2. **2000. Social security contributions**
    - 2100. Employees
        - 2110. On a payroll basis
        - 2120. On an income tax basis
    - 2200. Employers
        - 2210. On a payroll basis
        - 2220. On an income tax basis
    - 2300. Self-employed or non-employed
        - 2310. On a payroll basis
        - 2320. On an income tax basis
    - 2400 Unallocable as between 2100, 2200 and 2300
        - 2410. On a payroll basis
        - 2420. On an income tax basis
3. **3000. Taxes on payroll and workforce**
4. **4000. Taxes on property**
    - 4100. Recurrent taxes on immovable property
        - 4110. Households
        - 4120. Other
    - 4200 Recurrent taxes on net wealth
        - 4210. Individual
        - 4220. Corporate
    - 4300. Estate, inheritance and gift taxes
        - 4310. Estate and inheritance taxes
        - 4320. Gift taxes
    - 4400. Taxes on financial and capital transactions

4500. Other non-recurrent taxes on property

4510. On net wealth

4520. Other non-recurrent taxes

4600. Other recurrent taxes on property

5. **5000. Taxes on goods and services**

5100. Taxes on production, sale, transfer, leasing and delivery of goods and rendering of services

5110. General taxes

5111. Value added taxes

5112. Sales taxes

5113. Turnover and other general taxes on goods and services

5120. Taxes on specific goods and services

5121. Excises

5122. Profits of fiscal monopolies

5123. Customs and import duties

5124. Taxes on exports

5125. Taxes on investment goods

5126 . Taxes on specific services

5127. Other taxes on international trade and transactions

5128. Other taxes on specific goods and services

5130. Unallocable as between 5110 and 5120

5200. Taxes on use of goods, or on permission to use goods or perform activities

5210. Recurrent taxes

5211. Paid by households in respect of motor vehicles

5212. Paid by others in respect of motor vehicles

5213. Other recurrent taxes

5220. Non-recurrent taxes

5300. Unallocable as between 5100 and 5200

6. **6000. Other taxes**

6100. Paid solely by business

6200. Paid by other than business or unidentifiable

## A.2 Coverage

### *General criteria*

1. In the OECD classification, the term "taxes" is confined to compulsory unrequited payments to the general government or to a supranational authority. Taxes are unrequited in the sense that benefits provided by government to taxpayers are not normally in proportion to their payments.

2. The term "tax" does not include fines, penalties and compulsory loans paid to government. Borderline cases between tax and non-tax revenues in relation to certain fees and charges are discussed in §12–15.

3. General government consists of the central administration, agencies whose operations are under its effective control, state and local governments and their administrations, certain social security schemes and autonomous governmental entities, excluding public enterprises. This definition of government follows that of the 2008 *System of National Accounts* (SNA).[1] In that publication, the general government sector and its sub-sectors are defined in Chapter 4, paragraphs 4.117 to 4.165.

4. Extra-budgetary units are part of the general government system. These are general government entities with individual budgets that are not fully covered by the main or general budget. These entities operate under the authority or control of a central, state, or local government. Extra-budgetary entities may have their own revenue sources, which may be supplemented by grants (transfers) from the general budget or from other sources. Even though their budgets may be subject to approval by the legislature, similar to that of budgetary accounts, they have discretion over the volume and composition of their spending. Such entities may be established to carry out specific government functions, such as road construction, or the nonmarket production of health or education services. Budgetary arrangements vary widely across countries, and various terms are used to describe these entities, but they are often referred to as "extra-budgetary funds" or "decentralised agencies."

5. Compulsory, unrequited payments collected by national governments and paid to supranational authorities are also included as taxes under the definition in paragraph 1. Taxes that are collected by national governments and paid to a supranational authority are included as tax revenues at the level of the supranational authority in the SNA2008 (paragraphs 22.60-61, 22.88 and 22.99 refer) and the ESA2010 (paragraph 20.165 refers). In Revenue Statistics, these taxes include customs duties, contributions to the EU Single Resolution Fund, and any other taxes collected by EU member states on behalf of the European Union. They are included in the tax revenue amounts in the country tables (Chapter 5) of the country in which they are collected and are attributed to the supranational level of government (see §102).

6. In countries where the church forms part of general government, church taxes are included, provided they meet the criteria set out in §1 above. As the data refer to receipts of general government and to supranational authorities, levies paid to non-government bodies, welfare agencies or social insurance schemes outside general government, trade unions or trade associations, even where such levies are compulsory, are excluded. Compulsory payments to general government earmarked for such bodies are, however, included, provided that the government is not simply acting in an agency capacity.[2] Profits from fiscal monopolies are distinguished from those of other public enterprises and are treated as taxes because they reflect the exercise of the taxing power of the state by the use of monopoly powers (see §66–68), as are profits received by the government from the purchase and sale of foreign exchange at different rates (see §76).

7. Taxes paid by governments (e.g., social security contributions and payroll taxes paid by governments in their capacity as an employer, consumption taxes on their purchases or taxes on their property) are not excluded from the data provided. However, where it is possible to identify the amounts of revenue involved,[3] they are shown in Table 5.40 of this Report.

8. The relationship between this classification and that of the System of National Accounts (SNA) is set out in Sections A.9 and A.11 below. Because of the differences between the two classifications, the data shown in national accounts are sometimes calculated or classified differently from the practice set out in this guide. These and other differences are mentioned where appropriate (e.g., in §31 below) but it is not possible to refer to all of them. There may also be some differences between this classification and that employed domestically by certain national administrations (e.g., see §13 below), so that OECD and national statistics data may not always be consistent: any such differences, however, are likely to be very slight in terms of amounts of revenues involved.

### Social security contributions

9. Compulsory social security contributions, as defined in §40, and paid to general government, are treated here as tax revenues. They may, however, differ from other taxes in that the receipt of social security benefits depends, in most countries, upon appropriate contributions having been made, although the size of the benefits is not necessarily related to the amount of the contributions. Better comparability between countries is obtained by treating social security contributions as taxes, but they are listed under a separate heading so that they can be distinguished in any analysis.

10. The strict dividing line between tax revenues (compulsory unrequited payments to general government or a supranational authority) and non-tax compulsory payments (NTCPs) (payments that are either requited or made to other institutions) is clearly defined. However, within the range of different compulsory payments to governments existing across countries, it is not always straightforward in practice to decide whether specific payments are either taxes or NTCPs. For example, compulsory pension savings that are controlled by general government and that accumulate on an individual account earning a market return or a rate that compensates for inflation would at first sight be categorised as NTCPs as opposed to taxes. However, even these payments might still be 'unrequited' and therefore classify as taxes instead of NTCPs (for example if these pension savings are not paid out when the taxpayer dies before reaching the pension age and the funds are then used to provide a minimum pension to all taxpayers that are insured). These issues result in the social security revenue figures reported for most countries being based on the premise that all types of compulsory payments to general government are judged to some extent to have a re-distributional element. It should be noted that this conclusion is based on a typically broad interpretation of the term 'unrequited' in the tax definition.

11. Social security contributions which are either voluntary or not payable to general government (see §1) are not treated as taxes, though in some countries, as indicated in the country footnotes, there are difficulties in completely eliminating voluntary contributions and certain compulsory payments to the private sector from the revenue figures. Imputed social security contributions are also not treated as taxes.

### Fees, user charges and licence fees

12. Apart from vehicle licence fees, which are universally regarded as taxes, it is not easy to distinguish between those fees and user charges which are to be treated as taxes and those which are not, since, whilst a fee or charge is levied in connection with a specific service or activity, the strength of the link between the fee and the service provided may vary considerably, as may the relation between the amount of the fee and the cost of providing the service. Where the recipient of a service pays a fee clearly related to the cost of providing the service, the levy may be regarded as requited and under the definition of §1 would not be considered as a tax. In the following cases, however, a levy could be considered as 'unrequited':

*a)* where the charge greatly exceeds the cost of providing the service;

*b)* where the payer of the levy is not the receiver of the benefit (e.g., a fee collected from slaughterhouses to finance a service which is provided to farmers);

*c)* where government is not providing a specific service in return for the levy which it receives even though a licence may be issued to the payer (e.g., where the government grants a hunting, fishing or shooting licence which is not accompanied by the right to use a specific area of government land);

*d)* where benefits are received only by those paying the levy but the benefits received by each individual are not necessarily in proportion to his payments (e.g., a milk marketing levy paid by dairy farmers and used to promote the consumption of milk).

13. In marginal cases, however, the application of the criteria set out in §1 can be particularly difficult. The solution adopted — given the desirability of international uniformity and the relatively small amounts of revenue usually involved — is to follow the predominant practice among tax administrations rather than to allow each country to adopt its own view as to whether such levies are regarded as taxes or as non-tax revenue.[4]

14. A list of the main fees and charges in question and their normal[5] treatment in this publication is as follows:

| | |
|---|---|
| Non-tax revenues: | court fees; driving licence fees; harbour fees; passport fees; radio and television licence fees where public authorities provide the service |
| Taxes within heading 5200 | permission to perform such activities as distributing films; hunting, fishing and shooting; providing entertainment or gambling facilities; selling alcohol or tobacco; permission to own dogs or to use or own motor vehicles or guns; severance taxes |

15. In practice, it may not always be possible to isolate tax receipts from non-tax revenue receipts when they are recorded together. If it is estimated that the bulk of the receipts derive from non-tax revenues, the whole amount involved is treated as a non-tax revenue; otherwise, such government receipts are included and classified according to the rules provided in §33 below.

### Royalties

16. The ownership of subsoil assets in the form of deposits of minerals or fossil fuels (coal, oil, or natural gas) depends upon the way in which property rights are defined by law and also on international agreements in the case of deposits below international waters. In some cases, either the ground below which the mineral deposits are located, the deposits themselves or both may belong to a local or central government unit.

17. In such cases, these general government units may grant leases to other institutional units that permit them to extract these deposits over a specified period of time in return for a payment or series of payments. These payments are often described as 'royalties' but they are essentially rent that accrues to owners of natural resources in return for putting these assets at the disposal of other units for specified periods of time. The rent may take the form of periodic payments of fixed amounts, irrespective of the rate of extraction, or, more commonly, they may be a function of the quantity, volume, or value of the asset extracted. Enterprises engaged in exploration on government land may make payments to general government units in exchange for the right to undertake test drilling or otherwise investigate the existence and location of subsoil assets. Such payments are also recorded as rents even though no extraction may take place. These payments are therefore classified as non-tax revenues.

18. The same principles apply when other institutional units are granted leases that permit them to fell timber in natural forests on land owned by general government units. These payments are also classified as non-tax revenues.

19. These rents or royalties paid to general government should not be confused with taxes on income and profits, severance taxes, business licenses, or other taxes. If the payments are levied on the profits from the extraction activity, then they should be classified as taxes on incomes, profits and gains (1000). In addition, any severance payments that are imposed on the extraction of minerals and fossil fuels from reserves owned privately or by another government should be classified as taxes. Payments related to the gross value of production should be classified as other taxes on goods and services (5128). Payments for a license or permit to conduct extraction operations should be classified as taxes on use of goods and on permission to use goods or perform activities (5213).

### *Fines and penalties*

20. In principle, fines and penalties charged on overdue taxes or penalties imposed for the attempted evasion of taxes should not be recorded as tax revenues. However, it may not be possible to separate payments of fines or other penalties from the revenues from the taxes to which they relate. In this case, the fines and penalties relating to a particular tax are recorded together with the revenues from that tax and fines and penalties paid with revenue from unidentifiable taxes are classified as other taxes in Category 6000. Fines not relating to tax offences (e.g., for parking offences), or not identifiable as relating to tax offences, are also not treated as tax revenues.

## A.3 Basis of reporting

### *Accrual or cash reporting*

21. The data reported in the *Revenue Statistics* publications for recent years are predominantly recorded on an accrual basis for OECD countries, i.e. recorded at the time that the tax liability was created. Further information is provided in the footnotes to the country table in Chapter 5 of the Report.

22. However, data for earlier years and for non-OECD countries are still predominantly recorded on a cash basis, i.e. at the time at which the payment was received by government. Thus, for example, taxes withheld by employers in one year but paid to the government in the following year and taxes due in one year but actually paid in the following year are both included in the receipts of the second year. Corrective transactions, such as refunds, repayments and drawbacks, are deducted from gross revenues of the period in which they are made.

23. Data on tax revenues are recorded without offsets for the administrative expenses connected with tax collection. Similarly, where the proceeds of tax are used to subsidise particular members of the community, the subsidy is not deducted from the yield of the tax, though the tax may be shown net of subsidies in the national records of some countries.

24. As regards fiscal monopolies (heading 5122), only the amount actually transferred to the government is included in government revenues. However, if any expenditures of fiscal monopolies are considered to be government expenditures (e.g., social expenditures undertaken by fiscal monopolies at the direction of the government) they are added back for the purpose of arriving at tax revenue figures (see §66 below).

### *The distinction between tax and expenditure provisions*[6]

25. Because this publication is concerned only with the revenue side of government operations, no account being taken of the expenditure side, a distinction has to be made between tax and expenditure provisions. Normally there is no difficulty in making this distinction as expenditures are made outside the tax system and the tax accounts and under legislation separate from the tax legislation. In borderline cases, cash flow is used to distinguish between tax provisions and expenditure provisions. Insofar as a

provision affects the flow of tax payments from the taxpayer to the government, it is regarded as a tax provision and is taken into account in the data shown in this publication. A provision which does not affect this flow is seen as an expenditure provision and is disregarded in the data recorded in this publication.

26. Tax allowances, exemptions and deductions against the tax base clearly affect the amount of tax paid to the government and are therefore considered as tax provisions. At the other extreme, those subsidies which cannot be offset against tax liability and which are clearly not connected with the assessment process, do not reduce tax revenues as recorded in this publication. Tax credits are amounts deductible from tax payable (as distinct from deductions from the tax base). Two types of tax credits are distinguished, those (referred to here as wastable tax credits) which are limited to the amount of the tax liability and therefore cannot give rise to a payment by the authorities to the taxpayer, and those (referred to as non-wastable tax credits) which are not so limited, so that the excess of the credit over the tax liability can be paid to the taxpayer.[7] A wastable tax credit, like a tax allowance, clearly affects the amount of tax paid to the government, and is therefore considered as a tax provision. The practice followed for non-wastable tax credits[8] is to distinguish between the 'tax expenditure component',[9] which is that portion of the credit that is used to reduce or eliminate a taxpayer's liability, and the 'transfer component', which is the portion that exceeds the taxpayer's liability and is paid to that taxpayer. Reported tax revenues should be reduced by the amount of the tax expenditure component but not by the amount of the transfer component. In addition, the amounts of the tax expenditure and transfer components should be reported as memorandum items in the country tables. Countries that are unable to distinguish between the tax expenditure and transfer components should indicate whether or not the tax revenues have been reduced by the total of these components, and provide any available estimates of the amounts of the two components. Further information is given in Chapter 1 of the Report, which illustrates the effect of alternative treatments of non-wastable tax credits on tax to GDP.

### *Calendar and fiscal years*

27. National authorities whose fiscal years do not correspond to the calendar year show data, where possible, on a calendar year basis to permit maximum comparability with the data of other countries. There remain a few countries where data refer to fiscal years. For these the GDP data used in the comparative tables also correspond to the fiscal years.

## A.4 General classification criteria

### *The main classification criteria*

28. The classification of receipts among the main headings (1000, 2000, 3000, 4000, 5000 and 6000) is generally governed by the base on which the tax is levied: 1000 income, profits and capital gains; 2000 and 3000 earnings, payroll or number of employees; 4000 property; 5000 goods and services; 6000 multiple bases, other bases or unidentifiable bases. Where a tax is calculated on more than one base, the receipts are, where possible, split among the various headings (see §33 and §84). The headings 4000 and 5000 cover not only taxes where the tax base is the property, goods or services themselves but also certain related taxes. Thus, taxes on the transfer of property are included in 4400[10] and taxes on the use of goods or on permission to perform activities in 5200. In headings 4000 and 5000 a distinction is made in certain sub-headings between recurrent and non-recurrent taxes: recurrent taxes are defined as those levied at regular intervals (usually annually) and non-recurrent taxes are levied once and for all (see also §48 to §51, §54, §55 and §81 for particular applications of this distinction).

29. Earmarking of a tax for specific purposes does not affect the classification of tax receipts. However, as explained in §40 on the classification of social security contributions, the conferment of an entitlement to social benefits is crucial to the definition of the 2000 main heading.

30. The way that a tax is levied or collected (e.g., by use of stamps) does not affect classification.

### *Classification of taxpayers*

31. In certain sub-headings, distinctions are made between different categories of taxpayers. These distinctions vary from tax to tax:

*a) Between individuals and corporations in relation to income and net wealth taxes*

The basic distinction is that corporation income taxes, as distinct from individual income taxes, are levied on the corporation as an entity, not on the individuals who own it, and without regard to the personal circumstances of these individuals. The same distinction applies to net wealth taxes on corporations and those on individuals. Taxes paid on the profits of partnerships and the income of institutions, such as life insurance or pension funds, are classified according to the same rule. They are classified as corporate taxes (1200) if they are charged on the partnership or institution as an entity without regard to the personal circumstances of the owners. Otherwise, they are treated as individual taxes (1100). Usually, there is different legislation for the corporation taxes and for the individual taxes.[11] The distinction made here between individuals and corporations does not follow the sector classification between households, enterprises, and so on of the System of National Accounts for income and outlay accounts. The SNA classification requires certain unincorporated businesses[12] to be excluded from the household sector and included with non-financial enterprises and financial institutions. The tax on the profits of these businesses, however, cannot always be separated from the tax on the other income of their owners, or can be separated only on an arbitrary basis. No attempt at this separation is made here and the whole of the individual income tax is shown together without regard to the nature of the income chargeable.

*b) Between households and others in relation to taxes on immovable property*

Here the distinction is that adopted by the SNA for the production and consumption expenditure accounts. The distinction is between households as consumers (i.e. excluding non-incorporated business) on the one hand and producers on the other hand. However, taxes on dwellings occupied by households, whether paid by owner-occupiers, tenants or landlords, are classified under households. This follows the common distinction made between taxes on domestic property versus taxes on business property. Some countries are not, however, in a position to make this distinction.

*c) Between households and others in relation to motor vehicle licences*

Here the distinction is between households as consumers on the one hand and producers on the other, as in the production and consumption expenditure accounts of the SNA.

*d) Between business and others in relation to the residual taxes (6000)*

The distinction is the same as in c) above between producers on the one hand and households as consumers on the other hand. Taxes which are included under the heading 6000 because they involve more than one tax base or because the tax base does not fall within any of the previous categories but which are identifiable as levyable only on producers and not on households are included under 'business'. The rest of the taxes which are included under the heading 6000 are shown as 'other' or non-identified.

### *Surcharges*

32. Receipts from surcharges in respect of particular taxes are usually classified with the receipts from the relevant tax whether or not the surcharge is temporary. If, however, the surcharge has a characteristic which would render it classifiable in a different heading of the OECD list, receipts from the surcharge are classified under that heading separately from the relevant tax.

### *Unidentifiable tax receipts and residual sub-headings*

33. A number of cases arise where taxes cannot be identified as belonging entirely to a heading or sub-heading of the OECD classification and the following practices are applied in such cases:

*a)* The heading is known, but it is not known how receipts should be allocated between sub-headings: receipts are classified in the appropriate residual sub-heading (1300, 2400, 4520, 4600, 5128, 5130, 5300 or 6200).

*b)* It is known that the bulk of receipts from a group of taxes (usually local taxes) is derived from taxes within a particular heading or sub-heading, but some of the taxes in the group whose amount cannot be precisely ascertained may be classifiable in other headings or sub-headings: receipts are shown in the heading or sub-heading under which most of the receipts fall.

*c)* Neither the heading nor sub-heading of a tax (usually local) can be identified: the tax is classified in 6200 unless it is known that it is a tax on business in which case it is classified in 6100.

## A.5 Commentaries on items of the list

### *1000 — Taxes on income, profits and capital gains*

34. This heading covers taxes levied on the net income or profits (i.e. gross income minus allowable tax reliefs) of individuals and enterprises. Also covered are taxes levied on the capital gains of individuals and enterprises, and gains from gambling.

35. Included in the heading are:

*a)* taxes levied predominantly on income or profits, though partially on other bases. Taxes on various bases which are not predominantly income or profits are classified according to the principles laid down in §33 and §84;

*b)* taxes on property, which are levied on a presumed or estimated income as part of an income tax (see also §48(a), (c) and (d));

*c)* compulsory payments to social security fund contributions that are levied on income but do not confer an entitlement to social benefits. When such contributions do confer an entitlement to social benefits, they are included in heading 2000 (see §40);

*d)* receipts from integrated scheduler income tax systems are classified as a whole in this heading, even though certain of the scheduler taxes may be based upon gross income and may not take into account the personal circumstances of the taxpayer.

36. The main subdivision of this heading is between levies on individuals (1100) and those on corporate enterprises (1200). Under each subdivision a distinction is made between taxes on income and profits (1110 and 1210), and taxes on capital gains (1120 and 1220). If certain receipts cannot be identified as appropriate to either 1100 or 1200, or if in practice this distinction cannot be made (e.g.,

because there are no reliable data on the recipients of payments from which withholding taxes are deducted) they are classified in 1300 as not-allocable.

### *Treatment of credits under imputation systems*

37. Under imputation systems of corporate income tax, a company's shareholders are wholly or partly relieved of their liability to income tax on dividends paid by the company out of income or profits liable to corporate income tax. In countries with such systems,[13] part of the tax on the company's profits is available to provide relief against the shareholders' own tax liability. The relief to the shareholder takes the form of a tax credit, the amount of which may be less than, equal to, or more than the shareholder's overall tax liability. If the tax credit exceeds this tax liability the excess may be payable to the shareholder. As this type of tax credit is an integral part of the imputation system of corporate income tax, any payment to the shareholders is treated as a repayment of tax and not as expenditure (compare the treatment of other tax credits described in §26).

38. As the tax credit under imputation systems (even when exceeding tax liability) is to be regarded as a tax provision, the question arises whether it should be deducted from individual income tax receipts (1110) or corporate income tax receipts (1210). In this Report, the full amount of corporate income tax paid is shown under 1210 and no imputed tax is included under 1110. Thus, the full amount of the credit reduces the amount of 1110 whether the credit results in a reduction of personal income tax liability or whether an actual refund is made because the credit exceeds the income tax liability. (Where, however, such tax credits are deducted from corporation tax in respect of dividends paid to corporations the amounts are deducted from the receipts of 1210).

### *1120 and 1220 — Taxes on capital gains*

39. These sub-headings comprise taxes imposed on capital gains, 1120 covering those levied on the gains of individuals and 1220 those levied on the gains of corporate enterprises, where receipts from such taxes can be separately identified. In many countries, this is not the case and the receipts from such taxes are then classified with those from the income tax. Heading 1120 also includes taxes on gains from gambling.

### *2000 — Social security contributions*

40. Classified here are all compulsory payments to general government that confer an entitlement to receive a (contingent) future social benefit. Such payments are usually earmarked to finance social benefits and are often paid to institutions of general government that provide such benefits. However, such earmarking is not part of the definition of social security contributions and is not required for a tax to be classified here. However, conferment of an entitlement is required for a tax to be classified under this heading. So, levies on income or payroll that are earmarked for social security funds but do not confer an entitlement to benefit are excluded from this heading and shown under personal income taxes (1100) or taxes on payroll and workforce (3000). Taxes on other bases, such as goods and services, which are earmarked for social security benefits are not shown here but are classified according to their respective bases because they generally confer no entitlement to social security benefits.

41. Contributions for the following types of social security benefits would, *inter alia*, be included: unemployment insurance benefits and supplements, accident, injury and sickness benefits, old-age, disability and survivors' pensions, family allowances, reimbursements for medical and hospital expenses or provision of hospital or medical services. Contributions may be levied on both employees and employers.

42. Contributions may be based on earnings or payroll ('on a payroll basis') or on net income after deductions and exemptions for personal circumstances ('on an income tax basis'), and the revenues

from the two bases should be separately identified if possible. However, where contributions to a general social security scheme are on a payroll basis, but the contributions of particular groups (such as the self-employed) cannot be assessed on this basis and net income is used as a proxy for gross earnings, the receipts may still be classified as being on a payroll basis. In principle, this heading excludes voluntary contributions paid to social security schemes. When separately identifiable these are shown in the memorandum item on the financing of social security benefits. In practice, however, they cannot always be separately identified from compulsory contributions, in which case they are included in this heading.

43. Contributions to social insurance schemes which are not institutions of general government and to other types of insurance schemes, provident funds, pension funds, friendly societies or other saving schemes are not considered as social security contributions. Provident funds are arrangements under which the contributions of each employee and of the corresponding employer on his/her behalf are kept in a separate account earning interest and withdrawable under specific circumstances. Pension funds are separately organised schemes negotiated between employees and employers and carry provisions for different contributions and benefits, sometimes more directly tied to salary levels and length of service than under social security schemes. When contributions to these schemes are compulsory or quasi-compulsory (e.g., by virtue of agreement with professional and union organisations) they are shown in the memorandum item (refer to Table 5.39 of the Report).

44. Contributions by government employees and by governments in respect of their employees, to social security schemes classified within general government are included in this heading. Contributions to separate schemes for government employees, which can be regarded as replacing general social security schemes, are also regarded as taxes.[14] Where, however, a separate scheme is not seen as replacing a general scheme and has been negotiated between the government, in its role as an employer, and its employees, it is not regarded as social security and contributions to it are not regarded as taxes, even though the scheme may have been established by legislation.

45. This heading excludes 'imputed' contributions, which correspond to social benefits paid directly by employers to their employees or former employees or to their representatives (e.g., when employers are legally obliged to pay sickness benefits for a certain period).

46. Contributions are divided into those of employees (2100), employers (2200), and self-employed or non-employed (2300), and then further sub-divided according to the basis on which they are levied. Employees are defined for this purpose as all persons engaged in activities of business units, government bodies, private non-profit institutions, or other paid employment, except the proprietors and their unpaid family members in the case of unincorporated businesses. Members of the armed forces are included, irrespective of the duration and type of their service, if they contribute to social security schemes. The contributions of employers are defined as their payments on account of their employees to social security schemes. Where employees or employers are required to continue the payment of social security contributions when the employee becomes unemployed these contributions, data permitting, are shown in 2100 and 2200 respectively. Accordingly, the sub-heading 2300 is confined to contributions paid by the self-employed and by those outside of the labour force (e.g., disabled or retired individuals).

### *3000 — Taxes on payroll and workforce*

47. These consist of taxes payable by enterprises assessed either as a proportion of the wages or salaries paid or as a fixed amount per person employed. They do not include compulsory social security contributions paid by employers or any taxes paid by employees themselves out of their wages or salaries

### *4000 — Taxes on property*

48. This heading covers recurrent and non-recurrent taxes on the use, ownership or transfer of property. These include taxes on immovable property or net wealth, taxes on the change of ownership of property through inheritance or gift and taxes on financial and capital transactions. The following kinds of tax are excluded from this heading:

- *a)* taxes on capital gains resulting from the sale of a property (1120 or 1220);
- *b)* taxes on the use of goods or on permission to use goods or perform activities (5200); see §78;
- *c)* taxes on immovable property levied on the basis of a presumed net income which take into account the personal circumstances of the taxpayer. They are classified as income taxes along with taxes on income and capital gains derived from property (1100);
- *d)* taxes on the use of property for residence, where the tax is payable by either proprietor or tenant and the amount payable is a function of the user's personal circumstances (pay, dependants, and so on). They are classified as taxes on income (1100);
- *e)* taxes on building in excess of permitted maximum density, taxes on the enlargement, construction or alteration of certain buildings beyond a permitted value and taxes on building construction. They are classified as taxes on permission to perform activities (5200);
- *f)* taxes on the use of one's own property for special trading purposes like selling alcohol, tobacco, meat or for exploitation of land resources (e.g., United States severance taxes). They are classified as taxes on permission to perform activities (5200).

### *4100 — Recurrent taxes on immovable property*

49. This sub-heading covers taxes levied regularly in respect of the use or ownership of immovable property.

- these taxes are levied on land and buildings;
- they can be in the form of a percentage of an assessed property value based on a national rental income, sales price, or capitalised yield; or in terms of other characteristics of real property, ( for example size or location ) from which a presumed rent or capital value can be derived.
- such taxes can be levied on proprietors, tenants, or both. They can also be paid by one level of government to another level of government in respect of property under the jurisdiction of the latter.
- debts are not taken into account in the assessment of these taxes, and they differ from taxes on net wealth in this respect.

50. Taxes on immovable property are further sub-divided into those paid by households (4110) and those paid by other entities (4120), according to the criteria set out in §31(*b*) above.

### *4200 — Recurrent taxes on net wealth*

51. This sub-heading covers taxes levied regularly (in most cases annually) on net wealth, i.e. taxes on a wide range of movable and immovable property, net of debt. It is sub-divided into taxes paid by individuals (4210) and taxes paid by corporate enterprises (4220) according to the criteria set out in §31(*a*) above. If separate figures exist for receipts paid by institutions, the tax payments involved are added to those paid by corporations.

### *4300 — Estate, inheritance and gift taxes*

52. This sub-heading is divided into taxes on estates and inheritances (4310) and taxes on gifts (4320).[15] Estate taxes are charged on the amount of the total estate whereas inheritance taxes are charged on the shares of the individual recipients; in addition the latter may take into account the relationship of the individual recipients to the deceased.

### *4400 — Taxes on financial and capital transactions*

53. This sub-heading comprises, *inter alia*, taxes on the issue, transfer, purchase and sale of non-financial and financial assets (including foreign exchange or securities), taxes on cheques and other forms of payment, and taxes levied on specific legal transactions such as validation of contracts and the sale of immovable property. The heading does not include:

- *a)* taxes on the use of goods or property or permission to perform certain activities (5200);
- *b)* fees paid to cover court charges, charges for birth, marriage or death certificates, which are normally regarded as non-tax revenues (see §12);
- *c)* taxes on capital gains (1000);
- *d)* recurrent taxes on immovable property (4100);
- *e)* recurrent taxes on net wealth (4200);
- *f)* once-and-for-all levies on property or wealth (4500);
- *g)* stamp taxes not related to financial and capital transactions
    - i. Stamp taxes on the sale of specific products, such as alcoholic beverages or tobacco (5121);
    - ii. Stamp taxes restricted by law to imported products (5123) or to exported products (5124); or
    - iii. Stamp taxes not falling exclusively on a single category of transaction (6000).

### *4500 — Other non-recurrent taxes on property*

54. This sub-heading covers once-and-for-all, as distinct from recurrent, levies on property. It is divided into taxes on net wealth (4510) and other non-recurrent taxes on property (4520). Heading 4510 would include taxes levied to meet emergency expenditures, or for redistribution purposes. Heading 4520 would cover taxes levied to take account of increases in land value due to permission given to develop or provision of additional local facilities by general government, any taxes on the revaluation of capital and once-and-for-all taxes on particular items of property.

### *4600 — Other recurrent taxes on property*

55. These rarely exist in OECD member countries, but the heading would include taxes on goods such as cattle, jewellery, windows, and other external signs of wealth.

### *5000 — Taxes on goods and services*

56. All taxes and duties levied on the production, extraction, sale, transfer, leasing or delivery of goods, and the rendering of services (5100), or in respect of the use of goods or permission to use goods or to perform activities (5200) are included here. The heading thus covers:

- *a)* multi-stage cumulative taxes;
- *b)* general sales taxes — whether levied at manufacture/production, wholesale or retail level;

*c)* value-added taxes;

*d)* excises;

*e)* taxes levied on the import and export of goods;

*f)* taxes levied in respect of the use of goods and taxes on permission to use goods, or perform certain activities;

*g)* taxes on the extraction, processing or production of minerals and other products.

57. Borderline cases between this heading and heading 4000 (taxes on property) and 6100 (other taxes on business) are referred to in §48, §53 and §80. Residual sub-headings (5300) and (5130) cover tax receipts which cannot be allocated between 5100 and 5200 and between 5110 and 5120, respectively; see §33.

### *5100 — Taxes on the production, sale, transfer, leasing and delivery of goods and rendering of services*

58. This sub-heading consists of all taxes, levied on transactions in goods and services on the basis of their intrinsic characteristics (e.g., value, weight of tobacco, strength of alcohol, and so on) as distinct from taxes imposed on the use of goods, or permission to use goods or perform activities, which fall under 5200.

### *5110 — General taxes on goods and services*

59. This sub-heading includes all taxes, other than import and export duties (5123 and 5124), levied on the production, leasing, transfer, delivery or sales of a wide range of goods and/or the rendering of a wide range of services, irrespective of whether they are domestically produced or imported and irrespective of the stage of production or distribution at which they are levied. It thus covers value-added taxes, sales taxes and multi-stage cumulative taxes. Receipts from border adjustments in respect of such taxes when goods are imported are added to gross receipts for this category, and repayments of such taxes when goods are exported are deducted. These taxes are subdivided into 5111 value-added taxes, 5112 sales taxes, 5113 turnover and other general taxes on goods and services.

60. Borderline cases arise between this heading and taxes on specific goods (5120) when taxes are levied on a large number of goods, for example, the United Kingdom purchase tax (repealed in 1973) and the Japanese commodity tax (repealed in 1988). In conformity with national views, the former United Kingdom purchase tax is classified as a general tax (5112) and the former Japanese commodity tax as excises (5121).

### *5111 — Value-added taxes*

61. All general consumption taxes charged on value-added are classified in this sub-heading, irrespective of the method of deduction and the stages at which the taxes are levied. In practice, all OECD countries with value-added taxes normally allow immediate deduction of taxes on purchases by all but the final consumer and impose tax at all stages. In some countries the heading may include certain taxes, such as those on financial and insurance activities, either because receipts from them cannot be identified separately from those from the value-added tax, or because they are regarded as an integral part of the value-added tax, even though similar taxes in other countries might be classified elsewhere (e.g., 5126 as taxes on services or 4400 as taxes on financial and capital transactions).

### 5112 — Sales taxes

62. All general taxes levied at one stage only, whether at manufacturing or production, wholesale or retail stage are classified here.

### 5113 — Turnover and other general taxes on goods and services

63. These are multi-stage cumulative taxes and taxes where elements of consumption taxes are combined with multistage taxes. These taxes are levied each time a transaction takes place without deduction for taxes paid on inputs. Multi-stage taxes can be combined with elements of value-added or sales taxes.

### 5120 — Taxes on specific goods and services

64. Excises, profits generated and transferred from fiscal monopolies, and customs and imports duties as well as taxes on exports, foreign exchange transactions, investment goods and betting stakes and special taxes on services, which do not form part of a general tax of 5110, are included in this category.

### 5121 — Excises

65. Excises are taxes levied as a product specific unit tax on a predefined limited range of goods. Excises are usually levied at differentiated rates on nonessential or luxury goods, alcoholic beverages, tobacco, and energy. Excises may be imposed at any stage of production or distribution and are usually assessed as a specific charge per unit based on characteristics by reference to the value, weight, strength, or quantity of the product. Included are special taxes on individual products such as sugar, sugar beets, matches, and chocolates; taxes levied at varying rates on a certain range of goods; and taxes levied on tobacco goods, alcoholic drinks, motor fuels, and hydrocarbon oils. If a tax collected principally on imported goods also applies, or would apply, under the same law to comparable domestically produced goods, then the revenue from this tax is classified as arising from excises rather than from import duties. This principle applies even if there is no comparable domestic production or no possibility of such production. Taxes on the use of utilities such as water, electricity, gas, and energy are regarded as excises rather than taxes on specific services (5126). Excises exclude those taxes that are levied as general taxes on goods and services (5110); profits of fiscal monopolies (5122); customs and other import duties (5123); or taxes on exports (5124).

### 5122 — Profits of fiscal monopolies

66. This sub-heading covers that part of the profits of fiscal monopolies which is transferred to general government or which is used to finance any expenditures considered to be government expenditures (see §24). Amounts are shown when they are transferred to general government or used to make expenditures considered to be government expenditures.

67. Fiscal monopolies reflect the exercise of the taxing power of government by the use of monopoly powers. Fiscal monopolies are non-financial public enterprises exercising a monopoly in most cases over the production or distribution of tobacco, alcoholic beverages, salt, matches, playing cards and petroleum or agricultural products (i.e. on the kind of products which are likely to be, alternatively or additionally, subject to the excises of 5121), to raise the government revenues which in other countries are gathered through taxes on dealings in such commodities by private business units. The government monopoly may be at the production stage or, as in the case of government-owned and controlled liquor stores, at the distribution stage.

68. Fiscal monopolies are distinguished from public utilities such as rail transport, electricity, post offices, and other communications, which may enjoy a monopoly or quasi-monopoly position but where the primary purpose is normally to provide basic services rather than to raise revenue for government. Transfers from such other public enterprises to the government are considered as non-tax revenues. The traditional concept of fiscal monopoly is not generally extended to include state lotteries, the profits of which are usually accordingly regarded as non-tax revenues. However, they can be included as tax revenues if the prime reason for their operation is to raise revenues to finance government expenditure. Fiscal monopoly profits are distinguished from export and import monopoly profits (5127) transferred from marketing boards or other enterprises dealing with international trade.

### *5123 — Customs and other import duties*

69. Taxes, stamp duties and surcharges restricted by law to imported products are included here. Also included are levies on imported agricultural products which are imposed in member countries of the European Union and amounts paid by certain of these countries under the Monetary Compensation Accounts (MCA) system.[16] Customs duties collected by European Union member states on behalf of the European Union are reported under this heading at the supranational level of government in the country tables (in Chapter 5 of the Report). Excluded here are taxes collected on imports as part of a general tax on goods and services, or an excise applicable to both imported and domestically produced goods.

### *5124 — Taxes on exports*

70. In the 1970s, export duties were levied in Australia, Canada and Portugal as a regular measure and they have been used in Finland for counter-cyclical purposes. Some member countries of the European Union pay, as part of the MCA system, a levy on exports (see note 16 to §69). Where these amounts are identifiable, they are shown in this heading. This heading does not include repayments of general consumption taxes or excises or customs duties on exported goods, which should be deducted from the gross receipts under 5110, 5121 or 5123, as appropriate.

### *5125 — Taxes on investment goods*

71. This sub-heading covers taxes on investment goods, such as machinery. These taxes may be imposed for a number of years or temporarily for counter-cyclical purposes. Taxes on industrial inputs which are also levied on consumers [e.g., the Swedish energy tax which is classified under (5121)] are not included here.

### *5126 — Taxes on specific services*

72. All taxes assessed on the payment for specific services, such as taxes on insurance premiums, banking services, gambling and betting stakes (e.g., from horse races, football pools, lottery tickets), transport, entertainment, restaurant and advertising charges, fall into this category. Taxes on entry to casinos, races, other similar events or venues as well as stamp taxes on specific services are also classified under this heading. Taxes levied on the gross income of companies providing a specific service (e.g. transportation [including airport and other passenger taxes] insurance, banking, entertainment, restaurants, and advertising) are also classified under this heading.

73. Tax revenues from bank levies and payments to deposit insurance and financial stability schemes are also included here:

- Compulsory payments of stability fees, bank levies and deposit insurance should generally be treated as tax revenues where the payments are made to general government or supranational authorities and are allocated to the governments' consolidated or general funds so that the government is free to make immediate use of the money for the purposes that it chooses. This principle would apply regardless of whether the government is promising to make payments to guarantee the banks' customer deposits in some future contingency.

- If the compulsory payments are made to general government and placed in funds that are earmarked to be entirely channelled back to the sector of the economy that comprises the companies that are subject to the payment, they would still generally be treated as tax revenues on the grounds that the funds would be available for the government and would reduce its budget deficit, the fee is unrequited for an individual entity and the amounts raised could be unrelated to any eventual pay out to depositors or expenditure on wider support for the financial sector.
- Payments to made to the smaller long-standing schemes for insuring 'retail' deposits, where the payment levels are consistent with the costs of insurance should be classified as fee for service.
- Any payments which involve governments realising the assets of a failed institution or receiving a priority claim on its assets in liquidation in order to fund payments of compensation to customers for their lost deposits would be treated as a fee for a service as opposed to tax revenues.
- Compulsory payments that are made to funds operated outside the government sector and non-state institutions backed by the deposit takers and all payments to voluntary schemes should not be treated as tax revenues.
- Contributions made to the EU Single Resolution Fund are also included here and recorded under the supranational level of government in the country tables.

74. Excluded from this sub-heading are:

*a)* taxes on services forming part of a general tax on goods and services (5110);

*b)* taxes on electricity, gas and energy (5121 as excises);

*c)* taxes on individual gains from gambling (1120 as taxes on capital gains of individuals and non-corporate enterprises) and lump-sum taxes on the transfer of private lotteries or on the permission to set up lotteries (5200);17

*d)* taxes on cheques and on the issue, transfer or redemption of securities (4400 as taxes on financial and capital transactions);

*e)* general taxes on turnover (5113).

### *5127 — Other taxes on international trade and transactions*

75. This sub-heading covers revenue received by the government from the purchase and sale of foreign exchange at different rates. When the government exercises monopoly powers to extract a margin between the purchase and sales price of foreign exchange, other than to cover administrative costs, the revenue derived constitutes a compulsory levy exacted in indeterminate proportions from both purchaser and seller of foreign exchange. It is the common equivalent of an import duty and export duty levied in a single exchange rate system or of a tax on the sale or purchase of foreign exchange. Like the profits of fiscal monopolies and import or export monopolies transferred to government, it represents the exercise of monopoly powers for tax purposes and is included in tax revenues.

76. The sub-heading covers also the profits of export or import monopolies, which do not however exist in OECD countries, taxes on purchase or sale of foreign exchange, and any other taxes levied specifically on international trade or transactions.

### *5128 — Other taxes on specific goods and services*

77. This item includes taxes on the extraction of minerals, fossil fuels and other exhaustible resources from deposits owned privately or by another government together with any other unallocable

receipts from taxes on specific goods and services. Taxes on the extraction of exhaustible resources are usually a fixed amount per unit of quality or weight, but can be a percentage of value. The taxes are recorded when the resources are extracted. Payments from the extraction of exhaustible resources from deposits owned by the government unit receiving the payment are classified as rent.

### *5200 — Taxes on use of goods or on permission to use goods or perform activities*

78. This sub-heading covers taxes which are levied in respect of the use of goods as distinct from taxes on the goods themselves. Unlike the latter taxes – reported under 5100 –, they are not assessed on the value of the goods but usually as fixed amounts. Taxes on permission to use goods or to perform activities are also included here, as are pollution taxes not based upon the value of particular goods. It is sometimes difficult to distinguish between compulsory user charges and licence fees which are regarded as taxes and those which are excluded as non-tax revenues. The criteria which are employed are noted in §12–13.

79. Although the sub-heading refers to the 'use' of goods, registration of ownership rather than use may be what generates liability to tax, so that the taxes of this heading may apply to the ownership of animals or goods rather than their use (e.g., race horses, dogs and motor vehicles) and may apply even to unusable goods (e.g., unusable motor vehicles or guns).

80. Borderline cases arise with:

*a)* taxes on the permission to perform business activities which are levied on a combined income, payroll or turnover base and, accordingly, are classified following the rules in §84;

*b)* taxes on the ownership or use of property of headings 4100, 4200 and 4600. The heading 4100 is confined to taxes on the ownership or tenancy of immovable property and – unlike the taxes of 5200 – they are related to the value of the property. The net wealth taxes and taxes on chattels of 4200 and 4600 respectively are confined to the ownership rather than the use of assets, apply to groups of assets rather than particular goods and again are related to the value of the assets,

### *5210 — Recurrent taxes on use of goods and on permission to use goods or perform activities*

81. The principal characteristic of taxes classified here is that they are levied at regular intervals and that they are usually fixed amounts. The most important item in terms of revenue receipts is vehicle licence taxes. This sub-heading also covers taxes on permission to hunt, shoot, fish or to sell certain products and taxes on the ownership of dogs and on the performance of certain services, provided that they meet the criteria set out in §12–13. The sub-divisions of 5210 are:

- user taxes on motor vehicles paid by households (5211);
- taxes on motor vehicles paid by others (5212); and
- other recurrent taxes (5213). This sub-heading covers business and professional licences paid by enterprises in order to obtain a licence to carry on a particular kind of business or profession when the levies are on a recurring basis. Licences such as taxi and casino licences are included. Dog licences and recurrent general licences for hunting, shooting and fishing where the right to carry out these activities is not granted as part of a normal commercial transaction are also included under this heading.

82. Excluded from sub-heading 5213 are:

*a)* licences where the right to carry out such activities is granted as part of a normal commercial transaction (e.g., the granting of the licence is accompanied by the right to use a specific area which is owned by government);

*b)* payments relating to the checks carried out by the government on the suitability and or safety of the business premises or equipment, or on the quality or standard of goods or services produced as a condition for granting such a licence. These payments are not unrequited and should be treated as payments for services rendered, unless the amounts charged for the licences are out of all proportion to the costs of the checks carried out by governments.

### *5220 — Non-recurrent taxes on use of goods and on permission to use goods or perform activities*

83. This section covers non-recurrent taxes levied on the use of goods or on permission to use goods or perform activities and taxes levied each time goods are used. It includes taxes levied on the emission or discharge into the environment of noxious gases, liquids or other harmful substances.

- Payments for tradable emission permits issued by governments under cap and trade schemes should be recorded here at the time the emissions occur. No revenue should be recorded for permits that governments issue free of charge. The accrual basis of recording means that there can be a timing difference between the cash being received by government for the permits and the time the emission occurs. In the national accounts, this timing gives rise to a financial liability for government during the period.
- Payments made for the collection and disposal of waste or noxious substances by public authorities should be excluded as they constitute a sale of services to enterprises.

84. Other taxes falling under heading 5200 that are not levied recurrently are also included here. Thus, once-and-for-all payments for permission to sell liquor or tobacco or to set up betting shops are included provided they meet the criteria set out in §12–13.

### *6000 — Other taxes*

85. Taxes levied on a base, or bases, other than those described under headings 1000, 3000, 4000 and 5000, or on bases of which cannot be considered to be related to any one of these headings, are included here. Where taxes are levied on a multiple base and it is possible to estimate the receipts related to each base the separate amounts are included under the appropriate headings. If separate amounts cannot be estimated and it is known that most of the receipts are derived from one base, the whole of the receipts are classified according to that base. Otherwise, they are classified here. Other revenues included here are presumptive taxes not included elsewhere in the classification system, taxes on individuals in the form of a poll tax or capitation tax, stamp taxes not related to financial and capital transactions nor falling exclusively on a single category of transaction, expenditure taxes where personal deductions or exemptions are applied and unidentifiable tax receipts. A subdivision is made between taxes levied wholly or predominantly on business (6100) and those levied on others (6200).

## A.6 Conciliation with National Accounts

86. This section of the tables provides a re-conciliation between the OECD calculation of total tax revenues and the total of all taxes and social contributions paid to general government as recorded in the country's National Accounts. Where the country is a member of the European Union (EU), the comparison is between the OECD calculation of total tax revenues and the sum of tax revenues and

social contributions recorded in the combination of the general government and the institutions of the EU sectors of the National Accounts.

## A.7 Memorandum item on the financing of social security benefits

87. In view of the varying relationship between taxation and social security contributions and the cases referred to in §40 to §46, a memorandum item collects together all payments earmarked for social security-type benefits, other than voluntary payments to the private sector. Data are presented as follows (refer Table 5.39 of the Report):

*a)* Taxes of 2000 series.

*b)* Taxes earmarked for social security benefits.

*c)* Voluntary contributions to the government.

*d)* Compulsory contributions to the private sector.

Guidance on the breakdown of (a) to (d) above is provided in §40 to §46.

## A.8 Memorandum item on identifiable taxes paid by government

88. Identifiable taxes actually paid by government are presented in a memorandum item classified by the main headings of the OECD classification of taxes. In the vast majority of countries, only social security contributions and payroll taxes paid by government can be identified. These are, however, usually the most important taxes paid by governments (refer to Table 5.40 of the Report).

## A.9 Relation of OECD classification of taxes to national accounting systems

89. A system of national accounts (SNA) seeks to provide a coherent framework for recording and presenting the main flows relating respectively to production, consumption, accumulation and external transactions of a given economic area, usually a country or a major region within a country. Government revenues are an important part of the transactions recorded in SNA. The final version of the 2008 SNA was jointly published by five international organisations: the United Nations, the International Monetary Fund, the European Union, the Organisation for Economic Co-operation and Development, and the World Bank in August 2009. The *System* is a comprehensive, consistent and flexible set of macroeconomic accounts. It is designed for use in countries with market economies, whatever their stage of economic development, and also in countries in transition to market economies. The important parts of the SNA's conceptual framework and its definitions of the various sectors of the economy have been reflected in the OECD's classification of taxes.

90. There are, however, some differences between the OECD classification of taxes and SNA concepts that are listed below. They arise because the aim of the former is to provide the maximum disaggregation of statistical data on what are generally regarded as taxes by tax administrations.

*a)* OECD includes compulsory social security contributions paid to general government in total tax revenues. Imputed and voluntary contributions plus those paid to private funds are not treated as taxes (§9 and §11 above);

*b)* there are different points of view on whether or not some levies and fees are classified as taxes (§12 and §13 above);

*c)* OECD excludes imputed taxes or subsidies resulting from the operation of official multiple exchange rates or from the central bank paying a rate of interest on required reserves that is different from other market rates;

*d)* there are differences in the treatment of non-wastable tax credits

91. As noted in §1 and §2, headings 1000 to 6000 of the OECD list of taxes cover all unrequited payments to general government or to a supranational authority, other than compulsory loans and fines. Such unrequited payments including fines, but excluding compulsory loans can be obtained from adding together the following figures in the 2008 SNA

- value-added type taxes (D.211);
- taxes and duties on imports, excluding VAT (D.212);
- export taxes (D.213);
- taxes on products, excluding VAT, import and export taxes (D.214);
- other taxes on production (D.29);
- taxes on income (D.51);
- other current taxes (D.59);
- actual social contributions (D.611 and D613), excluding voluntary contributions and payments to employment-related schemes that are not social security schemes
- capital taxes (D.91).

## A.10 The OECD classification of taxes and the International Monetary Fund (GFS) system

92. The coverage and valuation of tax revenues in the GFS system and the 2008 SNA are very similar. Therefore, the differences between the OECD classification and that of the 2008 SNA (see §90 above) also apply to the GFS. In addition the International Monetary Fund subdivides the OECD 5000 heading into section IV (Domestic Taxes on Goods and Services) and section V (Taxes on International Trade and Transactions). This reflects the fact that while the latter usually yield insignificant amounts of revenue in OECD countries, this is not the case in many non-OECD countries.

## A.11 Comparison of the OECD classification of taxes with other international classifications

93. The table below describes an item by item comparison of the OECD classification of taxes and the classifications used in the following:

*a)* System of National Accounts (2008 SNA);

*b)* European System of Accounts (2010 ESA);

*c)* IMF Government Finance Statistics Manual (GFSM2014).

94. These comparisons represent those that would be expected to apply in the majority of cases. However in practice some flexibility should be used in their application. This is because in particular cases, countries can adopt varying approaches to the classification of revenues in National Accounts.

| | OECD Classification | | | 2008 SNA | 2010 ESA | GFSM2014 |
|---|---|---|---|---|---|---|
| 1000 | | | Taxes on income, profits and capital gains | | | |
| | 1100 | | Individuals | | | |
| | | 1110 | Income and profits | D51-8.61a | D51A | 1111 |
| | | 1120 | Capital gains | D51-8.61c, d | D51C, D | 1111 |
| | 1200 | | Corporations | | | |

| | | | | | | | |
|---|---|---|---|---|---|---|---|
| | | 1210 | | Income and profits | D51-8.61b | D51B | 1112 |
| | | 1220 | | Capital gains | D51-8.61c | D51C | 1112 |
| | 1300 | | | Unallocable as between 1100 and 1200 | | | 1113 |
| 2000 | | | | Social security contributions | | | |
| | 2100 | | | Employees | D613-8.85 | D613 | 1211 |
| | 2200 | | | Employers | D611-8.83 | D611 | 1212 |
| | 2300 | | | Self-employed, non-employed | D613-8.85 | D613 | 1213 |
| | 2400 | | | Unallocable as between 2100, 2200 and 2300 | | | 1214 |
| 3000 | | | | Taxes on payroll and workforce | D29-7.97a | D29C | 112 |
| 4000 | | | | Taxes on property | | | |
| | 4100 | | | Recurrent taxes on immovable property | | | |
| | | 4110 | | Households | D59-8.63a | D59A | 1131 |
| | | 4120 | | Other | D29-7.97b | D29A | 1131 |
| | 4200 | | | Recurrent net wealth taxes | | | |
| | | 4210 | | Individual | D59-8.63b | D59A | 1132 |
| | | 4220 | | Corporations | D59-8.63b | D59A | 1132 |
| | 4300 | | | Estate, inheritance and gift taxes | | | |
| | | 4310 | | Estate and inheritance taxes | D91-10.207b | D91A | 1133 |
| | | 4320 | | Gift taxes | D91-10.207b | D91A | 1133 |
| | 4400 | | | Taxes on financial and capital transactions | D59-7.96d; D29-7.97e | D214B, C | 114114; 1161 |
| | 4500 | | | Other non-recurrent taxes on property | D91-10.207a | D91B | 1135 |
| | 4600 | | | Other recurrent taxes on property | D59-8.63c | D59A | 1136 |
| 5000 | | | | Taxes on goods and services | | | |
| | 5100 | | | Taxes on production, sale and transfer of goods and services | | | |
| | | 5110 | | General taxes on goods and services | | | |
| | | | 5111 | Value-added taxes | D211-7.89 | D211; D29G | 11411 |
| | | | 5112 | Sales taxes | D2122-7.94a; D214-7.96a | D21224; D214I | 11412 |
| | | | 5113 | Turnover and other general taxes on goods and services | D214-7.96a | D214I | 11413 |
| | | 5120 | | Taxes on specific goods and services | | | |
| | | | 5121 | Excises | D2122-7.94b; D214-7.96b | D21223; D214A, B, D | 1142 |
| | | | 5122 | Profits of fiscal monopolies | D214-7.96e | D214J | 1143 |
| | | | 5123 | Customs and other import duties | D2121-7.93 | D2121; D21221, 2 | 1151 |
| | | | 5124 | On exports | D213-7.95a | D214K | 1152-4 |
| | | | 5125 | On investment goods | | | |
| | | | 5126 | On specific services | D2122-7.94c; D214-7.96c | D21225; D214E, F, G, H; D29F | 1144; 1156 |
| | | | 5127 | Other taxes on international trade and transactions | D2122-7.94d D29-7.95b D29-7.97g D59-8.64d | D21226; D29D; D59E | 1153; 1155-6 |
| | | | 5128 | Other taxes on specific goods and services | | | 1146 |
| | | 5130 | | Unallocable between 5110 and 5120 | | | |
| | 5200 | | | Taxes on use of goods and on permission to use goods or perform activities | | | |
| | | 5210 | | Recurrent taxes on use of goods and on permission to use goods or perform activities | | | |
| | | | 5211 | Motor vehicle taxes households | D59-8.64c | D59D | 11451 |
| | | | 5212 | Motor vehicles taxes others | D29-7.97d | D214D; D29B | 11451 |
| | | | 5213 | Other recurrent taxes on use of goods and on permission to use goods or perform activities | D29-7.97c, d, f D59-8.64c | D29B, E, F; D59D | 11452 |

| | | | | | | |
|---|---|---|---|---|---|---|
| | | 5220 | Non-recurrent taxes on permission to use goods or perform activities | | | 11452 |
| | 5300 | | Unallocable as between 5100 and 5200 | | | |
| 6000 | | | Other taxes | | | |
| | 6100 | | Payable solely by business | | | 1161 |
| | 6200 | | Payable by other than business, or unidentifiable | D59-8.64a, b | D59B, C | 1162 |

## A.12 Attribution of tax revenues by sub-sectors of general government

95. The OECD classification requires a breakdown of tax revenues by sub-sectors of government. The definition of each sub-sector and the criteria to be used to attribute tax revenues between these sub-sectors are set out below. They follow the guidance of the 2008 SNA and GFSM 2014.

### *Sub-sectors of general government to be identified*

*a) Central government*

96. The central government sub-sector includes all governmental departments, offices, establishments and other bodies which are agencies or instruments of the central authority whose competence extends over the whole territory, with the exception of the administration of social security funds. Central government therefore has the authority to impose taxes on all resident and non-resident units engaged in economic activities within the country.

*b) State, provincial or regional government*

97. This sub-sector consists of intermediate units of government exercising a competence at a level below that of central government. It includes all such units operating independently of central government in a part of a country's territory encompassing a number of smaller localities, with the exception of the administration of social security funds. In unitary countries, regional governments may be considered to have a separate existence where they have substantial autonomy to raise a significant proportion of their revenues from sources within their control and their officers are independent of external administrative control in the actual operation of the unit's activities.

98. At present, federal countries comprise the majority of cases where revenues attributed to intermediate units of government are identified separately. Colombia and Spain are the only two unitary countries in this position. In the remaining unitary countries, regional revenues are included with those of local governments.

*c) Local government*

99. This sub-sector includes all other units of government exercising an independent competence in part of the territory of a country, with the exception of the administration of social security funds. It encompasses various urban and/or rural jurisdictions (e.g., local authorities, municipalities, cities, boroughs, districts).

*d) Social security funds*

100. Social security funds form a separate sub-sector of general government. The social security sub-sector is defined in the 2008 SNA by the following extracts from paragraphs 4.124 to 4.126 and 4.147:

"Social security schemes are social insurance schemes covering the community as a whole or large section of the community that are imposed and controlled by government units. The schemes cover a wide variety of programmes, providing benefits in cash or in kind for old age, invalidity or death, survivors, sickness and maternity, work injury, unemployment, family allowance, health care, etc. There is not necessarily a direct link between the amount of the contribution paid by an individual and the benefits he or she may receive." (Paragraph 4.124).

"When social security schemes are separately organised from the other activities of government units and hold their assets and liabilities separately from the latter and engage in financial transactions on their own account they qualify as institutional units that are described as social security funds." (Paragraph 4.125).

"The amounts raised, and paid out, in social security contributions and benefits may be deliberately varied in order to achieve objectives of government policy that have no direct connection with the concept of social security as a scheme to provide social benefits to members of the community. They may be raised or lowered in order to influence the level of aggregate demand in the economy, for example. Nevertheless, so long as they remain separately constituted funds, they must be treated as separate institutional units in the SNA. (Paragraph 4.126).

"The social security funds sub-sector (of general government) consists of the social security funds operating at all levels of government. Such funds are social insurance schemes covering the community as a whole or large section of the community that are imposed by government units." (Paragraph 4.147).

101. This definition of social security funds is followed in the OECD classification with the two following exceptions which are excluded

- Schemes imposed by government and operated by bodies outside the general government sector, as defined in §3 of this manual; and
- Schemes to which all contributions are voluntary.

### *Supranational Authorities*

102. This sub-sector covers the revenue-raising operations of supra-national authorities within a country. In practice, the only relevant supranational authority in the OECD area is that of the institutions of the European Union (EU). Tax revenues collected by member countries and paid to the EU are included in the *Revenue Statistics* at the supranational level of government. Income taxes and social security contributions collected by European Institutions and paid by European civil servants who are resident of EU member countries should not be included.

### *Criteria to be used for the attribution of tax revenues*

103. When a government collects taxes and pays them over in whole or in part to other governments, it is necessary to determine whether the revenues should be considered to be those of the collecting government which it distributes to others as grants, or those of the beneficiary governments which the collecting government receives and passes on only as their agent. The criteria to be used in the attribution of revenues are set out in §104 to §107 which replicate paragraphs 3.70 to 3.73 from the 2008 SNA.

104. In general, a tax is attributed to the government unit that

*a)* exercises the authority to impose the tax (either as a principal or through the delegated authority of the principal),

*b)* has final discretion to set and vary the rate of the tax

105. Where an amount is collected by one government for and on behalf of another government, and the latter government has the authority to impose the tax, and set and vary its rate, then the former is acting as an agent for the latter and the tax is reassigned. Any amount retained by the collecting government as a collection charge should be treated as a payment for a service. Any other amount retained by the collecting government, such as under a tax-sharing arrangement, should be treated as

a current grant. If the collecting government was delegated the authority to set and vary the rate, then the amount collected should be treated as tax revenue of this government.

106. Where different governments jointly and equally set the rate of a tax and jointly and equally decide on the distribution of the proceeds, with no individual government having ultimate overriding authority, then the tax revenues are attributed to each government according to its respective share of the proceeds. If an arrangement allows one government unit to exercise ultimate overriding authority, then all of the tax revenue is attributed to that unit.

107. There may also be the circumstance where a tax is imposed under the constitutional or other authority of one government, but other governments individually set the tax rate in their jurisdictions. The proceeds of the tax generated in each respective government's jurisdiction are attributed as tax revenues of that government.

108. The levies paid by the member states of the EU take the form specific levies which include

*a)* custom duties and levies on agricultural goods (5123),

*b)* gross monetary compensation accounts (5123 if relating to imports and 5124 if relating to exports);

*c)* contributions to the Single Resolution Fund (5126); and

*d)* steel, coal, sugar and milk levies (5128).

109. The custom duties collected by member states on behalf of the EU are recorded

- on a gross of collection fee basis;
- using figures adjusted so that duties are shown on a 'final destination' as opposed to a 'country of first entry' basis where such adjustments can be made. These adjustments concern in particular duties collected at important (sea) ports. Although the EU duties are collected by the authorities of the country of first entry, when possible these duties should be excluded from the revenue of the collecting country and be included in the revenue of the country of final destination

110. These are the specific EU levies that most clearly conform to the attribution criterion described in §102 above. Consequently, these amounts are footnoted as a memorandum item to the EU member state country tables (in Chapter 5) and are shown as supranational revenues against each of the tax headings identified in §108.

## Notes

1. All references to SNA are to the 2008 edition.

2. See section A.12 of this guide for a discussion of the concept of agency capacity.

3. It is usually possible to identify amounts of social security contributions and payroll taxes, but not other taxes paid by government.

4. If, however, a levy which is considered as non-tax revenue by most countries is regarded as a tax — or raises substantial revenue — in one or more countries, the amounts collected are footnoted at the end of the relevant country tables, even though the amounts are not included in total tax revenues.

5. Names, however, can frequently be misleading. For example, though a passport fee would normally be considered a non-tax revenue, if a supplementary levy on passports (as is the case in Portugal) were imposed in order to raise substantial amounts of revenue relative to the cost of providing the passport, the levy would be regarded as a tax under 5200.

6. A more detailed explanation of this distinction can be found in the special feature, 'Current issues in reporting tax revenues', in the 2001 edition of the *Revenue Statistics*.

7. Sometimes the terms 'non-refundable' and 'refundable' are used, but it may be considered illogical to talk of 'refundable' when nothing has been paid.

8. A different treatment, however, is accorded to non-wastable tax credits under imputation systems of corporate income tax (§37–39).

9. This is not strictly a true tax expenditure in the formal sense. Such tax expenditures require identification of a benchmark tax system for each country or, preferably, a common international benchmark. In practice it has not been possible to reach agreement on a common international benchmark.

10. Unless based on the profit made on a sale, in which case they would be classified as capital gains taxes under 1120 or 1220.

11. In some countries the same legislation applies to both individual and corporate enterprises for particular taxes on income. However, the receipts from such taxes are usually allocable between individuals and enterprises and can therefore be shown in the appropriate sub-heading.

12. For example, "… sufficiently self-contained and independent that they behave in the same way as corporations… (including) keeping a complete set of accounts" (2008 SNA, section 4.44).

13. In Canada — a country also referred to as having an imputation system — the (wastable) tax credit for the shareholder is in respect of domestic corporation tax deemed to have been paid whether or not a corporation tax liability has arisen. As there is no integral connection between the corporation tax liability and the credit given against income tax under such systems, these credits for dividends are treated, along with other tax credits, on the lines described in §26.

14. This may also apply where a scheme for government employees existed prior to the introduction of a general social security scheme.

15. In the 2008 SNA these are regarded as capital transfers and not as taxes (see section A.8).

16. This is the system by which the European Union adjusts for differences between the exchange rates used to determine prices under the Common Market Agricultural Policy and actual exchange rates. Payments under the system may relate to imports or exports and where these amounts are separately identifiable they are shown under the appropriate heading (5123 or 5124). In this Report, these amounts are shown gross (i.e. without deducting any subsidies paid out under the MCA system).

17. Transfers of profits of State lotteries are regarded as non-tax revenues (see also §68).

# Annex B. Interpretative Guide to non-tax revenue in Revenue Statistics in Asian and Pacific Economies

## Table of contents

## 1. Coverage

The definition of non-tax revenues and the main subcategories identified in this publication generally correspond to the concepts laid out in the 2014 IMF Government Finance Statistics Manual (GFSM). Non-tax revenues refer to increases in government net worth resulting from transactions other than tax revenues. They exclude funds arising from the repayment of previous lending by governments or from borrowing, or proceeds derived from sales of fixed capital assets, stocks, land and intangible assets or private gifts.

Non-tax revenues are made up of the following elements.

## 2. Grants

The GFSM 2014 states "Grants are transfers receivable by government units from non-resident government units or international organisations without the receipt of any goods, services, or assets in return. Grants are normally receivable in cash, but may also take the form of the receipt of goods or services (in kind)". These transfers are un-refundable and unrequited. Grants encompass reparations and gifts given for particular projects or programmes. The term "grants" is not used to refer to transfers to or from non-governmental units and excludes inter-governmental transfers. The remission of funds collected by one government for another in an agency capacity should not be shown as receipt of a grant by the beneficiary government but as its direct receipt of revenue.

## 3. Property income

This category includes income to government arising from their ownership of property, enterprises, financial assets, or intangible assets when government units place them at the disposal of other units. Sales of non-financial assets such as the sales of lands are not recorded as revenue because disposal of such an asset does not increase the net worth. Similarly, repayments on loans and loan disbursements are not revenue. Property income may take the form of dividends, interest, land rents, royalties, or withdrawals from entrepreneurial income. The main components are:

- Interest and dividends: Interest is the revenue earned by the government unit from a financial asset by putting it at the disposal of another institutional unit. Dividends are the revenue earned by placing equity funds at the disposal of a corporation (resident or non-resident corporation). This category also consists of profits of state-owned enterprises except those classified as fiscal monopolies (see §62-§64 of the OECD Interpretative Guide to tax revenue in Annex A), export and import monopoly profits (see §70-§71 of the same document) or those providing public utilities such as rail transport, electricity, post offices and other communications. In this category are included revenue from public financial institutions such as the central banks' profits, profits transferred or distributed from the operation of monetary authority functions outside the central bank and the profits of state lotteries transferred to the government. Transfers from public utilities enterprises are recorded as non-tax revenue under "sales of goods and services" whereas profits for fiscal, export or import monopolies are classified as tax revenue.
- Rents or royalties: Rent is the revenue generated from natural resources, such as land, mining, or oil resources, when a government unit places these at the disposal of private or foreign entities. The rents received relate to a resource lease-giving agreement for the exploitation and extraction of a natural resource by the lessee in return for a payment. Payments for exploration rights are also treated as rent. Rents should not be confused with other payments a government may receive related to the exploitation of subsoil and similar assets, such as severance taxes, business licenses, or other taxes (e.g. value added taxes, excises, taxes on exports, etc.). They should also

not be taken to mean incomes from the rental of buildings and equipment, which are treated as sales of goods and services. Revenues from rents and royalties are in some cases difficult to establish and depend on the agreement between the government unit and the lessee. For example rents, royalties and taxes such as corporate income taxes and VAT are sometimes encompassed in a single payment to the general government. In such cases the revenue should be classified under the category to which the majority of revenue belongs (see §71 of Annex A for further explanation.)

- Other property income: This includes revenue earned by a government unit placing funds at a disposal of quasi-corporations.[1] Conceptually this source of revenue is equivalent to that of dividends from a corporation but by definition, quasi-corporations cannot distribute income in the form of dividends. This category of "other property income" also includes retained or reinvested earnings, i.e. the percentage of distributable revenue not paid out as dividends, but retained by the corporation or quasi-corporation on foreign investment; property income from investment income disbursements and unidentified property income.

## 4. Sales of goods and services

Revenue under the category "sales of goods and services" is generally reported on a gross basis, without deduction of costs. Since these costs can represent a significant proportion of revenues, they cannot be regarded in total as funds available for governments to finance their general activities. This contrasts with tax revenues, where the collection costs are usually a small proportion of revenue. This difference implies that it may not be meaningful to sum tax and non-tax revenues as part of a calculation of generally available funds.

The proceeds of sales of nonfinancial assets such as the sale of buildings or lands are not classified as revenues since their disposal does not increase the net worth.

Sales of goods and services consist of:

- Sales by market establishments.[2]
- Administrative fees for services (i.e. fees for drivers' licences, passports, visas, court fees, harbour fees, fees for birth, marriage or death certificates, patent registrations, radio and television licenses when public authorities provide general broadcasting services).
- Administrative fees that are sales of services associated with a regulatory function of government (such as fees for the inspection of premises before delivering a business licence) and considered to be proportional to the cost of producing the service are included in this category. If the fee in return for the service provided by the government unit is disproportionate, then the fee will be classified as a tax. Specific examples of fees that are considered taxes include fees for permission to perform activities such as hunting, fishing and shooting; and fees for business registration where this is a legal requirement for the business to operate.
- Sales by nonmarket establishments such as fees at government hospitals, tuition fees at government schools and admission fees to museums and parks.
- Leasing of buildings and equipment.

## 5. Fines, penalties and forfeits

The GFSM 2014 states "Fines and penalties are compulsory transfers imposed by courts of law or bodies for violations of laws or administrative rules. Out-of-court agreements are also included (...). Forfeits are amounts deposited with a general government unit pending a legal or administrative proceeding, and that will be transferred to the unit upon resolution". For example traffic fines are included here. Fines and penalties charged on overdue taxes or penalties imposed for the evasion of taxes should be recorded in this category and not as taxes. However if it is not possible to separate the amounts paid in taxes and fines, the whole amount should be classified under the tax to which the fine relates (see §14 of Annex A for further explanation).

## 6. Other social contributions

This category includes the actual and imputed contributions to social insurance schemes operated by governments as employers on behalf of their employees that do not create a future defined liability. This category also includes the sum of the total voluntary contributions.[3] Excluded from this category are any contributions to funds in which the contributions of each participant and of his employer on his behalf are kept in a separate account earning interest and withdrawable under specified circumstances or any contributions to a pension fund autonomous to the general government. This category is not included in this publication.

## 7. Miscellaneous and unidentified revenue

This category consists of unidentified non-tax revenues or those that do not fit into any of the other categories listed above. It includes revenue such as gifts and transfers from individuals, private non-profit institutions, nongovernmental foundations, corporations, or sources other than governments and international organisations. Major non-recurrent payments receivable in compensation for extensive damages or serious injuries not covered by insurance policies are also included, such as payments of compensation for damages caused by major explosions; oil spillages; or payments receivable for damage to property other than payments from an insurance settlement.

## Notes

[1] Quasi-corporations are unincorporated enterprises that exercise some functions of corporations, but have not been granted separate legal personality by statute.

[2] A market establishment is an establishment that charges economically significant prices.

[3] The IMF includes these contributions as part of their total of social security contributions.

www.ingramcontent.com/pod-product-compliance
Lightning Source LLC
Chambersburg PA
CBHW061213240926
51846CB00006B/1207